BASEBALL LIVES

BASEBALL LIVES

Men and Women of the Game
Talk about Their Jobs,
Their Lives, and
The National Pastime

MIKE BRYAN

PANTHEON BOOKS · NEW YORK

Library of Congress Cataloging-in-Publication Data

Bryan, Mike.
Baseball lives.
1. Baseball—United States.   I. Title.
GV863.A1B79   1989   796.357'0973   88-43127
ISBN 0-394-56467-7

Book Design by Stephanie Bart-Horvath
Illustrations © Nancy Doniger

Manufactured in the United States of America

First Edition

For the Deke,
who three years ago
didn't know from baseball

CONTENTS

1 THE NATIONAL PASSION

Charlie Royals: bus driver, Clearwater Phillies   2
Bob Lurie: owner, San Francisco Giants   6
Andy Strasberg: director of marketing, San Diego Padres   11

2 OF ARMS AND THE MAN

Larry Rothschild: minor-league pitching instructor,
Cincinnati Reds   20
Dennis Eckersley: relief pitcher, Oakland Athletics   24
Glen Rosenbaum: batting practice pitcher, traveling
secretary, Chicago White Sox   33
William Bryan, M.D.: orthopedist, Houston Astros   39

3 FOOD, CLOTHING, AND SHELTER

C. J. Cherre: traveling secretary, St. Louis Cardinals   50
Bernie Stowe: equipment manager, Cincinnati Reds   58
Pete Prieto: visiting clubhouse manager, Houston Astros   64
John Adam: trainer, Milwaukee Brewers   67

4 BEATING THE BUSHES

Larry Rojas: coordinator of minor-league instruction,
Philadelphia Phillies   74
Bill Shanahan: general manager, San Bernardino Spirit   80
Mark Funderburk: coach, Orlando Twins   84

5 WHEELER DEALERS

Randal Hendricks: players' agent   90
Dave Perron: director of community affairs,
Oakland Athletics   99
Karen Williams: director of special events, Houston Astros   104
Joe McIlvaine: v.p. for baseball operations, New York Mets   110

6 SUPERSTAR

Andre Dawson: outfielder, Chicago Cubs   120

7 OUT OF LEFT FIELD

Ronald Bryant: working supervisor,
Louisville Slugger factory   126

Charles A. Steinberg, D.D.S.: director of
Diamondvision and team dentist, Baltimore Orioles   130
Stephanie Vardavas: assistant counsel, Commissioner's
Office   137
Joe Diroff: cheerleader, Detroit Tigers   145
Tommy Hawkins: v.p. for communications,
Los Angeles Dodgers   153

8 THE NITTY GRITTY
George Toma: groundskeeper, Kansas City Royals   162
Pat Santarone: groundskeeper, Baltimore Orioles   165
Joe Mooney: building and grounds superintendent,
Boston Red Sox   171

9 PICKING WINNERS
Buck Rodgers: field manager, Montreal Expos   176
Hugh Alexander: scout emeritus, Chicago Cubs   184
Tim Wilken: scout, Toronto Blue Jays   191
Harry Dalton: general manager, Milwaukee Brewers   201
"King": gambler, New York City   206

10 THE FOURTH AND OTHER ESTATES
Hank Greenwald: broadcaster, San Francisco Giants   212
Sherm Feller: public address announcer, Boston Red Sox   221
Tom Mee: director of media relations, Minnesota Twins   223
Joe Quasarano: television producer, California Angels   227
William Weiss: statistician   234
Bus Saidt: sportswriter, *Trenton Times*   241

11 PLAY AT THE PLATE
Bruce Benedict: catcher, Atlanta Braves   250
Manny Mota: first-base coach, batting instructor,
Los Angeles Dodgers   261
Bruce Froemming: umpire, National League   264
Rex Barney: public address announcer, Baltimore Orioles   274

12 THEY ALSO SERVE
Ethel LaRue: assistant administrator, Cleveland Indians   284

Al Forester: grounds crew, Boston Red Sox   290
Pete Cera: assistant equipment manager,
Philadelphia Phillies   294
Jack Mullany: usher, New York Mets   296

13   PEANUTS! POPCORN! SEASON TICKETS!

Lloyd Rutzky: vendor, Comiskey Park and Wrigley Field   300
Pat Gallagher: v.p. for business operations,
San Francisco Giants   305
Arthur D'Angelo: "The Mayor of Fenway," Boston   313
Jim Murphy: tavernkeeper, Chicago   318
Jim Toomey: front-office executive, St. Louis Cardinals   321

14   YOUTH

Jamie Lowe: general manager, Orlando Twins   330
Sharon Pannozzo: assistant director for media relations,
Chicago Cubs   336
Billy Fagan: baseball card collector, Brooksville, Florida   343

ACKNOWLEDGMENTS

The fifty-four men and women whose interviews are published here are the heart and soul of this book. Their names belong on the *cover,* and bigger than mine. It's their book. It also belongs to the dozens of other baseball people whose interviews are not here. I apologize for wasting their time, but, for what it's worth, assure them that it was not a waste of *my* time. Their interviews are just as "good" as the others. Such mundane matters as limiting the number of people with any one organization dictated the choices.

Before I talked with these folks, I had to *find* them. The truly indispensable sources were the public-relations directors with the major-league clubs, who time and again introduced me to people I would not have found otherwise. I could not have compiled the book without Jay Alves, Oakland; Bill Beck, San Diego; John Blake, Texas; Dick Bresciani, Boston; Bob Brown, Baltimore; Ned Colletti, the Cubs; Bob DiBiasio and Rick Minch, Cleveland; Dan Ewald, Detroit; Jim Ferguson, Cincinnati; Harvey Greene, the Yankees; Richard Griffin, Montreal; Jay Horwitz, the Mets; Kip Ingle, St. Louis; Duffy Jennings and David Aust, San Francisco; Paul Jensen, the White Sox; Greg Johnson, Pittsburgh; Rob Matwick, Houston; Tim Mead, California; Tom Mee, Minnesota; Bob Porter, formerly with Seattle; Jim Schultz, Atlanta; Larry Shenk, Philadelphia; Tom Skibosh, Milwaukee; Howard Starkman, Toronto; Dean Vogelaar, Kansas City; and Mike Williams, Los Angeles.

Add to this list Richard Levin and Stephanie Vardavas with the commissioner's office, Chuck Schupp with Louisville Slugger, and ballplayer Keith Hernandez, who got me started with a good list that included the inimitable Bruces in the book: umpire Froemming and catcher Benedict.

As usual, my wife, Patty, deserves co-authorship. She did much if not most of the transcribing and early editing—the work, in other words. She pointed the way, spotted the flaws, and tolerated the bad moods.

The book is dedicated to my agent, Joe Spieler. Enough said about how I feel about the Deke.

Heartfelt kudos to my editor, Wendy Wolf. After all, the idea was hers, and she entrusted it to a guy she had just met. She is also superb with the red pencil. In this context, writers always say this. I mean it.

Thank you also to Barbara Frederickson, my ebullient hostess in Florida for spring training, where it all started, and to Chuck Pool and Meribeth

Fuqua with the Astros, for help with credentials and fact-checking. Finally, thanks to all of the people in baseball offices and press boxes around the country who offered coffee, food, hotel tips, and, most important, interview tips. I forget who suggested I look up Charlie Royals, the bus driver for the Clearwater Phillies who is the first interview in the book. I had many such lucky days.

I've been a ball fan all my life, but for the 1988 season, while the players determined the world champion (and, in the end, shocked us with their choice, the Dodgers), I concentrated on the game *beyond* the white lines.

For purposes of logistics more than symmetry, I began—like the teams —at spring training. Kip Ingle, public relations director for the St. Louis Cardinals, took my call and I launched into my well-rehearsed description of the project: "A book of interviews with off-the-field baseball people, primarily. We hear from the players all the time, but there's a rich subculture the fans don't read about." (I didn't get into it then, but the scholar Jacques Barzun once asserted that no one can understand America until he understands baseball; my corollary proposed that no one can understand baseball until he understands, or at least knows more about, that secret game.) "Every job is interesting," I continued, "I just have to find the folks who don't mind tape recorders to prove the point. Whom do you have in mind, Kip?"

Pause.

"Why don't you start with Jim Toomey? He might be good for the book, plus he knows everyone in the organization."

The following day I did begin with Toomey, a seasoned front-office exec. He told me the story about the undertaker and Enos Slaughter as proof of his point that "even a guy who works in baseball day to day can't really grasp how deeply a lot of people want to be a part of it."

Toomey and I talked for a couple of hours, then I strolled out to the fields, where the earliest arrivals in camp were limbering up. About fifty fans were watching. Nothing was happening really, certainly no game, but it was still *baseball,* and therefore worth watching, especially on a sunny day. I recalled that my first idea had been to check out the off-the-field world of *all* the major team sports. But who cares about the hidden world of . . . hockey? An exciting game, yes, but not the national pastime. Nor is basketball. Nor is football. Those sports simply don't resonate in our lives in the same way. Their histories are not a part of *our* history. Football has its heroes, but baseball has Babe Ruth and a pantheon of hundreds, thousands. (And pre-season football, as New Jersey sportswriter Bus Saidt told me, is like watching paint peel.)

Over the following days and weeks in Florida I located all the PR guys. They gave me tips for interviews; those tips gave me tips. I raced from

Plant City to Haines City and tried to catch someone in Lakeland in between
—and missed him.

Then I flew to Arizona, where eight of the teams train. During the
season I went to New York, Philadelphia, Baltimore, Boston, Chicago,
Detroit, Cleveland, Milwaukee, Louisville (where they make bats), Oakland, San Francisco, Los Angeles, San Bernardino, and San Diego. In Houston, where I live, I talked with National League people as they rotated
through the Astrodome. I drove up to Arlington, Texas, to catch American
League personnel when they visited the Rangers.

The baseball fraternity, as it is often called (or, much less often, sorority), is something over five thousand people, including all the minor-league
organizations. I met, "officially" or otherwise, several hundred of them,
and, with the rare exception, they love, or at least enjoy, their jobs, although
those jobs often demand sixty, seventy, eighty hours a week—even more,
for the clubhouse personnel. I was surprised how many people also expressed pleasure in being a part of something that gives *other* people so much
pleasure. I heard this time and again, along with an interesting corollary
from Bob Lurie, owner of the San Francisco Giants, who explained that he
declined to pursue an equity position with the football-playing 49ers because
football, with just sixteen games a season, doesn't provide enough *pain*.

As the interviews piled up, the original problem of finding the interesting people was superseded by the new one of *selecting* from among all the
interesting people I had found, trying to balance personalities and job descriptions, geography and experience. By the end of the season I had talked
with men and women in all twenty-six of the major-league organizations,
along with some who are "unaffiliated." However, the alert reader may
realize that no members of the New York Yankee organization are included
in the book. The reason is simple: they are not allowed, by George, to talk
to the press. Broadcaster Hank Greenwald is here because he is an employee
of his radio station, not the Yankees—or *was,* when we talked in June. At
the end of the year he returned to his former club, the Giants.

Off-the-field baseball, mostly, but one manager, one umpire, and
three active players are included. Unlike the rest of the people, the players
are interviewed all the time, usually by a sportswriter who has some story
idea *of his own* in mind. The players respond only after consulting their cliché
catalogue. I'm not knocking sportswriters. I've conducted a hundred of
those interviews myself, for magazines, and that's the nature of the beast.
But it was a pleasure to sit down with Andre Dawson, Dennis Eckersley,

and Bruce Benedict and simply say: "Here, talk about baseball the way *you* want to." And they did.

Dawson and I had a two-part conversation late in the season when the Cubs were out of the race and playing the Expos at Wrigley Field. In our negotiations beforehand, conducted long distance through Cubs intermediary Ned Colletti, he had agreed to thirty minutes. I knew this wouldn't be nearly enough time, but I also thought that once he got involved, he might find the wide-open format a refreshing change. Time ran out on us the first day, and sure enough he invited me to return the following afternoon, when we met in the dugout after batting practice. Regulations require that all reporters clear the area thirty minutes prior to game time. We were pushing the limit and Dawson knew it, but he was too polite to run me off. Maybe the players have a pact for these circumstances. I don't know. At any rate, Ryne Sandberg came over to the bat rack next to where Dawson and I were sitting and rattled a stack of bats, eyeing me and my tape recorder. I looked up and laughed. He didn't. Dawson stared noncommittally at the field.

We were just about through anyway. If we hadn't been, I believe he would have invited me back for a third session.

"Talk about baseball the way *you* want to"—that was my tack with everyone, and often they surprised me, no one more so than Andy Strasberg, the marketing man for the San Diego Padres who didn't want to talk about marketing. He wanted to talk about Roger Maris. I let him.

National League umpire Bruce Froemming has great umpiring stories and insights, but the subject closest to his heart is one not many people in the game know about—his extended sojourn in the minor leagues, and the painful reasons for it.

At no time did the Giants' owner, Bob Lurie, talk much about ownership. That seemed of only passing interest to him. He related to the game as a fan—one with certain privileges, of course, such as being able to fire, rather than just yell at, the manager, or move the team out of town if the city fathers and voters don't come up with a replacement for Candlestick Park—but a fan nevertheless, and mainly.

In Louisville, home of Louisville Slugger, sales rep Chuck Schupp met me at the airport, toured me through the town, and then took me across the river into Indiana, where the factory is located. He introduced me to Ronald Bryant, a supervisor. Late in our conversation, Bryant pointed to a stack of product and said, "To me, that bat there *is* Dale Murphy."

The remark remains my favorite. I have always believed that baseball is rich beyond measure, or at least rich beyond the telling *so far*. Standing on the floor of that bat factory in my safety goggles, I realized that the men and women of the game feel this way, too, because so many of them speak passionately and often eloquently about what they do and what it means to them.

1
THE NATIONAL PASSION

His home for ten months of the year is Room 237 of the Quality Inn in Clearwater, Florida. Baseball shoes, uniforms, and other paraphernalia are stacked or strewn around. A short, round man, he gives me a beer from the little refrigerator but declines for himself. He has to drive the bus later.

In 1963, I was driving the Phillips 66 gasoline truck for the man in Spartan-burg, South Carolina, who also owned the franchise for the A-ball team there. I was parking cars and messing around and when Mr. Hughes bought his first bus he said, "Charlie, you're going to be the bus driver." And since they didn't have trainers back then, he said, "Well, if you're gonna drive the bus, we'll teach you to be the trainer, too." Guys taught me how to tape, how to stretch arms. Anything major I had to take them to a doctor. I'd haul gas all day and about three o'clock Mr. Hughes would say, "Charlie, time to go!" I'd run to the ballpark with my uniform on from hauling gas all day, grab my medicine kit, get my bus, and head somewhere, and when I got there do what I had to do: tape, treat a few strawberries, give out some aspirins, which is the biggest thing you have to do. Then I would take a shower and put on my whites, and I'd go from a gasoline man to a baseball man. Get home at five o'clock lots of mornings—breakdowns on the road—take a shower, put on a clean shirt, get in that eighteen-wheeler, head up into the mountains with a load of gas. I did that until 1972, when I became full-time baseball.

I never had nobody to help me. I'm too peculiar about things. But very easy-going. I do all the laundry, fix the pitching machine. I've even tried to throw a couple. And I'm always a nut about shoes, shine them all. I repair gloves, too, in my spare time. All the trainers and equipment guys do that, even in the major leagues.

I was in Spartanburg twenty-two years. When the Phillies moved the team into the Florida State League four years ago, I lacked just a few years of having a pension, and I wasn't old enough to retire, and I didn't really want to move, but I did because I go with the bus.

When I got the pension they said, "Well, what're you gonna do?" and I said, as long as you people give me the job, I want it, because I feel too good to get under them pine trees at home. I'm sixty-six years old. I'll be married forty-four years in June. She knows I've got to pay the bills.

I live at the motel during the season because we park the bus here and it's real handy—good places to eat, convenient to the ballpark. I've had Room 237 for four or five years. I drive for spring training for the major league team. Then when the minor leagues come in, about the eighteenth of March, I'll leave the major leagues and haul the minor league kids around. I assist the doctor. They take blood out of all the kids, get a cardiogram. I generally fill out the papers for the doctor because I write like the doctor —bad.

The season opens the eighth of April and goes to the thirty-first of August—144 games. When that's over we're off ten or eleven days unless we make the playoffs, but we haven't made the playoffs since we've been in the Florida State League. Then we're back for the Instructional League. By the time I'm home it's the middle of November, but then it's cold already. But you're home for Thanksgiving and enjoy that, and you're home for Christmas.

After the holidays they have three weeks of Dream Week—one with Baltimore, two with the Phillies—till the fifteenth of February. I haul them around to the motel, the ballpark, the parties, about 100 people each week. These are guys thirty-five to eighty years old. They pay like $3,000 a week, and after two days some of the poor old fellers can't even walk—pulled hamstrings and muscles and you name it. They wear a Phillies uniform with their name on the back, just like the major-league players do. Some of them guys still think they can play; they say, "I can't get my curve over like I used to," and I'll say, "There's a lot of curves you can't get over anymore, or see, either!" and they'll all laugh at that.

In the Florida State League we probably go fifteen, twenty thousand miles a year, but I used to drive fifty thousand when I was up in Spartanburg. When the bus pulls in, a lot of people say, "There're the Phillies," and then they look and say, "Oh, you're the minor-leaguers." But I say, "Yes, but these are the future guys. This is where they all start." Some'll stay excited, some walk off.

No stops. When we get on the highway, we go. When we're coming back from Fort Lauderdale usually we'll stop and let the kids eat. But once I close that door, next stop's Jack Russell Stadium. They're all asleep anyway. And on the bus they cannot have music unless they have earphones on. We'd have fifteen stations, every one with a different tune, everyone trying to play louder than the other. No radios in the clubhouse, either, or some of 'em be sittin' there jivin' and not doin' their work.

Ain't too many of the ball clubs that own their own bus. Most charter. That charter driver doesn't have a thing to do with the ball club. His job is to pick 'em up and bring 'em back and let 'em out. Knock on wood, I've never put a scratch on a bus all the years I've been driving. I've done mechanicking, too. Just yesterday, air conditioner worked fine going down to Port Charlotte, came home in a hot bus. So I got up at four o'clock this morning, got it fixed, and was at Jack Russell at nine o'clock. And those kids, they're so lazy about the trash sometimes they'll throw cans down in the hole and sometimes you have to stick your arm down there to get 'em out. I've done that, too. Wasn't no choice. That goes with the job. It's a long, hard life sometimes that takes special people that's dedicated. Just like everybody can't be doctors. But ain't never a dull moment, I guarantee you. Never.

The kids pay me clubhouse dues, $10 every two weeks. I've had 'em tell me they don't have it, and I say, "If you ain't got it, you can't pay it. When you get it, go ahead and pay me." Generally, they will when they get their meal money, but I've been beat out of many a dollar. They get transferred before they pay me and I lose that one.

The Phillies furnish the soap, the Clorox, and the equipment. I take care of the work, clean the clubhouse, the bathroom. When the ball game's over at night, I start the laundry. By the time the manager's done with his report, I'm about half through. At six o'clock in the morning, I come back to finish up. You get to where you pick up a T-shirt, you handle it every day, and just throw it in the right locker, backward, forward, everywhere. Then you hang up the rest of the things and you're out of there. At three o'clock I'm back for the game.

On the road, I've got to do the laundry every other day. You take it to the maids in the motel, and they'll do it for you. Some'll charge you $40, some $30. I bring it up to the room, separate it, and spread it all out. I tell 'em what time and the players come in. I'll say, "Number 20, right there," and point.

Once the game starts, I don't have anything to do till it's over because they've got all their clothes on. I listen to the big-league game on the radio in the laundry room. I run in and out between the dugout and report. I have to wear a uniform. They ask you ten thousand questions. You and the manager get to talking and he'll say, "You notice anything?" And I'll say, "Yeah, a couple things." You pick up a lot from them guys who've been around a lot in the minors. You watch the kids, this year, next year, and you soon get to where you know just about what they're gonna do. It's very tough when you see a kid that wants to play so bad and just doesn't have the tools. They've come by and said, "Bo, I've just been released," and they've been crying and I imagine I've had a couple of tears myself over the years. Because a lot of 'em didn't have any education and they wanted to be a ballplayer so bad. And a lot of 'em *had* the tools and didn't want to apply them.

I've seen all kinds of players and all kinds of people from all walks of life, believe me. I'm just like a father to some of the kids. I call 'em kids because they are to me. I'm old enough to be any of 'em's daddy or grandaddy, either way. They ask all kinds of questions. They ask if I think they're going to make it. They'll say their wife didn't want to love them last night, and wonder if they done anything wrong.

"No," I say, "that's common. How long you been married?"

"A year."

"Well, the headaches are startin' from now on! It's headache time!"

We generally keep a plate of chewin' tobacco and we sit there and chew tobacco and spit and cuss right with 'em, just have a good time. I expect I have more fun with 'em than anybody else over there because I don't have to get on their ass that much, unless they cross me on something —like putting their clothes in the wrong hamper, maybe get something in with the Clorox and ruin it. But that don't ever happen but one time; they learn right quick. Lot of 'em come in from spring training and hug my neck. A lot of 'em are managers or coaches now and they say, "This guy's the first one who ever hauled me when I started playing ball."

Just the other day George Bell said, "Hi, Charlie," and I said, "Hi, George, how 'bout a new car?" We all laughed.

I like 'em all, really, but I guess the guy I like the most would be the guy you see come up as a rookie and work his way up, and then one day I drive over to the major league camp and see him on the forty-man roster. He sees me and walks to the fence and says, "Charlie, I just want to thank you for the times you got on my ass."

Yes, I'll tell them a lot of times, "Hey, you know where you're gonna wind up, you don't get your shit together? Gonna wind up with a sniper" —what we call a lawnmower. I can see how bad they want it. You'd have to be a nut not to want it with the money they make up there. They start out here with $700 a month. They have to pay their room out of that, telephone, their food, and four or five of 'em has to live in one apartment. Then when we go on the road, they get $11 a day, and the first McDonald's or Kentucky Fried or Lindy's we stop at they'll eat $7 of that. And then they don't have any more money. I seen 'em eat crackers and just what they can scrape together. It's tough. A lot of 'em got that major-league appetite but that minor-league pocketbook.

I've been to two World Series, 1980, when they won, and 1983, when Baltimore smoked 'em. They make better plays and play quicker games in the major leagues. I enjoy seeing those kids play. I still call 'em kids. I like to remember how horseshit some of 'em played when they started out and you go watch 'em now and you see how good they play, it really makes you feel good.

The Phillies give you a World Series ring, they take everybody up to Philadelphia, they put you up in a motel, you don't even pay for your coffee in the morning, just sign your name. The cocktail party starts at four-fifteen and goes till six-fifteen, then they load you on the bus and take you to the ballpark. I don't drive. Then there's a big buffet dinner after the game with three or four vegetables and all you can eat. The band plays till four in the morning.

BOB LURIE

Candlestick Park, home of the San Francisco Giants, may be a pit, but the owner's office on the fifty-first floor of a downtown skyscraper overlooks a stunning panorama of bay and bridge. Fog hovers. A huge Louisville Slugger bat and a baseball glove big enough to sit in are appropriate decoration. A portable radio sits on a side table, but there's no game today.

I've worn a jacket for the occasion and am happy enough with that decision, but it should have been a pin-striped suit.

We own and operate office buildings, primarily in San Francisco and Chicago. We have a couple of hotels. It's a family business that I've always enjoyed. Owning a baseball team is something I never planned for. I've always been a fan, spent a lot of time at old Seals Stadium when we had a Triple-A club, and I played the game from grammar school on up. I was a slashing, slugging outfielder, not good enough to play in college. In 1958, the Giants moved out here from New York and in 1960 [then owner] Horace Stoneham asked me to be on the team's board of directors. It took me about three seconds to say, "Yes!"

In 1975, the Giants were going to be sold. I was hot and cold whether I wanted to get involved and had resigned from the board. By March of the next year, Stoneham had found a group in Toronto. The deal would have gone through but for some injunctions in court. The judge told Mayor George Mosconi that he couldn't hold it any longer. At the last second,

Mosconi asked me if I would talk to Bob Short about being partners in keeping the team here. So Short flew out from Minneapolis in the middle of the night, we go to court the next morning, and we agree to buy the ball club. We had approval from the National League to go ahead.

We were partners for about three weeks. Then he broke his hip and was in the hospital in Minneapolis, so I made three or four trips just to try to put this deal together, and then he decided he wanted complete control over everything, and wanted me to put up all the money, and that just didn't appeal to me.

I came back here on a Monday and had a conference call with other owners. A lot of them felt Toronto was a better city. They wanted to get out of Candlestick Park and were really putting on the pressure. In their great wisdom they said, "We want an immediate answer, this has been going on long enough."

I said, "I'd like forty-eight hours to get a new partner. I'm not going to do this alone."

Walter O'Malley, a wonderful gentleman and a great friend and a great help to me in learning about the baseball business, said we've got to give him a little time. He was, you know, looking out for his own interests. He didn't want to see anything happen to the Giants-Dodgers rivalry; he had been instrumental in getting the Giants out here from New York.

In their great wisdom the owners gave me five hours. This was at noon. There are a lot of people in this area who will always help you. They were all out to lunch and unavailable and whatever. By about three o'clock I was still saying to people in this office, "Don't worry," and they would say," What are you going to do?" and I'd say, "Something will happen."

About then a man by the name of Bud Herseth from Arizona called the mayor and said he understood there was a little problem and he had some money in the bank and would be interested. I had some friends in Arizona, mutual acquaintances, and we checked him out. The money was there. There were many phone calls, and about four-thirty, four-forty, we agreed verbally what was going to happen, and I went back on a conference call and said I've got a partner—a man I'd never met.

I told the mayor and he said, "What happens if the guy doesn't show up tomorrow morning?" and I said, "Then you and I go off the bridge or something."

He showed up and we went from there. We had an interesting two years before I bought Bud out. He's a character. I haven't seen him in many years.

I told people I bought the baseball team because San Francisco is a major-league city and should have a major-league team—which is true—but I also bought it for the personal involvement, a chance to get into an area that I loved and try to resurrect a franchise that had really gone downhill quite a bit. If I didn't really love the game and wasn't a great fan, I wouldn't own a baseball team. Why go through all this otherwise?

Even though I had been on the board for fifteen years, I didn't know very much about the operation of a baseball team. I think sometimes the owners in baseball get involved too much without really knowing what they're doing, and they become instant experts. It's like any industry, you've got to really have a background and have knowledge. Most owners don't, but they think they do. So it was a quick study for me in 1976. It was twenty-hour work days, just a million things to do, it seemed like.

There's absolutely no comparison between real estate and baseball. A lot of things happen that make real estate exciting and different, but baseball is a *daily* thing. At one time I had a great interest in getting involved with the 49ers, pretty much at the same time as this Giants thing. But I didn't do that—you don't suffer enough with football. There's only sixteen Sundays in a season. There's not enough pain. With baseball, I can live and die with it 162 times a year. It's a kick what you do sometimes to get scores if you're away someplace or in a meeting. I've been in major-league meetings when there's a break for dinner and people run to the telephone to find out the scores.

Now the organization has turned around. I'm not as active as I used to be, on a day-to-day basis, with Al Rosen being president of the ball club. In the fall of '85 I found out that he was available, got permission to talk to him, went and spent eight hours at his house, and one of the first things I said to him was I'm going to fire myself as president and you're it, you'll have the necessary authority to run the organization. However, I talk to him every day, I'm at Candlestick Park most of the time, I have an office out there.

I'll call Roger Craig, our manager, if I have a question about something, ask him what he was thinking about on some play. But I wouldn't question or challenge his reasons. He knows a hell of a lot more about running a baseball team than I ever will. But I want to learn. Managing, that's a great job, to be able to guide the destiny of a team. It's up to them to make it or break it and if they can't make it I've fired them. I've fired four, and one quit after his first year.

Craig is the only manager I've had that got the respect of the players, and that's quite an achievement in this day and age. He took a team that lost a hundred games in '85 and contended for the pennant in '86.

I remember the first day in September 1985, when I went down to the clubhouse and introduced Roger and Al. I made a few remarks and Al made a few remarks and then Roger got up and he made a few remarks. These guys have heard it all, but after about fifteen minutes they were all sitting up and listening to each and every word he was saying. On Opening Day the next year my timing was great. I had to go into the clubhouse to make a phone call and heard his speech. I never heard Rockne make a speech, but I'll bet on Roger Craig to be a motivator.

I know there are some owners that never go into the clubhouse and don't have any association with the players. I've enjoyed that association from Day One. It was a novelty, meeting people that I'd read about and watched play the game, you know. That was a thrill. I was like a little kid. I still go into the clubhouse, but not every day, and I'm not there for hours on end. I have a good relationship because the players know I'm interested and they know I'm a fan. I like to kid with them before the game. I take some road trips.

I've had seats right behind the Giants dugout since 1960, and I continued sitting there after I bought the club for another five, six years, but it got to the point where I couldn't really enjoy the game. There were just too many interruptions, people with great ideas and great questions: "How come they didn't bunt?"—or whatever. Now I sit in a mezzanine box. I watch the game much more intensely since owning the ball club. We do have friends come and sit in the box with us, but I don't spend that much time with them. I'm certainly polite and charming—certainly try to be—but, no, I watch the game. I won't allow any interviews during a game.

I worry about every game and every pitch. I do a lot of pacing. I consider myself a pretty good competitor. Al Rosen has said to me there's fifty games you are going to win no matter what, fifty you're going to lose, and it's the other sixty-two that make the difference. But I wonder why—I've said this half kiddingly but I *do* wonder—why we don't win *every* game. I mean, why *do* you have to lose any games?

I get so frustrated. The other night we're ahead 5–0 and two balls are hit, one to Chris Speier and one to Robby Thompson, who are as good a pair of defensive players as there are, and they booted both of them and we ended up losing the game. Still, it doesn't get to me on the level that it used to because I know there is always a game tomorrow.

If it ever got to a point where I wasn't a great fan and didn't really enjoy watching the game, I'd sell. Financially, the worst I wanted to do here was break even, and overall we are still in a loss position. We were very successful last year, but we've had some years that were big losses. I won't tell you what I think this club is worth, but I know we could recover any losses we've had. It's amazing how many people out there want to buy a baseball team, and it's a pretty lousy investment, overall.

The salary structure in baseball is starting to come down, but we've got a long way to go. I mean, the agents come in and ask for a million dollars and we say, "No, we'll only pay you $900,000," and then we walk out and say we got a victory. Well, we've got to do a lot better than that. I've never objected to a player's agent asking for whatever, and these agents are very creative and very bright and the players' association has done a terrific job. But too many times ownership has said yes instead of no.

We will not—I've repeated this again and again—we will not renew our lease at Candlestick Park. We take surveys from time to time. People are asked why they don't come to Candlestick Park, and the answer that you always expect—that the team is not playing well at the time—is out-numbered by the people who say it's the ballpark. The reputation, I think, goes back to Stu Miller getting blown off the mound in the All-Star game in 1961, when you had press from all over the country and the world here. Now, when the park becomes more important than the performance of the team, I think that's one heck of a message. There was an unusual week three or four years ago when the temperature at night was seventy, seventy-five degrees—just perfect baseball weather—and we put that on the message board. People wrote letters and said, "Don't lie to us! It can't be that warm at Candlestick."

We've got a mayor here, Art Agnos, who said, "Oh, he's bluffing." I'm not bluffing. When Proposition W [a proposal to build a new stadium near downtown San Francisco] went down to defeat, I got calls from eight to ten cities, government officials, potential owners.

People say we've got plenty of time until the lease ends in 1994. They ask, "Why are you being so strict by cutting it off at the end of 1988?"

I say, "No, we don't have plenty of time. In my opinion it takes four to five years from the time you find a site until you get the doors open."

I don't feel this city has been very responsive regarding the stadium. There has been a lot of apathy in the business community. I don't think they realize, economically, what the ball club is worth. The new studies now say $150 million a year economic impact, maybe up to $200 million.

And what about in '87, when we clinched the Western Division championship on Monday night in San Diego and we came back here Tuesday morning? After sixteen years the Giants had won the division and I know there was a heck of a lot of excitement and pleasure and it continued through the playoffs. You could just walk down the street and feel it. I mean, that's all anybody talked about. This was a happier city.

A few months after the '87 season, Lurie, citing encouraging efforts to find a new site in or near San Francisco, softened his threat to move the team and said that he was "committed" to keeping the Giants in the Bay area.

ANDY STRASBERG

He is the director of marketing for the San Diego Padres. When I ask him to talk about his work, the selling of baseball, he looks quietly disappointed. "Can I tell you about *before* I got into this job? Can I tell you about Roger Maris?"

I grew up in the shadows of Yankee Stadium—if it was a long, long shadow! We were really about five miles from the ballpark. One of my fondest memories is when my dad first took me to the Polo Grounds. In the middle of Harlem was this immense cathedral and inside was all this green, green grass. Incredible.

On that particular day the Giants were playing the Phillies and the Phillies were wearing the old-style uniforms, with the oversized red numbers on the back. My dad had purchased tickets to sit in the upper deck, general admission, and then in about the fourth inning he said, "I'll be back in just a minute," and went downstairs. I was sitting there all alone. After about fifteen minutes he came back and motioned for me to come with him and we sat down about four rows from the field. He slipped the usher some money and the guy wiped off the seat. And I just fell in love with baseball. That was 1957 when I was eight years old and throughout my life, every time I started to drift away from the game, something brought me back, something incredible, something very special.

In 1960, when Roger Maris came to the Yankees from Kansas City, I was burned in a fire in August and so I was laid up for a while. I followed baseball even closer because of that. I remember a headline in *Sports Illustrated* saying that Roger Maris "rejuvenates" the New York Yankees. I had never heard the word "rejuvenate," but it triggered in my mind that this person Roger Maris was someone special. That's just like yesterday to me. That was the year, you may recall, that Roger won the Most Valuable Player Award.

For me, there was just something about the way he swung the bat, the way he played right field, the way he looked. Now I had an idol. In 1961, the entire country was wrapped up in the home-run race between Roger Maris and Mickey Mantle and Babe Ruth's ghost. I cut out every single article on Roger Maris and said to myself when I get older and can afford it, I'm going to have these professionally bound. When I was in college I actually went back to microfilms of 1957, '58, and '59 newspapers and magazines and made copies of box scores and stories on Roger Maris. About eight years ago I had all of it bound into eleven albums.

I always sat in section 31, box 163-A, seat 1 in Yankee Stadium. Right field. I would buy a general admission ticket, but I knew the policeman so I would always sit there. You have to understand, I'd get to the ballpark about two hours before they'd open up and I'd remain two hours after. I would see Roger park his car and I would say hello and tell him what a big fan I was. After a while he started to notice me. He threw me a baseball in batting practice and I am embarrassed to tell you what happened. I was so stunned I couldn't lift my arms. The ball fell off and somebody else got it and I yelled to Rog that I didn't get the ball. So he stopped on the way in and spoke to Phil Linz, a utility infielder. Linz came over, took a ball out of his back pocket and said "Put out your hand." I put out my hand and he said, "This is from Roger Maris."

He put the ball in my hand. But you know how cruel kids can be. All my friends said, "That ball's from Phil Linz, not Roger Maris." So later on I asked Roger for a ball and he did give me a baseball. My friends kept pushing me, challenging me. "Why don't you ask him for one of his home-run bats?"

Well, one day he was standing by the fence during batting practice. He would not sign autographs when the players were on the field, and I don't recall anyone even asking him for an autograph, but I made the request for the bat and he said, "Sure, next time I break the bat."

The Yankees had a West Coast trip and they were playing against the Angels and I was listening on the radio late at night, in bed, with the lights out. You know how kids did it. I'm sure they probably still do. And Roger cracked a bat. He had to go back to the bat rack. The next morning my old friend from high school called me: "Did you hear Roger crack his bat? That's *your* bat."

I said, "We'll see."

When the club came back my friend and I went to the stadium and during batting practice Rog walks straight over to me and before I even open up my mouth he says, "I've got that bat for you."

I said, "Oh, my God, I can't thank you enough."

Before the game starts I go to the dugout and there's a police officer there and I mean it is just impossible to get close unless you've got tickets. I went up to this great policeman and just poured my heart out as quick as I could: "You have to understand, please understand, Roger Maris told me to come here, I was supposed to pick up a bat, it's the most important thing, I wouldn't fool you, I'm not trying to pull the wool over your eyes, you gotta let me—"

"No problem. Stand over here."

I thought, geez, this is too easy, because I was expecting the worst. Just before the game starts Rog comes up out of the runway and hands me the bat. One of the most incredible moments in my life. Here is the bat from my idol and he thought enough of me to bring it back and give it to me. I went to the right-field seats and I was the only kid, obviously, in right field with a bat.

I brought the bat home and told all my friends and they said, "Now that you have the bat, why don't you ask him for one of his home-run baseballs?"

So I ask Roger for one of his home-run baseballs and he says, "You're gonna have to catch one 'cause I don't have any."

This is when the story starts to get unbelievable. In 1967 I go off to college at the University of Akron, in Ohio. My roommate has a picture of Raquel Welch on his wall and I've got a picture of Roger Maris. Everyone throughout the school knows that I'm a big Roger Maris fan. Maris had been traded to St. Louis for Charley Smith on December 6, and it was a real dark day as far as I was concerned, because Roger Maris was no longer a New York Yankee.

One day in speech class, I had to give a convincing speech and the subject I decided on was going to a baseball game. The conclusion of my speech was that I think so much of going to a baseball game that I am leaving after this class, driving with five of my friends two and a half hours to Pittsburgh to see the St. Louis Cardinals play the Pittsburgh Pirates.

My five friends had said, "You told us that you know Roger Maris. Let's just go see."

It's May 9, 1967. We get to Forbes Field approximately two hours before the game and there is the red number 9. It's the first time in my life I had ever seen Roger Maris outside of Yankee Stadium, and I figured he doesn't know who I am because the setting is different and I'm very, very nervous. *Extremely* nervous, because I now have five guys with me. I go down to the edge of the fence and my voice is quivering and I just say, "Ah, Rog. Rog . . ."

He turns around and says, "Andy Strasberg, what the hell are you doing here in Pittsburgh?"

That was the first time I knew he knew my name. I look at him and I look at my friends and I say, "Well, Rog, I'm with some guys from college. They wanted to meet you and I just wanted to come out and say hello." The five of them paraded by and shook hands and they couldn't believe it. I wished Rog the traditional good luck and he said, "Wait a minute. I want to give you an autograph on a National League ball." And he went into the dugout and got a ball and signed it. I put it in my pocket and I felt like a million dollars.

I'm very superstitious when it comes to baseball. Out in right field I sat in row 9, seat 9. In the third inning Roger Maris hit his first National League home run off Woody Fryman.

I caught the ball.

It's the most amazing thing that will ever happen to me in my life. My friends were jumping all over me. Five friends. Tears were rolling down my face. I couldn't believe it. He came running out at the conclusion of the inning—you've got to remember that Rog knew where I was and it wasn't crowded that particular game—and said, "I can't believe it."

I said, "You can't? I can't!"

I asked Roger if he would sign it and he said, "Why don't I sign it back in New York?"

My friends and I got back to the dorm about one, one-thirty in the morning and it was like wildfire. The whole school found out what had happened and I just had people coming in all night long, asking to see the baseball, asking me to tell them my story. I stayed up the entire night. I was also afraid that someone was going to steal or hide the ball, so the next morning I did not go to class. I went to the Akron Dime National Bank, explained the situation to the president and asked if he would put the ball in a safe-deposit box until I left Akron. And he did. No charge.

I came home for the summer and Roger signed the ball when the Cardinals came to Shea Stadium. My family had moved from the Bronx to White Plains and the local paper there had the story and a picture of me with the bat and the ball—the first time I had ever been interviewed. I might as well tell you that the bat and the ball are part of the family now. The bat's name is Woodrow, we call him Woody, and we just celebrated his twenty-third birthday. The ball's name is Homer.

You would think that the story of Roger Maris is over with now. I had caught the baseball. But it just snowballs. I graduate from college and I'm still in touch with him. He has now retired. In fact in 1968 I flew out to St. Louis to see Roger Maris's last game. For me it was a real tough time because I knew my childhood was coming to an end. I got real emotional at the end of the game. He ran out to right field and then they sent in a substitute and he came running in. I was sitting somewhat behind the dugout watching the proceedings and he didn't acknowledge me and by now I felt that we had a pretty good rapport and I felt a little bit bad. But he must have seen me because then he popped his head out and winked and went back in. This really touched my heart. I was interviewed by *The Sporting News,* who found out that I had made that trip from New York expressly to see Roger retire. The reporter asked Roger Maris about me specifically and Roger said, "Andy Strasberg was my most loyal fan."

On the front page of *The Sporting News.* There it was in print for the first time. I was his most loyal, his number-one fan.

I continued with my life and he continued with his. We started exchanging Christmas cards and the relationship kind of grew. I graduated from college in 1971 with a degree in English Literature and was getting to be somewhat of an adult and traveled around the United States in a yellow Chevy off and on for two or three years, looking for a job in baseball, visiting every major and minor league club I could find. I was a dishwasher in Arizona, a gardener in Maine, an editor for a football publication in New York. I delivered flowers, pressed clothes, drove a cab.

One time I was on the road in Spokane, Washington, with a friend from college nicknamed "Maps" because that was all he ever read. Maps sat in the car while I made my pitch to the general manager. Usually I would wind up such a conversation by asking whether it would be possible to get a couple of tickets for tonight's game. "Sure," they usually said, but in Spokane the man said, "Young man, if I were to give free tickets to everyone trying to get a job in baseball, I wouldn't have any to sell."

Maps asked, "Did you get the job?"

"No."

"Well, at least we're going to the ball game."

"The hell we are."

Finally in 1973 I settled in a camera store in Long Beach, California. The traveling was getting to be too much. In the beginning I had said if I didn't find the job by the time I was twenty-one I wouldn't frustrate the family any further. I pushed that up to twenty-two . . . twenty-three . . . twenty-four . . . twenty five.

In 1975 I finally got a job with the San Diego Padres, from Elten Schiller, the man who had turned me down in Spokane. He denies that story about the tickets, but it's true.

When I drove down from Long Beach to talk about the opening with the Padres, Elten asked me, "How much money are we talking about? What would it take for you to come and work for the San Diego Padres?"

I figured that many people had probably said they would work for free, or at minimum wage, so I looked at Elten and said, "The most I could pay the Padres would be $100 a month."

Again, he denies this story, but it's true.

I contacted Roger, telling him that I had gotten the job. He wrote me a nice note of congratulations.

I got married in 1976, at home plate at Jack Murphy Stadium here in San Diego. A nice, small ballpark wedding. I wouldn't allow the media in because I didn't do it for the publicity. I did it because I had promised myself I was going to get married, if I ever did, at home plate. But I didn't think it would be a *major*-league ballpark. On our first date I had suggested a ball game. "No, too boring," Patti said, so we went to the movies. But she appreciates baseball. She understands it. She's just not obsessed with it. *Obsessed,* that's the word for me. I have half a million baseball cards— nowhere near the record—categorized by years, bound in books; seventy-one different recordings of "Take Me Out to the Ball Game," most of them in a jukebox, including the first one ever produced, back in the early 1900's; a collection of seats from the old parks.

Rog and his wife Pat sent me a wedding gift, which to this day is one of only two gifts that we still have in our house. I started to call Roger about once or twice a year and we would visit on the phone and it was great because, although he was still my idol and still my hero, I was a little more down-to-earth and able to talk to him about normal things instead of "How'd you feel when you hit your 61st?"

In 1980, Roger and Pat were in Los Angeles for the All-Star game and my dad, who had never met Rog, flew in from New York. He ran into Roger Maris in the lobby of the Biltmore Hotel. It was a great meeting and they started kidding about me. That night we went out for dinner, my wife and my dad, Roger and his wife, and someone else in this organization. I sat next to Roger throughout the dinner; I hadn't seen him for several years.

Roger started talking about his first National League home run and how I caught it. I had never heard his version of the story. I had told it a number of times and usually the response was, "It's not true. You're lying." It was great to hear his version about how he had an injury to his right hand, how it was tough to get around on the ball. When he was through, the fellow from our office, Jim Weigel, said to me, "I've got to tell you, Andy. Up until now, I never believed that story."

I guess the next scene is when Roger passed away, in December of 1985. He lived in Gainesville, Florida, but he grew up in Fargo, and I made arrangements to go to Fargo for the funeral. It was brutally cold. I went there not knowing anyone but his wife. After the ceremony I sat and waited because I didn't want to go up to Pat when everyone else was there. Then I went to her and expressed how sorry I felt and she hugged me and kissed me. She couldn't thank me enough for coming. Then she said, "I want you to meet the rest of my family." I had never met the kids. Six children. She turned to them and said, "I want to introduce someone really special. Kids, this is Andy Strasberg—" and Roger Maris, Jr., said, "You're Dad's number-one fan."

I couldn't keep my composure. The family reached out to me and I reached out to them and I thought it was just a nice ending to a great story, but it wasn't the end. It was just the beginning. I have gone back to Fargo every year for a charity golf tournament and auction to benefit the Hospice of the Red River Valley. I have gotten to know the family well enough that Randy Maris and his wife have spent a week with my family. I've spent a couple of days at their house. I wouldn't say I'm part of the family because I'm not, but I'm part of the many, many close friends that they have. If you open up the first page of last year's souvenir program you'll see what they did for me, which I thought was so super. My wife was embarrassed because my picture made the front page, and the Maris family made the second page.

One year I went out to the cemetery to pay my respects, at no scheduled time. I just did it on my own and without my knowledge there was a photographer present. In the Jewish religion, you place a stone on the grave. The picture of me placing the stone was on the front page of the little newspaper.

Another year I asked for the opportunity to address the banquet. There were about 700 people there. I said, "You've heard from Roger's family, Roger's friends, his teammates, but there is another side, and that is Roger's *fans,* and this video tells it all."

The lights went down and I played this three-and-a-half minute video I had put together with a friend—pictures of Maris, of Maris and me together, with Lou Rawls singing, "Did you ever know that you are my hero? I can fly higher than an eagle, you are the wind beneath my wings." It gave me an opportunity to tell everyone how he was no longer just the player Roger Maris. He was the *man.* He was a very frank person and some people took that as being surly, but he was just an honest, straightforward person.

One year in Fargo this gal came up in her wheelchair and told me how Roger used to visit her in the hospital before he even made the majors. Then Roger sent her an invitation to his wedding. She told him she couldn't go because she had no way of getting there. Roger said, "I'll pick you up an hour before the ceremony."

2
OF
ARMS AND
THE MAN

The youthful pitching instructor overseeing the Cincinnati Reds' minor-league organization insists that his protégés are different from other players. Cerebral and intense he certainly is. His dream job is general manager.

There's no doubt in my mind that pitchers are a different breed. In general, pitchers and pitching coaches are not looked on as baseball *players*. They're looked on as more needy of emotional support than the regulars. If the fans are throwing things—that's in winter ball—they're throwing them at the pitcher. The pitcher is the guy the manager jerks off the field; it's embarrassing. Even pitchers who are going good need support. Batters who are going good are fine.

For me it's a hard thing to see: an eighteen-year-old kid from some small town in Texas who comes to unfamiliar cities and all of a sudden he's with players who are just as good as he is. He has some failure and that's hard enough to accept, and then he's walking off the field and people he doesn't know are yelling at him. That's probably the first time he realizes he's paid to do a *job*. Those fans are paying to watch, and they're going to swing a little harder when they get unhappy. There are times when the rosin bag looks like it's out there so you can crawl underneath it.

But no one has put a gun to your head and said you've got to be a professional baseball player. It can be a great way to make a living and it's an opportunity very, very few people have the chance to do and a vast amount would like, so the intensity *must* be there. Some pitchers just don't realize that that's what they need. If you're throwing ninety miles an hour in high school, you don't know that you're not going to be able to do this automatically. You can get away with that in high school or maybe even college, but not in pro ball. In the pros, you can't afford to give away *one* pitch to a batter. If you go 1–0 on every batter—well, you just can't pitch that way. My job is to make the pitcher understand this.

As a coach, you have to realize when the point has come that the guy has got to do it *now*. That separates good from bad pitching coaches. You have to have a relationship with the pitcher to be able to get into his head—the kind of relationship the manager doesn't necessarily have. There are guys you constantly pat on the back and others you kick in the ass. In baseball, people are too reluctant to have a hard talk with a pitcher.

I won't talk to the pitcher until I'm certain he's not pitching with intensity. I might be certain after one pitch, or just one warm-up session in a bullpen, but I'll let it go for a couple of games. You don't know what's going through a kid's mind, you don't know what's going on at home. I'm on the other side of the fence. As soon as a guy has a problem he's not going to come up to me with it because he's afraid he'll get the reputation of being a baby, or whatever. You have to be able to listen and hear what they're saying, and it's not necessarily the *words*.

But I'll open the conversation and say, "I'm going to tell you what I see. Tell me whether I'm right or wrong." Every time that I've done this, the pitcher will tell me what I'm telling him. He'll mirror what I'm saying.

In a pitching coach I think you look for a guy who hungers for knowledge. I try to pick people's brains about baseball, and I always have. I've seen great baseball players who don't become good coaches or good instructors, and to me it's easy to see why: people with great ability never really had to learn their talent *as a process*. The people who spend a lot of time in Triple-A always seem to learn a lot. They're always that one step away, that one piece of knowledge away, so they're going to learn as much as they can.

In Triple-A you'll find people who really know a lot about the game. Some coaches *prefer* teaching in the minor leagues to the major leagues, where the winning has to be stressed. Money is the problem in the minors. If you're going to be there for a long time, you'd better prepare yourself for a very modest lifestyle.

My whole life has been studying baseball. I went to Florida State for two years and played there, then I went with the Reds' team in Billings, Montana, in the Pioneer League—a rookie league—in 1975. Then I went to Eugene, then to Instructional League. The next year I played in Double-A, then back to Instructional League. The next year in Triple-A, then back to Instructional League. Triple-A from then on, winter ball three times. I was drafted by Detroit onto their major-league roster in the winter of 1980–81 and was called up at the end of the year, in both '81 and '82.

In '82 I went back to winter ball and hurt my arm, a slight tear in the rotator cuff. In '83 I was traded to San Diego and went to Las Vegas on a rehab program. Ended up missing two months. If you've played six years in the minors and are not on a protected major-league roster, you become a free agent and can sign with anyone. I signed with the White Sox and played at Denver. The next year I was in Des Moines, and then I decided to take the instructor's job with the Reds.

I miss playing less than I thought I would. I was injured, so maybe it was easier for me to walk away. I was thirty-four and a marginal major-league player anyway. But I do miss the one-on-one, holding the ball on the mound and saying, "Let's go." My job review was down there in black and white.

You're not going to find one thing to fill the void left by the thrill of going to the mound. It's not there. That's not saying life isn't worth living after the playing days. It is. I enjoy life, but I *more* than enjoyed every minute on the mound. And of course, I didn't have a long way to fall. I spent a long time in Triple-A. I hadn't lived a life free from the ordinary concerns and worries.

I try to go in and see a complete home stand, or at the minimum a complete rotation of the starting pitchers. The set-up we have is to coordinate the programs so that everyone in the minor leagues is doing the same things regarding fundamentals—fielding, covering bases, bunt, so on. Also standard is our thinking about handling different counts, 0–2, 3–0, and so on. This way the players have a smooth transition when they go to another team. I'd like every pitcher to have a change-up, so we teach that.

My theory is real simple: you make the glove to fit the person. I don't think there's one way to teach a pitch. When I see someone throwing a really effective pitch, I find out how he throws it. Then when I come across another guy with a similarity, maybe I can teach him that way. Our job as pitching coach is to know when something's going to work and when it's not.

I don't believe in changing deliveries. The main thing I'll look for is the follow-through. Shoulder injuries occur due to poor follow-through. Elbow injuries occur through the point of acceleration, usually on the breaking ball because you've got a shorter arc and a shorter time to decelerate. But there's not a whole lot you can do with those elements. If you start changing somebody's delivery, you have to be very careful. Throwing a baseball's an unnatural motion anyway, but something the player has done maybe fourteen years by the time I get him. The muscles have become accustomed to that. Now if I see something I don't necessarily like and change him, the muscles are acting differently and that's when he's going to get hurt. So as far as changing arm angles and things like that, it's not hard but it is potentially dangerous.

I need to see enough of a guy so that I see him when he's successful and when he's not, so I can compare the two. I work with the local pitching coaches on watching guys very closely when they're successful. Really get a mental picture. And we use video tapes and set up a library of good games, so the pitcher can take these with him through the organization. Eventually

I'd like to set up a split screen—good and bad outings. When you slow a film down you'll see all sorts of things.

I can tell by a pitcher's delivery if he's being successful on a given day. I don't have to follow the game at all, or even pay attention to balls and strikes. Just give me some film shot that day and I'll tell you.

Every successful pitcher I've seen has a distinct stop-and-go, a balance point when he makes the transition from wind-up to delivery. It's very controlled and compact. When pitchers are throwing good they always find it; when they're going bad you won't see it.

I've always been big on the mental side of pitching and try to get that point across to every pitcher I deal with, how important that is. I tell the pitcher that when he reads the box score the next day the *W* or the *L* is next to *your* name, no one else's. You have to be in control. If the catcher drops a sign you don't like, don't throw the pitch. When you can go out to the mound and say to yourself that when I throw this ball the way I want to, make the pitch do what I want it to do, this guy's got no chance—that's when the confidence comes. Even if it's A-ball, you're not concerned if Wade Boggs steps up to the plate. You'll get him out, too. It might not be true, but you have to arrive at that degree of confidence. And it takes a long time. Guys who have been through more things in their personal lives get to that point quicker. There is something to having that street smart and street savvy. I'm not saying our scouts should go look for motorcycle riders to be relievers, but baseball is a part of growing up.

It's almost a state of hypnosis on the mound. When you're going good the home run doesn't bother you. In the first place, if you're going good it's going to be a solo home run. You still have to be in the frame of mind that everything that's happening is happening as part of the game. You still have the next pitch to throw and the next batter to get out; you don't let the last pitch leak into the next pitch. That's a snowball and when that gets away from you, you're in trouble. Different guys hide this differently. Some hide it well but it bothers them anyway. That's when the manager had better pop out of the dugout. Good catchers pick it up before anybody. They can see the whites of the eye. Most pitchers try to give you the impression they want to stay in the game. Some really do but some really don't. That's why you've got to know the pitcher.

When I first see the guy I try not to think about whether he's going to make the majors. Don't look at him as a great prospect, and so handle him differently. I stress this: the pitching coach's job is to make the pitcher the best pitcher he can possibly be. In fact, the best possible *person*. With the towns in our system we're very lucky. The people there really care about the players. That's one thing about the minors; you have more relationship with the fans. You might walk in the diner and everyone knows who you are but you're just another person in the town who happens to play baseball. You might be looked at in a little different light, but you feel like you fit right in. The pedestal isn't as high in the minors. They don't have to be afraid of the other people in their environment. A lot of times players in the majors will develop a shield around themselves, shut everything off. You become an asshole, excuse the French, but actually you're just concentrating on your job.

We're not just talking baseball here. We're talking livelihood and lives. I'm dealing with bubbles. People have their bubbles burst sometimes. A personality is fragile.

I'm not trading stocks on the New York Stock Exchange to make dollars and cents every time I make a transaction. Sometimes I wish I were, very honestly, because there are things you can't do in baseball because of the salary structure. But it's my choice.

If I make a player a better human being so he can be successful somewhere else, then I've done my job. When a player leaves the Reds system because he's been released or traded, I'd hope he could look back at some point and say he's benefited from being with this organization. That's more important than anything I can do. My job is to get pitchers to the major leagues and make them successful. But I go beyond that.

D E N N I S   E C K E R S L E Y

"Boston, that'll be a royal pain in the ass for me. People don't forget. 'Why didn't you pitch like this when you were here?!' Oh, please! They'll be all over my ass."

He's the ace stopper for the Oakland Athletics, and in the 1988 playoffs against Boston he picked up the save in every game. Then he gave up the homer to Kirk Gibson in the first game of the Series.

A month earlier, we talk over coffee and fruit plates in the team's hotel in Arlington, Texas, waiting for the haze to diminish so he can catch some rays poolside. He spends many idle afternoons catching rays poolside. Sometimes he plays golf. "I only pitch one inning. I'm gonna be *tired?*"

People say baseball players should go out and have *fun*. No way. To me, baseball is *pressure*. I always feel it. This is *work*. The fun is *afterwards,* when you shake hands.

When I was a rookie I'd tear stuff up. Now I keep it in. What good is smashing a light on the way up the tunnel? But I still can't sleep at night if I stink. I've always tried to change that and act like a normal guy when I got home. "Hi, honey, what's happening?" I *can't*. It's *there*. It doesn't go away. But maybe that's why I've been successful in my career, because *I care*. I *don't* have fun. I pitch scared. That's what makes me go. Nothing wrong with being scared if you can channel it.

I used to hide behind my cockiness. Don't let the other team know you're scared. I got crazy on the mound. Strike a guy out, throw my fist around—"Yeah!" Not real classy, but I was a raw kid. I didn't care. It wasn't fake. It was me. This wasn't taken very kindly by a lot of people. They couldn't wait to light me up! That's the price you pay.

I had this thing with Rod Carew. I had thrown at him or something, knocked him down, and he took me deep the next time and yelled at me around the bases. At the All-Star game in 1977 he came up to me and said, "What's your problem?" I didn't *like* him. I don't think he liked me, either. A year later I had an 8–0 shutout in Boston in the ninth inning with two outs, and he steals second base. Asshole. Next guy hits a ground ball between the second baseman's legs and Carew scores and yells at me from home plate. Coming from a superstar like him, I wondered why he would belittle himself. I guess I got under his skin.

Typical.

As arrogant as I am at times, which I don't mean to be, I don't like it if the batters take a long time to get into the box. I think they do it sometimes to piss us off. I take it personal too much. Knocked a few down. Drilled a few guys. I protect myself and my teammates—all that macho crap —but I'm not a headhunter at all.

I was terrible with the umps—the worst. For ten years I had trouble with 'em. I wanted everything! I'd yell at 'em. Couldn't help it. *Instinctive.* Coaches said shut up early so you get those pitches later in the game. I said, "Fuck that! I may not be around if he doesn't give them to me *now!*" There's a fine line between being competitive and being a baby. It doesn't look good, yelling at umpires. Not only that, they get pissed off. I guess I would too. I've been thrown out three or four times. Second year in the big leagues a guy hit a home run after I threw two pitches I thought were strikes. I walked off the field yelling at the ump, "That's *your* three-run dinger, you *cocksucker!*"

I guess you should get kicked out for that.

Another time a guy takes me deep after a couple of close pitches. Next guy up I throw a pitch in the dirt and the ump calls it a strike. I yell, "I don't need it now, you motherfucker!"

Gone.

I was just so wound up when I was younger. I try to tone it down now, as much as I can. Some days are worse than others. A couple of months ago an ump said, "Geez, you're not the same guy." And I said, "You're right." The calls don't bother me now. But I also get better calls. It goes by reputation.

Now that I'm relieving, *stopping,* I think, "That's the only way to pitch! Everything on the line!" I'd never felt that kind of pressure before. Everybody busts their ass to get to you and now you screw it up. As a starter it's not so final. You get knocked out in the third, the team still has time. We lost because of him? *No!* That all happened six innings ago! But if I mess up *now* . . .

As a reliever I feel a little more important. I get more attention. As a starter people look at you differently. You only get attention once a week: "Come on, it's your turn. Let's go . . . today!" You're lounging around for the other four days. I thought it was the best job in the world. Lots of pressure, though, the day you *do* pitch. As soon as I woke up, I was psyched. I bounced around all day. *Now* I look at the starter who pitched last night and think, "Pressure's off! You don't have to do shit! Get outta here!"

So I show my emotions as much or more. When I do what I want to do, when I throw the ball on the outside corner and he's going to either swing through it or I paint his ass, I'm pointing!

"Yeah!"

"Yeah!!"

That's why I get so excited. Especially in situations like this year, especially at home. We're winning. Fans are standing and cheering. "Yeah!"

I shake hands like a demon now. I've shaked hands thirty-seven times so far this year! Walking off! That's like thirty-seven complete-game wins! But the other side of it—losing! Brutal. Hopefully I'll get to the Series and find out what that's all about. I want a World Series ring. Bad. This may be my only chance. I want the ring. I want the memories. That's something I want to do—walk off shaking hands after a World Series game.

I was drafted out of high school by Cleveland in 1972, third round. I thought I was going in the first round but third round wasn't bad. Got about thirty-five grand. I was seventeen, and when the phone call came I was like,

"Oh! Cleveland?" But that was the best thing that could have happened: a chance to go to the big leagues fast. Threw a shutout first game in Reno. Beginner's luck, but that first year wasn't easy, adjusting to everything, playing with people as good if not better than me, being seventeen and trying to go to the nightclubs and gambling and everything! Then I went to my first spring-training camp in 1973, and got married. Eighteen years old. That was a mistake which ended in a divorce five years later. I was *young!* It took me a long time to grow up. Sometimes you wonder if you ever do grow up, playing this game.

I had a good year in A-ball that year, and then was real successful in San Antonio in 1974. In '75 I went to the big-league camp. Frank Robinson, the first black manager, took over that year—very vocal, the ultimate competitor. Frank must have liked me. He didn't *have* to bring me to the big leagues. I think because I threw real hard and had pretty good control, the right place at the right time. I was twenty. I was in the bullpen for fourteen innings, then he gave me a start. I shut out the As, the world champions, on a two-hitter. I was fired up, throwing *hard*. Fifty thousand people in the stands. Then the next start I beat 'em again, gave up my first earned run in the big leagues. Won thirteen games that year, which isn't bad, got rookie pitcher of the year.

Good timing, really. A good rookie year can get you four or five years in the big leagues: "Well, maybe he'll be good like *that* again." That wasn't the case with me, but it could have been.

1976, I started off my second year brutal, 4–8 with a 4.9 [ERA] at the All-Star break. I couldn't get anybody out. Confidence shot. Frank stuck me in the bullpen a few times, then gave me a start and I came out of it. Punched out twelve guys and was on my way again. Last half of the season I was 9–3 with 150 punch-outs, which is a *lot*.

Next year threw a no-no. It was important for me to throw one at that time because every time I went out I was thinking no-hitter from the first batter. I did it against California, against Frank Tanana, and I didn't think about it anymore, unless I was into the sixth inning or so.

My wife and I weren't getting along. It was awful. We had a place in Cleveland but kept going to California, where I'm from. Always had to go back to California. Couldn't get California out of my system. Maybe I should have. Maybe we would have grown up more. I don't know. I was more worried about home than I was about the ballpark. Right at the end of spring training in 1978 I went to the ballpark and they whistled to me.

There had been speculation. I was ready. Traded to Boston. Guys said, "Hey, great, Boston. They're supposed to win the pennant!" I was supposed to be thrilled, but I thought, "Oh, no!"

I didn't want to go *nowhere!* Very emotional. Crying. Leaving some close friends like Buddy Bell, Rick Manning.

I called my wife and asked if she was going to meet me in Boston and she said no. I went, "Oh, fuck." It was a crusher. I was dying inside. I was scuffling. She wanted a divorce and I've got the Boston Red Sox giving up five guys for me. I've got to perform! We were supposed to win the pennant. As it turned out, she ended up marrying Rick Manning. That's what that was all about. A goddamn mess!

The game became everything to me. And I won twenty games—on a great team, maybe the best team I've played on, till this year. If I hadn't done it the right way I could have been out of the damn game.

Boston was great. A real switch. Packed houses. First place all year. We blew that lead but at the time I didn't know how devastating it was, how much that hurt—the home run [by the Yankees' Bucky Dent in a one-game playoff]. I thought we'd do it again and again. Not the case. And, being a pitcher, I was more personal-goal oriented to begin with. I'd won my twenty games, we just didn't win the pennant. It sounds cold, but if you're a pitcher at 10–15 with a 4.5, you just didn't *do your job*. But if an infielder hits .250 and turns the double plays, fine.

Guys said, "Except you're here, you're just a .500 pitcher." In Boston I'd have been a .600 pitcher for the last three years. You are what your team is, as a starter. Pissed me off. My control was better, I was spotting the ball. [Carlton] Fisk made me throw all my pitches and stop trying to be just a strikeout pitcher. Which was smart. Writers used to go to him and ask, "How come Eckersley's successful?" and he'd say, "Well, I've got Eckersley throwing his change outside and I've got—"

He's got me doing this. He's got me winning twenty games. Well, he's got me doing shit! I got to throw it! He helped a lot but don't take credit for everything! Used to *piss me off*. He had the locker next to mine so I heard it every day. Maybe that's why I got irritated after a while. But he *was* good.

I played hard. I lived hard. Man, it was quite an experience, being single again, and being successful. I soaked it up. I go to spring training in '79 and I was *bad,* on top, right? As on top as you could be. Just turned twenty-four, they give me a five-year deal for almost three million. I'm locked! I'm one of the best, I thought. I deserve it. Rich forever!

I was 16–5 at one time that year, talking shit. I was pretty cocky. The press ate it up. Then I lost five in a row, ended up 17–10. I threw some innings, too. We won ninety-one games and lost bad! I'm not sure what we did. [Third, eleven and a half games behind Baltimore.]

Things went downhill from there. Looking back, I might have done things differently, but hey, fuck it.

In '80 I had back trouble. I guess I wasn't in good shape. I thought I was. I did just what you had to do to play ball. Now I'm obsessed with working out. I wish I was then. I started having arm trouble every year. That's my excuse now, but it truly was. Always had some fire in there. Give me a cortisone shot every spring training. I'm not telling stories that they shot me all the time! I was pitching like shit, feeling like shit. Ended up getting serious with my now-wife that year and we got married in November. I was happy, personally, and my life was starting to get back in order with relationships, but my career was stinking it up, for whatever reason. I can talk about being hurt, but the bottom line is I stunk. I didn't pitch well. I was 12–14. But it didn't stick me in the back: "Hey, let's get it together!" I don't know why. I took it like, "I wasn't sharp. Didn't feel right. I'll be all right."

In '81 I threw the ball fair. In '82 I turned it on, came out of the box good after working fairly hard in the off-season—for me. But I still had bad work habits. Still having a good time, still living hard. Started the All-Star game and lost it. Hurt my arm in the middle of August. Things started going downhill *fast*. Missed a couple of starts, didn't pitch that well, ended up 13–13.

Then 1983 was the worst goddamn year of my life. Awful. Brutal. Started out 3–1, had tendonitis in my shoulder, missed three or four starts, came back and got my dick knocked off for four months. Crushed. No arm speed. Everything I threw was cock high. It was the most humbling experience of my life. Oh, the fans booed me bad. I would never want to admit it but it had me *on my knees*. Literally on my knees. I had tears coming down that the people didn't see, that I took home with me. I don't even want to remember it. The only thing I can say now is, "I *took* it. I didn't shelve it. Give me the ball. I'll try!" Once you make a lot of money, then you have to be *worth* what you make. That sits on you. I told myself I was going to get it back together, whatever it takes. But also for the first time I wondered, "Can I get it back? Can I pitch successfully?" My confidence was gone.

I started a Cybex program, really got into that, got some arm speed back. Felt decent. In '84 I didn't throw real hard but the arm felt good. I wasn't the number-one guy anymore. Obviously. Roger Clemens was about to come on. Bruce Hurst was there. Bob Ojeda was there. I was fourth fiddle. In May they wanted to trade me to Chicago, for Bill Buckner. I didn't have to go. They were on my list of teams not to get traded to. But I felt like Boston wanted to get rid of me and I needed a new start. I needed to get the hell out. Nothing against Boston, but it's hard to forget all the shit you did bad the year before. And Don Zimmer was with the Cubs. He had been my manager in Boston, now was third-base coach in Chicago. He knew what I could do. I said, "Okay." Wrigley couldn't be any worse than Fenway, I thought. Then I got to Wrigley and said, "You wanna bet?"

I didn't start out well. I was 1–5. But I pitched real good for 'em in the second half, like 9–3 with a 2.0. I was on top again! I thought I was getting it back. I felt like a real part of that club. We won the pennant. I lost a game in the playoffs. What are you gonna do? We didn't go to the World Series.

Then Dallas Green gave us all the money. Remember? Rick Sutcliffe got ten million, Steve Trout four and half, I got three. I was thinking about winning 200 games. I had 134 at the time. I remember that distinctly because at the press conference they said, "We're giving you this kind of money and you're our third starter." I said, "How the hell can I be your third starter when I got as many wins as the other two sonofabitches put together?"

A little arrogant, I guess.

But they took care of me and I tried to pitch my ass off for 'em. But shit went downhill. I got shoulder tendonitis again. I threw like four complete games in a row and then in the ninth inning of a game I felt something. I woke up and my arm was killing me. Something's wrong. Remember, all our starters went down that year. I was the last to go. I had a pretty decent year, 11–7 with a 3.0, but the next year they were all saying, "Geez, these guys are all screwed up." They looked at me like I stunk the place up. Little did they know what was to come!

Brutal year, '86. The whole team had a brutal year. Dallas Green was hootin' on us in the papers: "I give these guys all this money and look what they're doing." Hey, I have pride! I was out there pitching as good as I could. Everybody was playing as good as they could. We just stunk. Chicago's a tough place to play. I was livin' too hard—still drinkin' too much. You know, this game will get to you after a while. Not being successful makes it worse.

At the end of '86 I changed my whole life. I just realized my life wasn't going anywhere, personally with my relationships and professionally. My priorities were screwed up. Life for me was just always havin' a good time. But baseball was very important. It's hard to explain without saying *exactly* what happened. But I changed. Best thing that ever happened. I got with the "Eat To Win" people on the right diet. I've gotten away from it, but it got me to knowing what I was doing. I started working out seriously, and I quit drinking. Two years now. I've got some bad shit that happened to me that I don't even want to remember. The drinking—with me it was always drinking to forget or to celebrate. There's a lot of people in baseball who drink a lot, sort of "old-school," right?

In spring training of 1987 I was in the best shape of my life. The Cubs didn't know what they had: a totally together person! How were they supposed to know? They thought they still had the *other* guy. I heard trade rumors but I also knew I made a lot of money and it would be hard for them to offer me. I was expecting to be in Chicago. On the last day Gene Michael found me.

"Come on in here."

"Oh, my God! I'm gone! Who?"

He said Dallas Green would be down in about ten minutes to tell me where I was going to go. I had ten minutes to think about it! Cincinnati? San Francisco? Who needs pitching? Who'd want to pay my salary?! It wasn't *immense,* but it was enough, especially with my recent track record.

"Oakland."

"Jesus!" I couldn't have asked for a better situation. Going back home.

When I went over there Tony La Russa said I'd be in the bullpen for ten days, two weeks, until they got things settled. "Give me a little while and we'll figure out what we're going to do."

Fair enough. It was hard for me to think of myself as a reliever after being a starter for *twelve* years, but I was ready to swallow whatever was necessary because I didn't deserve to start. After the year I'd had? You have a bad year when you're twenty-five, they say you had a bad year. You have one when you're thirty-one, they say this guy's just about *done.* You have to eat what you have to eat.

They had a stopper. Jay Howell. I was coming in games for Joaquin Andujar, Moose Haas. They were hurt. I was their caddie. It took some getting used to. It was a blow to your pride. Had to be! I'm only human. Starting is still where it's at, to me. I had to be in the pen from Pitch One, in case somebody blows out in the first inning. That was tough, the not-knowing. But I was in good shape and I was ready every day. Back in the olden days I was ready once every five days, when I had to pitch, but don't ask me any other days! The others I was *tired* from livin' hard.

They talk about all the differences between starting and relieving. To me, *accepting my career* was the issue. First of all, I had no choice. Either do this or you're gone. And you make a lot of money, so hey, you give these guys the best you've got. Give me that ball! I'll pitch! I'll pitch my ass off! It was a do-or-die situation.

I jumped in there a few times when Jay Howell's arm was hurting, and *did it*. I could feel that this might be it. I was throwing ninety miles an hour, on many occasions, and I could spot the fastball. At the end of last year, in Texas, Tony came up to me in the bar and said, "Hey, when you come to spring training next year, do you want to start or close? You can be the closer."

I said, "Give me a chance to start!"

We got Bob Welch in December. La Russa called me.

"Remember what I asked you in Texas? Never mind."

Obviously, once you get Bob Welch, you don't need me to start. And they traded Jay Howell. So I figured they were going to give me a chance to be the stopper, but whoever's hot gets the job. We have Eric Plunk, young guy who throws hard. If I *stink* I'm not going to get the job.

Two innings is the most I'll pitch. Mostly it's one inning, starting the inning. You get your own trouble. That makes it a little easier, right? Ninety-five percent of the time I come in with the lead. I'm not out there just to get my work in. We've got a good bullpen, probably the best in the big leagues, I would think, two lefties, three righties. I get the glory but it should reflect on the whole bullpen.

You think of a great stopper as having one nasty pitch—"Hit it!"—like Goose Gossage who throws a hundred miles an hour or Bruce Sutter with a great fork ball. But I'm different. I'm not the guy they say, "Oh, my God, here he comes." I can sink the ball. People say I cheat! I have a good breaking ball to a right-hand hitter. But the big thing for me is I'm aggressive, I go after people, I throw strikes. The hitter can't be as aggressive. He can't be too cocky, either, because that ball's *too small*. Not only that, you could hit it on the screws and be out, right?!

I envision the *end* of the pitch. I don't think about *getting there*. No mechanics. I don't zone in on the glove. I pitch off the *hitter* somehow. Some batters make me more tense than others. I'm a little more careful with certain hitters. Other guys I might just zone it away as hard as I can. That's *power* pitching when you throw to zones. Mostly that would be with right-handed hitters. I get cocky against right-handers.

I wish I was a little happier in this game. What is so great about this shit? You get the money, then you're used to the money. You start making half a million a year, next thing you know you *need* half a million a year. And the heat is on!

Used to be neat to just be a big-league ballplayer, but that wore off. I'm still proud, but I don't want people to bother me about it. I wish my personality with people was better. I find myself becoming short with people. Going to the store. Getting gas.

If you're not happy when you're doing lousy, then not happy when you're doing well, when the hell are you going to be happy? This game will humble you in a *heartbeat*. Soon as you start getting happy . . . Boom! For the fans—and this is just a guess—they think the money takes out the feeling. I may be wrong but I think they think, "What the hell is *he* worrying about? He's still gettin' paid." There may be a few players who don't give 100 percent, but I always thought if you were good enough to make that kind of money, you'd have to have enough pride to play like that, wouldn't you think? You don't just turn it on—or off.

I've been very fortunate to pitch for fourteen years in the big leagues. That's a long time for a pitcher. I'm afraid of life after baseball. Petrified. I'm not ashamed of saying it. I'll be all right, but nothing will ever compare with this. I will not stay in baseball. I think about commercial real estate and money—big money! Or maybe I'll grow up after I get out of this fuckin' game.

GLEN ROSENBAUM

We sit in the bullpen during a game in spring training. He talks about the art of pitching batting practice and also of the frustrations of a minor-leaguer from the old days who now, as traveling secretary for the White Sox, has to coddle today's major-leaguers.

I grew up on a farm in Indiana and played baseball from the day I was old enough to throw. My brother and my dad were good athletes. My high school had only thirty-two kids, but we had a real good ball club. We lost one game in four years. I pitched all the time, but never got any notoriety outside the local papers. I never saw a scout.

Then I played for an independent team in La Porte, Indiana. After my second game the umpire asked whether I had ever thought about playing pro ball. I said honestly it had never entered my mind. I'd always thought I'd be a farmer. The umpire knew a bird-dog scout for the White Sox, who then came out to watch me pitch. After the third or fourth inning he gave me his card and told me to be in Comiskey Park on Tuesday night for a tryout. I had my cousin take me because my dad had to stay home to do the chores and the milking. In Chicago I worked out on the side, threw some batting practice, and signed about a week later.

I played eleven years, all in the minor leagues. Never got a big-league contract. I was 16–3 my first year, 15–5 my second, then 10–4, 9–3, 14–4. Then I was moved to the bullpen and came to the big-league camp three times, each time got cut on the last day of training. I was almost called up during 1961 when I was at San Diego in the Pacific Coast League.

I had a fastball, curve, and slider that I could throw for strikes at any time in the count. In my first year, I pitched 165 innings with 164 strikeouts and thirty-two walks. One year I threw 125 innings in relief with seventeen or eighteen walks. And five or six of those were intentional. But my size was always against me. Al Lopez believed you had to be big and strong. If Marty Marion had stayed one more year as our manager I would have been in the big leagues.

The White Sox were a first-rank ball club in those years, finishing a game or two behind the Yankees. They brought up *one* pitcher during my first six years in the organization. Many times I asked for a trade, but in those days a minor-league team had to win—they had to support themselves —and they kept guys like myself who were valuable to the organization. I ended up with 98 wins and 42 losses in my minor league career.

I'm the one who quit. They didn't release me. I could have played for a few more years if I had wanted to. I quit when I was right in my prime: twenty-seven years old. It's tough to turn the page, it really is. If I hadn't been successful, it would have been easy. But when you're successful at the work you've chosen, it's hard to walk away from it. It's something you don't want to do. And leaving baseball, you go back to being an ordinary working person.

My family had moved off the farm after my dad passed away, but I had continued to live out in that area in the off-season, working as a machinist in the lathe department for Urschel Laboratories, which makes food-processing equipment in Valparaiso, Indiana.

My second winter out of baseball, I came home from work one day and my wife said I had gotten a call from the farm director at Comiskey Park. They asked me if I would come in and talk with them about throwing batting practice during spring training, at least.

Eddie Stanky was the manager and Marv Grissom was the pitching coach. They're the ones who started the idea of no pitchers throwing batting practice. It was a new thing at that time, 1968. Before that, pitchers threw maybe fifteen minutes of batting practice on the second day after a start. Stanky had the idea that he'd rather have his pitchers throwing to a catcher on the side, working on things. My name had come up as a batting-practice candidate because of my good control.

The plant manager gave me six weeks' leave of absence. I worked the whole spring, and about the second week before it ended they said they'd certainly like me to stay on as batting-practice pitcher. I signed a contract, and then I worked back at the plant in the winter. That's the way I did for about ten years, until I got in as the traveling secretary, too.

Pitching batting practice is *control*. Hitters want to step in and build their confidence. They would much rather hit off a live pitcher than a machine because that's how they get their timing, off your body movement. With no arm action, there's nothing for the hitter to gear off of. Basically they use the machine to toughen up the hands, get or keep their arms and legs in shape. When they're ready, they want to hit off live pitchers. But some—Dick Allen, for one—didn't think BP was important.

I don't care who you are, you always have some competitiveness left in you. But I was one of the few former pitchers who did not try to show a hitter up, who didn't bust one in on the hitter's hands, for my own ego. I was able to forget that part of me and try to make the hitter look good. This is what impressed the club. The average batting-practice pitch is seventy-five miles per hour, at tops eighty-two. Most hitters want something moderately fast—not a hummer, but not a looper either. The high seventies gives them timing. A few hitters move in front of the plate for batting practice in order to, in effect, speed up the pitch. That's telling me they want more on the ball, so I do it and they can get back where they belong. Some guys throwing BP can't put that extra on it.

When a batter asked me to throw the ball away, if they were having problems there, I was able to do that. If they wanted me to come in tight, I could do that. And if they wanted a good curve ball, I could do that. Very occasionally in a special morning session I would pitch to a catcher giving signs.

When Chuck Tanner was manager I threw forty-five minutes to the regulars, every day of the year. Three hundred and twenty-five pitches. Now I don't throw that much every day. I'll be fifty-two this summer and it's just not as easy. But I'll do it some. I take a lot of pride in it, I really do. If I didn't, I wouldn't be any good. Players are traded and word got around and in a *Sports Illustrated* poll in 1983 I was voted best batting-practice pitcher.

I had become a coach under Chuck Tanner in 1974. Then Bill Veeck bought the club in the winter of '76 and he brought Paul Richards in as manager, and Richards had his own coaches. So I was out of a job as a coach. But the job as traveling secretary opened up, I interviewed and got it, and stayed on as batting-practice pitcher, too. I've done both since then, and for the last three years I've been coaching, too, working with Dyar Miller in the bullpen, or taking over in the bullpen if Fregosi gets thrown out and Miller has to go into the dugout.

You don't have any time to yourself. If I get one job done I have to go to the other. The only time I'll have a problem in the bullpen is on travel day, and on travel day I'll usually go in and get dressed about the seventh inning, call the airport, call the airlines, make sure everything is set out there. If we're in Chicago and I'm in my office working on my secretary duties, they might call up to see if I can get free for BP. If I can, I do. But if I can't, I don't. I don't have a secretary or anything, so I do all my own correspondence. It's a one-person department—me. I use the baseball as the fun part to burn away a lot of my traveling-secretary frustrations.

The first couple of years were very nerve-wracking. Those years we had the energy crisis, then the grounding of the DC-10s after they had that terrible accident in Chicago on American. Then United went on strike. These things really caused stress.

The energy crisis might have been the toughest because it was my second year and I had five charter flights canceled on me for fuel shortages —one within five days of departure. I have a trip to make and I don't have an airplane! That is the first time I'd ever experienced that ache in my stomach and gone to bed with it a couple of nights and it never left and I never slept. I could not think about anything else. It took three days before I got that flight covered. We were jammed three abreast into commercial planes, and the team wasn't having that good a year, which doesn't help, either. By the time of the All-Star game that year I was a basket case. I said, "I'll never do this again. If this is what this job is, I'm getting out."

The longer you do it is a plus. At first, it wasn't second-nature. I had to think about everything, double check on myself. I'd stop and wonder: Did I talk with that bus company or didn't I? So the next day you call again to make sure. Never leave for an airport if you have any doubt. Never. Never.

If you've made three calls and it's going to take a fourth one to erase any doubt, you make the fourth call, because the airport is no place to have any doubt—the team will nail you to the wall. If the players see any crack, they will nail you. A lot of it is in fun, but some—if they see they can get under your skin—they will. They'll test you at all times, see if they can get a single room for nothing, just a lot of little things. They can make life miserable for you and they can just sit back and laugh about it. It's all part of a big mind game.

I have an advantage over some of the other secretaries because I was a player. I'm also a coach, and I travel with them so I'm not going to do anything second class. In those first years we also had a great player rep, Greg Luzinski. He knew there were two sides. He was willing to listen to what I had to say from the management side, and we could always strike an agreement. Then he would go to the players and say this is how it is, if you have any problems, come to me. He eliminated a lot of the nit-picking.

The players know what their rights are now, and I know, so there's only one way to go about solving a problem—you go immediately to your player rep. No surprises. They have more respect for me if they're sure I'm not going to try to pull anything on them. Say you're flying commercial. The players' agreement specifies that everyone flies first class or with an empty seat between two players in coach. Maybe the plane has a mechanical problem, and you have to switch from a 747 to a 737, which has fewer seats. The airline will come to me and say, "We have a problem. Will you give up some of your empty seats so that we can accommodate these people who have purchased tickets?"

I have to go to the player rep because I can't release those seats without talking to him. If I just handed a player a boarding pass and had him sitting three abreast, I would have a war. They'd file a grievance immediately, and I would be at fault.

If for some reason a charter plane isn't available until three hours after the game, I have to tell the players *well* beforehand to prepare for the waiting time. I can't spring that on them in the clubhouse.

Travel is not glamorous. On a ten-day road trip there are a lot of irritations. Guys are tired because we fly at terrible hours. We don't get to eat when we should. With forty-five people—twenty-five players, six or seven coaches, trainer, assistant trainer, equipment manager, two to three press, four announcers, radio producer, TV engineer, general manager, and so on—you have forty-five different personalities, and the anthill that doesn't bother one person looks like a mountain to another.

The biggest trouble with this business is we don't get a chance to recharge. We can't pick a vacation period. I go to spring training on February 11. People don't realize what it's like to work from the eleventh of February until the middle of October, seven days a week. Mentally you get burned out. Physically you get tired. It's not always easy to be cheerful and receptive to a player who may be asking for something extra, or something unreasonable.

Let's face it. Baseball's different than it used to be. Players have so many rights now, they're not used to taking orders like we used to. They told us we got only two tickets per game, and we didn't ask why. When I played, the traveling secretary came around with the itinerary, showed it to us, and walked away. Well, now I can have a kid two weeks out of high school join the club and he asks me why I'm doing something, why we're leaving the night before. I have to explain it. It tests my patience.

Only a couple of times, with a certain player rep, have I had a big problem. He had contract problems and was going to take it out on everyone, including me. On a plane he'd ask me why somebody was sitting up front. I seat according to seniority, and I have in my briefcase, every time I travel, the roster with the years, months, and days of seniority in the big leagues. He questioned me and I said, "Come here," and I handed him the sheet.

One time in Boston I'm doing the ticket work with the airline agent, filling out my boarding passes in the hospitality room, and I start walking around and passing out the passes. This same player rep looks at his and says, "Oh, for Chrissakes, I was sitting by the window the last time I was in here." I just looked him in the eyes and said, "I've got a lot of things more important to worry about than where you sat last time." Then I walked away. That's about the only time I've talked to a player without any respect. He was constantly going out of his way to make life miserable for me, and I'd had my bellyful of it.

A few years back we had some new players come on, and one was a black player, a free agent, established player. I was never prejudiced, and it bothered me back when I played minor-league ball to see the way the black ballplayer was treated, it bothered me to no end. So I've always had sympathy for the black ballplayer. I have *never* based any decision on what color a player's skin was. Well, that season was about two months old, and I was in the clubhouse after handling the players' pass list, getting in my uniform to go on the field and throw batting practice. This black player walked by —I don't know what had happened, but there had been some dealings in the clubhouse—and said, "Rosie, I've been watching you."

"What do you mean?"

"You're all right," he said, and he gave me a high five. "You're the most fair person I've ever dealt with."

"What are you talking about?"

Well, he was talking about black and white, but I didn't know that then. He had been watching me to see if I treated the black player different than I treated the white player. That startled me. And he treated me as well as anyone in baseball ever has. He told me later he had a world of respect for what I did for the ball club.

Whenever I talk with kids the one point I make is that no matter what courses they've taken in school, no matter what they know, no matter what they want to be, always go at everything with an open mind. You never know where that road is going to take you. You can say, "Boy, this is what I want to do," but it doesn't work that way. I never knew I was going to be anything but a farmer.

WILLIAM   BRYAN,   M.D.

The orthopedist for the Houston Astros is not much older than the veteran players. He is on the faculty at the Baylor College of Medicine, has a private practice, and is a big fan unless the game is too boring.

The arthroscope is of great value for the shoulder but in no way has it really changed the natural history of the baseball pitcher. We're not Doctor Goodwrench when it comes to these problems. We don't want to be merchants of false hope. We may help some people but we still have as many men going on the disabled list every year, as many people dropping out of baseball because of shoulder problems.

There's a lot of hype in sports medicine, and as honorable as we would like to be as M.D.s and orthopods, we have to be careful that some people don't use our athletes in their self-promoting schemes. There are people out there on the periphery, other physicians, who are trying to get famous taking care of pro athletes, who tell the young athletes, "Come get your shoulder 'scoped and you're going to be like new." That's just not true.

The public thinks that we are performing bionic surgery, taking ligaments out of legs and putting them in elbows, opening up shoulders, and sending people back out there to be superhuman. The fact is that none of that stuff works on a regular basis. These operations are done on sort of a desperation basis. I can understand that. A guy's about to have his career ended and the doctor'll say, "The only thing left to do is to have your arm operated on and rebuild the elbow ligaments." Only a few guys have made it back. Tommy John is one, and I like to think we turned the corner for Jim Deshaies. With Deshaies, we didn't exchange parts, we didn't put in a new carburetor. He had a partial tear of his rotator cuff. We got him on the right rehabilitation program.

Our goal is to try to pick things up very early, shut them down, rest them, and then we may have a positive effect. Total rest for six months. We get a lot of heat for that. There are many situations where rest will get it better, but rest is not glamorous. You tell a guy with a sore shoulder, "Look, I want you to sit down and rest it for six months," and he'll say, "The hell with you." If you *operate* on him and tell him to sit down for six months, he'll believe you. It makes you look like a hero. I see that mentality and I don't want to be part of that.

Most important for pitchers is that they change their mechanics. It's like with tires. If your tires are worn down crooked and you put on new tires, unless you get the front-end realigned, the new tires are going to wear down the same way. The same with the shoulder. 'Scoping it, cleaning it out, strengthening the muscles around the shoulder are just not enough to put up with the tremendous stress that the rest of the body puts on it as you deliver a baseball.

We had a guy by the name of Mike Friederich, highly touted prospect, a great big guy from Fredericksburg, Texas, who could really bring the heat. His first or second year he pitched a no-hitter and everybody was real excited. Mike was big, six-six or six-eight, and threw real hard *with his arm*. There was an argument as to whether he trained properly or not. I don't know. I think he was doing all his exercises, but as they moved him up through the ranks, as the batting got better, he just couldn't keep up. I think Mike went outside of his envelope and started throwing with bad mechanics. He tore up his elbow ligaments and the nerve running by that area was stretched and he was numb in his fingers. I tightened up the ligaments in his elbow but I didn't feel we should go and get the tendons from somewhere else in his body—go through all of that business. He rested six to nine months. I told him, "Unless you come out and throw with different mechanics, you're just not going to make it."

He came back and did good for about six months, and then the next season, that was it.

You know, baseball came out of cricket and in cricket you have to throw with a straight arm. You can't bend your elbow during the delivery. And they don't have any arm problems. Bending the elbow and externally rotating the shoulder puts incredible stress on the shoulder. And it demands that the legs and the trunk get the arm in the right position to get that final whipping action. If that smooth motion breaks down, then there's too much stress on the shoulder. It tends to loosen up, and the rotator cuff gets stretched. That's why a lot of people drop out.

We work carefully with the pitching coaches on mechanics, simple things like keeping your opposite shoulder in—if you open it too quickly your pitching arm drags behind—and your elbow above the horizontal. Where the hand is—overhead or three-quarters or side arm—doesn't matter. We just need that elbow *up*. The submarine pitchers aren't really throwing with the elbow below the horizontal. The trunk of their body is turning and their elbows are still *above* the level of their shoulders. Next time on TV, look carefully. You'll see.

What makes Nolan Ryan so different is he throws every single pitch with the same mechanics. He doesn't vary, whether it's early in the game, late in the game, ahead 11–0 or behind 11–0. He just doesn't change. He's been analyzed with some high-speed cinematography and there are a few little things about trunk rotation that look special, but otherwise his mechanics look like those of a lot of other people.

His build is about like yours and mine. He's not going to win a Mr. Universe contest. He's very powerful in his legs and his trunk muscles, but his arms look like John Q. Public's. The difference is his mechanics. And he has a very fastidious program of working out, doing light weight lifting, sit-ups, bicycling, running. He keeps in very good shape twelve months a year.

But Nolan got in trouble in '87 and I don't know exactly why. I think in spring training he probably came out and did a little bit too much too quick and he really didn't tell us immediately that he was having some trouble. Later, Dick Wagner, the general manager then, came to me and asked what was happening. I said Nolan had a sore medial collateral ligament in the elbow—tenderness on the inside of the elbow. The diagnosis didn't take any special tests. It's a very common injury and it can often be career-ending. Operations to fix that haven't worked very often.

Dick said, "Well, what do you think?"

I said, "If he blows it out, the horse is out of the barn and we're in big trouble."

Wagner had done an analysis of when Nolan didn't pitch well correlated with how many pitches he had thrown the *previous* outing. Dick showed me that and he showed it to our trainer, Dave Labossiere, and he said, "I think we're getting into trouble here. Looks like if he comes out and throws 135, 145 pitches a game, we're in trouble."

Dick was of the opinion that the coaches probably were a little afraid of Nolan because he is a senior person, although he's not an angry kind of guy. He does command respect and Dick was afraid that they were just going to let him keep throwing. So Dick, bless his soul—he's an excellent businessman but was known to be a little gruff—rather unceremoniously put the pitch limit on Nolan without consulting him. Nolan wasn't very happy about it. I believe that he thought *I* had stabbed him in the back. I wasn't too happy with the way it was done because most of the time we get together with the players. But if you look back at last year, Nolan had one of his more successful years, he stayed off the disabled list, and I'll defend that decision until my dying days.

Nolan also went to see another doctor, who told him he should be operated on after the season. This is Nolan speaking. I never talked to that other doctor about it. I knew Nolan wasn't grossly unstable in his elbow; he didn't need tissue brought up to strengthen it. I said, "Nolan, you're crazy. You don't want your elbow rebuilt. You're forty years old. You rest it and it's gonna be okay next year."

He rested it and he seems to have healed up this year. We're letting him throw as much as he wants.

Players can go see anyone they want to, but the Astros' policy is if they have a medical problem on our team, I have to know about it. They can't sneak off with their agents and see somebody else behind our backs. Players have talked to me and then gone to someone else. I was away on sabbatical in Australia one winter when Kevin Bass's shoulder got sore. I wanted him to see my partner who just does shoulder work, but Kevin's agent wanted to consult someone else, and that doctor told Kevin he should have his shoulder ligaments tightened up with surgery. They got hold of me in Australia and I said, "No. Don't do that." I know Kevin is a little loose-jointed and can get shoulder pain. But if you tightened the ligaments, they'd stretch back out to the way they genetically were. He rested the shoulder and was okay the next year.

The Joe Sambito situation is one that taught me to be conservative.

My predecessor, Harold Brelsford, had told Sambito to treat his elbow conservatively, but Joe and his agent wanted a quicker solution, so they went to someone else. Joe was operated on, but there's a complication that can occur even in the most flawless procedure—damage to the ulnar nerve. That's what happened, and Joe was left with weakness in his hand. Of course, then he came back to our club and tried to make it again and it was just kind of hard to see him struggle and not throw well and know that his hand was weak. Joe is a very endearing person and I like to consider him a friend. On the other hand, I had to tell management, "Look, he ain't gonna make it."

He was released by us, and lo and behold, he popped up with the Red Sox and they went on to play the Mets in the World Series in '86, and he contributed, sort of. [Sambito is now out of baseball.]

I'm very impressed by how fastidious good baseball players are. They are not the impulsive, knock-down-the-walls kind of people. To put up with the process of coming up through the minor leagues, riding those buses, sleeping in those strange beds every three or four nights, getting your tits lit, as the pitchers say, by a couple of rockets now and then—being able to weather that takes a lot of maturity and a very steady, calm personality. You look at Ryan and [Bob] Knepper and [Mike] Scott. They just don't get nonplussed. You don't seem them down there pounding walls and breaking up furniture.

I see the ballplayers at one of two extremes. They have either football minds or track-star minds. The football mind is a guy that loves pain. He seeks it out, in a way. He may feel better if he's hurt and that's what makes him a great football player or hockey player. Billy Doran, our second base-man, has a football mind. It's not that he's dumb and ignores his body, but he just wants to play. If you were going to have an army, you'd want a million Bill Doran's out there in the front lines. In fact, I chew my finger-nails worrying about him. The trainer and I have to be careful that we don't send him out there too quick.

Dickie Thon is a guy with a football mind, ready to play. When Dickie got hit with the Mike Torrez fastball in 1984, I happened to be sitting in the owners' seats at the Astrodome, right next to the rail. I heard the crack and knew it was either the helmet or a bone breaking. He went down like he was shot. It's the only time I've ever jumped over the railing and run onto the field. I thought, "God, the guy's dead or brain-damaged or something."

It broke the bone around his left eye, temporarily changed the shape of his eyeball, and wrinkled the retina. I gave numerous interviews with reporters asking if I thought Dickie would become gun-shy, and I said, "Look, with a kid that has the ability to make it to the majors—for every two hundred we draft, three or four become everyday players at the major-league level—don't be asking me whether Dickie Thon is mentally prepared to play the game, even with an injury."

Then there are guys who have track-star minds. They know every little ache and pain that bothers them and they're constantly telling me, "I've got to make a living with my body and I don't want it abused out there. I need a little more medicine, a little more therapy."

Cesar Cedeno was like that. Cedeno lived in the training room. He was into aspirin, anti-inflammatories, vitamin B-12 shots. And I always saw him complaining to the trainers. Often you couldn't substantiate it with any objective findings. He'd go 0 for 4 and he'd hurt. The next day he'd go 3 for 4 with a home run and miraculously all those aches and pains would be gone. But I can understand that. We all handle stress in a different way.

"Happy" Brelsford, as he was known, had done this job for eighteen years. After that long, one gets a little tired. And 1981 was a horrendous year for him because J. R. Richard, the pitcher, had a stroke and filed a lawsuit against Brelsford and some other physicians.

The case was settled a couple of years ago. One physician, Dr. Michael Feltovich, still the team's internist, felt really miffed and held out. They eventually dropped the case against Feltovitch. Also, the agents were becoming more a part of the medical treatment. It was almost like talking to a kid's mother up here in our office. You had to talk to the player's agent and that wasn't like the good old days. Happy said he didn't like dealing with that. Then he had a personal tragedy, his wife had cancer. So he was clearly looking around for someone to take over. I'm a baseball fan, but I was never an inveterate fan. I didn't spend all my medical-school days out there at the Dome. But I had done a sports-medicine fellowship and I was interested in rehabilitation of the total athlete. I could look after upper- and lower-extremity athletic problems.

One day I just happened to read an article in *Sports Illustrated* on Bob Horner, and the next day I was sitting down in the little lunch bar here at the Methodist Hospital talking to Brelsford about Horner, because I knew Brelsford liked to talk about baseball. He thought it was pretty keen that I had read the article. The next week I got called to his office. I thought maybe I had screwed up on one of his patients and he was mad at me. And he put his feet up on the desk—big ol' cowboy boots—and took a couple of puffs on a cigarette and said, "I'm getting tired of this shit. I'm gettin' out. Why don't you take over?"

I told Happy, "Hey, I'll hang around and see what happens." So for a couple of years I worked with him. The club trusted Brelsford. Whomever he named to take over, the club accepted. I kind of got the hang of things, although there are a lot of political things I'm still learning. There are more politics in this aspect of what I do than in private practice at the Methodist Hospital, certainly.

Then one winter—this must have been before the '84 season—Happy called me and said, "That's it. I can't take it. I'm out. You go to spring training."

"What happened?"

He was mad because Art Howe, one of the Astros whom he had taken care of over the years and considered a friend, had suddenly gone to somebody else for his medical care. His agent had jerked Howe away from Brelsford.

It's been easy for me because I'm young and I don't have that barrier of age. I've kind of gotten along with the guys, my kids are the same age as many of their kids, so they've come to accept me. I have to be careful with the players so they don't think that I'm a stooge for the management, trying to use their bodies for the glory of the Astros. I try to impress on the players that I'm their physician, I'm their advocate, even though I'm management. On the other hand, I might say that the management at times feels that I may be, you know, giving the players a little too much leeway, letting them stay on the disabled list and whatever. But there may be a misconception that the managment, à la *North Dallas Forty,* is down there injecting corti-sone in the guys and pumping them up with pills and making them play. Baseball's not like that. These players are valuable commodities and I have never felt pressure to send people back out there prematurely.

I think the players are apprehensive. The public thinks, "Those sons-of-bitches making all that money ought to be on top of the world." But what has happened with all that money? They've had to invest it and shelter it. These guys are not educated. They're high-school grads and their wives are high-school grads, for the most part, and I can see they're a bit concerned about what's going to happen. They are depending on their agents. I see that the great income has created a lot of tension and stress. They're driving Mercedes and it's going to be quite a crash, you know, from making $500,000 a year, back to whatever.

I get a lot of jocular grief from the players about the amount of money

I make in my private practice, and the fact that I will continue to make that until I retire. I don't make as much as the players on an annual basis, obviously, but I will still be making my present income in my fifties and maybe sixties and they won't. So they bring that to my attention.

The job at the Dome is certainly different than sitting here in my office and seeing private patients. Here, I may have to talk to the guy's employer, or his wife may call, wanting to know what's going on. Out there, it's the doctors, management, the athlete, the media—and occasionally the agent, even though I don't put people on the disabled list. That's done by the club.

I try to channel stuff for the media through the general manager or the publicity director. I learned the hard way. Gary Carter was here and had me look at his knee and I said, "You've got torn cartilage," and he said, "I know, what should I do?" and I said, "See your doctors."

Then I said, "I'm not telling you how to run your business but I think you might skip the All-Star game, get 'scoped, and get back."

So somebody called me from the *New York Post* or one of those tabloids and I made the mistake of talking to him and saying that Carter *could* be operated on. Well, the next day friends from New York called me and said, "Gee, says here you said Carter *should* be operated on."

People often ask me why I do it. The pluses are that I rapidly built my sports-medicine practice and got away from general orthopedics, which I didn't have an interest in. I see a lot of baseball players locally, high school and college kids, which is kind of fun. Many of the team physicians are strictly private practice and don't have academic interests and don't enjoy talking about baseball problems and analyzing a series of cases, but I do. I'm frequently asked to talk about baseball problems to national audiences.

When I first started, it was great fun to meet famous people. In fact, when I took the job, all I could think of was I'd get to meet one of my childhood idols from Pittsburgh: Bill Virdon. So I closed my eyes and said I can't believe it but I'm going to be talking to Bill Virdon. I've kind of gotten over that rush of meeting famous people and now I want to meet nice people, and I do.

I've got three sons, a daughter, and a wife who love baseball, so it's a family affair for us. The kids' stock in school has increased since they've known the players. My oldest boy was a batboy for the Mets games in New York. That was a big deal for him. It was a big deal for *me*.

And the playoffs in 1986 you can't take away from me. To see how big a thing it is, the tensions, it's really impressive. On the other hand, it's very frustrating to be close to the people who are winning and losing and not be able to do anything about it. You say to yourself, "Am I going to be more excited if we win or more disappointed if we lose?" I can still close my eyes and see our locker room and training room after we lost to the Mets. Pretty heavy duty. Worse than a funeral. I was surprised. That statement, "It's only a game"? It's *not*.

One downside is the threat of litigation. These guys are making a lot of money and are all tied up with attorneys as their agents. So the insurance industry is not willing to write "excess coverage" for my activities as team physician for the Astros.

The other downside is the amount of time put in, including phone calls. The Dickie Thon situation, for example, went on and on. I go to about sixty games a year; a resident goes to the others. Someone has to be there, even though the rules of baseball are generous to the physicians. Unlike in football, if the baseball player goes out of the game he can't go back in, so I don't have to be down there making split-second decisions about somebody that's hurt. That decision is not where the pressure of the job is. The pressure is to give accurate expectations of *recovery*.

3
FOOD, CLOTHING, AND SHELTER

He joined the St. Louis Cardinals in 1977 as summer help in the sales department, then shifted over to public relations before getting his present job as traveling secretary in 1981. He turned thirty-six and got married just a month before we talked, during spring training, 1988.

"This is my second marriage and it was tough on the first marriage and I have a little daughter whom I miss greatly and don't see very often just because I'm gone and then when I'm home I'm at the ballpark from ten in the morning to ten or eleven at night."

Sitting in the office he shares at the Cards' training camp in St. Petersburg, Florida, he greets several veterans as they report for duty and fields a query from Willie McGee about where to get a check cashed. General Manager Dal Maxvill drops by. Someone asks about car rentals. Phone calls come through regularly. He excuses himself to see someone out front. But this morning, he assures me before the camp really gets humming, will be the best time for our conversation. The only alternative is during a game.

What I try to do is think of things that *may* happen, and how I'm gonna react to them. You can't be prepared for every problem that comes down the pike, but you have to try. We normally carry forty to forty-five people, and if something goes wrong and the plane or bus breaks down, the players and coaching staff—even though they realize I'm not the one flying the plane or driving the bus—they're gonna sit there and say, "OK, C.J., how are you gonna get us out of this? What'll we do now?" If you sit there and say you don't know, like a raving lunatic, well then all hell breaks loose.

We had a situation in New York in 1981, my first year. We had a Sunday afternoon game, and then we had like a six or six-thirty commercial flight to Cincinnati. The ball game went long, and it was gonna be cutting it close whether we were gonna make the plane. With a lot of commercial aircraft they're only gonna give you a hold of, say, thirty minutes, because that plane leaving New York to go to Cincinnati might be going on to Atlanta or Chicago, and they can't hold it for an hour and a half and screw up everything all down the line. They will hold it a little, mainly because we're using so many seats. Usually what happens if we're late, then we'll open it up, you know, buy everybody a drink, appease them.

Anyway, the day was sunny but it had rained all Saturday night. And the bus driver, instead of parking in the lot, pulled the bus up behind the scoreboard, and instead of being on the concrete he was on the dirt part—only this time it wasn't dirt. So he revs up to go and that wheel sunk into the mud all the way up to the axle and we aren't goin' *anywhere*. I was sittin' there next to our trainer, Gene Gieselmann, and he says, "What are you gonna do? What are you gonna do?"

Whitey was just sitting over there looking at me.

This was one of my first trips! Our first thought was to just start hiring taxis. We were asking policemen for help. Then I asked somebody where the nearest city bus terminal was and fortunately for us there was one just on the other side of Northern Boulevard, a dispatch center for city buses. I saw a bus pull out and I went up to the driver and asked if he'd take $100 to take us to La Guardia Airport, $200—we just got to get there. The bus driver says, "I can't do it; I'm going out on my route." Well, then I told everyone else to wait by the stuck bus, don't go scattering all over because we'll never find you, and Gene and I walked over to the terminal and got ourselves a bus and they only charged us like fifty cents a guy or something like that. They held the plane for us and we barely made it, running like the Hertz commercial.

Approaching the airport on the flight, you have the pilot call in when you're about ten minutes away and make sure the bus and the equipment truck are there. When you're landing somewhere between twelve midnight and six, that's when you want to make sure everything is right. The guys are tired, they've had a long day, especially if they've lost a tough game. That's when you least want mistakes. People's resistance is down. If that bus isn't there then, you got forty guys sittin' there, gettin' ready to yell at you.

In September 1985, we were in the pennant race. I don't remember where we were coming from or even if we won or lost the game, but we had played extra innings and arrived in Philadelphia about three in the morning. I told them to have *two* buses there because we had extra writers and also, in September, extra players. Well, two buses were there but one of the drivers decided five minutes before we landed that he was going out for something to eat.

I was livid. "Why in the *bleep* would the other guy leave?" And the driver we had goes, "I don't know. I told him not to." Mike Shannon said, "Don't worry, C.J., we'll just get on here, no problems." We had to load like sixty-five people onto one forty-five-passenger bus. Guys were standing and everything, but they didn't say one word because they knew I was hacked off.

In January I start lining up the airlines, sending out for bids. We use predominantly charter and we send our schedule out to three different airlines. We mix and match because not all carriers can handle you. This year we're making thirty-five movements—mostly charter.

In St. Louis, TWA controls 72 percent of the flights, so they can give us an airplane at ten o'clock in the morning, where Delta or USAir wouldn't have the plane available, so therefore they can't even bid on those flights. The only times that people really bid are for either Sunday afternoon or the eleven o'clocks at night, but for us in St. Louis, since Whitey's come on board we like to fly the day of the game. This gives Whitey another night at home and saves on the meal money. You could therefore justify the cost of the charter. Whitey also figures one less night that the guys have to spend on the road is better. I think he's right, too.

When he first came over there were a few people that didn't like it, and there were some players that bitched and moaned about it, but after a while they finally got used to it. The record does show that we've had just as much success whether we've traveled the day of the game or the night before.

When we charter for an aircraft with TWA, say, we can request a certain pilot, and he's one that I'm usually satisfied with—that I feel is, one, safety first, and, two, has an interest in the ball club. To me this helps. He'll go out of his way, be a little more friendly to the people, be more enthusiastic about the job, and take it more than just a regular nine-to-five job. I had airlines call up before the World Series saying they'd like to fly the Cardinals. They enjoy it and there's a certain amount of prestige, you know. I've just found out that if they're fans, it's better.

Say you pull out on the runway and all of a sudden the pilot finds out an engine isn't working. You want a pilot who instead of just saying, "Well guys, I'm sorry but I'm gonna have to take this plane back in," will come up and say, "Hey, C.J., we got a problem here. I don't want to fly at this point. I'm gonna see what I can do."

The chances of his getting another plane right away are much better than mine. This hasn't happened to me, but I know when Lee Thomas had the job they had a problem in New York and the airplane sat on the runway, I believe, from twelve-thirty or one in the morning until seven A.M.

Bill Calvert, one of our pilots, works like a dog. He can go in and try and pull some strings, call the airport, call the traffic control and say we've got this ball club and we've gotta get them out and I think it does help out. I *know* it does in St. Louis. Very seldom do we have to sit there and wait.

Sometimes the charter flight is just as cheap, considering that the agreement with the players calls for either first-class seats or an empty seat between players in coach. Also, if you have a charter you just take the bus out to the airplane and that makes it easier, too. But the great thing about charter is that, in most cases, the plane is there when you are ready to go. That's the thing that you really need to try and stay on top of, because after a guy plays a game at night and especially as the season winds down and you are in a pennant race, that's when you want things to go *perfect*.

You'd have to be darn near dead not to get involved in the situation as summer turns to fall and you're either two or three games out or two or three games up. Each game means a little bit more and tempers get a little short—everybody's, because there is so much at stake.

I've been blessed with our ball club over the years, though. I've had people on airplanes come up and say, "Gee, your players are so nice, so polite." People that we don't even know say the ball club is a very nice club. They can't believe that it's "Yes, ma'am" and "No, ma'am." And you like to hear that. That's why it doesn't matter really how we go, how we travel, because these guys are first class. The only dress code we have is for commercial flights they need to wear a sport coat, no jeans. They can wear anything they want on the charter. However, it's gotten to a situation where the players really police themselves. Whitey's rule is, if I remember correctly, you can't look like girls or dogs. If they wear jeans they have to be designer jeans or dress jeans and it's gotten to the point where even on charters we have a lot of guys that wear sport coats and some wear ties. If somebody comes on with even a shirt that's not a normal shirt, maybe it's a funny color or a little out of the ordinary, the guys will say, "Hey, we don't want to see that again!"

During the playoffs and Series we make it even a little bit nicer for 'em. During the season there are no wives on the team bus and they can only make three flights with the ball team—and no moms, dads, children, or girlfriends. But during the playoffs and Series, it changes. We provide all transportation and we allow each player to take his wife and kids, and a guy who isn't married could take his father or mother or his girlfriend.

While you're on the road invariably you'll get phone calls from hotel people. They'll take you out to lunch, tell you they're interested in having the ball club over and all that kind of stuff. Happens all the time. Every year, every city. Most of the time I go over. Again, you're always anticipating a problem. You always want to be prepared in case something happens, and you *never* want to go into a place that you haven't seen.

We probably get as good a rate as there is. You're booking a lot of places in the summer, which is tourist season, but you're talking midweek, too, not just weekends, and it's consistent business. They know that every year they're gonna have a ball club into that city three times, for clubs in that division, nine nights in a city every year. You're talking 360 rooms. That's a lot of business, plus a lot of the guys eat in the coffee shop, and a lot of guys will frequent the hotel bar.

It's not like the old days when it was like bringing in a college fraternity. Most of these guys are making more money than a lot of corporation executives. My policy is to try and stay at the best hotel possible for the money, and the people here, the players, pretty much leave it to me to do what I want. I won't say expense is *not* a factor. We wouldn't stay at the Plaza in New York or the Four Seasons in Philadelphia because it's $190 a night or whatever the heck it is. We stay at the Grand Hyatt in New York. As a matter of fact they have just about everybody at the Grand Hyatt.

When I look for a hotel I make sure that the rooms are nice, that the bell service is good. I remember when we were in Montreal—this was back about '81, '82—we went into the hotel about three-thirty in the morning and four guys went to their rooms and the rooms were filthy. They came down and were upset. Not too upset, just tired. And the guy behind the counter started talking to me in French and I kinda lost my temper. Then in broken English he said he didn't have any more rooms.

I said, "You *gotta* have more rooms. The rooms are filthy."

He said, "Well, I can't help it. It's not my fault."

I said, "It *may* not be your fault but I guarantee you it's not *my* fault." I ranted and raved. I was really teed off. I usually give people a break. If it was one room, fine, but it was four rooms. We later moved out of that hotel. Somebody else happened to come up with a better offer and we've been there ever since.

We're getting to the point where when we make up our contracts and deal with the representative, we want the rep there when we check in the hotel because, once again, if there's somebody that comes down and says their room's dirty, the rep can go get them another one. They're always hiding a few.

The only time I really jumped on a *player* was in Chicago. He came down complaining about something with his room. I said "Well, wait just a minute, I'm taking care of somebody else."

He said, "No, I want it right now."

I said, "You just wait a minute. I'm trying to get this other player taken care of and make sure he's got a room, and then I'll take care of you."

Then he said he was gonna check out and go to another hotel. I said you go ahead, and the guy behind the counter said all the other hotels are booked in Chicago, which I could believe.

So this player started yellin' at me and I started yellin' at him and he started cussin' at me and I started cussin' at him. He was a veteran, a big star, and said, "Don't talk to me like that." I said, "Look it, if you start acting like a man I'll treat you like a man, and if you're gonna act like a seven-year-old then I'll treat you like a seven-year-old."

The trainer was standing right there, and another player; they knew who was right.

That guy's still in baseball. He later apologized and I said I was sorry too. It was at the end of the year, an also-ran season.

Things get grim around when you're losing, and I'll tell you what, it's a lot more fun when you win. I guarantee it. It's the way the players act, you know, and *my* mood changes whether we win or lose, too. It's not radical, but you know how it is when you win—you're excited, can't wait to get to the park and everything doesn't seem to be a chore—and you know how it is when you lose—it becomes a job.

Nineteen eighty-six is a perfect example. We were sixteen games behind the Mets by June 1. It doesn't take a Harvard graduate to figure out that we're not gonna win. You can't throw in the towel for the rest of the season, you have to go out there and try, but each day is a struggle. The team may not be, you know, performing up to the level expected, but that doesn't mean I can sit there and say "Shoot, we're not winning, who gives a damn if the plane's on time." I can't afford to have a bad night.

The part of things I really hate are the end of the year or the beginning of the year when you have to make those two-days-in-a-city trips. You're gonna go two, two, and three in those squeeze weeks—that's really brutal. You can't even unpack. We get into a hotel in Pittsburgh on Monday, say, if we travel the day of the game, leave out Tuesday night and go to another city on the East Coast and play Wednesday and Thursday and then leave Thursday night after the game to go play somewhere else. So you're only spending like a night and a half in each hotel, you know, by the time you get in at two-thirty or three.

In '83 we had a killer schedule where in September we had five cities in thirteen days. We were in the pennant race till then. We won two out of the first three in Chicago and then we went to Pittsburgh, New York, Philadelphia, and Montreal. We ended up winning only four out of the thirteen games, I think. That's where we bit the bullet in '83.

Tickets are a hassle but I try not make them more so. What I do with tickets for players—in all cases, whether it's a rookie or a star—is take care of their family first. If we're in Philadelphia and Tommy Herr's from Lancaster, nearby, I'll take care of his family. If we're in Atlanta and I know Danny Cox is from around there and Vince Coleman is from Jacksonville, I'll take care of those two guys, sometimes as many as fifty tickets for their people alone. In our meeting before we start the season, I sit there and say you guys have got to understand I'll always take care of a guy's family first.

I really had it out with the ticket guy in—let's make it an unnamed city. This guy's a real jerk. We had a deal with the former ticket director in this unnamed city. He was a real good guy and a friend of our ticket director. Well, we had our pass list there last year for about two hundred tickets, pretty much standard. And this new guy wanted to put our people in the standing room!

I made a comment, something like, "You can tell the *other* guy isn't here anymore."

I was probably wrong in saying what I said, but too bad. I felt that we were getting jilted. Well, this new guy heard the remark and came around the corner and started cussing at me, "You know so-and-so isn't here anymore. I'm running this. You're gonna take this and you're gonna like it."

I said, "Well that's fine but you people were just in St. Louis last week and you used a lot of tickets for a lot of your people."

And we started cussing at each other. I said you want to do it that way, *we're* gonna do it that way to you in St. Louis. All polysyllabic cuss words. He turns around and says if you say one more thing I'm gonna have you thrown out of here. He called the security guards and he told them to throw me out and if I didn't leave he was going to arrest me, so with that I went up to the traveling secretary of the ball club, who happens to be a very dear friend. I told him what happened. He was horrified. Outraged. He and the other guy had a big argument.

Two hundred is a set standard. Some places do give you more. The Dodgers are always real good on tickets. I mean, everybody's from California anyway. I like to get the tickets done by five o'clock, two and a half hours before a seven-thirty game. It can take forty-five minutes to an hour to write up the passes and assign the tickets. I decide who goes where. The family seats are usually very good in all the parks. After their moms or dads or brothers or sisters or wives are taken care of, our guys just say, "Get 'em in the ballpark." With the playoffs and World Series, all the tickets are paid for; there are no comps. Each player gets twenty seats. It's funny because I remember in '85 one player told me that he really didn't enjoy the Series so much, it was too distracting. He had all these people asking him for all this stuff and he really couldn't enjoy it himself. I must have had half a dozen players come up to me and say, "Boy, now we know what you go through every night with tickets, handling these things, they're a pain in the ass."

I try and sleep at least till ten, ten-thirty in the morning because I don't usually get to bed till two after night games on the road. I don't eat my first meal till noon and I'll eat a little snack at seven or so, and then I'll eat after the game. It's a different type of day, you know. After a ball game you can't just go home, turn off the lights and go to bed. You're geared up, pissed off, or whatever, especially as the season goes on and you're having a season like '82, '85 or '87 where you're in it all the way. Then you get to your room and you're not even cold in the grave and you're thinking about tomorrow.

I'm often in the clubhouse during the game, especially if we're leaving that night, to make phone calls, to make sure that the plane is on time, and then make sure we get all our stuff packed, see if we got any problems, pay any type of bill, like uniform cleaning, and also in some cities the equipment truck people want to be paid right then, so you just pay them.

If I'm in the clubhouse in the sixth or seventh inning and a guy comes in and he's had a bad night, I'll look over and maybe if he looks at me I'll roll my eyes or somehow tell him don't worry about it, without saying a word. If a guy comes in who's just got knocked out of a ballgame and he's just sittin' there on his stool, you might come up and put your hand on his shoulders—after the first five or ten minutes, so they can cool off—and say don't worry about it. I probably wouldn't have done that when I first started, but now I know these guys a little bit more. My office in St. Louis is in the clubhouse so I probably know these guys as well as anybody else. I live with them for nine months a year. But I know I'd *never* say, "You should have done this or you should have done that."

I see these guys in a different light. I see them just as human beings. That's why I never, or very, very rarely sit in the stands, unless my family is there. I'll sit in the press box because I can't stand hearing people yell, "Herzog, you bum," or "McGee, you're a bum," or "Get off it, Coleman."

You hate to see and hear all that. These guys are friends. I usually have lunch with a couple of players and maybe every now and then if they ask me to go out, I'll go out for a while with them and get something to eat after the game. But I don't force myself to be around them. I never go up and say, "Can I go with you tonight?" That's just not my style.

I usually go out with the coaches or Whitey and I eat a lot with Red Schoendienst or Jack Buck and Mike Shannon, our announcers. After a game, if I can't find some people to eat with, I'll just go out by myself and get a sandwich, but if you want to be with somebody there's always a coach or a player that'll go get a pizza or something to drink with you. If I was a player I'd eat at a good restaurant every night. I very seldom have anything to drink but, boy, I do love to eat.

B E R N I E   S T O W E

He lounges in the box seats along the third-base line in the Astrodome, two hours before the scheduled night game with the Astros. As equipment manager for the Cincinnati Reds, his duties on the road are less rigorous than when the team is home, but perhaps more varied. A young woman interrupts the interview, wanting to know where a certain prominent member of the squad is. Stowe glances at me, asks for a five-minute recess, and departs to take care of the matter.

This is my thirty-eighth year with the Reds. I grew up around the old Crosley Field in Cincinnati, played Little League but never went no higher: my size. I never missed a ball game at Crosley. If I knew the game was still going on when school let out I got right down to the ballpark. The visiting clubhouseman at that time was Chesty Evans. I used to hang around and he used to chase me out—"Get out of here, you little four eyes"—or throw a hose on me. So one day a kid got sick and Chesty had no help and he asked me if I wanted to come in. That was 1947. I've been here ever since.

I started out as the visiting-team bat boy. I was home-team bat boy from '50 to about '54. I was a minor-league trainer for two years in Douglas, Georgia, and I was assistant equipment manager for about fifteen years. I was hired full-time twenty years ago as equipment manager. I wouldn't want to do anything else. I always wanted to be a ballplayer, you know, like all kids, and this way was the closest thing to it.

I've been here when Dave Bristol was manager, Sparky Anderson, John McNamara, Russ Nixon, even Rogers Hornsby when I was the bat boy. I've seen a lot of 'em and they all operate the same. They try to get their players up and they have patience with a kid if he needs a little help.

Sometimes a manager has asked me about somebody's attitude, and I just tell 'em if I can. If we hit a losing streak, you can't miss it; you see a few heads down. The players care, it's in their blood from when they were little kids. If I see a kid going bad I might just kid with him, act like I'm the batting coach, tell him to get them elbows out or something. I don't know what I'm saying. And they laugh at me and it kinda keeps the pressure off of them thinking about their slump. Or take spring training. You know the kid's gonna feel bad when they tell him he's going back to the minors, so I got a little thing where I drop hand grenades or I get a tommy gun out, shoot 'em down. They start saying I'm goofy or crazy and then they cool off a little bit.

When Sparky was managing he used to give me the job to go out and get the player and tell him that Sparky wanted to see him. We had one kid —this was toward the end of spring training—and I walked out on the field and this guy, Danny Osborne, saw me heading his way. He took off! He climbed the fence! He wanted that extra day's meal money and he came back the next day for that extra pay.

When you know they won't be back, that's the rough part. Or with a veteran like Bill Gullickson. He's such a great guy, all my personnel and kids loved him. That makes it pretty rough after you're around the guy for two or three years because you get to really know him and his family and then they're off to other parts of the country. When George Foster left us, he gave me and my wife a trip to Hawaii for two weeks. When Tony Perez retired, Johnny Bench retired, I got goose bumps when they had different things at different stadiums for them.

The most exciting years were with the Big Red Machine, the World Series, the playoffs, nothing like them. That team was amazing. In the fifth inning we'd be behind and there'd be a little chatter on the bench, players talking about what the pitcher's throwing and what he threw last time. Soon they'd put two and two together and just start hammering.

In spring training in '75 Sparky came to me and said we're going to win this year, we're gonna win it all. Sure Spark, here we are in spring training. But he was right. The next year he says we're gonna win again and he was right.

In 1987 we were playing Detroit, Sparky's team now, in an exhibition game in June. I think they were about eight or nine games below .500 and he told me they were gonna win the division that year. They did. Now that's amazing.

The most enjoyable part of the job is just being around your Andersons, Benches, Roses, Morgans, and Tommy Helmses. I go back to Gus Bell—Buddy's father—Rocky Bridges, Lee May, ah, gee, you could go on and on with names. They're the kind of guys that keep everybody loose and cracking jokes.

In all my years there might be three guys that I really didn't like. And they knew it, I guess. We had one kid, a catcher, that was demanding all the time—everything had to be just right. He'd look at his shoes and say they weren't right and throw them at the clubhouseman. I jumped him one day in L.A. and said you just don't treat people like that. You've only been in the league about three years and you think you're a superstar, you're lucky you're a catcher because you're only hitting .170 and they're keeping you.

But then recently, when we were in Atlanta, he called me and I left him tickets. We sat down and talked and he said, "Now I know what you mean." He's been out of baseball for about eight years.

Quite a few of the guys come back to see me. They get out of the game and then they can't wait to get back in. For instance, last year, Dave Collins. He was in spring training with Montreal and they released him the last day when they heard Tim Raines was gonna come back and play. Well, he lives in Cincinnati and he called me in July to leave him some tickets, so I did. Some of the former players don't like to come back into the clubhouse, why I don't know, so Collins was in the stands and I was talking to him. I said, "Oh, I got to ask you something, come on down to the clubhouse." I really never asked him anything, I just wanted some of the other players to see him again. About four or five days later, Pete [Rose] is talking about problems at this position and that position and I said, "Well, Dave Collins was in here the other day and says he's in great shape," and Pete said, "Call him and tell him I want to talk to him." And they signed him, sent him to Nashville for two weeks and he joined us and he's been doing a good job for us ever since. [Collins was still with the team at the end of 1988.]

I purchase all the bats, all the balls, all the uniforms, and do all the special ordering for different players. It's all my job. Whoever they signed a shoe contract with I get a hold of and make sure that they get the right spikes to us, and a back-up pair or two. Some players might just go through two pair and others might go through a pair a week—they just wear 'em so long and then switch. Most of our guys wear spikes, even on the turf.

One of the most embarrassing things ever happened was just this year. We called up a rookie and I called Rawlings and had 'em make up a uniform for him and express it out to me in L.A. Like always, I checked to make sure they got the name spelled right and the right number on it. So we're on national TV and after the game Johnny Bench [now a Cincinnati announcer] comes down to me and says they had the *Cincinnati* spelled wrong on the shirt. That was a first! I never did check the *front* of the uniform.

I would say each player's got at least two dozen bats left over from the previous year, and I'll order two dozen more for spring training so if something would happen this fall, like the bat company could be on strike or something so I couldn't get bats, I'll always have enough. I always try to keep a dozen ahead for each player. I'll hide a dozen someplace in the clubhouse, just to be safe.

You get some guys who'll go through six and seven different models a year and then you got other guys who from Day One use the same model. Some day a guy will come running in and say, "Bernie, get me some P-72s." We're lucky being so close to Louisville—we use mostly Louisville Slugger bats—so I can call down there and maybe a week later I got 'em. But teams from L.A., they might have a real rough time getting the wood on time.

Some players who live in Cincinnati get a van and go down and pick their own wood. You'll see players that come into Cincinnati with other teams, like Joel Youngblood with the Giants, who get up early one morning, rent a car and ride to Louisville to pick out the wood they want. There might have been five San Francisco players went down there. The wood's just in big bins, and the guy there tells them how the grain will run after he cuts it down.

When we travel during the season I gotta make sure the stuff gets on the plane, make sure the truck's there to meet the plane, make sure everything gets off the plane. I know the baggage handlers in most of the cities. It's a little rough when you fly a commercial flight because then I gotta pick out all the personal luggage down there at the conveyor belts and get it onto the bus to the hotel. With all the collectors nowadays, it makes it a little bit rough. Say with Pete and Eric Davis, all the superstars, what I try to do is put a code on their bags instead of their numbers because otherwise people will say, "Hey, number forty-four, that's gotta be Eric Davis's bag," and then you'll be missing something. I put maybe three Xs on his bag or an extra number two on that bag. I make sure all the personal luggage gets dropped off, then come back out to the airport to help the visiting clubhouseman with the equipment going onto the equipment truck. It makes it easier on them late at night, when it usually is. I don't care if it's two o'clock in the morning, I'll go out there. Only me and about four other equipment guys do this. I would say there might be one or two of the trucking guys in the league that you're kinda leary about—wondering if they're gonna be there when we get there.

Two days before I get into town I'll call the clubhouseman and give him the roster for the team, tell him if there was any changes, so he's ready for them with new name tags. Once everything's in the clubhouse I won't be that busy till we leave town, when the pack-up begins. Like today, sometimes a kid working in the clubhouse misplaces something in the wrong locker and the player hollers for me and I go around trying to find it. The first day in town I'll go down and clean the helmets and the catcher's equipment and then I'll come back and help, say, Petey here [Pete Prieto, visiting clubhouseman in the Astrodome]. But Petey, he's nervous in the service, he wants to do everything. "Sit down," he keeps telling me. But I'm as fidgety as he is, I can't sit down.

On the road the visiting clubhouseman is in charge of running people —visitors—in and out, but we'll work together on it, look at each other and say we better make sure this guy's got a tag. Or somebody wants to bring in his brother and the clubhouseman wouldn't know the guy so I would have to say, "Oh, he's all right."

With the press you usually look for the credentials right away, but you can tell the ones that aren't pros because they'll come in with a pen and a pad and want to get autographs. You know something's wrong there.

Home games, I get in about eleven in the morning and leave about two A.M. Ballplayers start coming in about one and two o'clock, then it just gradually starts picking up, the pitchers being first, then the extra men, then the regulars. They'll get a card game going or some of 'em work crossword puzzles. I never join in. Some have their music with the headphones. Maybe some of their kids come in and the first thing they ask for is some punch or a candy bar or something. Those afternoons go by fast.

Pete's rule about players in the clubhouse is that once the bell rings, they gotta be out there on the bench. Don't miss the first pitch. So my crew is pretty much alone in the clubhouse. I might have the pitcher that's pitching the next night, or somebody with an injury, that's about it. But there's always stuff to do. At home I see very little of the game.

You've got your laundry to do—the practice uniforms—and then clean everything up. You have players doing a lot of sliding and they don't want to change pants and I'm down there trying to get them to change, but unless they get a lot of mud on them and they get heavy they won't change. Some players they're having a pretty good series and that's the uniform they like and they won't change. They'll go out there with a big hole in the behind.

Your regulars go through four sets of home uniforms and about three sets of roads a year. But Dave Parker was the toughest I ever had. I must have got him about ten pairs of home uniforms and eight road uniforms.

The biggest headache of this job is the food. Feeding them after the game. You spend so damn much time doing that when you could be keeping your clubhouse a whole lot better. Before the game I have hard-boiled eggs out, carrots, celery sticks. I'll have melons. Whatever's out there, that's what they get. On day games I put out cereal and strawberries, sliced peaches. I give 'em fruit cocktail once in a while.

After the games we try to mix it up, steak one night, roast beef the next, some fish or shrimp, chicken. We start from scratch sometimes, maybe two times a homestand I'll come up with meatloaf or something like that. I make salads, grill hot dogs, hamburgers. But I also have a butcher and three other restaurants that cater for me. I like to have plenty of food and I'm always overordering. Say a guy gets on TV after the game and comes in after doing that and there's no food left. I might hear about that, for sure, so I don't want to take no chances.

Way back they never had food in the clubhouse—you might have had pretzels and dip and that would be about it. Then they had what they called the swindle sheet. If you had a doubleheader you were allowed to have a sandwich between games, so before the first game you'd put down on the swindle sheet for one sandwich. It was an honor system. If the player goes in and gets a coke he puts down for one coke and when that series is over, he pays what he owes.

Now the players pay me so much every payday. Everybody pays the same. I make a little but not much. You get some that'll pay you extra at the end of the season, a couple hundred dollars maybe. Buddy Bell and Ron Oester bought me and my wife some tickets for a trip to the Bahamas last year.

In the off-season I get everything cleaned and packed for spring training and then if we have a trade I just go back in the box and take the player's uniform out and get the name taken off and another name put on it. I'll do all my inventory. It's pretty much a regular eight-to-five job then, and some days I might leave at three.

Spring training is really the most difficult period, with all the extra men and extra coaches and A games, B Games. The total gets up to about fifty, fifty-five guys, and you got one guy leaving on one bus, one leaving on another. We have to keep the bats separated, the helmets, everything. I have four kids working for me. We start out at about six-fifteen in the morning and get done about eight or nine o'clock at night. Back the next day. When you've got a ten o'clock game in the morning and a seven-thirty game at night, that really kills you. If the games are separated I'll send my son to one and I'll go to the other. I've got two sons working for me, seasonal. One is twenty-eight and the other twenty-three. I think my oldest might take over after me. He's pretty into it.

PETE PRIETO

A thin, fiery man, he smokes a lot of cigarettes as he directs operations in the visiting team's clubhouse in the Astrodome. He got his start in baseball in 1951 when he inherited $5,000 and bought a club in Cuba. He did some scouting, then came to the States as a trainer ("I wanted to learn to speak English, but I don't speak *good* English now!"). He quit for a few years but came back and worked all over the country as a trainer for the Astros organization. In 1978 he heard about the job opening at the Dome.

Tal Smith was general manager. In this business we hear a lot of true and we hear a lot of lies, we hear both ways. I don't care what anybody say about Tal Smith, he's my friend. I fly to Houston and talk to Tal Smith and he says, "Pete, you work for Houston for many year, we love you, everybody thinks you're a good man, but I don't think this is the right job for you because you got a lot of temper. You get fired and I can't do anything for you."

On June 29, 1978, I take the visiting clubhouse. The next day, the Houston Oilers play in the Dome after the baseball game and I see a few players and the equipment manager for the Oilers come from behind the clubhouse to take a chair and I say, "Listen, I need the chair."

After the game Phil Garner, who was with the Pirates then, asks me, "Pete, where's my chair?"

I run into the Oilers' clubhouse and fight with this guy for the chair. It was my first experience in the clubhouse—a fight with the football players! I remember the peaceful ballplayer Willie Stargell went in there. Everybody went in. We got a big fight. Couple of players with pistols—big fight.

The next day Tal Smith says, "Hey, what happened over there?"

I say, "I got a little trouble. You already know what happened, Tal."

I don't think I'm supposed to say it but I don't take shit from nobody. From the first day I take the clubhouse the players know I don't take it from nobody. I never tell the player what he has to do to hit the ball. It's not my business. How I run my clubhouse is my business. I try and be nice, I try to treat the guy making one million, the guy making a hundred thousand, everybody, the same. I don't care white or black because I come from Cuba. In Cuba we don't look for the color. We look for the inside of the man.

Some guys say, "I don't like Pete." Maybe a lot of people, I don't know. There's no way you can please all twenty-five guys. I've been married seven times, I'm the only man in the world who likes all seven mothers-in-law. All beautiful. It's the same with ballplayers. I try to treat every ball-player the same way, the tip don't matter. When a guy don't tip me good somebody on the ball club finds him and says, "Hey, listen, you gotta tip this guy." Only *one* guy I really don't like, but I never show it. I try to please this guy sometimes *more* than everyone else.

I know what player likes to dress in one corner of the clubhouse. I know what player in the league don't like to dress next to his own ball team. I put him in a different corner. I know the player who don't like to dry the uniform. We hang it. Five years ago the equipment manager for Chicago, Yosh Kawano, said to me wash but don't dry his uniform. He said to me ten times wash and no dry. I said to him, "You know what you gotta do with that uniform? Take that uniform and stick it right up your ass." I know how to dry the uniform.

I know what team likes fish, but I know three guys in the league don't eat fish. Willie Stargell is one, so I bring fried chicken for Willie.

Everybody's different. Like day and night. When we had Pittsburgh three years ago, four years ago, everybody got different music: twenty-five ballplayers, twenty-five musics, and very loud, you know. There's some players don't like it but, I be honest with you, when Pittsburgh come I feel good because I feel relaxed. I know the players won't call me for coffee, get me this, get me that. I know he listens to music. I know it's loud. What the hell? It's nice to see the team relaxing, you know. It's better than to see everybody in one corner worrying about the game or something.

I don't know why, but when Nolan Ryan pitches for the Houston Astros, the other team, whoever it is, drinks a lot more coffee. I don't want to say the other team's afraid; I don't know what happens. I have to buy extra coffee. Normal is about ten pots of coffee—don't forget you've got a lot of newspapermen go to the clubhouse. I spend a lot of money making coffee when Nolan Ryan pitching. Between batting practice and the game, five pots just like that.

When the team wins you can hear from a hundred feet away; people come happy in. When the team loses, you can see everybody's face, you know. Ballplayer when he lose is like a piece of liver; when he win, like sweet apple pie.

What happens to the old, old ballplayer, the guy playing eight, ten year in baseball, when they lose he's the guy to control the other ballplayers. Every ball club needs one old guy. Willie Stargell, he's great. Another guy I really miss in the league is Dusty Baker, the guy who played for L.A. And Keith Hernandez, he's like a godfather to the Mets.

I try and keep my eye open and my ear open to watch and see, you know, if everybody got everything he want. I keep my mouth closed. I don't know anything. I don't wanna know anything. Sometime when the team's low you can't smile. Best thing is stay away. The player make a lot of money today and everybody wants to do good, everybody wanna play good, everybody wanna win, nobody like losing. There are some times I hear people say, "Ah, the player no care, he make a lot of money." Wrong. When the ballplayer come to the big league, he wanna stay. He care.

In minor league you have to work hard, very hard. I remember Pete Rose when I work for Cincinnati in 1959. You know the spring training, you have to work hard from nine sometimes to five. At five o'clock everybody go take a shower, everybody go eat something. Not Pete Rose. What Pete Rose used to do was run two, three miles and take a bat and swing and swing and swing. Everybody used to say he's crazy, but that's why we don't find many Pete Rose in baseball today.

My life is already made. Fifty-four years old, I don't got too long to go. I know I'm going to retire at sixty-three year old, eight year from now. I hate to see Pete Prieto walk into clubhouse at sixty-five year old, fall asleep in every corner, and everyone say, "Hey, old man, when you gonna retire?" I don't want to hear it. I gonna retire just in time.

In the winter I'm the trainer for the Caracas club. That was my agreement with Tal Smith. I work winter ball because if I stay home I don't have any money to live. Venezuela is my second home. It's a beautiful country, beautiful people. Baseball atmosphere is better than here. You get thirty thousand to the game. Last year we had Tony Armas, Bo Diaz, Andres Galarraga, lot of big-league players. First thing I do is talk to their trainer and see if they have any special exercise. If anything happens we call the trainer or the doctor in the United States. "Hey, your man has a broken finger. You want us to send him home?"

My worst time in baseball in many years was when Steve Sax from Los Angeles wrote a book and he said a lot of stuff about Venezuela. I was really pissed off. I said to Sax, "Why you say that about Venezuela? It's a nice country and I know the people there treat you nice. Why you got to say all the bullshit you say about Venezuela? Why you take their money for three months to pay your bills in the United States?"

Really, I don't like that. When I have to say something I say it.

J O H N   A D A M

We talk twice. First, in his training room beneath County Stadium in Milwaukee, and again when the Brewers are on the road in Arlington, Texas. During batting practice in Texas he leads a small group of players, the starters, mainly, in a rather desultory set of calisthenics. It's about 100 degrees. The home-team Rangers are prepared for this. They wear shorts during the workout.

You can figure these guys out in about two minutes. I rate players in three categories. There are the ones that will play no matter what. If there is a bone sticking out, they play. You cannot pull them out of the line-up. Those are your gamers. I'm not saying that's great because sometimes they do more harm than good. Robin Yount is one. Paul Molitor is one. Jim Gantner's one. The trainer should know the players better than anybody. I *do*. I can see how they are taking their jacket off, how they are warming up. I think it is my job to watch the players who will play no matter what, and tell the manager what I see.

Then there are players that will play hurt but they want everyone to know beforehand that they are hurt, so they have that excuse: "No wonder I went 0 for 4, shit, I got a bad leg."

Then there's the players that just won't play unless they feel 100 percent, and those guys will drive you mad. They don't last long, 'cause, let's face it, who feels 100 percent every day? You're lucky if you do once a week in this game, with only getting one day off every eighteen or twenty days.

All you have to do is look in the standings. When you're twenty games out on September first, not too many guys want to play hurt. Ask the Seattle trainer in September.

I'm the only ex-player among the trainers. It's not a great advantage, but I'll go out there on the road and take early batting practice, and I'll take ground balls. I'm not near the caliber of these guys, but they see, "Hey, he's not a klutz, he's not a bookworm. This guy can field ground balls, he has a good arm. He *knows* what I feel like when I say my arm hurts. He knows why, and what to do for it."

I got drafted out of high school, a sixth-round pick for the Baltimore Orioles in 1972. I played a year with them as a pitcher. The following spring training I was released and then I signed with the Angels, and that summer, on July 4, 1974, in Idaho Falls I injured my right elbow pitching and I never really threw the same after that. I couldn't even reach home plate. I went from prospect to suspect in one year, and that was pretty much it. Maybe it was a blessing in disguise that I left the game so early. I had my shot. I'm pretty realistic and even when I was healthy I was mediocre, so I don't think I missed the major leagues. I probably would have ended up with one year in Double-A or something.

I'm from the Los Angeles area so the Angels sent me to Dr. Frank Jobe. And it was actually while I was sitting in his office that I was overwhelmed by his knowledge of the human body. It sparked an interest that I never, never had before.

It's a little bit of a shock, obviously, when you can't play anymore and you're only nineteen years old. A big void. I didn't want to give myself any time off 'cause I was afraid I might enjoy it too much, so I really pressed myself hard. I went back to school. Like twenty milllion other ex-jocks, I was gonna be a coach and a teacher. I had always been a pretty fair student, and behold, I made the dean's list three of my four semesters in junior college. I found out that I *really* enjoyed school, a lot more than I had ever dreamed I would. Here I was your basic jock in high school who had always thought how in hell can someone go to school and not play athletics. But now when I'm going to college I thought just the opposite! How the hell can someone play athletics and not study? My father was Phi Beta Kappa at UCLA, speaks three languages fluently, and, while I was growing up, was president of a union. I wanted to show that I had some of those abilities, too.

I graduated and went to Long Beach State University for a year and then transferred to Cal State at Domingus Hills, a little college close to my parents' home, where I was living. I really got into athletic training. The kinesiology, the anatomy, the physiology of exercise, all that really came into play, and became so interesting. Then you have your other sciences. It's not just a lot of PE classes. My teachers were great, but there wasn't an official athletic-training curriculum and that's what made it difficult for me to pass my boards for being a certified trainer.

The boards—a one-day, six-hour test that involves an oral, a written, and a practical—are extremely difficult. In fact, they make the test so ambiguous it's ridiculous.

The practical: If you come upon an unconscious football player, not breathing, what do you do? Do you take the helmet off? How do you do CPR? Show me how you do the CPR with a possible neck injury. There's tons of different ways you can do it, but they don't give you any guidelines. They have you tape different parts of the body for time. You have to be able to do an ankle in three minutes, which is a long time—you *should* be able to do an ankle in a minute and a half—and it has to be good, stiff, no wrinkles, the whole thing.

Right before I graduated I realized I'd better get things going. I called up the scout that had signed me, a man named Ray Poitevint, who is still with the Brewers organization. We talked and he said it sounds like you've really changed; when you were younger you were a lot flakier. He called me a month later and said they had a rookie-ball job for me. The last thing he told me was, "Look, you blew it your first chance as a player. This is your last shot, you've got a chance to start a baseball career all over again as a trainer."

I spent only three years in the minor leagues, which is really unheard of for a trainer. Many times they will spend ten, twelve years, and most of them *never* get out.

I arrived in the big leagues in 1981 as assistant trainer and in '84 I became the head trainer. I've seen the good times and the bad times with the team and as a trainer I know I've grown and gotten better and better. Continuing education has never stopped for me.

I let the player think that he's the boss a little bit, but if a guy oversteps, I tell him what my policy is in the training room. I'm pretty sarcastic. I get on the young players the first day and let them know that it peeves me if they act a certain way, like they are a gift to this team. We *drafted* you, we didn't *adopt* you.

I had a rookie this year come in the trainer's room in spring training. He's reading the paper, eating an apple, and tells me to ice his knee. I looked at him. I walked over to where some supplies were and took out a media guide and said, "You know, it says here that you've only got six months service time in the major leagues. God, that's odd, 'cause you know the way you're acting, it looks like you've got about ten years."

And he just kinda looked at me.

And I said, "So finish your apple, take your paper out of here and then come back in about six years."

He laughed and realized it and folded the paper and put it away. And it never happened again. He didn't make the team.

We test our players on the Cybex machine twice for fitness levels, in the spring to get a base, and again in the fall to see if our worst fears are realized: players regress as the season goes on. It's a very accurate test of strength, flexibility, and endurance of a muscle, shoulder or knee joint, whatever, and, yes, *everyone* regresses, except a couple of guys who don't play much, the twenty-third and twenty-fourth men on the roster who stay in great shape because they are not getting beat down as much. In spring training the regulars run and throw more than at any other time of the year, and they've worked hard in the off-season. Then the season begins and the weather's cold and they do a little less. The games start and it's a lot more comfortable to spend another hour or so at home, come to the ballpark and say, "Oh, I won't do my weights today." Before you know it it's July and hotter than hell and you don't feel like doing anything because you *haven't* been doing it. A vicious circle.

And you *don't* get in shape by playing every day, just like a guy doesn't rehab his arm by pitching in a game. It doesn't work that way. You have to do specific exercises and that is very difficult for a player to realize. Some never do.

We are constantly doing preventive measures for pitchers during the season, because the shoulder, the number-one injury in baseball, just wears down. The focus of my job is to prevent those insidious little injuries so that come July, all of a sudden it's not, "Hey, I can't go! I can't lift my arm!"

Every pitcher on the Brewers is on a maintenance program designed for him, but basically they're about the same—five-pound exercises for the shoulder through all the planes: external rotation, internal rotation, isolating the rotator-cuff muscles, supraspinatus, infraspinatus, teres minor. They do three sets of ten reps with the light weights, or they can use surgical tubing or theraband. Tubing and theraband are resistance, and basically they're the same thing as the weights. They break the monotony, number one, and number two, some patients like them better. Some guys like jogging, some guys like the exercise bicycles.

Compliance is fair at best, even among pitchers. *Fair* at best. It's frustrating. Nobody can make the players do anything, but I suggest and I try to convince them that it's better for them. I never use threatening tactics or anything, like, "If you don't do this your career will be over." Everyone has done their own little shtick and it *has* worked for them, that's why they are up here. But they need more sophisticated exercises and many times their resistance is a mental factor: "Hey, this little five-pound weight ain't doing shit." But the rotator-cuff muscles are only *this long,* a couple of inches or so.

It's a trainer's job to convince, to show them that it works. If you're lucky enough to have someone on your team that is a great example, you play it up to the hilt. I have Paul Molitor here with a reconstructed elbow. He sat out all of '84, missed the whole year, but he came back and had a great season last year, thirty-nine-game hitting streak, top of the world. No one has done that in a decade. He worked his butt off. He easily could have said no. He makes a million dollars. Paul still does his elbow exercises. Robin Yount has come back from two shoulder surgeries. He's on the exercises. I have more guys with reconstructed elbows than any other trainer. Tom Candiotti, pitching for the Indians now, he was with us. I can go on and on.

I've gone to the general manager for everything from a guy being way overweight to a guy being sort of negligent in off-the-field habits. I've done it for many other things than just exercises. Unfortunately, if the person is still performing—doing all these things wrong but things still turn out right on the field—those are the guys who are tough. I've had many of them.

When I became the head trainer I started doing quarterly reports on each player and turned them into the GM three times a year, to make it easier for my manager and GM to look at guys. When did he hurt that shoulder and how long was he out? I take care of workman's comp reports and league injury reports. If a player misses one day or one month we make a note of it and send it to the league, where it's all computerized.

For a seven-thirty ball game at home I get to the park no later than two o'clock, maybe a little earlier. I live ten to fifteen minutes away, in an apartment. I prepare the daily report from the night before, every treatment of significance. I might have to call a doctor to see what the diagnosis is on a player he saw that morning, what our plan is going to be. Or I might set up appointments with dentists, doctors, eye appointments, whatever. People say, "These guys are adults!" But I'd rather do it myself. Many times they can't get in to see an ophthalmologist or an optometrist or a dentist.

The girl in the dentist's office may not know them, or even if she does know them, it's, "Well, yeah, we'll get you next week." If I call I'm always able to get them in quickly, and I know when they are supposed to show up.

I get the whirlpool ready, call for any supplies we need, check with the pharmacy, get dressed, and start treating the players. It's like any job, there are some drags to it. I make about one-eighth of what I think I deserve, but a tax man told me that seven-eighths of life is enjoying what you are doing, and I believe that.

The trainer is there to tell you what to do. He can't make you do it and even if you did it all, you still may not be 100 percent. The only thing I can promise you is you'll be healthy and that's a pretty big promise—ask any guy that's spent time with surgery rehab. They'd give anything to be healthy again. That's the bottom line.

And then you can do everything right and still come in last. It's a bitch, it really is.

4
BEATING
THE
BUSHES

As coordinator of minor league instruction and spring camp for the Philadelphia Phillies, he makes decisions about careers.

He signed out of Cuba in 1961 and over the following decade played in Decatur, Jamestown, Lakeland, Nashville, Syracuse, Rochester, Hawaii, and Eugene. But he never played a major-league game.

I got close by one day in 1969 when the California Angels broke camp. Bobby Knoop was supposed to have a broken toe. If he had, I would have gone with the team, but the doctors had a look, said give it three days, and that was my last chance. A lot of it is being in the right place at the right time.

I was just a utility player at the end. I had a family and I wasn't concentrating at the plate. I got hit and I said I don't need to play this anymore. Baseball didn't hold any special thing for me *then*. I had already played so many years.

This was 1970. I was living in Clearwater, Florida, and had a very good job in the carpet-cleaning and sales business. Andy Seminick, who had been my last manager in the minor leagues, must have told the Phillies that I had a chance to be a coach. Years before I had played *against* the Phillies team managed by Seminick and I liked the way the Phillies handled themselves in a little incident. I was knocked down by the pitcher because somebody hit a home run. Well, *I* didn't hit a home run so why should he throw at *me?* So I went to charge the mound—but I weighed 145 pounds then. That wasn't a good way to challenge a man six-two, six-three, but I was going to the mound anyway. The whole Phillies ball club came out—Seminick told his clubs, if somebody starts a fight, we all fight, and I liked that. I looked around and *my* teammates were nowhere to be found. I was going to be the only one fighting against a whole ball club. I don't remember the pitcher's name. He was throwing nothing, anyway. Someday, I thought, I might be able to get this guy, but not today.

My boss in the carpet business said I could always have my job back, so I said to Dallas Green, "Sure, why not? I'll give it a chance since I live here." I would just go to camp and see whether I liked it or not. I hadn't liked the way I had been treated as a player by the managers and coaches, and I knew there had to be a better way to do it. I'm a black Cuban, and don't forget, that was before civil rights. There weren't any black managers —still are very few—and many of the managers and ballplayers came from the South, so there was a cultural difference there, because in Cuba we didn't have any problem with the races.

As a player I had learned most from my teammates and not from the coaches. Al Federoff for Detroit really took his time to help me, but for the most part he was the only one. No ifs, ands, or buts about it: there was a difference in how we were coached, but that was understood by all the black players, and we helped each other and we knew how to play the game.

Even in the sixties they [white players] stayed in hotels downtown while we stayed in private homes or fleabag motels somewhere. But in 1963 in Macon, Georgia, I roomed with Tom Matchik, a red-headed white guy from Pennsylvania. We were roommates for four years. He played short-stop, I played second base. We were inseparable. That was unheard of.

When I had to go to a different place to eat—this was so unlike my country—I complained once in a while and that got me a reputation for being outspoken. For the most part the black players would not say any-thing. I was a little bit of a rebel and that didn't endear myself to the managers. In the Detroit organization, I was a troublemaker. If there was an injustice like "You got to go eat in the kitchen," I would speak up about it. I've never eaten in the kitchen, but it was either that or nobody eats, so I was a troublemaker. However, I would never say that was a reason I didn't make the majors.

In 1971 the Phillies sent me to Walla Walla, Washington. I walked into the parking lot and this tall gentleman, very well dressed, called out, "Hey, Larry!"

Who knew me in Walla Walla, Washington? I wondered.

He came over and introduced himself and put his arm around my shoulders and we walked into the restaurant. That was the time I finally met Paul Owens, the general manager.

I've been a roving infield instructor, a coach, a manager, a scout. Now I'm coordinator for the Phillies' minor leagues, and that includes how the managers manage. If I see something, I tell them. They can manage any way they want, but we try to help them. If he's going to bunt with the third hitter, I'm going to question him. We don't play like that with the Phillies, but I've seen it in Double-A ball in other organizations. When I see a pitcher miss three times on the sacrifice bunt, that's not coincidence. That's because the coaches haven't been working on it, or haven't done a good job during batting practice. The manager writes in his report, "We lost the game because we did not execute." Yes, but who's in charge of execution? The manager. Do something about it. It's up to me to say to the manager and coaches, "You guys are not working enough on this." I might discuss the situation with Jim Baumer, my boss, but I usually talk to the manager first because I don't want anyone saying I talked behind his back. I don't tell lies. They know that. If the play called hurts the player, I tell the manager because if he hurts the player he hurts the Phillies. I can't accept it.

People make too much out of managing. There's no challenge to it. It's not that tough in the major leagues, either. But not many share my opinion. Some managers aren't afraid to make things happen, the Billy Martins, the Whitey Herzogs. You can call all the little plays you want, but when you call a tough play in the ninth inning with the bases loaded, that's when you earn your money as a manager. Or when you tell the pitcher to get up in the bullpen, even though you know you're not going to use him but make the other manager make a decision.

The *key* to managing is respecting people as individuals. When the players come out of high school they don't know a thing. Many of the high-school coaches are history teachers. I appreciate that. By the time the players get to Double-A they pretty much know how to play the game, now they have to polish their skills. Watch them on the field, watch them get off the bus, in the lobby of the hotel, and you can tell which is a good organization and which is not. We *strive* for our players to be good on and off the field. Watch infield, watch batting practice. We have a standard which is the Philly way.

We use what we call step-teaching, starting in rookie league: how to run the bases, throw the cutoff, receive relays, and so on. If the minor-leaguers are at home, they work out in the mornings at least four days of the week, from ten to twelve. We've learned through years of study that if we stay on one fundamental more than forty minutes, we've lost the player. The workout goes soft. So you go on to something else. In spring training everybody has to be working for every minute on different fundamentals. We have lectures and demonstrations because they've been home forgetting about baseball; we play pepper games to get them back to thinking baseball. The fields are full with 140 players doing something. The players, even other coaches, ask how we control so many people.

The players at the lower levels don't know if the instruction is good. That's my job. I am a perfectionist. I believe in working hard because I worked very hard when I started. When I was playing I went to the people who were best to ask them about things. Why teach the pickoff play before teaching something else? When is the best time to teach the bunt? I went to George Myatt, George Kissell, Ron Plaza to ask him about coaching third base, I talked to Johnny Sain about pitching, Seminick about catching.

Last year the managers had a meeting with the scouts, suggesting things to look for. Take infielders: people talk about good hands, but the feet are more important. Good balance takes care of everything—tennis, golf, baseball. If a guy has good feet, he can play the infield. Bad hands are *not* bad hands; that's fundamentals and that can be taught. I had bad hands when I started. But good feet you cannot teach. You can jump all the rope you want. Ask any scout. Good feet.

How do you lose the most ball games? Three ways: bunt plays, relay throws, or the pitcher doesn't cover first base. Once that happens, all hell breaks loose. Now you've got a man on base and the pitcher's mad, he's not concentrating as hard, he gives up a base hit.

Mental mistakes bury you every time. You play good defense, you don't give the extra base, you don't give them four outs, and you win. Once you give the extra base, all hell breaks loose. No outs, man on second base, single to center field, you miss the cutoff man, the runner goes to second base. Now they bunt the guy to third base, you have to bring the infield in, a high hopper goes through, you got two runs in, a man on first *still*. All because you miss the cutoff man.

I'd rather have *the* best manager and *the* best instructors at the *lower* levels. They can recognize who's scared, who's timid, who's a pop-off trying to cover up that he's scared, so they can channel this. All the players are terrified at first. They were big fish in a small pond and suddenly they are just small fish in a big pond.

Of the 140 players in the minor-league spring-training camp, about a hundred have already been here previous years. So the guys who are here for the first time see the huge guys who run fast as hell—excuse me!—and that can be intimidating. Their minds tell them, "I can't play against all these people. I can't play this game." Some of them are thinking about going home.

I see the people the first day and say, "Good morning, how are you?" and they appreciate this, that someone recognizes them. I know everyone from the name tag above the locker. Those first days, they're not going to move around! They stay right in front of their locker. They don't even talk to each other. Very seldom. I've had a couple of people later in their careers tell me how much it helped them that I said hello to them their first day in camp.

That's why I always tell the managers, "Don't sit in there and talk. Go and say hello to a kid. You might save a career just by doing that."

I've been sitting in my office after everyone goes out to the field and I see a kid walking down the hall and I know what's coming.

"Mr. Rojas?"

"Yes, but you can call me Larry."

"Mr. Rojas—"

"No, no, call me Larry, please."

"I, I don't think I really want to play this game."

"Why?"

"Well, I was talking to my girlfriend at home—"

Dadadadada. This way I got a way out, they think. Most of the time when they tell you that, they're not talking about *that,* really. And I talk them out of leaving. We have to keep the new players *away* from those older people and *with* people on their own level, to build their confidence. Step-teaching.

With pitchers, the scout's report may say he's very good but very crude, he's going to take some time to mature. Well, now it's up to Jack Pastore, the scouting director, to inform me so I can inform the coaches we'd better take our time with this guy. Don't push it too fast. He's from the country. He hasn't pitched too many games. Don't let him bury himself. Don't put him in a ball game and let him walk twenty guys. Don't let them beat him up. This pitcher might take three or four years before he blossoms. We tell the *player* it will take a long time or he will get discouraged. Once you lie you've got to keep lying and the players will catch up to you, and then they won't trust you. So I don't lie to the players.

We have a meeting near the end of spring training and go through all the names, and it's up to me to say the word "release." If any manager says for any reason, "Hold the guy," we hold him. For the most part we try not to make the player feel bad. It's got to be done with taste. We don't tell a player he can't play the game, so why not get the hell out of here, like old managers used to do; we tell the player we don't have a club for him to continue with.

This year we have four clubs—Maine, Reading, Clearwater, and Spartanburg—which take about ninety players. The two rookie teams report in June, and we have extended spring training for about twenty, twenty-two players for that. The others we have to figure out something to do with. It has happened that many players have found jobs right away with other organizations. We help them make phone calls. Everybody calls each other. I don't know, but it seems like Phillies players get more jobs than other players.

The biggest frustration is the player with talent who would not use it and winds up being released and five years later calls and says he should have listened. I don't say there's anything wrong with pumping gas, but you could have made a lot of money for your family and yourself by just doing what we asked you to do, working hard, keeping your nose clean. It happens too often. They want to do all the wrong things, be the bad guy. They don't want to just play the game, behave, go to bed on time at night. That's too easy. I've seen thirty, forty, fifty guys in the Phillies organization with the talent who didn't want it enough to really grind.

The ballplayers are not as motivated as we were. To us, making it to the big leagues was everything. There were not so many opportunities. To these guys, if I make it, fine, if not, I'll do something else. Even with the money. They complain about the buses, the hotels, the managers. I spent *one whole year* and I never spoke with the manager! I said, "Don't talk to me at all! Don't say a word to me! Don't say, 'Good Morning.' If you write my name down on the line-up I'll play 150 percent, just don't talk to me." The man was one of those persons we have talked about before. He didn't like blacks.

"Don't let the manager bother you!" I tell the players.

Twenty or thirty guys with minimal talent work so hard they make it. People call them organization-type players, guys who can help with the ball club: they keep working and working and all of a sudden someone says, "Hey, this guy can play." Greg Legg for instance, he came to us as a short-stop. We had Franco, Sandberg, and Bowa. We moved Legg to second base. He was adequate at the beginning. He didn't hit that much at the lower levels; he moved up to Double-A and did a little better, but all of a sudden was a *good* second baseman. He works hard, he knows the plays, he doesn't make mistakes on the field, so you want him around. Legg goes to the big leagues.

I am not a very good fan. I enjoy seeing minor-leaguers who play their hearts out, but I'm not a very good big-league-game-watcher. When players get to the big leagues, it's tough for me to see them make defensive mistakes. Don't players back up bases anymore? Their thinking goes two ways: "These guys are so good, he won't overthrow the base, so I don't have to back up."

I've seen the Phillies do this.

BILL SHANAHAN

The general manager urged me to make it out for a game. He didn't want to just sit in his office on some off day and *tell* me about the San Bernardino Spirit. He wanted me to feel it in the ballpark.

A miniature Chavez Ravine: beyond the fence, the dusty hills of southern California, Douglas firs, palm trees, and azaleas; within the fence, sparkling grass, grounds, and people. Sharp scoreboard, freshly painted advertisements, large speakers hanging above the stands.

Wearing shorts and a Spirit T-shirt, he greets me behind home plate and answers my unspoken first question.

You walk into this ballpark and hear the sound and you say, "Wow! That's something else!" Well, that's a synthesizer instead of an organ; it's more upbeat. You go to a lot of ballparks and you hear this old-time baseball announcer. Our announcer is a morning radio man, the Number One morning man in the San Bernardino area.

We knew we were going to get the kids; we knew we would get the older segment, but we needed to reach that younger segment, the eighteen-to-thirty-four age group. It's really very difficult to reach that group with baseball. They like sound. It's very important to have a good system. You definitely have to get your speaker system up to a level that people are used to hearing. It's not like AM radio. Why do people listen to FM radio? Because they want to hear better sound. It's the same thing when you come to a ballpark. Why are there clubs that are still running the old system? I mean, come on! The newspaper did a survey with that eighteen-to-thirty-four group on the best places to go around here on a date. We were number two, after the local night club.

I've received over thirty requests from other minor-league clubs this year for advice setting up their sound systems. I put together a whole package for them, free. I look at it this way. In September there's a four-day seminar for all the minor-league operators and I got a lot of help from that seminar, and I want to make sure that we help other people, too. But you can't just go into a park that's been sitting there and do this electric atmosphere. Try it without building it over a long period of time and the fans would probably go nuts.

Starting from scratch here with fans not really knowing what to expect, we were able to create our own tradition. There have been some complaints from baseball purists, but I thought I would get more.

I don't get frustrated anymore whether we win or lose. Sure, your best promotion is a winning team, but from a marketing standpoint, as long as you have a club that's in the hunt, that's competitive, you can be successful. I want people walking out of here not worrying about whether the team wins or loses, but knowing that they had a good time.

When you walk in the ballpark you see some very all-American Diamond Girls greeting you. When you *leave* the ballpark, they're saying, "Thanks for coming." You see the vendors wearing bow ties and white shirts and aprons, always with smiles on their faces. I go over to Disneyland a lot to catch different ideas—flowers around the ballpark, landscaping, a very colorful atmosphere. We have young kids who literally walk through the ballpark with their little sweepers, like Disneyland.

We tried a Harpo Marx type of guy who strolled through the stands and tried to keep them entertained, and a Crazy George type of cheerleader. Bring them in and see what works. We do dot races, you know, up on the scoreboard. I learned that from Oklahoma City. The crowd likes it for maybe three home stands and then we'll fade away from it for a while. Throughout the game we do a lot of different things with our mascot, the Baseball Bug, a bug with a baseball head. He gets up on the dugout and dances to "Bad" by Michael Jackson, or whatever. We do a thing called Beat the Baseball Bug, where we put him on second base and he has to walk from second base to home and a guy or gal has to run from home all the way around and it's always close at the end, but the bug always loses. We play "Happy Trails" when the other team changes pitchers. Watch the crowd start to wave to him. The thing is, we aren't doing it to get anybody mad, and the teams know that now. It's just another entertainment angle. We're in the process of purchasing a laser system that would be run throughout the game. Keep the fans pumped. Keep the adrenaline flowing.

We have TV monitors throughout the park so you can watch the game while you wait for your food. We make our money from the concessions operation. In minor-league baseball, as I look at it, all you want to do is to get people in the ballpark. A family of four can come here for six dollars. We're in the restaurant business.

I don't sit during games. I walk the stands. I guess I'm the security in a sense and I want the people to know me. Most do, and I'll go sit with them 'cause they're the ones who are going to make it successful. With about a hundred people working the games, I'm the producer that makes sure that everything is working with continuity. We have ten walkie-talkies for our ten key areas, to stay in touch. If I feel that the crowd's a little dead, let's throw in some more sound effects, or whatever it might take.

This club will cost half a million dollars this year. That's our budget and we'll make money. This is a business. It's not the old days of minor-league baseball like in the TV commercial with the dog running around after the player, or when you opened the ballpark and got two hundred fans in. We market baseball as an entertainment product.

A lot of local fans are coming here instead of driving an hour over to L.A. or Anaheim. I'm not saying that we are pulling people away from the Dodgers or the Angels, but this is our team now and the fans are pretty much supporting this club and they like the excitement. They go back over to Dodger Stadium and they say it's not like Spiritland. We call it Spiritland.

This city was ready for it. People were looking for something to hang their hat on because the town itself didn't really have a lot of civic pride. When we did the contest for a name, "Spirit" just jumped out. It's pretty much the number-one thing in this community now. It's not really the San Bernardino Spirit, it's the Spirit of San Bernardino.

I grew up with baseball in San Francisco and was a Giants fan all my life. I played high-school ball and did real well, but not good enough to make it. We moved to Wichita, Kansas, in the Midwest, and when I got out of college—my major was speech and communications—I got into radio. I did the producing for the local indoor-soccer club, the Wichita Wings. And if you are familiar with major-league indoor soccer, those games have extremely high sound levels and an electric atmosphere, and those games are always sell-outs. I learned a lot about lights-camera-action from indoor soccer.

There was a Triple-A club in Wichita, the Arrows, that had been there for fourteen years with about eight different major-league affiliations and twelve general managers. The ownership had heard about what I had done over at the Wings, and they were trying to get that kind of atmosphere at the ballpark. So not knowing that I'd ever end up in baseball on the business end of it, I took over as vice-president and general manager of that club. We tried to establish the electric atmosphere, in 1984, but it was like putting on a Band-Aid. The club was sold at the end of the season and moved to Buffalo and I was out of baseball. I went to work for the local beer distributorship as a manager bringing new products into the marketplace, and I was working with the owner of the distributorship to bring baseball back to Wichita. That didn't happen.

A friend of mine heard that a group trying to bring a club to San Bernardino was looking for a general manager. One of the owners contacted me, flew me out here, and I made the decision to get back into baseball and start up here from scratch.

Nineteen eighty-six. Brand-new team. We had five months to put together a ballpark, find the players, hire the manager, sell the season tickets, sell all the advertising for the '87 season. We were busy. Real busy. This park was just a baseball field with some bleachers, and now it seats 2,880, not including the beer garden, which is a private club for the season-ticket holders.

The club came from Ventura, where it had been affiliated with the Toronto Blue Jays. It was failing there, and Toronto made a decision to move to the Florida State League, so we were left high and dry. There was no major-league affiliation last year. I went down to the winter baseball meetings and tried to at least get some co-op players, and was able to work that out with the California Angels, the San Diego Padres, and the Blue Jays.

We hired Rich Dauer, the local hometown hero, as manager. He had just retired and was getting in the insurance business and so we brought him in and had open tryouts—over four hundred guys showed up.

The fans really enjoyed having their hometown boys running the club. Most of the guys on the field had been released by other clubs and by the end of the season we even had some major-leaguers, such as Terry Whitfield and Rudy Law. Our goal was just to get this ballpark open and to work at creating excitement, and we ended up breaking the forty-year-old California League attendance record, with 161,000. We were number three among all Single-A baseball teams, and we outdrew eight of twenty-six Double-A teams and four triple-A clubs. Everybody said, Can they do it again this year? And we sold all of the season tickets and we're at 75,000 in attendance already and we hope to break our own record.

A lot of it has to do with local community ties. I go to at least two luncheons a week in the off-season, one every other week during the season. I eat it up. Go to any successful minor-league club and you're gonna see that the club is very much involved with the programs that are meaningful in that area, whether it be the YMCA or the Boy Scouts or the Little Leagues. I think the biggest compliment to the Spirit is that we have set up twenty-three Little League teams in Spirit uniforms. They have their own exhibition games here Saturday mornings. We're very much involved with the local "Say No to Drugs" program. Just three weeks ago we had the 2,500 sixth-graders come out for a rally and we had kids who had been on drugs get up and talk about their problems. I believe that's our responsibility.

Also, one of the owners is Mark Harmon, the TV actor. Back in February they filmed *Stealing Home* here. Mark is the star and he's wearing a Spirit uniform. Rich Dauer, the manager of the Spirit team, and all the guys are involved, so that's more exposure that's going to hit for San Bernardino and the Spirit come August. We'll have the world premiere here.

And this year we put together a two-year player development contract with the Seattle Mariners, and they told us we were going to get Ken Griffey, Jr., which is nice. Already this year Ken has had a four-page article in *Sports Illustrated,* there's been a show on *ABC News* about him, he's been on ESPN, *This Week in Baseball,* you name it. Normally you would never market a player in the minor leagues, but with a Ken Griffey, Jr., my gosh. A ballplayer like him comes around once a decade. He's going to leave and we know he's going to leave but we marketed him anyway, saying, "Hey, you're going to see a ballplayer that within the next two years is going to be playing in the majors, and has a chance twenty years from now of being in the Hall of Fame. We did an "It's Griffey Time" poster, the first poster of an A-ball player ever, that we know of.

There's nothing like minor-league baseball, but I think it's the wrong word these days. I don't think we are *minor*. We are an entity of entertainment and business that just happens to have ballplayers on the field. But it *is* awfully neat to be in baseball. Going to the winter baseball meetings, you get to hobnob with the major-league guys. We are a part of it. We're part of a tremendous tradition in America. This same ownership group—about ten owners, and I'm one of them now—wants to own about five minor-league clubs. This would be the "flagship station."

I have a staff of four full-time people in the office: the business manager, the office manager, a concessions manager, and myself. It's not like everyone has a job description here. Hey, listen, I was cleaning the toilets and the windows yesterday in the office. Somebody has to do it. Last year, being an independent, I had the opportunity to suit up and throw a lot of batting practice. I was a wild lefty.

MARK FUNDERBURK

Drafted as an outfielder by the Minnesota Twins in 1976 in the sixteenth round, converted to first baseman in 1978, he played with "the big team" at the end of the season in 1981. Released the next year, signed with the Royals

organization, released in the middle of the year. Then Mexico, Italy, and back with the Twins organization in 1985, where he had a big year with thirty-four home runs. For the second time, he made it to the big team at the end of the year. A disappointing spring training in '86 was his last real chance for the majors.

A large, soft-spoken man, he wears a dark suit and tie because he's on his way to a function at the church. Spring training hasn't started yet, and it will be a new kind of spring for him. Thirty years old, he's no longer a baseball player. He's a coach with the Orlando Twins.

Let me put it this way: there's a *lot* of luck involved in getting to the majors. In Toronto they've got Barfield, Moseby, and Bell in the outfield. If you've got a high prospect in the minor leagues, where're you going to play him? That man has to suffer. If he goes to another organization he'll have a chance to play but maybe his organization says no, we want to keep him in case someone gets hurt. You know. He's good enough but the luck isn't in his favor.

I felt like I was in that situation. In 1981 Kent Hrbek was having a good year at Visalia and there was a place for him on the big club. Two years before *I* was having a good year at Visalia but Rod Carew was on first base for the Twins. I can't go over Carew. See what I mean? But Hrbek did a good job when he got the chance and he made the best of it. So Hrbek established himself and I had to step back. Give credit where credit is due. That's the way baseball is.

I became a lot better hitter the last two or three years because I moved the ball around, hitting it where it was pitched, making the pitcher work more. Lot of times before that they would get on the mound and I would go to hacking at the first two pitches and be done with it. Pitcher says, "Thank you very much." In 1985 my manager taught me how to work the pitchers and set them up. Tony Oliva in winter ball worked with me on the same thing. I wish I had had them back when I first started. That's the kind of luck you do or don't have, too.

Red Robbins, the scout who signed me, said, "You're one of the chosen. Now make the best of it." And that's how I played every day— make the best of it. Every time I put on a uniform I thought, "I can play in the big leagues."

Some of your best baseball is in the minors because you're striving so hard to make the big leagues. There's only one day in my career when I didn't give 100 percent and I'll never forget it. The manager was Tom Kelly in '82. I thought I had hit a home run and I was in my trot but the wind caught it and they threw to second base. I wasn't out, but I had to go back to first. Kelly called me off the field and said, "Look, if you don't want to play, get on out of here." I apologized to him and the team. I should have raced on around to second base.

Playing-wise, the toughest part of the minor leagues is the travel—the buses. I'm the type of person that when the sun is up, I'm up. To get off a bus at ten o'clock in the morning and go to the field at four in the afternoon and try to play is a mental thing. If you can overcome that mental part of it you can be successful in this league, the Southern League. I usually get a seat by myself because I'm so big. I suggest they find a smaller guy to sit next to. I can't stand smoke. I just can't handle cigarettes. I can't stand drinking either. I lost one of my favorite uncles—he was drinking and smoking in bed and ended up killing himself. When I saw that I said I'll never drink or smoke.

I talk to guys and tell them they have to find a way to cope with some of these long bus rides. That's what I'll stress to the guys during spring training: getting yourself mentally prepared. Think about how some great ballplayers have played in Birmingham, say, and think about how you're one of the chosen ones, and make the best of it—instead of thinking about that ten-hour bus ride you just got off of, and the back hurting and the guy throwing a ninety-mile-an-hour fastball. You have a small slump and you have to get on that bus and you have to find some kind of way to handle that ride because it can get to you and cause you to play not to your full potential. You might not think it's the ride, not getting proper sleep, but they can get you—they got me, at least—on the second day. I might hit a homer on the day we get off the bus. On the *second* day I come out and say, "What happened?"

Columbus, Georgia, one year we had a two o'clock game. Left Memphis at one o'clock, lost an hour crossing zones. We got to playing and it was three up, three down, three up, three down. The hardest day of my career. Hot, tiny dugout about ten-feet wide, two rows of seats. I come up to the plate in the ninth inning and told the catcher and the ump, "I'm taking one swing and one swing only. I don't care where it goes." First pitch a ball, the next pitch I hit it out of the yard. Umpire jumps around saying, "He said he was going to do it!" That was one of my better yards to hit home runs in.

It can be rough on the family, too, but it all depends on what kind of wife you have. If she's understanding and willing to go through the hard times and the good times, you can make it. If you've got one who's jealous, who can't stand you being away from home so much, it's going to be tough. You'll have *that* when you come home, and if you had a bad road trip it makes things even worse. I've seen a lot of that. To be honest with you, I try to not take baseball home with me. I know what I've done wrong after a game, I try to correct it then, so when I go home I don't have to worry about it.

When I see the big-league guys getting all the money I can say, "They deserve it." They deserve it because of all they've gone through. But it's not the money. It has to come from your heart. Me? I could play for free. I enjoyed playing the game that much. Of course I wouldn't tell the minor-league director that! It can be a tough life in the minors. You're not making any money.

But whether it's *worth* it? That's a totally different question. I learned to handle it in two ways. The first way, I turned my life over to God, the other way was just totally blocking out those bus rides. Don't even think about it. Get a good book and read.

We'll see what happens this year. Basically I'm thinking of going to the park, not seeing my name in the line-up, not coming up batting fourth or fifth in a key situation, needing a hit, thinking, "Oh, we need a hit. Let me hit."

As far as coaching goes, after being in the game twelve years, basic instinct takes over. Experience. What the situation calls for. I'm not the best hitter but I know I'm not the worst one, so if someone comes to me I'll give him some advice and if he can't use it, I advise him to let it go in one ear and out the other. A manager once told me if I couldn't use something, let it go on out. Advice can destroy you—trying to hit like Carew, Killebrew. There's only one Carew, Killebrew, Ruth, Mantle.

So it's kind of been up and down for me. So now my playing days are over. It's kind of hard to swallow sometimes. My little kid asks, "Dad, will you be playing this year?" and I answer, "No, son, I'll be coaching." It first hit me that I might be through when my agent called me and said, "Mark, you can't make it to Japan, that deal didn't go through, and right now there's only one team I haven't heard from about next year."

That's when I thought, "I'm not going to make it back to the big leagues again." That was last fall. The spark left. I talked to my wife. I knew it was time for me to step aside and let some young guys go in and try to make it. And I had a good year last year, so I don't have anything to hold my head down about. You go into the big-league stadiums and look around and say, "Wow, all the greats have played here." Well, I'm one of the chosen ones, too. I've been successful. It's better than going out hurt.

Now I'll just be out there with rubber spikes instead of steel.

5

WHEELER DEALERS

His clients include Mike Scott, Dave Smith, Joaquin Andujar, Roger Clemens, George Bell, Rance Mulliniks, Keith Moreland, Mark Thurmond, Alfredo Griffin, and Mike Krukow.

He helped create the role of sports agents, but he can't see doing this work forever: "Most sports agents are young. Going out to have a couple of cool ones with the boys when you're thirty-one is not as much fun when you're forty-three."

In 1970 I was with a law firm in Houston, in the real-estate department, and my brother Alan was a real-estate investor. This was when the stories were coming out about Mickey Mantle and Lance Allworth and Jerry Lucas losing lots of money in failed restaurants and so forth, and being wiped out financially. We thought, "We could do better than *that*." We were introduced to Elmo Wright, the receiver at the University of Houston who was the first-round pick of the Kansas City Chiefs in 1971, and he became our first client. He brought in a few friends, all young Texas players. I left the law firm.

In 1975 Alan and I realized the real-estate business in Houston was going to be more cyclical than we had thought, and we had this *serious* hobby, sports representation. All we were doing was a player here and a player there, and we realized we could do really well if we concentrated on it. Only 10 percent of all baseball players had agents, but now that they were becoming liberated slaves, we felt we both would have great opportunities. We set up Hendricks Sports Management and became more aggressive looking for clients. And representing the players was a lot of fun.

One of our real-estate partners had moved back to Cleveland, where he was from, and he invited us up there to speak to an investment group, a member of which was Fritz Peterson, the pitcher who had been traded to Cleveland from the Yankees. We sat down and talked about his situation. The net result of that conversation was that at one point we represented fifteen of the twenty-five players on the Indians. The team had some talent but as a whole they were a bunch of underachievers. One of the best things that happened to us was that they started getting traded all over, so instead of a lot of players on one team and none anywhere else, we had a few here, a few there, a few all over.

From 1976 to 1978 we built a large firm quickly, in football and baseball. We were almost saturated with players, and the differences between the two sports were becoming obvious. Football entailed recruiting players who were used to being entertained by colleges. Players were auditioning the recruiters. The feeling on our part was that we had earned our reputation, we knew the quality of our work, and yet we were expected to audition for children—or at least not fully developed adults, people who had not lived in the real world, never held a real job, never filed a tax return.

Football is a more militaristic game than baseball. There's this mind control: "Don't think independently." The players are more aggressive and less sensitive.

We compared that to baseball, where there is almost a familial atmosphere. Major-league players have played together in minor league and winter ball, and players are traded more often. Often they are married, have held down other jobs while in the minors, have filed tax returns, and they were willing to talk about their lives with each other.

They are what we considered *educated consumers*. Baseball players wanted to know whom we had represented. In football every year a new generation of players said, "Hey, how about spoiling me?" At one time I've held five records for highest-paid player at his position in the history of pro football, but that kind of achievement generated *not one call* from a player to check on our firm.

Baseball was easier. The players would call us. So we have made no effort in football since the '79 draft. We still have ten or twelve clients from that era, and have added a couple of younger players that were exceptionally good friends with some of our clients, but even those players had to go through some of the recruiting games with other people.

I don't want this to come out as antifootball—I like watching football games—but the difference for us *as a business* is profound. Plus I've seen what football does to players' bodies. Also, the baseball legal system is much better, and the quality of the people in the baseball union is far superior.

When we started, a $100,000 salary was excellent. Average was $30,000. Average today is $430,000. The players, taken together, used to earn about 10 percent of the gross revenues of the teams. Now it's up to about 50 percent. We worked hard. We developed the high profile and the "brand name," if you will.

I'm very sensitive to the fact that these players perform in public before fans with unrealistic expectations. It's not just "Be a good athlete." It's "Be better than *all the other* good athletes." And there are a lot of good athletes. In my opinion, the player who makes it does so thanks to his mental make-up. I give him credit for this, but the fans don't.

On the other hand, he can be a self-indulgent guy who has been told since Little League how great he is. So the sum total is a strange combination of self-indulgence and those special mental qualities that got him to the majors, with a lot of insecurity mixed in, too, because the player is always being told, directly or otherwise, "If you don't do good we'll *replace* you." A player can never rest on his laurels. The better he does the higher the expectations.

I'm a fan but I'm no beanie-wearer. I'm a professional. No matter that I love baseball, I don't mix any of that emotionalism with doing my job *for you*. I can't estimate how many times that kind of comment to a prospective player has elicited a grin of approval. They don't want a rooter. They want someone shrewd enough, streetwise enough, to go through this *minefield* of management, money, hangers-on, and injuries. We don't teach them how to throw the split-fingered fastball, but we teach them how to deal with the system.

The player has hope. The parents have hope and pride. All of them are naïve. In the early days I'd try to make those players and their parents think about all the reasons they needed competent representation.

I'd say, "Let's talk about the system. The owners are in business to win and make money, and this goes right down through the organization. The general manager is the *agent* for the owner. The fans are there to win, too, and when they cheer, don't make the mistake of believing they're cheering *you*. They're cheering *what you did*. And when you can't play they'll forget you, unless you're Stan Musial or Willie Mays."

Then I'd give them a list of four or five people in the previous generation who had played for fifteen years and made the All-Star team a couple of times, and usually this twenty-one-year-old player had never heard of them.

"Okay," I'd continue, "now let's talk about the player. You. You've been well trained to be a great athlete, but what do you know about the business of sports, the labor system, the legal system? If you really think the general manager or the scout wants to pay you as much as possible, if you don't think they celebrate a cheap signing just as you would celebrate an expensive signing, you're *wrong*!

"While we mean no disrespect, certainly no antagonism toward the fans, the managers, coaches, whomever, we represent the player and we are not concerned that we may be vilified from time to time because we represent your interests. If you're a great player and someone doesn't want to pay you what you're worth and the whole town's against you, it doesn't matter to me. I'll be for you."

Now that we're known by our reputation and our clients, it tends to be, "Oh, you're Randy Hendricks. Great to meet you." Alan and I represent sixty-five major-leaguers—about one-tenth of the total, more than anyone —and another twenty or thirty players in the minor leagues who are on the forty-man major-league rosters. Our staff includes three CPAs and a young lawyer.

The fee structure in the business differs from agent to agent, depending on the services provided, but it's usually some floating percentage, anything from 3 to 7 percent. We have a scale where the percentage goes down the more you make. A full-service firm like ours charges 5 percent above the minimum salary up to $500,000, 4 percent from $500,000 to $700,000, 3 percent thereafter. It doesn't matter whether it takes us three hours to settle or we have to go all the way through arbitration.

We don't want to represent 20 percent of the league. Our clients would start banging into each other. There would be jealousy. I would be too strung out. But every year a few retire and we want to add a few, like an upcoming Roger Clemens or Greg Swindell, players we think have a real shot of going to the major leagues. A lot of people want us to represent them, especially considering the way we charge, which is we *don't* charge them until they reach the major leagues. We thought about this wife sitting in the stands thinking, "If we hire this guy we don't get the new sofa," so we call it the sofa theory, and we don't want the sofa to stand between us and a real good prospect. So we're a bargain for young players. That has become pretty standard, and so it becomes very important to select the *right* players. It's just like drilling wildcat oil wells. You need five or six good, solid wells or a couple of gushers to make up for the dry holes.

Taking on ballplayers and drilling wells are no different. Alan makes it his business to follow college and minor-league baseball. I'm not real good with young talent, but I think I'm a good scout of high minor-league talent and major-league talent. That doesn't distinguish me a great deal from shrewd veterans, I realize. However, I remember watching Don Robinson in spring training in about 1978, when he was about twenty, and I said to Alan, "I'm going to go get Don Robinson before anyone else figures out how good he is."

All the good agents I know fit a certain mold. They have charisma, boldness, self-confidence. They're all *smart*, first-rate minds with high energy levels. They understand the mentality of the game and have a love of the business. It's not necessary to be a lawyer, but it's helpful. As a lawyer, I'm part contract, tax, antitrust, and labor lawyer—as well as a psychologist and student of the game itself. I don't want to work in a system where you're supposed to conform to some role model, wear a pin-striped suit every day and talk and act in the corporate way. I do some of my best work late at night or with loud music on. My body chemistry isn't conducive to a regular nine-to-five schedule. Without exaggeration, I might work twenty-four hours in a row.

I read the sports pages every day for at least two hours. When we were building our business, I was out of town at least one day out of two, maybe two out of three. Now it's probably about three months out of the year. I watch two hundred baseball games a year, most at home. I have two satellite dishes and the equivalent of a TV studio. It's not a pathological addiction, but you just can't wear me out. If something has to be done, I'll do it.

Teams tend to reward former players. You see them in the broadcasting booth. You also see them in management. Now, imagine a fair fight between someone like me—a person who never missed an honor role or dean's list in his life, who ranked in the top four or five of every class, who loves sports, who has fanatical determination—and some of these people, who in general are not as intelligent or as well educated and are not willing to work as hard. I know this sounds self-aggrandizing, but the record shows the result of that kind of fight. If you can't have this kind of candid description, then the description ought to be, "I guess it's just luck, shucks, that we succeed."

Peter Ueberroth views baseball as one conglomerate with twenty-six divisions. His question is, "How profitable is each division?" He has intimidated owners and general managers, telling them how they've let our side run all over them. We've pushed the legal system to the limit. We're like the Indy racers, roaring all the time. We've had more talent on our side. That might not read well in print, but it's true. Our side has been the big winner and collusion is the response: "We can't beat 'em any other way, so let's get together and rig the market." No offers to Tim Raines? Andre Dawson? Every man on the street knows the market was rigged. It was their convoluted way of saying, "We can't cope. We're losing money. Our labor costs are getting higher and higher. This has got to stop."

I raise my hand and say, "Who's accountable for that? How about doing *your* job? Say *no*. Say *no* to me, if you like, but say it the right way."

The first time I went over to the Astrodome with my client Dan Larson, the assistant general manager at that time was John Mullen. He was assigned to meet with us because his boss, Tal Smith, didn't want to do it. And he asked me, "What are you doing here?"

He asked the player, "Why do you have this man with you?"

My response was, "You don't believe in the U.S. Constitution? You don't believe in the right of representation?"

Phil Seghi, another GM, said to one of my clients, "Why don't you just do this on your own?"

The player was a pitcher, and I said to Seghi, "When you step into the batter's box to face my client is the day he'll walk in here to meet with you on his own."

Now I have a warm relationship with all those men, although Phil died recently. The clubs resented the loss of control over the players, and I understood that, but today a lot of clubs say they're very happy to have an agent because the agent can *de-emotionalize* the situation. If you have a player from the "me generation" coming off a good year and demanding as much as the player who has accomplished that level for three or four years, maybe it's the agent, not the club, who educates the player.

I have compared free agency in baseball to the demise of the old contract system in the movie industry. Has the movie industry broken down now that "free agency" has come to the studios? No. I'm proud to have been part of the wars of liberation for the athletes.

Management people have said kind things about Alan and me over the years, because they're making comparisons. Yes, their real first choice would be dealing with the player by himself, because they know they'd get a better deal, but if they have to deal with an agent, they'd like one who values his word, who has ability, who sees the bigger perspective, who does *not* have indiscriminate greed.

I used to tell teams—I haven't had to say this recently—they need to understand our role in the game. If it's not us, it will be somebody else. That's *inevitable*. Second, we intend to be long-term players with the same kind of credibility a general manager has. I can't stay in business if I don't bring in superior results, just as the general manager can't, so it's also inevitable that we're going to have conflict. If you expect me to take an inferior deal, I must fight. I don't care whether Detroit wants to be hard-nosed while the Yankees are generous. I deal with the industry. I'm not giving any discounts to Detroit. They might say, "This is what we pay. We don't care what the Yankees do." I can't tell my client, "Sorry, you're in Detroit."

But this business isn't like reading that AT&T sells at thirty-two and knowing that that's the market. I might be wrong sometimes. Management might be. But I'd rather be pleasant, with professional flexibility and rapport, so we'll make proper financial arrangements for our client more expeditiously than if we have the mentality of a couple of gunfighters trying to shoot each other down. If the general manager tries to get me with one client this year, guess what, I'm going to try to get him. It might be ten years, but I'll get even, and they know it. If they want to go behind my back with my client, I'll play that game. However, I prefer the logical, rational game.

I also get a perverse satisfaction out of all the gamesmanship when there's enough rapport so that no one is entitled to get offended and we can kind of holler a little bit. In those situations nothing is more fun than to engage in this raging debate about how good the player is.

"Your client was 5 and 8, Randy! How can you expect a raise?"

"I'll tell you how I can expect a raise. He was 5 and 8 with a 2.90 ERA, with the worst defense in the league, with no hitting. The facts are he should have been 12 and 2 and you should be embarrassed by your offer. And what about the game where he was ahead 3–0 in the seventh inning and he gave up a hit and a walk, then there was an error, and you took him out and the reliever gave up the grand slam and he lost that victory? What about that lousy reliever?"

I've had that discussion more than once. It's really just fun. Sometimes it'll get down to the team telling me, "You've got a lot of gall asking for this. On July 13 we had to have the game in Cincinnati," and then proceed to tell me the story, probably true, about my client who didn't come through in the clutch. *One* game in the season.

This unadulterated discussion, including the good things you have to say about the other side, is almost as good as salary arbitration.

One negotiation could involve a phone call with the player every single day for two months, and twice a week with the team. And sometimes you know where you're going but no one can get there quick. Markets are dynamic and you watch what everybody else does, and if my player is just about like three other players who have signed for $430,000, $440,000, and $450,000, then the market has spoken and both sides better get off our original numbers of, say, $400,000 and $500,000.

Maybe I want to get $455,000 to say I won, and the GM wants $430,000 to say *he* won, and sometimes battles are waged over that difference and the sportswriter writes, "It is hard to believe that in this era of big money, player X is now into his third day of holding out in spring training due to a difference of $25,000. Nevertheless, Randy Hendricks, reached at his office in Houston, commented that $455,000 was as low as he intended to go because the market had been defined and his player was markedly better than three other comparable players signed to inferior contracts. The general manager said that as far as he was concerned the player is not quite worthy of the higher end of the scale, for reasons he'd rather not go into, and how could any fan work up sympathy for the ballplayer turning down $435,000? The young man needs to sign his contract and get into camp."

There you have it. It's ego or standards or *will*—no different than a 3–2 count. The first quotes to the press are posturing. As it drags on the quotes get more provocative. Meanwhile the player isn't benefiting and everyone may lose, so you don't want to get to that position unless you're willing to play the game. People know I am. I go down that road. It's well known that I'm very sincere. If I cave in this year, I'll have trouble with the next contract and the wrong message will be sent to everyone else in the game. So what happens is you look for a different way to do it, so everyone wins. For example, you might sign for $435,000 plus two $10,000 bonuses, which are feasible goals. And I'll issue a statement saying that the contract acknowledges the legitimacy of the perspective of both sides. And six months later the GM, the player, and I will say, "Can you believe we got worked up to a point of confrontation over a 6 percent difference?" But that might have been good for me in subsequent negotiations.

Pitchers talk about pitching inside, keeping the hitter off balance. Likewise, even my friends in this business will take advantage of me if I let 'em. If I said to ten general managers, "Just give me the fair number and I'll take it," there might be *two* who put the right number in. Likewise, if they told me to fill in the numbers for my players, I'd probably resolve every doubt in favor of my client. I'd probably tell some GMs, "I'd rather fight than fill in the blank. Don't make me play the role of adjudicator. I prefer the role of advocate."

Roger Clemens? My view was that Roger was thirty days short of what he needed for arbitration, and under the system in existence the year before he would not have been short those thirty days. That was terribly unfair. He'd been the Cy Young winner, MVP, and his team had gone to the World Series. Plus the team had asked him to assume a leadership role. And he did. And they offered him a $60,000 raise, patronizing us as part of an industrywide plan to roll back salaries. We didn't intend for the Red Sox to take him for granted. I didn't intend to wear the Neville Chamberlain hat. Neither did Roger Clemens.

The Boston Red Sox don't understand Roger Clemens. One of the things that's a joy about representing Roger is that neither of us wants to be denied the benefits of our talents on account of age or whatever. We both want to be as good as we can be. We don't want to *get in line*. We don't want to be patronized. Roger has conditioned himself mentally and physically to be one of the all-time great players. He doesn't say it publicly, probably would prefer I not say it here because it sounds too egotistical, but Roger is great because he has high standards. Being an All-Star hasn't gone to his head, winning the Cy Young hasn't gone to his head. And you know why? How about being the best pitcher ever, or one of 'em? That's his goal, and with that goal you can never be satisfied.

Now, Roger and I got matched up. Imagine the Boston Red Sox thinking they're gonna take us! Imagine them thinking they're gonna keep him under those terms. We thought, "Pay me what I'm worth as a ball-player. Don't talk to me about being a young man, wait my time. When you say that, how about asking who's the best pitcher on the team? The team's best pitcher in the past ten years? Who took you to the World Series? Who has pumped up the other pitchers on this team? Who has preached winning and good attitude? So don't patronize me by telling me I'm too young. I want to play in Boston till the day I can't play, but you should acknowledge me for what I am and pay me fair market price."

Just treat Roger right and he'll love you. I told the Red Sox, "Look, I understand you need to be tough, but within reason. Your signal to Roger is, 'We don't care what you did. You're not going to get paid.' "

They offered $400,000, then raised that to $500,000. We said we'd sign for a million a year. We wanted relative fairness: look at the salaries of Bret Saberhagen, Dwight Gooden, Orel Hershiser.

Six months beforehand Roger and I talked about what might happen. He asked, "You really think they'd do this?" And I said, "Yeah." We didn't plan it, but we were *prepared*. Hardly any agent in America would have engaged in that battle, let alone won that battle. It looked too unwinnable because Roger's only alternative was to say he wouldn't play. You have to go back to when Koufax and Drysdale had their tandem holdout back in the sixties for something comparable. I thought I could do it.

Part of the Red Sox's problem was that they were pretty much ordered to have their attitude, as part of the industrywide plan to pay young players not based on merit but with token raises based on a lack of rights. They were not really acting autonomously. They were free to break ranks, but I don't think they cared to pay the price. Makes it difficult to negotiate, but Roger was the wrong guy to trifle with.

The general manager, Lou Gorman, and counsel John Donovan, both nice men, were in the initial meetings, but I knew that they didn't have any discretion or authority. If you want to interview me and I send down a press spokesman, which I don't have, you'd quickly figure that I don't want to talk candidly, or you're being patronized.

So I tried to outflank all that very simply. "He won't play." They thought this was all emotion, so we went through about one week where we didn't talk at all simply to let them know that I was serious. If they thought it was just a matter of time before we lost our emotional energy, then they wouldn't budge.

I have a responsibility to think down the road to the next step or two steps. Would he have sat out part of the season, not just spring training? Yes. The whole season? Highly unlikely. If he had had to sit out part of the season would it be likely he would play for one day beyond his free-agent year with the Boston Red Sox? No. There would have been no amount of money to get him to do that.

The final contract was two years and Roger has already earned $2.15 million guaranteed right now, plus whatever he makes from the Cy Young balloting. Some people thought we were foolish and that amuses me. The holdout was worth at least $500,000 to Roger, net. And a poll showed that 70 percent of Boston fans supported him.

This Clemens thing was so intense. I didn't understand how much emotion, cynicism, and, in some cases, hostility the reporters would bring to it. One article said, "Negotiations with Clemens were going smoothly until Randy Hendricks entered the picture." That reflects a stereotype about Alan and me as the good-cop/bad-cop routine. Alan as the low-key diplomat, Randy as intense and aggressive. It's true that there is part of me that *enjoys* being tough, and Alan doesn't particularly enjoy being tough, but that statement in the press was nonsense. Alan did all the talking but the whole concept was mine, including the prediction of the ultimate adversarial action on our part.

A lot of what I say sounds outrageous at times, but I like the word "professionalism." Being a truly competent professional is what we're called to be and what we are.

D A V E   P E R R O N

The Oakland Athletics is one of the more laid-back organizations in baseball. Their director of community affairs wears jeans (the owners also own Levi's) and employs phrases like "exploring myself and the rest of the world" and "pure altruism"—unusual language for the baseball world.

My experience in getting into baseball is highly unusual. I taught first grade for about seven years in Marin County and was fortunate enough to have in my class the daughter of one of the A's owners, Wally Haas. He and I became acquaintances and then semi-friends. This was five or six years ago. I took a sabbatical and then decided not to go back to education, for various reasons. I worked in the garment business for a while. I didn't like it. Then the gentleman who was running the youth programs for the A's was leaving and Wally heard that I was out there looking. He said, "Dave, why don't you come on over?"

A consolidation of three or four jobs ended up developing eventually into the title I have today. It's an unbelievable job. It has a lot to do with what I am about, and also with the way the A's manage people and allow them to create and explore. I'm very close to the owner. I sit right next to him in his office; the joke is that Dave is Wally's "Bobo." He's a young guy, like me—well, he's thirty-eight, three years older than I am. The job is almost carte blanche, in a way, and it touches so many different parts of the organization, so many parts of the world, too.

Wally is adamant that he doesn't want community affairs consolidated into public relations and diluted. It has never been an arm of our marketing department. The marketing department is selling and promoting and everything. We're doing the same thing but it has a different kind of slant.

How can we take baseball, this very powerful entity in our society, and make it more than just selling hotdogs and watching a baseball game and listening to the umpire call balls and strikes? What we've established is a way that we can make baseball more than what baseball really is.

"Cause marketing" is essentially what I do.

I'm really the candy man in this place. I am not bringing in any revenue. It's all expenditure. I go through probably 550 letters a year—everything from the Boy Scouts to convalescent hospitals to the Association for Mothers' Milk—asking for tickets. I give out, literally, a hundred thousand tickets a year, and our marketing people are trying to *sell* these tickets. I have consciously tried to instill in them that this philosophy is what the Haases believe in. Number one, it's coming from them and they are paying my salary so I can't argue with that. Number two, the team benefits from this program because it's good community relations. The marketing people are not stupid. They know it's good business practice.

We have a broadcast guy in our organization, this Eastern sales type who is very good. We've developed a relationship and work together. He'll sell the Toyota folks his package that includes the sky box, thirty-second spots, and everything, and they'll want to do a community thing, so he'll bring me in and I'll create a community thing for them that will make them very visible. I'm just adding to the package and helping him sell, and we have the community involvement using someone else's dollars. So everyone wins.

I think I can say unequivocally that we are the biggest and the best in baseball, maybe all sports. Again, it comes from the top.

We have thirty to fifty community programs, from food drives and book drives at the ballpark and CPR Saturdays and a Cops' Corner, which are not unique to this team, to some very unusual things. We have a project called the mammal project where we bus kids—inner-city kids who never get the opportunity to do this—out to the Marin headland for a day of education in the mammal center out there, a hospital-resort for wayward and sick sea lions and sea otters and so forth. We have Black Adoption Night, where we're encouraging black families to look at the critical need for blacks to adopt blacks. We have a reading program in the summertime. When the kids complete ten books we give them a free ticket to a ball game. I can go on and on and on.

Take the Scleroderma Foundation, a new group that's trying to combat this terrible fatal skin disease that afflicts women between the age of twenty-five and forty-five. You've probably never heard about it. They came to me and asked what can you do. What we did first was set up a way to use our tickets in their fund-raising pursuits—three hundred tickets to a night game to give to their supporters. Then we established an inner circle. They might charge $300 per ticket, and we give each person two hats, two shirts, two wristbands, and great seats. Then I said, "Let's give them something that *nobody* can get. Let's do a pre-game chalk talk where I bring in our hitting coach and pitching coach. Finally, after the chalk talk let's take them down to stand around the cage and watch batting practice. Let's do that and raise some money for you. Let's raise $15,000."

Well, you can imagine. They were booked up. It was called Scleroderma Night. We passed out fliers. Dennis Eckersley was with the lady who has scleroderma, who threw out the first pitch. We absolutely did not go into that with any kind of intention at all except pure altruism. We weren't trying to get people to come out to the ballpark.

Other packages might include eight field-level seats and a tour of the facility as well as batting practice. Because a lot of people don't ever get on the field their whole life, sometimes those seats will go in an auction for $2,000.

With the mammal project, I had to sell the folks at Marin Airporter bus service. The president and the vice president of the company are sister and brother. The sister didn't like baseball but her brother loved baseball so he was trying to sell his sister, and all she could see was the bottom line. Now, what are the A's getting out of that? We're actually getting nothing, but the company was negotiating with me and I almost said, "Wait a minute. I'm dealing with a different mind-set. All they care about is what they're getting out of it."

I said you give us thirty trips from the Oakland public schools to the headlands, which they said cost them about $10,000, and here's what we will give you: five hundred tickets, a page of advertising in our magazine, which is worth about $8,000, scoreboard recognition in forty games, throwing out the first pitch one night, front-row seats.

It was a turnabout for this lady. At the game she must have said to me 150 times how great it was, I know that I was hard to sell, I can't wait until next year.

My relationship with the players is important. A lot of people are scared of these guys and want them always to be their friends, or they allow them to do whatever they want to do, and there is a real line you have to walk. You don't want to set yourself up by being self-righteous and lose some of them. Sometimes I look at them and say, "Would you donate your services?" Sometimes I have to get some money out of my budget. Oftentimes I will do that with coaches just because coaches don't make a lot of money and I like for them to get involved. They do a half-hour-, forty-five-minute thing and I give $150 to each one of them. I don't have to.

I go to spring training a couple of times, which you don't find community-affairs guys doing. I travel with the team at the beginning of the season. I'll go down to the clubhouse and sit with the players in their lunchroom during the game, although usually the only players you find in there are the DHs or the relievers or the next day's pitcher.

I spend a great deal of time procuring this relationship because I want to be able to ask Mark McGwire to go to the mammal project. I had a contractual agreement with the bus company that we would provide a photo opportunity with a player. Mark McGwire and his wife went with me in a limo to the mammal center. He signed autographs and walked around the mammal center. It just so happened that the day before they had received a baby otter that had been abandoned. It was red like Mark's hair and they named it McGwire. Mark and his wife and I had lunch in Sausalito and we went home, and Mark, who gets $4,000 to $10,000 for a two-hour stint, donated all his time.

I want to ask José Canseco to be the spokesperson for United Way Day. José is from Miami. He doesn't have an instant strong urge about wanting to do something for this community, because he's not here. He's young and maturing, and when you're twenty-four and have had all the adulation and whatever they've had, what do you care about? So there has to be another way, and it has to be pretty much how they respect *you*.

I want Dave Stewart to do a public-service announcement and he'll spend an hour before or after a game to do it. He cares in a very genuine way. Last year we gave him the first-ever Walter A. Haas, Jr., Achievement Award—named for Wally's father, the principle owner, who would never put his name on a trophy, except that one. It was created pretty much because of what Dave Stewart did last year. He never said no and always wanted to do things on his own with us. He's a pretty remarkable guy.

I want to ask Storm Davis, Dave Parker, and three other players to do a reading-program spot where they come on and they say, "My favorite book when I was a kid was *The Yearling*. You guys go read *The Yearling* and tell me what Jody's father's name was." Or Curt Young, one of our pitchers, says, "Hello. When I was growing up, I loved *Ol' Yeller*. Can you tell me the animals that bother Yeller's family?" Dave Parker is doing one on Huck Finn. The kids write to the television station and give the right answer. That was my idea. The winner gets a *television*.

I don't mind speaking a little bit, as you can tell. I love public speaking and I'm the guy running that end of things. I just took over the speakers' bureau about a year ago. I make dozens of public appearances. Wally will do one if it's real big, or our general manager will do it. We talk about A's baseball and I can do it extemporaneously for a long time and answer questions and I love the exchange. I always give a brief history about what our community-affairs department is all about, and then I'll talk about the sexy part, the players, and the questions are almost always pertaining to baseball players.

I did a diploma ceremony at some junior high school and when I left they wanted my autograph and I've never, ever done that. I said, "You don't want mine, I'll devalue the ball. You want a baseball player." But that's the connection. The power that baseball has permeates every part of the business. I always remind people that the whole thing revolves around those nine guys on the field, and you can't lose sight of that.

No matter how much you do in community affairs, how much you do in marketing, how good the promotion is, things work better, food tastes smoother, smiles are a little wider when we win, particularly for me because I sit next to the owner and he's got so much invested in time, money, energy and all that. I want us to win mainly because of my boss, really. I can remember when I'd see him after a loss and I'd say, "Wally, you must feel horrible," and he'd look at me and say, "Hey, Dave, you've got to feel horrible, too!"

The only thing that I *don't* like is that I don't make the kind of money that I should be making. The people that are making the money are a few people in the front office and the people on the playing field. The rest of us make better money than teaching school, and my job comes with a lot of perks—tickets, car—but I should be making, you know, 30 to 50 percent more than I'm making now. I don't believe I have a frustration. I do have a *concern* that might grow to a frustration after being here a few more years. Movement in this organization looks like it may be tough. But if I wanted to go to another place, knowing a little about a lot, where would I put myself? You know, I'm thirty-five years old.

KAREN WILLIAMS

She wears two hats: executive with the Houston Astros and ballplayer's wife. She married Houston outfielder Billy Hatcher following the 1987 season.

It's funny how you feel like you get breaks. I started working with the Houston Sports Association, the parent company of the Astros, in January 1983, during an internship out of the graduate Sports Administration Program at Ohio University. In September, about two weeks before I was to finish, I went in to talk to them about where I might go after this. To be perfectly honest, my idea had been to come down here, stay for eleven weeks, get my degree and move on. I'm from Ohio, near Pittsburgh, I hadn't spent much time in the South and I just really didn't have an interest in sports in the state of Texas. But I got down here and it was a real awakening. I started liking Houston and I learned so much that I really did want to stay. I'm inquisitive and aggressive and I have the tenacity to stick with it, but I realized that I was really so green. I learned that I wasn't going to knock the world dead with what I had learned in college. There were so many talented people here and every day was something new and they were real open to teaching me. I was like a sponge. I probably put in fourteen to twenty hours a day, literally. When the team was in town, I was here.

They said, "Well, let's think about what's good for you and we'll get back to you." Nobody had gotten back to me.

One evening shortly after that I was serving as a receptionist, basically, and a gentleman came in looking for our sales manager, whom he wanted to go speak to a group from Houston Lighting and Power up on level eight. I figured this man was with HL&P. He asked me about what I was doing and I said I was hoping that I could work with the Astros but it didn't seem that there really was a position for me.

This man said, "Well, what do you *really* want to do?"

I said, "If I had my druthers I'd like to be the Astros' director of promotions. If there's any area where they are lacking, it's in that area, but apparently they really don't realize talent when they see it and they are going to pass me by."

That kind of ended the conversation and I asked for his name so I could pass it along to the group sales manager.

"Yes, my name's Mike Storen."

That night some people were talking in the stands and they said we had gotten a new senior vice-president in charge of sales and marketing, coming from the American Basketball Association. Right away, it clicked, because I'm a basketball fan. I knew that the guy I thought worked with Houston Lighting and Power was my new boss.

I figured I was pretty much in trouble. I hadn't really bad-mouthed the organization, because I wouldn't do that, but I had said that they didn't realize talent when they saw it.

The next morning I came into work and at nine-thirty Mike Storen called me down to his office and told me to give him three days because he was going to work something out for me. On the fourth day he called me in and said I was going to be the director of promotions.

Now I'm director of special events. Right after the playoffs in 1986 we restructured the department and renamed it because we do a lot more than just promotions. And since that time we've taken over a lot of other things, too.

We're in charge of stadium atmosphere. Our department builds baseball fans. We now have all advertising sales, except for broadcasting. I feel like I finally have an area of responsibility that is very challenging—you're talking about a significant amount of revenue to the company—and one that

I've wanted for a long time. I have commissions and bonuses, so I make more money. I do a lot of coordinating, but coordination comes after the selling. I sell you something and then I coordinate for you and have you feel good about what you bought so that you'll buy it again.

Let's just say you're Kroger and I'm going to sell you a promotion. I'm going to sell you, maybe, Diamondvision and other of our advertising means, too, but let's look at the promotion alone. You decide you're going to do baseball night in the stadium, say it's going to be an autographed-baseball night. We get your logo. We find a vendor that can service that product. It gets in here and you have to handle the advertising of it. You're going to use your own resources and then I'm going to go to our director of communications and say, "Look, can you run something on radio, something on TV, can we have an ad in the newspaper?"

Then we have to alert all our operations people. How are we going to get the baseballs to the fans? We don't just set them in a big box and when people come in they take one. We have to print the coupon they get when they come in the gate because baseballs can't be given out until after the seventh inning because you're afraid that people will throw them on the field.

When I came in we were realizing about $50,000 worth of promotions revenue, and in three years we took it to practically half a million dollars. That was nice but it then became *science,* because you knew that in April you were going to do this and in December *this.* It wasn't fun anymore. When I realized that I was getting burned out, I got more responsibility of a different type.

I correlate a baseball team with a business, and selling tickets or selling an ad in the scorebook is the same thing to me as selling airplanes. You have to have a basic ability to do it. I really feel like I could sell bananas on Loop 610 and make money if I really wanted to. I just really believe that.

And I like the baseball fraternity, or sorority. The beauty of baseball is if I didn't know anyone at a particular club, I could just call and say, "Hi, my name is Karen Williams with the Houston Astros," and the other person would say, "Hey, how are you doing? What's going on? What can I help you with?"

When I met Billy I thought he was the biggest jerk. In April 1986, I asked him to do a promotion and he told me that he couldn't because Shawon Dunston, one of his friends, was coming into town with the Cubs and they were going out to chase skirts. That was his phrase. I pretty much stayed clear of him after that because I just thought, first, he's not too intelligent to say something like that to me and, second, what a jerk, you know. And then in June we were doing a city-wide promotion with J.C. Penney, including tying in the players to each of their seven locations around Houston. The day before the promotion Billy came to me and said he wasn't going to go do the promotion out in Baytown, after he had said he would.

I was pretty upset but he just said, "I'm not going out there." Well, about ten minutes after that I saw one of the guys in the clubhouse and he said that some of the veterans on the team, like Alan Ashby and Denny Walling, had been kidding Billy and telling him he really shouldn't go out to Baytown because it was a strong Ku Klux Klan area. They were just pulling his leg but he was pretty afraid to go because he believed them. He's from Williams, Arizona, up in the canyon from Flagstaff.

So I went back to him and said, "Look, it's really not that way."

He said, "I'm not going out there unless somebody goes with me." There wasn't anyone else who could go except for me and I really was not too wild about that, but he was adamant. And so I rode out there with him and I didn't talk to him the whole way. The person with whom I had set up the promotion ended up going to that location, too, so while Billy did the appearance I was able to put together some business.

Then Billy said, "What do you say we go catch something to eat?"

"I'm not hungry."

"Well, I am," he said. "How about you just go and watch me eat?" He was pretty much fed up with my attitude.

So we sat down. He started talking about his family and he got me talking about mine. He comes from a big family, eleven kids. I come from a family of six and there were so many similarities.

I found out that he is a really hard worker, that he wants some of the same things in life that I want. He had a lot of aspirations, like the fact that he didn't sign right out of high school, but went to junior college first. It was kind of scary. After a horrible first impression of this guy I find out that he's not so different from me. I thought, Oh, he's not so bad, after all.

We became friends and we did things together. Dutch treat. When I came here I had said I didn't want to be around the ballplayers because I didn't want anyone to think that I was in baseball to get a husband. Not long after I had met Dick Wagner, the general manager at the time, he asked me, just as a joke, if I was in baseball to get a husband. And the statement I made to him was, "The guys that you have on your team aren't smart enough to be my husband."

We laughed about that later.

In September or October of 1986 I really found out that I had feelings for Billy, and he had feelings for me, too. During the off-season we spent time together. He stayed here and worked for Budweiser in the PACE program—Professional Athletes' Career Education. Three days a week he wore a uniform and rode a route truck. Two days a week he was in the office, learning how to forecast sales and all those things. He obtained a much better appreciation for my job. He saw that marketing for me wasn't just having fun and watching games. There's work involved.

Billy asked me to marry him in February, and I said no, and he asked me for ten straight days and finally I said, "Are you going to ask me anymore?" and he said, "No," so I said, "Yes."

I was at a point where I had just taken over a lot more responsibility and I was moving in the direction that I wanted to with the company, and I was concerned about how they would accept this. We hadn't by any means tried to hide our relationship, but we didn't broadcast it. Staff meetings are very open and honest. People speak freely about what players we're going to tie in to our advertising campaign, or who's going to be on the front of our calendar, and I was concerned because I wanted there to be this free flow of communication, so people wouldn't feel like they *couldn't* say, "Billy stinks. He's 0 for 24 now."

We really got engaged on July 6, and on that day I met with Dick Wagner. I said, "Dick, I just wanted to let you know that during the off-season I'm going to get married."

"Are you proposing?"

"No. Somebody else already has."

We got married last November. Billy Doran was the best man.

I kept my maiden name because I didn't want any of my clients to ever feel like they had to tie Billy to something. Some of them know that I'm married to Billy, some don't.

I was working with someone with a civic organization in the city and she said, "We're going to tie three players to the event. I don't care who it is as long as it isn't Billy Hatcher because, you know, he's such a liar and cheat after he got caught with the corked bat."

And she said he's just a worthless human being. It was evident to me that she didn't know him personally but she had read the paper—but not all of it or she would have known the other side of the whole corked-bat incident. But she made her statement and it was fine. I have to deal with that on my job. I said we'll do the best that we can to get you who you want.

Right after that I went to an event with this lady, and she said she'd like to meet my husband. Well, Billy was going to be there.

I said, "I want you to meet my husband. This is Billy."

She asked him what he did for a living and he said he played baseball and she said for whom and he said for the Astros.

She said, "Billy Williams?"

"Oh, no. Billy *Hatcher*. Karen goes by her maiden name at work."

Well, she was very, very upset and apologized and I said, "Listen, it's no problem, I totally understand." I didn't really want to slam it in her face, or embarrass her, but I wanted her to get to know him as a person. I knew that she would feel a little bit differently about him. Since then she's made it a point to get to know him and we ended up tying him in to that event, after all.

It's really hard when both of us work in the same field. My busiest time happens to be when Billy's in town, so it's difficult sometimes. We decided we weren't going to talk about baseball at home, but that hasn't worked so well, partly because I'm still so much a student of the game. I feel more comfortable asking him questions than asking other people. So I ask him what was the rationale behind that play, or when did this rule come about. A couple of things that I had never seen before have happened this season. I asked Billy about them. For instance, a switch hitter came in and literally switched after he'd been in the batter's box. But you can't switch after two strikes. Or I might ask him about something as small as why players on base go back and touch the bag after every pitch. I've never played baseball, never played softball in college or anything, so I don't know the rules as much as I'd like to and I'll ask him things like that.

When Billy was in his 0 for 24 slump, I tried to make light of it. I told him I thought he really hadn't gotten a hit because he was wearing hideous red batting gloves. He had started the series using them and hadn't gotten a hit the whole time. "You need to go back to the blue ones." We kid and joke and I do ask him things and we talk about baseball but I try to really let him do his job and enjoy it. Because I want it to be fun for him and not just a job. And we talk about my job, like the fact that twenty thousand sun visors came in and the Gulf logos were upside down and we've got a promotion tomorrow and I don't know what I'm going to do. I had to coupon it.

We spend so little time together, it becomes a matter of quality instead of quantity. This month, for instance, July. The team is in town for ten days and the rest of the time they are out. It's good that I'm such an independent person and so is he. And let's say Billy has come in from a long road trip. He doesn't get home until one forty-five in the morning and he's in bed by three. I'm up at seven and off to work and I'm up for probably forty-five minutes after he gets home from a game and then I'm in bed. We don't probably go out as much as we'd like because what is really important is spending time together, just the two of us. Maybe we'll rent a movie or go out to a movie, have dinner, make total use of that time that we have. We're both selfish with time, clear down to when it's our families. I mean, we won't want our families to come visit because we know we only have this weekend to spend time with each other after day games.

I have to plan my vacations around the baseball season. I might take a long weekend during the season and go see Billy somewhere, but I don't take a vacation. I miss the high-school reunions, the college reunions, the family reunions, because they tend to be on days of games.

You think about the possibility of a trade; not a lot, but you do. We want to live in Houston. My career is very important to me, as much as his is to him, and if he got traded we'd probably not decide till after the season if was I going to look for a job in the new city, or look for something else in sports. A new owner could come in here, or a new general manager, and wipe out the marketing department. We have learned, with his job and with my job, not to plan the next year. Just take it a day at a time.

I talk about the downside of all this but there's an upside: he's doing something that he really loves, I'm doing something that I really like, and it's going to afford us a lifestyle that we will be able to give to our kids. And beyond that, I think it's exposing us to a lot of different people, a lot of different things in life, good and bad. It's helping us to become more worldly. We want to have kids and that's something else that we can offer them.

J O E   M c I L V A I N E

One of the men who put today's Mets together. Big and tall and wearing cowboy boots, he sits in the dugout a couple of hours before a game in the Astrodome. He tells the story of the boots: "We had a guy in the Mexican League one year who came to the winter meetings looking for ballplayers. I said we'd be interested in talking about it. A few days later, during our first

conversation, he asks me what size shoe I wear. I thought it was a funny question, but didn't think any more about it. Three days later he calls me to his room and here's this beautiful pair of boots. I said thank you and got a nice pair of boots, although I still haven't sent him a ballplayer.''

Gerald Young walks by the dugout and McIlvaine jumps up to greet the Astros' young center fielder. The Mets had drafted Young the same year they got Dwight Gooden.

I spent four years studying to be a Catholic priest before I decided to get into another line of work. I had pitched a few games during school, but we never played outside competition. During the summers I played semi-pro in Narberth, just outside Philadelphia. I pitched against Lee Elia, who's managing the Phillies now, and Granny Hamner, Stan Lopata, Doug Clemens, Art Mahaffey, players like that who played in that league after they retired. It was an interesting experience for a nineteen- or twenty-year-old kid to pitch against these former major-leaguers. It helped.

The Tigers had seen me in the semi-pro league and they said if I ever decided to give baseball a try, let them know. They drafted me in January 1969, and three or four days after I left the seminary I was in spring training.

This is important: I did *not* leave the seminary to go play baseball. I left the seminary because I didn't feel I was going to become a priest. I had this opportunity to do something in baseball, so that's what I did.

I was a player in the Detroit Tigers organization for five years, from 1969 to 1973. The first three years I could only play a two-month season, because that was right at the height of the Vietnam War and my draft number was forty, which was a sure thing to go to Vietnam at the time. So I taught elementary school for two and a half years from September to June, then played professional baseball from June through August. That was really a handicap. The first year I played the full season I was twenty-four years old, playing in the Florida State League against Keith Hernandez and a few other notables, and it was my best year. I was 9–6 with a 1.57 ERA.

I went back the next year to Clinton, Iowa, where my manager was a young man named Jim Leyland. It was a depressing town, a radical change from living in the East all my life, and the type of situation that made my mind up. At twenty-five years old, I was still in A-ball. The clock was ticking away. I was engaged, too, and lonely. A lot of factors went in, but things work out for the best. Some things aren't meant to be. My career won–lost record in the minors was .500, so that's how good a pitcher I was.

That five years in the minors has been a tremendous help to me every day of my baseball career.

I wrote to what I thought were the twelve best teams in baseball and told them I'd like to stay in baseball in some kind of capacity, manager or coach or scout. One team, the Orioles, gave me an interview, then another interview. Three of their scouts had retired that year, 1973. The general manager at the time was Frank Cashen.

I suppose they were looking for somebody with some degree of intelligence, some analytical ability, playing background preferable. Rather than grizzled veterans they wanted some fresh blood. It's interesting that the three guys they hired that year were Bob Engle, now the scouting director of the Toronto Blue Jays, Tom Gamboa, director of field operations for the Detroit Tigers, and me. They said at the time that the three most important people they would hire that year were the scouts. I now understand exactly what they meant.

I lived in Florida from 1974 to '81. I worked for the Orioles for three years and then I just couldn't make enough money, and Frank Cashen left there and a new regime came in, and I got an opportunity with the Angels. That's how you get a raise sometimes as a scout—you change teams. I worked for the Angels for two years and then a third time I switched and went to the Milwaukee Brewers for two years. And that's good. I was exposed to a lot of different people.

In 1974 I had Florida and Georgia. In '75 I had Florida, Georgia, Alabama, Mississippi, Louisiana, and I became a supervisor for Latin America. I spoke Spanish. Then each year I scouted I added more territory. I went farther up the East Coast, then the whole East Coast, then the East Coast and the Midwest. Finally by the end I was checking the whole country plus Latin America. There, in the early years, I would run tryout camps. I would go to every little outpost I could find with Eddie Toledo, our man in the Dominican Republic; we had camps at every field and condition imaginable. One time we went to have a tryout camp and there was a little student uprising down the street. The police came to quell the semi-riot with tear gas and all the tear gas floated onto our field and we had to call off our workout because all our players got tear-gassed. Just another day at the yard in Santo Domingo. José Bautista, now pitching for Baltimore, was signed from one of those camps, and Manny Lee. We signed a lot of players, but the success rate of all players signed in the Dominican is probably 2 percent.

Over the course of a year I saw between eight hundred and a thousand games, or more—three or four games just about every day. I loved it. It's different than if you're following a team. Some of the games are painful to sit through, they're so poorly played, but it's easier when you're watching every move that the selected kid makes. When you walk into the ballpark you've got a clean slate, your mind is a *tabula rasa,* as they say in Latin. The player is like a jigsaw puzzle. Let's see, he's got this and this and this. You're trying to fill in as many pieces of that puzzle as you possibly can. The more you fill in the better chance you have of making an accurate judgment. How much money would you invest in him? At what level would you draft him? Can you even sign him? You hold in your hand a lot of power. You have to like making decisions. I like to make decisions.

Sometimes I had to commit on a guy on a one-shot basis, which, if it's not the hardest job in baseball, is close to it. If I only had the one look, I hoped I saw a game where the kid had some trouble, when he came up with the bases loaded and struck out; when the pitcher faced bases loaded and the umpire made bad calls on him; when the shortstop booted the ball. Adversity is a mirror of what he has inside of him, almost a clear indication of how well he's going to do in the future. The player has two choices: he could be determined to do better, or he could hang his head. Feeling sorry for oneself is a very, very bad quality, and very hard to get over. The ability to bounce back—mental toughness—is usually instilled by the time you're seventeen.

The player has to make you like him, even if he doesn't have a good day. If at the end of that game you have your doubts, you're better off to pass.

Probably the most bizarre thing that happened to me was the night I went to see Ty Gainey, who's now in the Astros organization, in a little town called Cheraw, South Carolina, where the lights at the field are about as high as this dugout roof. I flew to Charlotte and drove down and got there right at game time, and Gainey was playing first base. The pitcher on his team threw a perfect game! He struck out eighteen guys or something, and the team didn't hit a ground ball. I saw Gainey for seven innings, he did not field a ball, he did not throw a ball, he did not swing at a pitch—he came to the plate four times and they walked him intentionally four times. About the sixth inning I went down to the trunk of my car where I had about a dozen baseballs, and I went to the coach and said, "Coach, I'll give you these balls if after the game you'll throw the boy ten pitches just so I can see him hit." And he did and Ty hit six of them out of the park and ran to first base in four flat. Thank you very much. Another scout goes down and watches Gainey get off the team bus, put on his spikes—before a cloudburst came. He never saw him play, either. We didn't get Ty Gainey.

In November 1980, I took the job of scouting director with the Mets at the age of thirty-two. I had played for one organization and worked for three others. My wife, Marty, had a baby in April of '81, and we moved up to New York in July. The Mets were a baseball man's dream then, almost an expansion-type situation where you're kind of the doormat of the league and the challenge is taking that team and building it up to the point of, well, becoming world champions.

Now our team is more in a position of maintenance than of building. That's different, but still just as challenging. The moment we rest on our laurels and think everything's rosy, that's when we get knocked down. Last year we had an inordinate amount of injuries to our pitching staff, but I like to think that with a few more resources we still could have won.

I was the scouting director till '85, then became director of player personnel, then vice president for baseball operations during '86. I'm in charge of any baseball facet of the operation, the scouting of players, the development of players, anything not strictly business-related, which is run by Al Harazin. Frank Cashen [the general manager] lets us do the work, but we report to him, so he's still the main man who gets the credit or the blame.

I probably spend 200 to 225 days a year away from home. About 25 percent of that time will be scouting our minor-league teams and the rest will be with the Mets. I have three young children—seven, three, and six months—and it's very difficult for me to pack up and go. The only reason I would ever leave baseball is if it got to be too much on my family. My family is still worth more than the game.

There are different types of scouts. There are scouts who strictly scout the tools. Can this boy run? Can this boy throw? All the necessary qualities. They don't care if he's a criminal. All they say is, "This boy's got tools. Sign him."

The second type of scout, the in-depth scout, scouts tools, yes, but also psychological make-up, family background, everything. Is he mentally tough, self-confident, aggresssive? Does he have the intuition and desire to become a baseball player?

Ability can take you to the major leagues, or the periphery. But what you have inside decides who becomes the fringe player, the average player, the star. Talent becomes somewhat neutralized at the major league level. It's not that Darryl Strawberry's talent is not greater than Al Pedrique's, say. It is. But when you get down to comparisons of *average* major-leaguers, what really separates them is what they've got in their guts and their hearts.

It's difficult to try to read this in an eighteen-year-old, but you have to try. We use psychological tests and evaluations. Teams are starting to do it more. When I became the scouting director, a young guy coming onto a veteran staff, and I telling these guys we weren't drafting anybody unless we got a psychological profile on them, they thought I was crazy. But after a year or two, when they saw the players we were taking and the success we were having, they all began to believe in it. Now with the Mets it's a given. But you can go too far and get too analytical. Unless there are some really bad tendencies, ability is still going to get you to the big leagues.

Ninety-three percent of the players you sign, on average, *don't* make it to the major leagues. What you try and do is beat those odds. That's when you're doing a good job. On opening day this year [1988], they did a survey of all the rosters in the major leagues to find out what team originally signed each of those 650 players. The Mets had more players on the rosters than any other team in baseball.

In 1982, when I was scouting director, the first player we drafted was Dwight Gooden, second was Floyd Youmans, now with the Expos, third was Roger McDowell, fourth was Tracy Jones, now with the Reds, and fifth was Gerald Young, now with the Astros. Wes Gardner, Barry Lyons, and Randy Myers were also selected in that draft. We had a helluva draft that year, and the next—as many players in those two years as some teams get in ten. It just fell that way—good scouting.

The most enjoyable part of the job, maybe even more than winning the World Series, is looking at a seventeen-year-old player, saying that guy is going to be a big-leaguer, going against the grain, watching him progress and make it. For me, Dwight Gooden was probably the most satisfying. In 1982 we were the fifth pick in the country, and that was my second year as scouting director, and there were a lot of people in the room who wanted someone else. There was another pitcher in Tennessee, Mark Snyder—I saw him pitch probably the best game he ever threw—and then there was Sam Horn. Our thinking was that Sam Horn was a guy who would hit thirty home runs in the big leagues, but I really wanted Gooden. We argued and argued and argued about it, but the choice finally was mine and I chose Gooden. I went against the grain. Percentage-wise, the worst draft you can make in the first round is a high-school pitcher. More of them fail and come up with problems. A college pitcher is less of a gamble; you see more of what you're getting.

There are so many beauty queens out there in the first round—you have to decide which one will it be. When you're drafting you're playing craps. You like to have the odds in your favor, and Gooden is the only high-school pitcher we've ever taken in the first round, but I just felt this was as good-looking a high-school pitcher as I had ever seen. The only guy who compared with him in my mind was Lee Smith when I saw him as a high-school kid in '75 in a little town in Louisiana. Lee was from the woods and no one had ever showed him one thing about pitching, but he was a natural —perfect delivery, great arm, and the kind of body that was going to get bigger and stronger. He was a perfect projection. Gooden was the same thing. He was six-three, 180 pounds maybe, long arms, long legs, and a body you could just see fill out. In hindsight that was a great choice—and Youmans, too, another pitcher in the second round—but at the time it was a gamble.

After the '86 championship season we perceived the biggest weakness on our ballclub was still the lack of a good right-handed, power-hitting outfielder. We made a list of the players around baseball who might fit that need, and Dale Murphy and Kevin McReynolds were at the top of that list. We went to Atlanta and Ted Turner told us he would sell WTBS and CNN before he would trade Dale Murphy. We went to the Padres and they indicated that we were the only team in baseball who could give them enough to satisfy what they wanted for Kevin McReynolds. That was what we wanted to hear. Originally Jack McKeon, their general manager, asked for a center fielder, a third baseman, and two pitchers. But we were trying not to trade pitching; we wanted to keep the pitching we had.

We let them choose the center fielder and the third baseman; those were the two places where we seemed to have a little excess, more than we needed. They choose Stanley Jefferson and Kevin Mitchell. We still had to bridge the gap of the pitchers. I wanted to get them out of the trade. The key player in that trade was Shawn Abner, the number-one pick in the whole country in 1984. And we hated to trade him, but when we looked at our team what we really needed was the guy we could put in left field who was going to hit for power. Abner had a chance to be a good player, but we also felt if we had McReynolds, who's in his twenties, our outfield would be strong for quite a few years to come. As soon as we mentioned that we would include Abner in the deal, that turned the trade around. Those conversations took about three months' worth of work, including pretty much the whole week of the winter meetings in 1986.

Sid Fernandez we got in one day. The Dodgers needed a left-hand reliever real bad because of the Steve Howe situation, and Carlos Diaz had had a real good year for us the year before when we were still in last place.

They wanted Diaz, who they thought was the best available left-hand reliever for something that wasn't going to kill them, and we suggested in the first meeting that we'd trade our Hawaiian for their Hawaiian. They kind of laughed and twenty minutes later Tom Lasorda called back and that trade was done. Sometimes it hits that way.

When you're in charge of personnel, you have to have them believe in you and have confidence in you, and you have to have a rapport with them, and not fear governing. If you ask others about me, one of the things they'd tell you as one of my best assets is my ability to handle and understand people, and that came from the seminary, where I did social work. Every Thursday we'd go out into Philadelphia on a particular assignment, and I worked with the housing authority, finding homes, working with families having housing problems. The motivation you have going into seminary is you want to help people. Whether that avenue becomes the priesthood or some other avenue—that's what you're in there to find out. For me, it didn't become the priesthood. I just didn't think I was being called to do that. So I got out, and into this, and it's not that I've aspired to become what I've become, it's just that God has had a hand in it.

My job is to work for the New York Mets and do the best I can for the New York Mets, but hand in hand with that goes the responsibility to do the best we can for every player we sign. If we're not able to use them on the big-league team, we try to put them in a situation that's going to be better for them.

Baseball and the Catholic Church are similar in a lots of ways. They really are. They're run by fallible individuals—there've been good popes and bad popes, great baseball commissioners and not-so-great ones, and owners, and general managers. They're very similar as institutions. I see such a parallel. You like to think as you get a little older you understand some things. Baseball's not going to die. It's a lasting institution. In the seventies people were saying baseball's dull, and so on, but the strength of the game, the solidity, the *sanctity,* will always keep it there, despite players' strikes, bad owners, whatever. And I look at the church the same way.

I'm not a big Jim Bouton fan, but I'll always remember a line in *Ball Four* because it's absolutely true: All the time you thought you were the one holding the baseball, in the end you found that it was the other way around, the baseball was holding you.

6

SUPERSTAR

ANDRE DAWSON

Most Valuable Player in the National League in 1987, his first season with the Cubs, and runner-up in two previous years with the Montreal Expos, he's the reluctant superstar.

I don't really like crowds. In Montreal, you never got quite the exposure you get here in the States, in Chicago, where you become a household name. Everyone feels good within, when they're recognized, and you're only in the game so long, but I stay away from all that as much as possible. I stay by myself a lot. I rent a condo downtown, on the lakefront, and I don't go out a lot for the simple reason that people come on to you, pull at you from all different directions. I go directly home with my wife. I like to get off my feet, kick back, watch some television, listen to some music, read on occasion.

The key in this game is to do the things that it takes to stay, day in and day out. Nobody's going to feel sorry for you. My first year in the majors, 1977, I was on the verge of being sent back to the minors. It was going to happen within a week or so, but I got a chance to play against a right-hander, which was unusual because they were platooning me, and I hit my first major-league home run. Buz Capra was the pitcher in Atlanta, a good breaking-ball pitcher. I had two strikes on me, fouled off some tough sliders and curves before he hung one. It was a thrill to get that behind me. I had come up the previous year and played about twenty-four games without hitting one. The following night I got three hits. They delayed the decision to send me down and I got hot and went on ahead and won the Rookie of the Year.

When you're young, you're not as aggressive and you take pitches, and it seems like when you do that the guy throws the ball right down the middle of the plate. On the other hand, you look for one down the middle and he throws a breaking ball outside and you look totally bad, over-matched. You begin wondering, what am I going to have to do to get this act turned around? I tell young guys, stay within yourself but stay *aggressive*. You can't let the pitcher take that away from you.

There are certain ways pitchers back someone off the plate, but they don't do it throwing up and in, certainly not around the head. No one can convince me Eric Show wasn't throwing a knock-down pitch on purpose last year. I had been doing a job on San Diego pitching. I think I had seven home runs off the staff before the All-Star break, and I'd hit a home run off Show the week before in San Diego to knock him out of a game, and I had a home run my first at-bat in Chicago. Show's a sinker-ball pitcher and they have control problems when they get the ball up. You get hit upside the head it feels like your head explodes. It's scary. Your eyes close and don't want to open, and when they do, you see blood and don't know where it's coming from. I got a letter of apology from him. That's not the first time I've been hit in the head. I was hit by Bobby Castillo of the Dodgers two years earlier. Right on the cheek. I still have some problem with nerve damage there, but it's gradually coming back.

I get nervous today, but not as nervous as ten years ago, when I put a lot of *undue* pressure on myself. Now, it's the cat-and-mouse game with the pitcher. Fifty thousand fans screaming, guys huddling around the mound and you don't know what they're talking about. But those are the situations I like the best, when the game is on the line. That seems to be when I concentrate the best. You hate not to come through. This past Sunday I was pinch-hitting against Todd Worrell. I went up thinking he was going to come right at me because I sat on the bench all day, with no batting practice. He knows I'm cold. But he started me off with two sliders away, I swung at both pitches, fought off two more, hit a third one just foul down the right-field line. Then he decided to go with a fastball out of the strike zone and I chased it and the ball game was over.

When I get in the batter's box I've done my thinking. I know how I want to approach the at-bat, how he's pitched to me in the past, where the runners are, so I have an idea how he will likely pitch me this at-bat. Pitchers have patterns. I don't *guess*—well, I suppose you could call it guessing, but I won't go up there guessing *curve ball*. I'll look for location.

I want to see the ball *before* I stride. I'm looking to the release point. I don't watch the motion at all. Some pitchers have breaking balls that break about halfway to the plate. Other curves break late. A lot of times you can identify the fastball from the spiral effect of the seams, but I don't try to read seams. I just pick up the ball in a certain area.

I usually anticipate the fastball and make the adjustment to the curve. Now with John Tudor, say, it's different. His fastball runs away from me as a sinker, and he throws a change-up as his out pitch. Rarely does he throw a right-hander a slider or curve ball. So he's going to try to make me pull the sinking fastball and hit it on the ground. I have to stay behind that ball and drive it back up the middle or to right field, make sure I don't get out in front on the change-up. You can't think about pulling a home run against a guy like Tudor. The only way you'll ever do that is if he makes a mistake.

Against Dwight Gooden I look location and lay off a pitch in any other location. If he starts a breaking ball out over the plate, it's going to end up out of the strike zone, so I look for the breaking ball starting out *at* me and breaking over the middle half of the plate. Hopefully I'll get him to throw the fastball on the inside part of the plate, where I'm looking, and I can pull that pitch.

Nolan Ryan is one of the toughest opponents. You know he's going to come right after you every at-bat and give you something to hit. There have been times I've struck out my first two ABs before I even made contact off him, but you don't mind striking out against a guy like that. You walk back shaking your head but sincerely thinking that if he throws you the same pitch next time you're going to hit it hard. I've hit four or five homers off him.

I keep a book, a little black book full of notes. I fill it out after every at-bat, documenting everything that happened.

Once I realized that I would test the free-agent market, two cities came to mind: Atlanta, because it's a natural playing surface and closer to my home in Florida and someplace I would consider making a permanent residence, and Chicago, because of the grass and it's also in the Eastern Division. My main priorities were getting off the Astroturf and staying in the National League. I didn't want to adjust to a new league, new pitchers, and I *knew* I had to do get off the Astroturf, for my knees.

All the knee problems go back to my senior year in high school. I was a defensive back, and it happened about two minutes before the end of the first half. Quarterback threw a pass downfield and I was attempting to make an interception and the wide receiver pushed the cornerback and his helmet hit me on the knee. I had all the basic problems: stiffness, some fluid build-up. I did very little rehab. We didn't have the facilities in high school. But the speed finally returned and I didn't think I'd have the problems I've had.

In 1984, I actually thought about retiring. That year was my worst slump and I got off to a very slow start. When I got up in the morning I had to get in the shower and run hot water on the leg, just to be able to move it around, and it got so bad I was taking pain pills in order to play, and this was only two months into the season. It was a turning point. A lot of people felt I was finished, washed up. I was sitting in a bar in St. Louis after a game. Disgusted. I wanted to be alone but a scout was sitting there. I don't know whether he was drunk or not, but he told me I couldn't move, I was finished. He was more or less rubbing it in. I got tired of hearing this and politely got up and left. I didn't want to be responsible for what might have happened after that. Management decided to take X-rays and detected the crack. I got on a strengthening program and it eventually healed. I hit a *hard* .248. I had to hit well over .300 the last two months to get up to that.

So in 1987, the monetary matters didn't really come into the picture. We gave the Cubs a blank contract and told them to fill in the dollar amount. The figure [$500,000] was embarrassing at first, because it represented a six or seven hundred thousand dollar cut in pay, and I felt in all honesty that that proposal was given to me in an effort to get me to turn it down. The collusion going on was pretty obvious to everyone. The owners around the league were surprised when I *did* sign it. But I thought my best years were ahead of me and if I stayed healthy, I could make up the difference later on. The game now is business-oriented: how much can management save, as opposed to how good a ball club can it put on the field.

The fans in Montreal are more subdued, more laid back, and generally are hockey fans. They're not that knowledgeable about baseball. Chicago is totally different. The fans love the ball club and are right on top of you. It makes it a lot easier to go out and enjoy yourself. My first at-bat here I got a standing ovation from a full house. Right away I felt like a part of it. John Tudor for the Cardinals was the pitcher, a runner on third. He threw me a change-up that I hit off the end of the bat, a little nubber, but the run scored. The fans cheered again.

My first home run for the Cubs—my first hit also, I believe—came off Bill Dawley, also with St. Louis. I had hit about eight homers in twenty games in spring training and people said, "He'll hit forty in Wrigley Field," but they didn't realize the wind blows *in* here as much as it blows out. A lot of balls are crushed, in the early and late part of the season, especially, and *don't* make it out. It can be an intimidating ballpark but you can't try to hit home runs. I never let the wind put pressure on me.

My *last* home run at Wrigley that year was probably the most exciting I've ever had, after I had put together the type of season I thought I was capable of. I worked the count to 3–1 off Bill Dawley, the pitcher I'd hit the first one off, but who had then given me some problems before I figured out what approach to take. He threw me all off-speed pitches, and the 3–1 change-up was a good pitch but it didn't fool me. The ball just jumped out of the park. The fans were on their feet chanting "M-V-P, M-V-P!"

The average fan thinks it's *all* glamorous. You play a kid's game and get paid tons of money for doing it. It gets rubbed in all the time: "Get a real job." They don't realize that something like this is short-lived. Most of the time it's envy and jealousy. It's not our fault we're blessed with this talent and the job.

I'm not worried about retirement. The players who have the toughest time leaving are the ones who still think they can perform, but I still plan on leaving the game far before I think *I'm* done. I want to play, at the most, three more years. That would make fifteen years. That *is* a goal. I'd be thirty-seven. I want to leave healthy. I don't want to be hobbling around. I believe I'll look forward to hanging the spikes up. I'll just pack up my belongings and take my family home.

Some players want to live this life style for the rest of their lives. I don't feel that way. I can live a very *normal* life style. I don't have to have a million-dollar home and worry about the upkeep. I cherish the time I've had in the game but you have to realize it's all going to come to an end. Of course everyone wants to play in a World Series, but I stopped setting personal goals about midway through my career. I feel that when you reach the goal you become content. I try to play the game day to day.

7
OUT
OF LEFT
FIELD

He's a slight man with thinning hair, safety goggles, a direct gaze, and a cigarette. His domain is the Louisville Slugger bat factory in Jeffersonville, Indiana, right across the Ohio River from Louisville. On the other side of the plant they make Power-Bilt golf clubs. The facility is as large as a football field, with stacks of timber and bats in various stages of production jammed everywhere. His job is to know the status of each one of them.

If we got the timber the way we want it we could produce a lot faster. But when you're fooling with Mother Nature, it's not like an iron golf club. Man-made stuff you can push, this stuff you just have to wait until it grows. We cull about 40 percent, maybe 50 percent, because it's not good enough for a ballplayer. It's a good bat but it doesn't have the cosmetics, the straight grain; it just doesn't *look hard*. The ballplayer's not going to take it. He'll say this is just trash. But that doesn't mean we throw it away. That goes into your store bats.

I've been here going on twenty-eight years, but it seems like ten. It goes fast. Twelve years to go; they'll come quick enough. I'm too old to be on the softball team anymore—fifty years old and I'm shot.

I started off as a flame-burner—that's a hand operation, a completely different system than they got out here now. Then I went to packing for about five years, and then I went into "ballplayer," where we make the major-league bats. I've been here about eighteen, twenty years. I'm a working supervisor. I supervise plus help do the work. Consequently I'm running the tracer lathe, the automatic lathe, picking out timber, checking weights, checking models, checking orders. Gets to be quite a job.

If they're not good bats I'm the one who hears about it. We just got a bad bat back from Dave Concepcion. Chuck [Schupp, the sales representative] brought it back in here the other day, said Concepcion was griping about his model. I look at the bat and says, "He's right. It's not even close." We can't figure out what happened. We checked the master model and it was a little off but not that much off. We allow one-tenth of an inch for sanding. After they're turned on the lathe they get rough sanded, then fine sanded. But if they happen to put new sandpaper in there, it cuts a little more. What somebody done maybe, they pulled that machine in until it fitted the exact model, and they didn't allow for the sanding. Plus they had just put new sandpaper in there. It changed that whole bat. Thirty-second of an inch. Enough that you could see it. Concepcion could tell by *feeling* it. These guys can start with the handle and work their hands up and tell you whether the barrel is big or small. They can pick 'em up and I guarantee come within half an ounce of what it weighs. I can do it and they can do it, too. Concepcion's been using our bats for nineteen years, and that type of person we don't like to give a wrong bat.

Kal Daniels sent some bats back; the handles were a little small. They was a little small, but not that small. He said they just weren't right, but if he'd been hitting, he wouldn't have paid any attention to it. I'd be the same way. These guys make a living with that bat.

They can specify from one end to the other, from the end of the knob to the end of the barrel, how big, how they want it tapered. And they know it, too. Handles, say, come with cone knob, semi-cone, then you've got your extra-large knob, your regular knob, and your small knob.

In every case but one the letter of the model stands for the player's name. The C-243, that's Rod Carew. If Ricky Henderson wanted to use that model his name would be on the bat, but it would be Carew's model, and that model number will never change. If Carl Yastrzemski had a model made it would be Y so-and-so. There's one exception: the C-271. That C actually stands for "cup bat." Lou Brock brought one of them back from Japan, a cupped bat, because the Japanese had trouble getting wood and that's the way they took weight off. Brock liked it and it really caught on. What it is, they can get a heavier, harder piece of wood and still get it lighter, because a cup takes an ounce off. That is a very popular model. We can't keep it in stock.

The T-141: you've got players all the way down to the lower and all the way up to the higher use that bat. The most popular are probably your C-271, M-110, and P-72.

With a lot of 'em, I know what they want. Some change so much it's hard. Don Mattingly is using the T-141. The T is Cesar Tovar. Mattingly's also got one out now that's his, M-1728, the birthdays of his kids.

They know you can't always find exactly what they want, but you've got to give them the best. Particular ballplayers like knots in the barrels, some like wide grain, some like narrow. Most of 'em like the wide grain. They think it's harder. It's in their head. There's no science to it. I've always been told, actually, your narrow grain is your stronger bat because the narrow grain has took its time by nature and grown, and the wide grain has been shot with juice, growing fast.

Ted Williams, as great a player as he was, wanted narrow grain. He didn't want the wide grain. He said that tree grew too fast.

Harmon Killebrew kept calling me saying, "I want narrow grain, narrow grain." He got this from Ted Williams. I kept sending him narrow grain, so narrow you couldn't hardly see it.

"Too wide, too wide."

He raised cattle, and right before he retired he came down here to the big cattle show at the fairgrounds, and he came over and I just asked him personally, "Harmon, show me what you're talking about, 'narrow grain.' " And he went over and picked out a bat that in my opinion was a cull; something we probably wouldn't give a minor leaguer. He wanted *no grain at all,* what we call brashie, no texture at all, going all over the place. I said, "For two years I dug craters trying to get narrow as I could and I could have walked up and picked any of them out of the rack for you."

And he said, "Well that's what I want. That's natural-grown wood. That hasn't had the juice shot to it."

But most of your players today want the wide grain. Mattingly has to be real wide grain—half inch or better—or he'll send it back.

With the knots, I think there is science. You ever sawed a piece of wood and got a knot? It's hard. I think the knots help in the barrel. They do not want them in the *handle;* it makes the handle weak. The older ballplayers almost all asked for knots in the barrel; they don't do it as much today. A lot of the new ones coming up don't even know about it. Babe Ruth was one of the first who started asking for knots in the barrel. We've got a record of it. Carl Yastrzemski, he'd ask for knots. Ted Williams would. Willie Stargell would. It's on the order. "Knots in barrel if possible."

Hickory went out about when I came in. It has no grain at all, just fiber; that's why they put the dark finish on hickory, to cover it up. It's all ash now, mainly because it's more workable, I think, and it's got a grain to it and you can get a bigger bat with lighter weight—and nowadays these ballplayers they want lighter bats. They do not use heavy bats. I'd say your average weight now is between thirty and thirty-one ounces. Used to be thirty-three, thirty-four, thirty-five. We had some guys using forty-one-ounce bats. Back then the pitcher comes up after being in the minor leagues for years; he's in his thirties when he makes the big-league club, so he wasn't throwing that hundred-mile-an-hour fastball. Now you get these kids coming up, they're eighteen years old throwin' that dude a hundred, a hundred and ten miles an hour. You're not going to get no forty-one-ounce bat around on *that.* You've got to get that bat *through* there, the way they pitch today.

You get your order, get the model he wants, the specifications, the finish, then you go over and pick out the timber by weight to make the certain length and model of bat. That piece of wood is called the billet. You have to really dig through the racks, the trucks, the bins, keep looking till you find what they want, to the best of your ability. Coming out of the hothouse they can be 8 to 10 percent moisture. That's what we want. You don't want them completely bone dry, but you want 'em dry enough to where they won't lose weight.

My favorite job is picking out the billets. That's the whole job, to me. If it's not right at the front it's not going to be right at the back. These clubs'll order 450 to 500 bats for spring training, then they'll turn around three weeks later and order another 500 for their Opening Day. That hurts our timber situation, really takes it down. Right now [May] we're behind. Right now I've got 12,000 bats on order to get off that [computer] screen. Imagine. It'd probably take me a half a day to get out a special order. If I walked right over and found the timber ready, I could probably get them out of here in three hours. I've done it.

The billets used to be square or round. Now they're all round because they're easier for us to turn. After I pick the billet I mark the barrel end, turn it so the knots will be in the barrel. Then we semi-rough it down to what's called a rough-out. Then it goes to either the tracer lathe or the lathe, and it's turned into a bat. The only difference in the lathes is that the tracer is automatically fed, instead of manually. And it's computerized; that machine is exact and twice as fast. The hand turners can turn pretty close to the model, but that tracer spits 'em out exact. But if the tracer's not set up just right it will turn the bat wrong. Or a lot of times on your automatic lathe over here, where you slide the bat in, if there's a lot of wood chips behind it and you don't notice it, it'll make a difference in that bat. The slide won't go all the way in.

The hand turner averages four bats an hour, and we only use it if we don't have the templates. They hope to get all the templates but in my opinion they're not going to. There'll always be something new. I think eventually they'll get another tracer.

After the bat is turned it's checked for size, for weight. If it's okay it goes on to the brander, then on to the finisher.

They can specify eight different finishes: flame-burned; hickory; filler; Hornsby (a lighter brown than the hickory); Walker (hickory halfway down with a light-brown handle—that's the two-toned bat I like, that's a pretty bat); black; unfinished; and waxed. A lot of 'em like the black bats; they think that gives them a hard look. Don Mattingly uses the plain bat.

You have the sawing man, the man roughing out and weighing, the tracer lathe is two more people, the rough sander is a person, the fine sander is a person, your brander is a person, your sealer is a person, your dipper is a person. You're talking roughly fourteen, sixteen hands handle that bat. Right now our seniority here is fifteen years, on the average. It seems like once people come here they stay. I'd say for every six people they hire, five of 'em retire from here. It's hard work. You'd classify it as manual work. You have the machinery but still the man has to pick the bat up, feed the machine most of the time.

For as many bats as we put out I think we do a super job. We don't get many back. Not satisfying the ballplayer—not getting it to him on time, not getting it right—that disturbs me more than anything. To me, that bat there *is* Dale Murphy. The bat is his personality. It's him. I think he's a super guy, and I try to give him what he wants, give him the best. Of course I do that with all 'em. I don't do any favors. My favorite team's Boston, but they don't get any better bats than the Reds, the Yankees—which I hate, of course.

When guys at the plant hear we got some bats out late they'll come up to me and say, "How come we got his bats out so late?" Or, "Why'd those bats come back? What was wrong with them?" I'll have people from the factory come up, people who don't even have anything to do with the ballplayer bats, and ask what was wrong with those bats? They want to know.

C H A R L E S   A.   S T E I N B E R G,   D. D. S.

As far as anyone knows, the only practicing dentist who also has a full-time job in baseball. From a windowless office jammed with recording and play-back gear, he directs the Baltimore Orioles' video and Diamondvision operations.

I became a big Orioles fan in 1967 when I was about eight or nine years old. I haven't missed an Opening Day since.

I went to a small private school and in the last month of the senior year they have a program of internships. The school recommends choosing either something you want to go into when your education is finished, or something you'll never have the chance to do again. So "Mr. Practicality," the son of an orthodontist who had worked in his father's office on Saturdays and completely enjoyed what he saw, said he'd work in a dentist's office. But a couple of days later a friend stops me in the halls and says, "Hey, Charlie, how about working for the Orioles? I heard someone did that before."

Practicality went out the window! What a chance! On April 12, my friend—his name is Chris Lambert, now a lawyer—and I came in to be interviewed by Bob Brown, who gave us the rundown of what we'd be doing, menial but important tasks; if we did them we could then do other things, like go to the clubhouse for autographs. My friend and I looked at each other: "Oh my goodness, that would be great."

On May 10 we started. That was an off-day and Reggie Jackson, who had just joined the Orioles ten days before, was coming into the office to go over biographical information. I was dying! In that month I was doing menial work—pasting articles in scrapbooks, stamping names on slides— but I was thrilled. In the eyes of those who were watching me, this was unusual. They had previously experienced people who wanted instant glory, not someone willing to sit in the closet all day pasting articles. I was in every morning and every afternoon, and stayed for the games. Well, when the internship was over they asked whether they could call on me during the season for part-time help and I said, "Sure." My real job was swimming instructor and lifeguard at a camp in Baltimore.

I came in occasionally, and sometimes I got "thrill" kinds of things to do. ABC needed a runner and I got to sit on the field and cue the umpire when we were out of the commercial. Twice I worked for NBC, sitting in the booth behind Tony Kubek and Joe Garagiola, keeping the line score up to date. Dreams come true every day, and it went on like that off and on through the year, but it didn't occur to me that this was a way into baseball management, and dentistry was still as appealing as ever. I started college that fall at the University of Maryland at College Park.

Bob Brown asked me to work for the club the next summer, as a full-time assistant. My first day Bob dumps a bunch of 11-by-14 envelopes on the countertop they called my desk and said this was my project. Those were Earl Weaver's statistics.

Mark Belanger was 10 for 14 against Jim Kern, at that time a hard-throwing pitcher for Texas. The crowd was surprised when Belanger pinch hit against Kern. He made an out. Ten for 15. The statistics behind those moves became my job. I had been a statistics buff but it was still a little exciting learning that the statistics I'd heard about for years, that Weaver used, were going to be my job to prepare. I soon realized that they're time consuming, tedious, and have to be perfect. I did them by hand with paper and red pen, no computer.

At that time the stats showed how each Orioles pitcher did against Cleveland, say, as a whole, and how each Baltimore hitter did against each Cleveland pitcher. Earl used these figures to rest players on a certain day, or determine pinch hitters. We didn't use a hard-hit ball category at first, just at-bats, hits, doubles, triples, homers, RBIs, walks, and strikeouts. At one point we went to an expanded form where we recorded line-drive outs, ground-outs, fly-outs, which is a *lot* of work, and Weaver said, "You know, I don't really use that stuff anyway. I just go by the batting average, how many at-bats it's based on, and whether there's any home-run potential."

When a new team came to town I gave Earl a sheet on every opposing pitcher. One thing I tremendously respect about Weaver is that he never got on me if I made a mistake. I worked for Bob Brown, and if Earl wanted to get mad about something, he knew he should go to Bob Brown. But he'd still come marching in and say, "Is that right?" and I'd go look it up. And I was lucky, a lot of the things he questioned were right.

In 1979 the stats got blown up into a brief bit of national attention when one of my mistakes had a happy ending, in the first game of the playoffs against the Angels.

Nolan Ryan started for the Angels. It's a 3–3 game in the eighth inning. They take Ryan out and bring in John Montague. Big deal. I'm up in the press box doing my game work—a whole different set of things, in this case counting pitches, typing the play-by-play, and scoring the game. The phone rings from the dugout. It's Ray Miller, the pitching coach. Very even tempered, he asks, "Charlie, where's the sheet on Montague?"

I nearly died. My mistake was not double checking to be sure we had *every* Angels pitcher. We had last played them on August 30, and I knew no pitcher they acquired after September 1 could play anyway, and I must have supposed that no one had joined the Angels on August *31*. John Montague had been acquired on August 31 from Seattle. His sheet was not in there. I still get chills when I think about it.

We had the Seattle stats on file, so I called downstairs to get the latest Seattle stats. When I got them I learned they were updated only through the third series, and we had played them four times. I hadn't updated for the fourth series because I knew we wouldn't be playing them again that year.

"Okay," I said, "Take that sheet anyway and run it to Weaver in the dugout." This wasn't the most up-to-date information, but it would be better than nothing. Then I looked in my scorebook to see whether he had even pitched in the last series against us. I looked and found zero official innings in one game, but six hits. Then he pitched in two more games.

The bottom of the eighth is over by now. I start writing down the new stats: Kiko Garcia, 0–2, Lee May, 1–3, John Lowenstein, 2–2 with a home run and two RBIs.

I called downstairs and dictated the new stats to the captain of the "Basebells," the PR assistants, who happened to be Earl's stepdaughter. She ran them over to Earl and by the time that had happened we had gone out in the bottom of the ninth. But at least I knew now that in the tenth inning, when we were getting to the bottom of the order and a possible pinch hitting situation, Earl had the information.

Who comes out of the dugout to pinch hit but Terry Crowley. "Oh my God," I thought, Earl doesn't have the stats. It was real clear from the stats that Lowenstein had done very well against Montague. He had something like three home runs in four at-bats. I call downstairs and asked if they're sure Earl got the stats. Yes.

Well, he was outsmarting us again. He put in Crowley, the weaker of the pinch hitters, against Montague, because first base was open. It would make a better story if they walked Crowley, but they pitched to him and he made an out. Then they walked Al Bumbrey, the lead-off hitter, bringing up Mark Belanger, who had started because he had a good record against Ryan. Weaver pinch hit Lowenstein, who hit a three-run homer to win the game.

I wish I could have enjoyed it but I didn't. I was numb, sure that those were my last minutes working with the Orioles. How could you make a mistake like that and survive? I told Bob Brown right after the game, but first asked him what was the worst mistake he'd ever made. "Gosh, I've made so many," he replied. So I told him my story. And he said, "What a great story!"

I knew I had to apologize to Weaver. Ray Miller's locker was the closest to Weaver's office, and I looked at Ray.

"Is he in there?"

"Yeah, but he's okay. Go on in."

I walked in. Usually it's "Earl," but this time I said, "Hi, Mr. Weaver, I'm very sorry."

"Siddown! Have a beer. You won us the ball game!"

I totally admired the way he chose to see that situation. He could have really pasted this intern, me, but instead he chose to see the department facing adversity and getting the job done. I kept trying to apologize as he was telling me to shut up and have a beer.

I did the stats in the summers throughout college, interspersed with other research jobs and, sometimes, cleaning the storeroom. This made me realize that no matter how long I've been here, I still have to sweep out. Bob Brown does it himself.

I got into the University of Maryland Dental School, in downtown Baltimore, and I can't count the number of people who said, "Well, now you'll have to give up the Orioles."

I said, "We'll see."

I worked for them in my free time in the summers and Bob gave me more duties, in addition to the stats: researching for press notes, writing the two-line messages for the scoreboard—we didn't have the big Diamondvision screen at that time—and taking part in the choice of music played in the stadium. Music has always been a passion.

Still, when I graduated in 1984 I didn't conceive of a career in baseball. I just pictured myself as Bob Brown's assistant until my practice got so large it would prohibit me. That winter, John Blake, our assistant PR guy, was made the PR director for the Texas Rangers. Well, *that* was no time for me to withdraw.

I had started my practice in the evenings, in offices with three other dentists who were working during the days. It was the Orioles during the day and dentistry at night—an evening practice is not completely novel. I had worked for the team during parts of my freshman year in dental school, when I spent thirty-seven hours a week just in the classroom, so why wouldn't I be able to stay on when I was practicing on my own, and able to set my own schedule? I never understood what all the fuss was about.

We were about to leave for Christmas break that winter when Bob said that the club was negotiating for a Diamondvision video board. If it came through, he wondered, would I have time to work it? Yeah, I said. It didn't seem like a big deal to me, although I hadn't seen one. What's the atmosphere of a ball game? I knew that. Are you going to play the hardest rock songs? No. Concertos? No. I had learned what the right attitude was for the stadium: family atmosphere, fun, taste, not too many PA announcements.

Bob Aylward, director of business affairs at the time, Bob Brown, and I went out to dinner to discuss the concepts, the philosophy. There's the option of having the board say CLAP! CLAP! CLAP! and those other wonderful things in other ballparks, and we unanimously decided that this was exactly the *opposite* of the tone we wanted. The Orioles were still feeling the fun of some great seasons. We knew our fans didn't need to be told when to make noise. Let what happens on the field tell them. I mean, we're talking about people who eat the dirt on the infield. The "Charge" trumpet is fine, and enough. They enjoy the hot dogs and the trivia questions and "Thank God I'm a Country Boy" in the seventh inning, but they come out for the *ball game*.

The board would not be a prompter, but a mirror. The game must always be the dominant feature, with nothing else even a close second. The board will never interfere with the game or question an umpire. The board does not belong at second base. Show a replay, but be modest. Between the innings, go wild. Be a TV set. But during the game, mute yourself. It may bring the fan in the upper deck closer to the field by way of showing a close-up of the batter, but the board shouldn't be active when someone is batting at the plate. That's a sacred rule at Memorial Stadium.

Now I wasn't a PR intern anymore; I had a budget to draw up and try to meet. I was full-time with benefits and salary. The board was installed on March 19 and the season opened three weeks later. I started with six or seven part-time game technicians; today, three years later, I have six full-time people, all of them studio staff technicians.

Judge our performance by how well we bridge the "conflict" between the hard-core fan and the other fans. Everything on that screen must have a purpose. We're not going to deviate to the ends of the spectrum, hard-core music or baseball statistics only. You offend the hard-core fan with CLAP! and NOISE! but the entertainable fan wants to get up between innings and move around. Maybe there are some hard-core fans who want *no* music, but Memorial Stadium was the first in baseball to play rock music, back in the seventies—Bob Brown's innovation. We haven't lost any old-fashioned fans, and we've increased our here-to-be-entertained fans.

We keep the hard-core fan informed about a Wade Boggs RBI ground-out, or a triple by Glenn Davis, say, whom the fans will also know has been hot. We quickly find out how hot and relay this information: "Davis, with ten hits in his last twenty at-bats, drives in two runs with a triple to give Houston a 6–4 victory over the Mets." The casual fan is not *im*pressed or *de*pressed by this note on Diamondvision, but the hard-core fan appreciates it.

When you see the bloopers replay at Memorial Stadium, you're not going to see any Oriole bloopers or bloopers of the opposing team. If you see an Oriole, it will be doing something funny. We get the same footage everyone gets, put out by Major League Baseball Productions, but we re-edit it entirely. Let's realize these ballplayers are heroes, and let's humanize them. We take cameras and follow them on community visits, we see them kissing the wife good-bye when she drops him off at the ballpark. We've got baby pictures and Little League pictures of our players.

We put all of this into a couple of different formats. Heroes of Birdland is one—a player's highlights set to a song. I knew when I took over Diamondvision that I would need to take over the music completely, because they go hand in hand. I have a good background in pop music of the past thirty years, and some knowledge of classical music as well. My father is a violinist as well as an orthodontist.

Heroes of Birdland is still my favorite feature to make. I first think about the song. Last year we choose "Sonny" for Cal Ripken, Jr., as a play on words relating to his father, the manager. "Center Field" by John Fogerty has been Fred Lynn's song for three years. Fogerty's sound works very well in the ballpark.

It didn't take long to map things out and get them organized. Now we try to be flexible to go with the flow of the game. Say we have Billy Ripken set to be the Hero of Birdland, but Eddie Murray hits a grand slam the previous inning. Quick! Get the Eddie Murray Hero of Birdland. Or Fred Lynn makes a great catch. Quick! Get Fred's Hero of Birdland and edit into it the catch *he just made*.

The fans are amazed!

We can do that if we're really clicking, if we make the right judgment on the amount of time we have. Is this a slow or fast pitcher? Zero or one or two outs?

There's another time I tried to be too good and I blew it. It was our biggest blunder, no getting past it. We learned a lesson: "Don't panic and believe you must show something." It was in June 1986 when Alan Wiggins was our second baseman, and he had had some troubles, personal and otherwise. At the end of the eighth inning we were going to show some highlights of the Yankees–Red Sox game. In the top of the inning I got the replays, but without a log. I didn't know what was on it, and I didn't have time to find out, build the graphics, then get it up there.

We can't just show nothing, I thought, we've established a standard of having something every half inning. That was the mistake, and I made the split-second decision to show something that I thought would be innocuous, a "Who Am I?" feature, where the pieces of the puzzle come together to show an Oriole player. That's simple, so I called for a "Who Am I?" tape.

Which one? Who cares. As the pieces of the puzzle start coming together I get this sick feeling because in the top of the eighth inning Wiggins had made two errors, giving him three for the game. He wasn't a fan favorite anyway. Oh no, it's not! It couldn't be! But everyone in the booth realized who it was at exactly the same time as the fans did, and there was nothing we could do by then. There was a collective, "Oh, shit!" Wiggins turned and saw his picture and heard the boos. We had set him up. Not good. He thought the media was in charge of the board and lashed out at the writers after the game. But it was our mistake and he was right to be angry.

I still have my practice with the same three dentists; it includes some of the players and front-office people. When the team's home, I don't practice, with occasional exceptions for a player. When they're gone, it's fifteen, twenty chairside hours a week. But I'm also counseling, examining, or taking immediate care of players in the clubhouse at the stadium. The Oriole hours are roughly sixty, seventy per week; when they're home, eighty-five to a hundred.

The practice has led to a lot of research into the contrived but legitimate field of sports dentistry. I'm one of the charter and founding members —there are a hundred of us—of the Academy for Sports Dentistry.

You don't learn in dental school that the musculature that supports the opening and closing of the mouth is part of the same musculature with which the pitcher throws the baseball. The trapezius muscle, an accessory muscle of mastication, if you will, goes right to the top of the shoulder. We've seen clearly in some players how a loss of teeth or significant imbalances in the way they bite can cause stresses on those muscles. Those stresses can affect pitching performance. We have cases in which a guy comes up here not knowing that his lack of back teeth is likely to cause that stress. When they're young and strong it may not affect them, but when they're thirty-two, it may be too late to realize they need additional support from the teeth in back. Some pitchers would say I've helped them. Storm Davis of the Oakland A's.

STEPHANIE VARDAVAS

She's a lawyer in the commissioner's office with plans to take over the place.

When I was a kid I wanted to be president, just like every other little kid, but when I was around nine or ten it dawned on me that commissioner of baseball is the best job in the world. It's just like being president except you don't have to worry about the Middle East or arms control, you get to go to as many games as you want, you get the best seats, and people are nice to you. It's more fun.

It doesn't embarrass me to say that I want to be the commissioner of baseball. It's not impossible, but I don't think it's likely. I may have done the wrong thing by being an insider. However, league presidents tradition-ally come from the inside. At any rate, there isn't a *bad* spot for me to land in, as long as I stay in this game.

Here, I love having my finger on the pulse everywhere, but when I worked for the American League I was even closer to the trenches, which are the clubs. I'd also like to take a stab at working for a club. They are really what baseball's all about, and I only had a brief taste of it interning with the Mets. When you get up every morning and live and die with what happened on the field the night before, that's a part of what it is to be a baseball person that I would really like to have.

I don't know anything about player development, and freely admit it. This may change for women as more and more girls play Little League and even high-school baseball—hardball—and there will come a time when there will be women with the same tools for evaluating talent as men have. How the game will deal with those women is an open question. It's difficult to have credibility. A lot of clubs will be bifurcating the traditional respon-sibilities of the general manager: one person in charge of player develop-ment, someone else in charge of player-personnel administration. And I'm certainly qualified to be a pretty fair in-house counsel.

Ownership? You tell me where to find a group of people who are going to install a woman as the general partner of a club and let her run the show. I don't expect to get a call from Reggie's investor group saying, "Stephanie, we've been hearing about you . . ." I don't mean to sound defeatist, but you have to be realistic.

Being a woman with my aspiration has more assets than people might think, but I still believe they're outweighed by the liabilities. As a woman it's easier to develop friendly relationships with the people who run the clubs because, at some level, you're not threatening to them. I'm not bashful or self-effacing. I'm friendly and don't try to take advantage of people, and person-to-person I have no trouble dealing with the men who populate this game, because they're nice guys. But the baseball establishment—the people *plus* the baseball tradition that hangs over all of us, and that I revere as much as the next person—is a male establishment. Remember, I went to Yale, so

I'm not a stranger to male-dominated institutions. There are a lot of women in baseball who are very bright, hard-working, fabulous people, a large number of whom will never be anybody other than someone's secretary. A lot of them may be the victim of being twenty or only ten years older than I am. They came in as secretaries and got to be good enough so that no one wants to give them something else to do.

I'm from Baltimore, so these days, being an Oriole fan, I feel cold doom closing around my heart. I don't know whether that's clairvoyance or existential dread. My parents still live there. My father loves baseball— loves, loves, loves baseball—and he liked the idea of having a kid to take with him to the games. Since I came along before my brother, I was handy and got drafted.

I went to Yale and blush to admit that I was active in an organization called the Yale Political Union, basically designed to keep former student-council presidents off the streets. I didn't bother to rejoin my senior year but a good friend called me up one night and said that he had invited Bowie Kuhn to speak, and he knew I would be interested in coming.

I showed up at the restaurant early, and I had been to enough dinners to know how to scope out where people were going to sit. I knew etiquette established that the president of the union sits to the right of the guest, but whoever lucked into it would sit on his left. I just selected the seat I thought would be to the left of the guest and sat down. I call it legitimate manipulation. I have never been bashful. I guessed right and so had the opportunity to talk to Bowie Kuhn throughout dinner and found him a delightful, funny, charming person, without a lot of false friendliness and bonhomie but not at all the stiff-backed prig the newspapers make him out to be. Anyway, there's too much false friendliness in this business.

So I shot the breeze with him and had a wonderful time. I asked him how to go about getting a job in baseball. My major was American studies, and I was planning my senior paper on the Black Sox scandal, with Bart Giamatti as my senior adviser. Kuhn gave me the standard-issue answer: "Well, when the time comes, send us your résumé. If we have any openings, we'll keep you in mind." He had brought with him Alexander Hadden, who was at that time baseball's secretary treasurer. That position is traditionally a lawyer, and Sandy is a Yalie, so while Bowie was besieged for autographs after his speech, I buttonholed Sandy and had a nice chat with him about my plan for the Black Sox paper, and asked whether the commissioner's office could recommend research sources. He suggested I write him and he would follow up. I did that and it happened that there was a guy working in the commissioner's information office who was a big White Sox fan, and he took a personal interest in the inquiry. The paper had to do with the relationship between the scandal and the establishment of the office of the commissioner. There wasn't a commissioner at the time, and the scandal exposed the existing structure as being completely inadequate for dealing with a problem of the magnitude of the Black Sox.

So anyway, when the time came I sent in my résumé and got a letter back from Sandy saying that baseball was about to start some kind of training program for college graduates to develop potential executives. Was I interested in being considered as the first applicant? It didn't take me long to write back and say "Count me in!" At that point I was still in school and hadn't embarked on serious interviewing, but I was asking around all over baseball. I was also thinking about law school, but sometime in the future, not then.

Six men and two women were the finalists. I was twenty-two years old, this was the job I most wanted in the world at that time, and it was scary. When I went to my interview, two of the people's names just terrified me: Frank Cashen and Lee MacPhail.

They asked me what I thought about women reporters in the clubhouse. This was 1979, when it was a very hot issue. I said that I thought any accredited reporter should be allowed in the clubhouse on the same basis as any other reporter, and that if the club felt it required five or ten minutes of privacy after the game, it should be five or ten minutes of absolute privacy, after which the clubhouse should be open to accredited reporters. I still don't understand why this was such a big deal.

They didn't mean this next question the way it sounded, but it was very weird. They asked me if I could type. I thought to myself, "What do I say?" This is the question that causes the hair on the neck of every woman coming out of college with a bad attitude, like mine, to stand up. But I was unbelievably disposed to like these people and brush aside any possible bad vibes, and it was a reasonable question, in fact. They weren't in the mode of taking a couple of young puppies out of college and setting them up with little fiefdoms and secretaries and dictaphones, and who can blame them? I said I wasn't a touch typist but made it through college typing my own papers.

At the time I was convinced I wouldn't be hired because I was certain they wouldn't hire a woman in the first year of the program, but later on I thought that maybe they viewed the program as an opportunity to make a statement about where they were going, that they were going to use it to broaden the base a little bit. Yes, I was a woman, but I went to Yale and had done the paper on the Black Sox.

Pretty quickly after the interview—less than a week—I was at my parents' beach house and Frank Cashen called me up and offered me the job. I managed to keep my composure long enough to ask when they wanted me to start.

I was in the program for sixteen months. The first fourteen I worked with Barry Rona with the player relations committee, then I went to work for the Mets as an intern in the promotions department, then I worked for Major League Baseball Promotions Corporation, planning the logistics for the 1980 World Series and helping to produce the program.

In November 1980, I was offered a permanent job with the American League, as the manager of waivers and player records, and I did that for five years. I don't mean to boast but I'm one of three or four people in the game who really understands a couple of the rules concerning waivers and transactions. But I wasn't in the American League office because I was always right. I was always right because I was in the American League office. It's kind of like the Supreme Court.

One of the things I found in that job was that I'd have a lot of trouble with male fans who would call and ask a question and not believe me, largely, I believe, because I had a female voice. A guy wanted to know whether Bobby Grich was on injured-reserve. That's football. In major-league baseball we have the disabled list. First a secretary in the office told him this. He hung up and called back and said, "I'd like to talk to someone who knows the difference between injured-reserve and the disabled list."

I said, "That's very easy. The injured-reserve is football and the disabled list is baseball."

He just wasn't coping, and it happens that he was going to keep getting women picking up the telephone. The way it worked then was that whoever happened to be passing by a ringing phone picked it up, and numerically there were more women than men in the office. It turned out that this guy had read in the *New York Post* that Grich was on injured-reserve, and never mind that he was dialing the American League, he was refusing to accept the word of a female voice answering the phone over something he had read in the *Post*. Maybe that's really cynical of me.

At night I went to Fordham Law School. Everyone knew that I wasn't interested in going out into the world to practice law for a living, but there were never any guarantees here. I didn't know whether there would be a job for me when I got out of law school. I knew I didn't want to do the job I had forever, as much as I liked it. I knew I wouldn't be happy doing it when I got out of law school. I was setting myself up for some kind of life decision. I don't want to seem like some horrible ambitious monster, but I wanted a credential, something to get ahead in this business, to get a job I really aspired to, because I could see then, and maintain to this day, that a woman with a bachelor's degree will not get as far as a man with that degree, though there may be an exception here or there.

Now I'm assistant counsel to the commissioner. I've been on his payroll since January, after I graduated from law school and passed the bar. I was lucky because the activities of the commissioner's office were expanding to the point of needing another person in the legal department. Peter Ueberroth doesn't particularly like lawyers, but he likes women, so I had only one strike against me.

I do trademark licensing. We have tremendous problems with counterfeiting. A lot of people don't know that it is a felony to counterfeit a registered trademark. If you go into business making a sweatshirt that says *Yankees* or has the crossed *NY,* and you do that without a license, we'll go after you and make you sorry. It's not possible to get a criminal conviction in every case, nor would we want to, so we try to confine ourselves to the collection of damages and making people stop. We handle all of the licensing and enforcement for the teams, who divide equally the income from the licensees. We're all in the same business. My boss and I both spend a substantial portion of our time dealing with our national law firm, which has private investigators in every major-league city, looking for counterfeiters. A tremendous amount of this stuff comes from offshore.

There are over two hundred different licensees, ranging all the way from caps to kazoos in San Francisco that say "Humm baby." And because the kazoo says "Humm Baby," that manufacturer pays royalties to both major-league baseball and Roger Craig, because that phrase is his slogan. You don't have to register something to have the right to collect royalties.

The way the trademark laws are written, if you don't police your trademark, you lose it. If we let people counterfeit, and didn't have evidence that we had sent cease-and-desist letters, that we had sued people and collected damages and extracted acknowledgments of right from people and promises they would not do it again, then at some point our trademarks would be vulnerable to legal attack, and they wouldn't belong to us. They'd be in the public domain and anybody could use them. The law demands we maintain a certain level of care, and that's what we do. When we bust people with federal marshals, we often put out a press release. We're trying to get the word out that it isn't tolerated. We had a seizure last year—apparel and novelties, in the New York area—from a guy who actually had tacked on his bulletin board a clipping about major-league baseball clamping down on counterfeiters!

The biggest damage award without a lawsuit that I have personally handled was a $24,000 settlement, from someone who had been in business less than five years. Last year the office made a private settlement of about $140,000. I wish I was on commission.

Counterfeit stuff is sold by street peddlers and in stores where you would never expect stuff like this, stores that don't know what they're buying. They have such high standards they assume no one would bring illegal stuff to them. A New York department store, which I cannot name but one of the major ones, had some bogus Yankees and Mets T-shirts. One of the women who works here was shopping for clothes for her son, bought them, and brought them in to us.

Last year during the World Series I spent a few hours one afternoon riding around in an unmarked police car with three fabulous, very amusing plainclothes St. Louis cops, because someone had received a report that out at the Day's Inn near Lambert Airport some guy had nine rooms full of St. Louis Cardinals merchandise. We hung around the parking lot. It was great. No one answered the door at any of the rooms he was registered to, and we later found his truck in the parking lot of the International House of Pancakes, with some young guy driving it. The plainclothes officers went over and showed him their badges and my business card, and said we wanted to search the truck. He let us, even though we didn't have a warrant. Everything was licensed.

The absolute top counterfeit trademarks are not likely to be sports franchises—a couple of months ago the hottest property in licensing was Spuds MacKenzie—but the Yankees, Mets, and Dodgers generate a steady stream of counterfeiters. When the Twins won the World Series, it was accompanied by an enormous outburst of spending by Twins fans, as if they had had this pent-up lust for Twins merchandise for twenty-five years that only now was able to achieve full expression. They went nuts. Anything they could lay their hands on that said *Twins* on it. That was an opportunity for anyone with a silk screen in his garage to try and make a few bucks, and they did.

There are a lot of unlicensed trading-card issues, issues you have never heard of. Two guys in a basement get the idea of doing a series of cards featuring players who hit thirty home runs in a year. They go to a printer and arrange for a limited card set of, say, ten thousand, distributed by mail via the magazines that cater to the card market. We subscribe to them, naturally. Often these card sets represent an infringement on the players' rights, as well, because no right to their likenesses has been acquired. You can't put out a card without two permissions—the players' for their likenesses, and ours for the logo on the uniform. The players' association has a very active licensing program, but their situation is more complicated because each player can go out and make deals on the side, in addition to any group deal made by the association.

After nine years in baseball, I find that I don't have any clubs I hate anymore, like I did when I grew up in Baltimore, and I don't say this in order to sound like a good management soldier. What happens is you get to know people.

When I worked for the American League, every year around All-Star time I had to try hard not to get psyched, not to let resentment build up. This was when the American League was losing every year. Finally, 1983 rolled around and the American League really kicked butt and Fred Lynn hit the grand slam, the first ever in the All-Star game. I'm not a big autograph hound but this time I sent the souvenir pennant to my friend Mike Port, the Angels' general manager, and asked him to have Lynn sign it. And he did. The other things I have are weird, like the beginnings of a collection of baseball cards of players who later became executives, which I get them to autograph. I have a Tom Grieve, but there's a lot of room for growth in that collection.

I have a record album of Gene Autry singing Christmas carols, including "Rudolph the Red-nosed Reindeer," which I bought somewhere, and again I called my dear friend Mike Port. Mr. Autry wrote this lovely inscription.

My sophomore year in college I was trying to think of a really high-quality Halloween costume. The year before I had gotten myself a long, stringy, blond wig and some fishnet stocking and a real short black skirt and a papier-mâché lamppost and gone out as a hooker and spent the whole evening with a friend dressed as a sailor. But that was a drag because I couldn't wear my glasses; no self-respecting street hooker wears glasses.

It occurred to me that wearing Brooks Robinson's uniform would be a really neat thing to do. I picked Robinson because he was my favorite. I thought he was cool, terrific. I got some nice engraved Yale stationary and wrote to him: "Dear Mr. Robinson: If your uniform isn't doing anything near the end of October would you consider letting me borrow it for Halloween? I promise I'll take really good care of it and send it right back"— you know, the whole thing.

I got this letter from him, in his handwriting, a week or two later, saying that he thought it was a great idea but the uniform didn't belong to him, it belonged to the Orioles, and I should write to Jack Dunn and tell him Brooks said it was okay. I don't know what that letter would be worth now on the collectors' market. I showed it to an Oakland A's fan and he said, "Wow! That's like getting a letter from God!"

I wrote the next letter and then I received this package with Brooks Robinson's home uniform, and the cap, the socks, and the stirrups. You could tell it was real because there was a button missing and the leg was worn from sliding. I had it for about a week before Halloween and every night after dinner I would lay it out on my bed and people would come over and just view it. The word got out and people would say, "We heard you've got Brooks Robinson's uniform. Would you mind if we looked at it?"

I was on cloud nine. I didn't actually put it on until Halloween, and it was really a thrill. People were really blown away, like Beatlemania. No one thought it was real; an incredible simulation.

I sent it back and a couple of years later I went to photo night at Memorial Stadium and took with me this picture someone had taken of me in the uniform, and asked Brooks to sign it.

Maybe someday I'll be the answer to the trivia question, "Who's the only other person to ever wear number five for the Orioles?"

JOE DIROFF

Strung above the front door of his modest red-brick house not far from downtown Detroit is a hand-lettered sign reading, WELCOME MIKE.

I retired from teaching school and coaching in 1980, and I had the opinion that when you retired you hit the rockin' chair. You played golf, you traveled if you could afford it, which I couldn't. For two years I operated on that basis, but I was feeling sort of down. I didn't know what I was supposed to do, and I got to the point where I said a prayer. I said, "God, what talent did you give me over the years that I could use to help or entertain people?"

It was after that that I came up with this thing about cheerleading. I had started cheerleading in high school in 1938, fifty years ago, in an all-boys school. I went out for all sports but never really made it, and cheerleading was an opportunity to be close to the action. Then for many years I hadn't done anything relating to sports particularly, but I was following every Detroit team all the way, like mad. No cheerleading, but a lot of yelling. One time in Fenway Park a little old lady tapped me on the shoulder and asked, "Would you mind moving? I'm getting hit with everything they're throwing at you."

Then came the dancing. One day the team wasn't doing too good and the fans were down on 'em, and the guy on the organ started playing. Well, I started to dance, which in my case is a matter of kicking about as high as my shoulders. The crowd went a little bananas.

And the third thing, these signs, I'm doing because I got in trouble in the sixth grade. I was in class the first day of school and I was talkin' to some guy and the teacher stopped and said, "I can see you and I aren't going to get along." After class I went up to her and asked her what I could do. She asked if I could cut out letters and make signs. I said no. She said you can learn.

The reason why I'm in this is I really believe God gave us sports. The athletes can pump up the people in the area by their play and so forth, and the fans in the stands can pump up the athletes. I've got a sign that says, IT'S IN THE HANDS OF THE FANS IN THE STANDS. They need someone to lead them, and that's where the cheerleader comes in, see. But there are people who see no significance in it. To tell you the truth, I consider myself a failure at the present time, as far as getting people going at the start of the game. Not easy to do. Some people think it's boring if the Tigers aren't getting hits, but I tell them I don't care what's going on out there in the field, it does not have to be boring in the stands. We can make it so it's not. You can keep that darn place hyper. That's the word, as far as I'm concerned. *Hyper.* It's funny, the answers you get from people, like somebody'll say, "That guy's making plenty of money; he can pump himself up!" Stuff like that. But the money they make doesn't have anything to do with it. They're not a better player because of that.

The players call me the Brow because Whoever made me forgot to stop going across, you know. As best I remember it was the Tigers who gave me that nickname, because it was with the Tigers that I first started going to the airport. Some player said, "Look at those eyebrows" or something like that. I got to know the Tigers at the airport. I never asked for autographs—really I have no desire for autographs—but I would bring signs and put them around and sort of move into the background. I might say hi to a player and that's it.

When Kirk Gibson came into the airport he would always say, "Hi, Brow. Thanks for coming." There ain't another guy who ever said "Thanks." They meant it, I'm sure, and show it in different ways, but they never *said* it. So everybody I run into who has something to say against Gibson, I let 'em know. He's intense. He's fired up. Not only that, I've seen him get off a plane at midnight and sign autographs, while most of the rest of the team was getting in a bus, right from the plane.

When I go to the airport I call every one of the media and tell 'em the Tigers are leavin', and tell 'em when and what airline. They don't relate to this too much, so ninety-nine times out of a hundred I'm the only guy there at two or three o'clock in the morning. One guy said to me in May, "Joe, call me back in August when we clinch the pennant."

Well, what the heck good does it do to pump up a team *after* they've clinched it? But that's all right, I know they had a bad incident in August of '84, when some disc jockey got on there pumpin' things up and six thousand people showed up at the airport. A lot of them guys were drinkin' to the high heavens. It got so bad that the word got to the plane and it landed thirty miles away in Ypsilanti. Supposedly things were burned down and vandalized. And of course the World Series was bad, too. Next year I was bound and determined to do what I could to eliminate such malarkey as that. I went to one of the councilmen, Jack Kelly, whom I knew. We sat down and went over a plan on what to do if we won again.

Anyway, when I'm alone at the airport I go up and down the concourse and let the people know that the big team is coming in. Before I do this I've got these signs plastered on the walls. Sometimes I can get 150, 200 people. Then I ask whether they'd care to hear a cheer, and so possibly for the first time they hear the "Strawberry Shortcake."

> Strawberry shortcake,
> Gooseberry pie,
> V-I-C-T-O-R-Y!
> Are we in it?
> Well I guess!
> Can we do it?
> Yes! Yes! Yes!
> That's no lie,

> That's no bluff,
> We're the Tigers,
> RED HOT STUFF!!!

Then you jump up. They like that. It's an old cheer with lots of variations.

One time, the Tigers were sittin' around waitin' to go on a trip, and I asked them if they wanted to hear a cheer.

"Okay, Brow."

Well, I've got to ask the boss first, Sparky Anderson. So I goes over and asks, "Sparky, is it okay if I give 'em a little cheer here? Pump 'em up?"

"Sure thing, Brow, go ahead."

So I start my count—I always do a count to lead into it—and I hear a lot of yellin', and the players are all lookin' over my shoulder. I turn around and there's two businessmen on the telephone. They're yelling at me that they can't hear and the players are yelling at *them,* "Don't you dare yell at the Brow! Go on, Brow! Give us a cheer!"

Mike Heath was really going strong. He's right up there when it comes to pumping. Well, heck, I'm not going to get involved in this darn thing, so I quit. To this day, Alex Grammas, one of the Tigers' coaches, cracks up every time he thinks about what happened.

Usually when they go to Cleveland or Chicago I make those trips. The others I just can't afford. When I go on the road I don't always go to the game. What I do, a lot of times, is to go over to the hotel before the game with signs and stuff. If I do that, they don't know whether I went to the game or not. They would take it for granted that I would be at the game. It's not a matter of not wanting to see the game, because I love to watch a game, but, I don't know, I'm busy or something. Many a time I just hop on the plane and go back home. I don't know how to explain why I would do such a thing as that. My wife does not approve of this stuff at all. The whole family doesn't approve of what I'm doing. I'm just a crazy old man to them.

Great woman, my wife, took care of the nine kids like it was nothing. Great woman, I love her dearly . . . I think—yeah, sure! She loves the game, but will not go to a game at which I'm performing. She's quite conservative and her folks are the old, traditional Irish. She has gone far beyond the call of duty. She's been called a saint, I've been called the opposite.

The Red Wings' plane is the only one I've flown on. Also the only clubhouse I've been in. My signs go in the other clubhouses. The players pick one out and leave it there as long as they want it. I had one in the Tigers' clubhouse for three weeks: "Tiger uprising! Not surprising!" They related to that.

Last year I went to Edmonton with the Red Wings. About halfway back on the flight, I had to go to the restroom and got up and started walking down the aisle. You know Steve Yzerman, he scored fifty goals this year before he got hurt, he's the captain of the team, he got out of his seat and set up a blockade. I thought what the heck is this. "Brow," he said, "the rest of the team has got a presentation to make to you for coming out to the airport all the time." Well doggone it, he reached into his pocket and pulled out a wad of bills—fifties, twenties—almost $400 those guys collected. I almost cried. In order to ease the tension one of the guys asked for the "Strawberry Shortcake." That's an all-purpose cheer. Those Wings gave me a jacket, too, and a sweater with all their signatures. I haven't even washed it yet, I'm afraid they'll wash out.

Me and baseball go back to the thirties. I was the oldest of nine children, the same combination my wife and I have: six boys and three girls. In the stores they used to have inning-by-inning accounts of the games, and I used to make up line-ups at home and keep score. We were in Ypsilanti about six years and then we moved to Detroit, and we didn't live too far from the ballpark. I was peddling papers right around the ballpark, which at that time was called Navin Field, then Briggs Stadium, finally Tiger Stadium. Before that it had yet another name, Bennett Field.

I don't recall just how I did this but some of us guys, trying to get closer to baseball, went over to the ballpark and asked if there was anything we could do to get in. We were given a stick with a nail in the end of it and a burlap sack, and given a section and we'd go through that section and clean it up. Then at the end of the day we were given a pass for the bleachers. This was really a big deal. My favorite players were Charlie Gehringer, Hank Greenberg—I could just about name the team at that time. But Gehringer stands out in mind: he never swung at the first pitch, and when he had two strikes on him he was the most dangerous man in baseball. He's still living, in his eighties; the nicest guy you'd ever want to meet. He must have had an inner desire that really kept him up there, because he never showed it on the outside.

One day in 1955 I looked in the newspaper and they had an ad for a baseball administration school in Florida. The fee was eighty-eight bucks. I thought I could make that, and applied for the school. Anything to do with sports, that was the idea. I took a leave of absence from my teaching job. Then I turned down jobs in Batavia, New York, and Erie, Pennsylvania. In Erie they wanted me to take the job on a percentage basis. There was no way I could have afforded that. I had about given up for that year, and one day I received a telephone call from Chuck Comiskey, the grandson of the original owner of the White Sox. He and I had gone to the same small college in St. Paul. He asked if I was still interested in getting into baseball. He offered me a job in Davenport, Iowa, Class-B ball. That was where I first got the idea of going out to the airport—although of course there was no flying in that league. They went on the road by station wagon or bus. They had seventeen men on the team, and the manager and the trainer. If you can imagine putting nineteen people plus all the equipment and uniforms into four station wagons and then traveling three or four hundred miles. I always said I'd never boo anybody after seeing what these guys went through. I got the idea to meet the bus because you could tell those young guys got home-sick, and they're going to really love to get their mail, so I waited there no matter what time, day or night. They appreciated it. They cut me into a share when they won the first-half championship.

One day I was walking down the street in Davenport with my daughter and she said, "Dad, are you coming home tonight?" Well, in two years on that job we went on one picnic and went swimming once. That's all I did with the family. The rest of the time I was married to that job. And I suddenly got the feeling, "Hey, this ain't worth it." I quit and went back to teaching.

You don't crack a smile. At least pretend that you're dead serious and that you want to get things pumped up to a feverish pitch, even though you don't feel that way inside. That's my idea of a cheerleader. I carry a pump and a plastic banana. You'd be surprised how they relate to the pump. I used to have real bananas but with the warmth of your hand, that banana is no longer firm like it should be. Not only that I've had them to split, and I'd just tell the crowd we now have a banana split.

I've got to be careful because I can really yell. I don't need a mega-phone. Some people jump if I pull up and a play happens and I let out a blast. Some people want to just sit quietly and watch what's goin' on. One guy said to me, "They want you way up there in the corner." You've got to have one-liners ready for these guys, so I said, "Gee, that's funny, I just came from up there. They sent me down here!" The crowd gets a bang out of that, but I'm not smiling at all.

One time a guy in front of Tiger Stadium said, "You're sick." They've got some idea I ain't a young guy doing this. I'm sixty-six. I had this ready for him: "When was the last time you had a check-up?"

Sometimes I cheer outside for a big game, give 'em a cheer to pump things up if there's a long line for the bleachers. But strange to say, I don't usually go early. I'm slow and I procrastinate. I know that. I don't sit, ever. I move around the whole stadium, although there is a part of Tiger Stadium where my presence is undesirable, where the big boss, the director of park operations, is. He has never related to all this. He tolerates it is the way I look at it. He thinks I'm out there for an ego trip, to get the exposure and all that—I get on TV quite a bit, too—but it's not so!

He has a bunch of guys around him, ushers, they're almost like body guards. Of course, they're an extension of his feelings toward me. One guy said to me one day, "Say, every time you come around here and get in an argument with Ralph [Snyder], and you leave, he takes it out on us. Would you stay away?"

I've never met Tom Monaghan, the owner. I've only passed him and said "Hi" and he said "Hi." He flies in on a helicopter. There's a Checker Cab building that's about as old as the hills across the street from the stadium, and he lands on top of that.

The closer you get to the field of action, the less the response. In other words, your high-priced people are down there. I don't want to say anything to insult them, but it's beneath their dignity to get out there and yell and everything. There's no problem in the bleachers, but they closed our bleachers here because of a certain amount of rowdiness, drinking, so on. If I had my way there'd be no drinking at any athletic event.

Something happened last night that has never happened before to me. There was a big guy in the boxes, and he was carrying on a tirade with the pitcher on the other team. All of a sudden one of the guards come over and told him to keep quiet, he had to calm it down. It seems as though this pitcher took exception to something he had said. Well, the guy yelled at the guard. It went back and forth and the guy said that the pitcher was the one who cussed at him. I was right there telling the guy he had the right to yell all he wanted as long as his language was what it's supposed to be. Finally, I told those ushers, if he can't yell, *I* can't yell. He's not doing anything different from what I do. That's the only way I could see it. Somebody called out, "Should we let him yell?" and everybody hollered, "Yes!"

The game is an outlet. It's also a place to take the kids, and there's a certain amount of hero worship, and you can believe this or not, but people all the time are asking me for my autograph. I couldn't believe my eyes when the first guy came up. Then they had my picture in the yearbook, and the fans were bringing the yearbook up. You know what I tell 'em? "Hey, I'm just a fan like you. I'm nobody." But I sign.

You've got to be making up new things all the time. Instead of "Old MacDonald Had a Farm," I go "Good old Tigers, what a team, s-c-o-r-e." As recent as this week a new thought came up. We were losing 7–0, and the eighth inning came along. How the heck do you think, if you were a ball-player, that you could be pumped up if you looked up and saw people leaving in droves when you were behind? You couldn't get yourself up to it, not unless you had a super "K-I" factor—Killer Instinct. The thought came to mind, "Let's pretend that we're ahead!" What do you do when you're ahead? You start pumping and going bananas. Then the other team starts to wonder what's wrong with this outfit? That's what we want them to do, start wondering. I don't know whether this will catch on, but we've got something to go on.

Something happens every night. There's fights once in a while, I help to break them up. That's another thing. There's a tremendous opportunity to set some kind of example, especially to all those young people, who relate to an old man doing something. So you've got to think, "What am I doing? What should I do? What shouldn't I do?"

I get into it, but I tell a lot of people that when I find somebody who will take my place, I'm going to hit the rocking chair, and I would. I'm not doing it to make money. I lose money. I was offered a spot on a commercial for Beck's beer, but because I'm a former schoolteacher and a big family man, I turned it down. I wouldn't be in a beer ad. I sort of have the feeling that when it comes time to stop what I'm doing, I'm not gonna be sorry or miss it that much. It takes all kinds of time, especially the signs. I've used over 300,000 staples over the past four years.

I put up other signs too, outside of sports. You know this town's had problems like mad, so the idea came up that maybe I could contribute something. What I started to do is take the names of the streets and do a sign —like my street is Hayden and Kenfield is the next street over, so the sign is HAYDEN LOVES KENFIELD. And then reverse it for another sign over on Hayden. I want to get them all around. Another thing is we're going to have voting on casino gambling. That's a big item in this town, it's going hot and heavy, I think most of the people are against it. So I'm making signs: CASINO. [The voters subsequently agreed.]

I feel that whatever effort is made here can be of help to the community. I believe that. If I were out to have fun why would I be out all night? I don't get any sleep. I got to bed about two-thirty this morning, I was up at six. But there are a lot of good things, too. A couple of days ago I was in the upper deck and a guy comes down and grabs me: "Remember me?"

I didn't remember the guy from Adam.

"Remember the screwdriver?"

Oh! I had loaned one to the guy in a parking lot a week earlier. Now, *who* does that? Of course, if you told someone that "something happened," they'd say you're nuts.

TOMMY HAWKINS

In his office looking out over left field is a basketball goal with his new team's logo. A former star for the Los Angeles Lakers, on the baseball payroll for only a year, he already bleeds Dodger blue.

In June 1987, I got a note from Peter O'Malley, the Dodgers' owner, asking me to give him a call. I got off my television show and called him and he said he was doing some restructuring and he'd like to pick my mind. We talked about twice a month until late October, early November. We discussed the Al Campanis incident, which had been in April, and it was a motivational factor for many higher-ups in baseball to take a look at minorities.

But I don't play that game. Never have. I'm a legitimate graduate of the University of Notre Dame. I went to graduate school at the University of Southern California, I taught two years at Cal State, Long Beach. I'm no token. I told Peter and everybody else, "If I make this move, I don't want to be your affirmative-action window dressing for the Al Campanis incident."

A lot of people have said that indeed I am, but not *racial* affirmative action. I'm *personal* affirmative action. I'm not running scared. I get things done. I work with all people, I understand all people. I'm a sociologist by education, I've had just about every social experience that anyone could have. I've traveled extensively.

I wasn't hurting for a job, but I've always been an eclectic person, doing a lot of things. I'll be fifty-two years old in December—a classic Capricorn, if you think of the goat as constantly climbing that mountain. I played pro basketball from 1959 to 1969, four years with the Cincinnati Royals, six years with the Los Angeles Lakers, and I got to know sports management as a player representative and as a labor negotiator for the players during the time when the NBA was just getting into pension plans, major medical plans, per diems for training camps, and all of those things. I know the interworkings of managerial sports.

During my playing career some of the other jobs that I held were life-insurance underwriter for North American Life and Casualty; loan solicitor for Great Western Financial Corporation; management-training program, dealing in credit and contracts, for Hallmark Financial Corporation; director of public relations for Merchants Title Insurance Company; teacher for two years at Cal State, Long Beach; partner in Bishop, Hawkins & Associates, an advertising and public relations agency.

As a matter of fact, I ran into trouble when some coach said I wasn't completely concentrating on basketball, but I always felt that you've got to start concentrating on other things because when it's over, it's over, and the game doesn't serve a person any good unless he's going into coaching. I had other plans. Now, of course, the players can do what they want to do and live happily ever after, if they take care of their money. We didn't enjoy that luxury.

Then I got into broadcasting. Being the eclectic that I am, I was doing three different shows last year: *Mid-Morning Los Angeles* on KHJ-TV, an hour and a half live on current events and issues—loved it; two daily sports reports for KLOS, a rock station; and on Saturdays I had a jazz show for KKGO, which I dearly loved. I'm a record collector, have been since I was thirteen years old, and when I originally got into broadcasting I thought I would become a disc jockey, but I never had the time to do it. I have over seven thousand records. I've got some CDs now, too. If it spins, I collect it.

I had also been sports director of KABC radio, the Dodgers' flagship station, for fifteen years and we broadcast from Dodger Stadium each home game, so coming over here wouldn't be like coming into a strange situation and strange people. I had gotten to know the front-office staff very well, coordinating some of our broadcast activities with promotions that were going on here.

So I had been in broadcasting for twenty years—in this town, that's a nice record—and one of the stipulations of Peter's contract was that I had to give that up. It was a very big decision. Can you say, "Okay, I'm going to give this up and go do something else and be just as successful?" In my mind I felt that I could do that—the Capricorn continues to climb—but reality has to be proof of the pudding. And I wanted to eventually get into broadcast management. This isn't too far away from that, so I decided to get in and make this challenge a successful one for me. I became vice-president of communications for the Dodgers on December 1, 1987.

There was a lot of controversy within the organization, the press, everywhere, about this ex-basketball player being put into this baseball position. It was a big deal. I didn't buy into it and I would tell people, "Don't insult Peter O'Malley. He talked to a lot of people and he made a decision based on intelligent assessment. The man knows what he is doing, so let it go at that."

Sitting at this desk and functioning in this capacity has *community* meaning because this is a step that no minority has ever taken. We're talking *working* vice-president. We're not talking token. It means an awful lot. My mom, who's going to be eighty years old, was out here recently. She walked into this office and she cried. I asked, "Why are you crying?" and she said, "Because I can think of you as a little boy and I've watched you grow every step and I'm just grateful at eighty years old to be able to share this and know that you are functioning successfully at this level." It kind of chokes me up when I think about it.

I oversee publicity, promotions, marketing, and community services. My background has been infinitely important to me. Without it, I don't think that I could assume this job as comfortably as I have. I'm functioning with our legal counsel, our head of finance, our head of ticket operations, our head of stadium operations, all of our people. I work and share decisions with about twenty-five people: six or seven in the publicity department, same number in promotions and marketing, same number in community services. We would be here forever talking about the number of things that have to be done and coordinated, but it's that kind of job. I'm very diplomatic. I don't want to bowl anybody over. I want to blend my energy with yours to see what we can best achieve.

For example, the Dodgers are coming up on our centennial year in baseball, in 1990. So I am making plans and working out things that we are going to be doing, checking on various directions. These things have to be coordinated, but *now*, not when you get there. We hope to have a Dodger Museum built right here on the premises by 1990. When you talk about which is truly America's team, you're talking about the Dodgers. I think there should be a place where the people can come to see what America's team has been all about.

Once in spring training we had to decide whether we were going to close the training room to the media after the games—not the clubhouse, but the training room. The player representative, Dave Anderson, and his assistant, Mike Scioscia, came to me because I'm an ex-player representative and I understand what's happening. What the players didn't want was just the same as you don't want—twenty people looking over your shoulder during an examination in the doctor's office.

We got together with the beat writers but nothing was resolved. Back in Los Angeles, I personally called every major-league team to see what their practices are, and why. All of the training rooms around the league, except ours, are closed. I talked to the National League office. I talked to some of the players. I talked to the trainer. Then I presented all of my facts to the executive board. The decision was made to close the training room to the media, as long as the players don't hide there and make it a sanctuary.

Now, today, I'm having a luncheon at noon for the electronic media. We're working out some of the problems that they have in scheduling our players during the pre-game period. Mike Williams, our media-relations man, came to me and said, "Hawk, there's some ill feelings between the players and the electronic media and we have to come together in terms of handling these problems. What are your thoughts?"

If the program is live, it wants the player at a certain time, but then maybe they get into a commercial cluster or another news story comes in, and that means my player is standing down there for five, six, seven minutes and nothing is happening. Well, we're on a very tight schedule—batting practice, running, calisthenics, and infield work. These things have to be handled. Timing is of the essence.

Another example. The little people, the Hispanic media, the smaller newspapers, came to me and said that except for the *Herald Examiner,* the Los Angeles *Times,* Associated Press, and United Press International, nobody can get a spot down in the camera wells. These people wanted space too, especially for the big games.

I said, "Hey, come show me what you're talking about." I'm a hands-on person. My style is face-to-face. I won't do it with a memo if I can sit down and talk to you. So I went down with these people and Bob Smith, the director of stadium operations.

I said, "Bob, is there anything that we can do?"

He said, "Well, we can extend the camera well to the start of the auxiliary scoreboards and we can make them two-tiered without obstructing the view of the fans, so we more than double the capacities."

That's what we did and we get more photographs in the newspapers all around.

I'm a troubleshooter in many senses. Anything that falls through the cracks is my responsibility. I've got to see that these things *don't* fall through the cracks. Anything can happen. George Bush comes here. I have to escort him throughout the stadium.

The baseball is ultimately important to what we do here because if the team is unsuccessful, no matter how good we are at what we do, we're unsuccessful. It's a numbers game, putting people in the stands, making them comfortable. Yes, we sell 27,000 season tickets a year and that would be humongous for some teams, but we have a stadium that seats 56,000. We want to fill this park. We're not satisfied with 30–35,000. We want to bring over three million people a year into this park and there have to be special-event days, group sales, marketing, publications to keep the product in front of the people, a courteous staff of people who take care of our guests in one of the most beautiful surroundings in the world. The press has to be taken care of by a publicity department that understands their needs.

And we're competing with so many things. This is Los Angeles. This is Tinsel Town! We can't sit back and take for granted that they're going to come here because we have a clean ballpark and a pretty good team. The food has to be *good*. The entertainment has to be *good*. There's a Dodger way of doing things and a lot of people say, "That's a lot of baloney." It's not baloney.

Look at baseball compared to the other major sports. Baseball is Middle America. It's not the pace of Hollywood. It's not Old Town in Chicago or Greenwich Village in New York. It's the pace of Middle America. It's where you come to have a beer or soft drink and a hot dog, visit with your neighbors, cheer for the Dodgers, second-guess the manager. It is not basketball, where they are up and down the floor every twenty-four seconds. It's a slower, more pastoral game.

This is our home. The trees that you see on the hills, the stands, the parking, everything. We invite you into our home. We want you to know that if something happens there is someone to take care of it. When any ball goes into the stands, for example, our ushers will follow that ball into the stands and make sure that the person is okay. We don't allow banners and beach balls and things like that because they interfere with another person's opportunity to enjoy the game. When you show people that you respect them, most will try to meet you halfway. What people don't like is to become just a number, part of a herd—move 'em in, move 'em out. We strive to maintain the human touch.

I'm always in touch with the game, but there's no such thing for me as sitting down and unobtrusively watching the game. Having been a Laker, then a broadcaster all those years, I have immediate identification. I'm a public person. To a lot of people in Los Angeles, I'm "Tommy" or "Hawk."

"Hey, I got a problem. There's the Hawk, maybe he can help us."

Thank God I have that visibility, but sometimes it can be difficult. It's open season on the Hawk. People just want to talk to you. One man had his grandkids with him who didn't know Tommy Hawkins from Noah Webster, but there's an old tradition in the sports world that the grandfather would stop me and explain to his grandkids who I was and when I played and all of those things. Now, if the grandfather cares enough to do that, I've got to care enough to spend some time with those people. I'm moving at a pretty rapid pace and if I walk through the parking lot or walk down the corridor I may talk or shake hands with fifty, a hundred people, literally.

"Hey, Tommy, what about this?"

"Hawk, what about that?"

I do a lot of motivational speaking. I get an incredible number of speaking invitations from all sorts of places. In seven months, I've probably done thirty, maybe more. I try to keep it to one a week because it interferes with my paperwork, but sometimes I get loaded. There are certain things that I have to do. We have an adopted school in the neighborhood, Salano Elementary School. They're going to have their graduation at Dodger Stadium and I've been asked to give the graduation speech, and I will do that.

With this position you also get the bigger speaking engagements: the Presidents' Circle at the University of Southern California. California First Bank: we went down and did an hour with all of their executives throughout southern California. They understand what the Dodgers do in a marketing way, and they want to share those things. The corporate world is coming closer to the sports world in understanding what the two have in common: teamwork. I will tell a bunch of bank presidents, "Don't be afraid to take off your vest and put on the company uniform. Check your ego at the door." They're kind of shocked.

I'm not bragging but I think that since I've been here I have made a very strong impact. I have answered the challenges. If someone puts you in a management position, it's not a trial run. You're put there to *deliver*. It's sort of like when I first broke into pro basketball. I was the sixth man who comes off the bench and makes something happen. He increases the pace and adds strength and impetus. For a couple of years the best sixth man

in basketball was a toss-up: Frank Ramsey with the Celtics and Tommy
Hawkins. We were considered the best in the business. That's the way I
look at my job. I'm on the starting team of an executive staff, but with a
sixth-man mentality.

THE
NITTY
GRITTY

One of the most famous groundskeepers working today, he greets me on the field at the Kansas City Royals' new spring-training complex in Central Florida, adjacent to the "Boardwalk and Baseball" amusement park. Just across the street a loud roller coaster rumbles past. The baseball field is an oddity in another respect, too: artificial turf infield and grass outfield—the latter to save money.

I am the groundskeeper for the Kansas City Royals and director of fields for the Kansas City Chiefs and for the past twenty-two years the playing-field consultant for the National Football League, for both natural and artificial grass. It's an art, it's a science. When the Super Bowl field is beautiful they say George Toma's an artist. He's not an artist. He's just a nitty-gritty dirt man. To be a good groundskeeper you have to have pride and a lot of knowledge of grass.

I've been in baseball for forty-three years. I'm from a little town outside Wilkes-Barre, Pennsylvania, called Edwardsville. My first job in high school was picking beans or tomatoes on a truck farm for ten cents an hour, ten hours a day, six days a week. I didn't want to work in the coal mines and our next-door neighbor was a groundskeeper. I used to go over and drag the infield for him and see the ball games—it was the Class-A Eastern League then. He finally offered me a job, probably $25 a month, back in 1945. A couple of years later Bill Veeck bought the Cleveland Indians and also several farm clubs, and one of them was the Wilkes-Barre Barons. He came into the stadium one time and told the groundskeeper, Stan Schlecker, that he was now the bus driver and trainer. I was only a sixteen-year-old kid in high school, and he looked at me and said, "You're the new groundskeeper."

Schlecker taught me a lot and Mr. Veeck used to send me to Florida when they started mass spring training in 1948. I went with Emil Bossard. Everyone knows of Emil Bossard, the world's greatest groundskeeper. He was the groundskeeper for the Cleveland Indians, his son Gene was the groundskeeper for the Chicago White Sox, now semi-retired, and Gene's son Roger is now that groundskeeper.

I worked in Wilkes-Barre until 1950 when I was drafted and went to Korea, fought in the Korean War, then came back. Wilkes-Barre lost its team to Reading and the man there was forty and I was twenty and I didn't want to take his job. In the meantime Wilkes-Barre got a community-owned team. New York and Detroit and a couple of other teams supplied some players and I did a pretty fair job there and Detroit hired me to handle their Triple-A field in Buffalo, New York. That teamed moved to Charleston, West Virginia, in 1956, so I went there for two years. Then one day John McHale called me and said "George, we just gave Kansas City permission to talk to you. They need a groundskeeper."

The first thing I did was call Emil Bossard and he said, "Stay out of Kansas City. I helped Lou Boudreau on the field. You don't want to go there. The weather's too bad. Every spring it floods you out and every winter it bakes you out." I went into Kansas City in September 1957 and the field was pretty bad and I said, "Heck, I'll stay here because I can't mess this one up."

We were making a transition from bluegrass to Bermuda, and in June the sportswriters were writing, "Send that guy back to Charleston." But three weeks later the field became an oasis in the desert. It became beautiful. The trick with Bermuda is the hotter the weather the better it grows.

I had offers almost every year to go to Yankee Stadium. Tony Kubek, Bobby Richardson, and some of the players wanted to give me some money to take over Yankee Stadium. When Ralph Houk sees me he says, "You little farm boy, afraid to live in the big city!"

I never went to college. I picked up everything by myself, working with Emil Bossard and others, reading books and learning from trial and error. When Charles O. Finley bought the Kansas City A's he dressed up the grounds crew so we'd look sharp like the players, and he first started calling us the world's greatest grounds crew. You hear of George Toma but there's no George Toma. If it wasn't for the grounds crew I've had over a period of forty-two years, George Toma wouldn't be here today. We used high-school boys. The stadium was in the ghetto section, they called it, and those boys, fourteen, sixteen years old, did a tremendous job for me. About six of them. Mel Allen timed 'em one time putting the tarp down in forty-five seconds. We used to change bases, drag the infield, brush the baselines, wipe off home plate and the pitching mound in twenty-eight seconds. Sportswriters used to time us and announce it. I was the only full-time guy. They were tremendous kids. They had what it takes in this job: pride.

Grass is important but more important is the skinned area. Major-league clubs would call me and say, "George, how about shipping us a coal car of your infield? Players say that infield is the best in the world." Agronomists said we had the world's worst dirt in Kansas City: no drainage, poor soil, no automatic irrigation. But I'm only worried about the top inch, not usually what's under the dirt. Some places the dirt is only a few inches.

Might be gravel, sand, anything underneath it. People say their dirt's I-70, like concrete, or Iwo Jima, all sand, but sometimes the dirt gets a bad reputation. I'd tell these people you have just as good wherever you are. It's not the dirt, it's the man who works the dirt. You just have to be a chef. In Fort Myers, Sparky Anderson said we had the best infield—after people had called it I-70 or Iwo Jima. It was the same dirt. We added the knowledge of working it.

About four years ago we put in a field for Tommy Lasorda and the Los Angeles Dodgers. John Schuerholz, our general manager, said, "On your way back from the Pro Bowl, I want you to stop off and help them with their infield." I always said that was part of the Joe Beckwith deal. I do their infield, we get Joe Beckwith. That was man-made dirt.

The United States is trying very, very hard to get the World's Cup for soccer [and has succeeded], and my job will be to cover up artificial turf at maybe six or eight stadiums around the country with natural grass for one month. The World's Cup won't play on artificial turf.

Right now we go into stadiums for Mud-a-thons, tractor pulls, that kind of thing, we cover up the turf or grass with plastic, plyboard, and sometimes as much as eight feet of dirt.

No way is George Toma against artificial turf. I can work with anything. What George Toma is against is poor artificial turf *installation*. A good installation is like the Kansas City Royals' installation of 3-M Tartan Turf. Omniturf, a system from Europe in the infield here, is excellent, over a crushed stone base on a natural foam-rubber pad, and then an inch and a half of polypropylene fiber with sand worked into it, to give it a natural grass feel. I think it's going to come a long way.

If you had natural grass you could give your groundskeeper $200,000 a year to maintain it and still be way ahead of an artificial-turf installation. Grass is much cheaper. And there's more work to artificial turf. We have a natural-grass infield across the street and artificial turf here. We're finished faster over there. With artificial you have to get the dirt out of the turf, get the bubble gum and tobacco juice out of the turf, the sunflower seeds, you have to water, scrub, and shampoo it. And the players prefer natural grass. Your spring-training field should be just as good or better than your major-league field because you don't want to have a bad field and get in bad habits.

My son Chip and Dr. James Watson from the Toro Corporation built the grass practice field for the Kansas City Chiefs for $25,000, and it works better six years later than artificial turf, which would cost two million. The reason sometimes they put in artificial turf, even though it's more expensive, is that a grass field might not be built up and maintained right. When people put in natural grass they forget to put in good drainage, they don't get a good root-zone structure. Like I explained before, we have a $25,000 Chiefs practice field. If it gets two inches of rain on it, they practice. We have a *million-dollar* artificial turf field at Arrowhead Stadium, and when it rains it takes two and half hours and a $100,000 machine to get the field ready for practice.

When I consult for high schools or colleges which might have the money to pay for artificial turf the first time, I ask them whether they'll have it *again* five or eight years down the road, to replace it. Otherwise the kids are playing on concrete. Each year the turf gets harder.

The Chicago Bears are going back to natural grass. The new stadium in Denver is natural grass. Down the road I think some major-league parks will go back to grass. If a stadium has baseball, football, concerts, tractor pulls, it's detrimental to natural grass but it's also detrimental to artificial turf. All that weight breaks down the cells of the padding, which gets harder and harder. It's not indestructible. It's destructible.

PAT SANTARONE

His office is the Baltimore playing field, and not much coaxing is required to get him to explain, at length, the intricacies, pitfalls, and subterfuges of groundskeeping—and the damnable effects of artificial turf. "So what the *hell* do you want it for? If the new stadium here is artificial turf, I won't be around. I'm absolutely a grass man."

Sure the field can make a difference. Hell, yes. One of the reasons I'm in Baltimore is that Earl Weaver knew I could do what he and the ballplayers wanted me to do. In 1969, we had an extremely good infield—Davey Johnson, Mark Belanger, Brooks Robinson, and Boog Powell, how the hell do you beat that?—and they could catch the ball and turn the double play with the best of 'em. A slow infield isn't conducive to that kind of play, so Earl asked me if I could speed it up. Of course I could, and I did with shorter grass, de-thatching that grass, top-dressing it to get more bounce, keeping the infield dirt a little firmer by watering it and letting the sun bake it a little, where normally you wouldn't want to bake it. There's a whole lot of ways to do it. We were in the World Series in 1969, '70, '71, so something worked then.

When Horace Clarke played second for the Yankees back around '70, he couldn't move too quickly so we made the field as hard as possible between first and second, because he couldn't go to his left and field the ball —and our guys could. You have to watch the papers to make sure he's not injured or out of the line-up for some other reason.

Campy Campaneris with Minneapolis, well, he could really go get them, especially to his left, so we'd *slow* the infield down for him so he'd have to come get the ball and by the time he got to the ball he couldn't turn the double play. Of course that might have been a detriment to our pull hitters at times. It depended on who was pitching against us, whether we done that or not. If Boog Powell hit a ball on the ground that slowed down, he'd give me hell because the infield was too slow: "Hey, what's going on out there? You trying to grow nightcrawlers?"

I remember when we played Minnesota in the 1969 playoffs. I got the infield grass right along the base line real long—didn't even mow it, in fact. Then before the game I told Paul Blair, "Take a look at that third-base line."

"I already saw it in batting practice."

By God if he didn't dump it right up that line. They couldn't have thrown him out with a cannon and that won the game and the pennant. That's the most pleasure, going all the way and knowing perhaps you had a little part of it. I'm not going to tell you anything recent because it's still viable or whatever you want to call it. The opposing managers look around when they come into the park, sure they do. But it's all legal.

I got started in baseball because I was born into baseball. My dad was a professional baseball groundskeeper before I was, in Elmira, New York, in the old Eastern league. Twenty feet past the right-field fence is where we were born and raised. The three boys would go with our dad, sweep the stadium, shag balls. We had a herd of goats right in the ballpark, where we used to pasture them. We had anywheres from four to eleven, twelve goats. The players bellyached about the droppings, so we had to clean that up before batting practice. The old Eastern League scorecard had a picture on the cover of the goats in the outfield.

My dad was a hell of a groundskeeper—really, *really* good. He was from the old country, of course, a man of the earth, a farmer, a laborer in Italy. He got into it when he migrated to the United States, and he taught me. He understood dirt and what dirt did. He died in 1952 and I took over the team in Elmira, in the Dodgers organization. I was twenty-two or so.

In 1959–60 Baltimore took over the franchise and that's when Earl Weaver came to Elmira as the manager. So when Weaver come up to the big leagues during the '68 season, that winter the Orioles called and asked if I would come up to the big leagues. We had guys in Elmira who came quickly to the big leagues, like Davey Johnson and Mark Belanger and those fellows, and they raved about my infield. So Earl thought, "Why not transfer that to Baltimore?"

I played seventeen years of semi-pro baseball myself—pretty fair pitcher, back when we got $35 if we won, $25 if we lost—so I know what it takes to have a decent infield, what the dirt should consist of, what makes a bad hop, that kind of thing. Hands-on knowledge and intuition. It's just getting a *feel*—it's hard to discuss. If I see a bad hop I remember it and take a look after the game, hoping it's not a matter of the infield being too dry or too wet, too hard or too soft. I can tell by walking on it. We make up our infield base, mostly river-bottom loam if I can get it, with about 7 percent sand and about 10 percent clay. And then we put a soil conditioner on it and get it to the consistency we want so it doesn't hold water or shed water too darn quickly; get it so they can play through a rain and don't have to stop the game because it's too nasty and muddy, but without it being too dry and hard when it isn't raining. This used to be an old clay mine, so there's a lot of clay underneath here. It's hard as hell to grow grass on clay, so we continually doctor it up to try to make decent topsoil. Through the year with all the tilling we bring in about a foot of decent topsoil.

All groundskeepers have their own mixes, and basically it's what the ballplayers want. They have to make their living on it. But almost always the groundskeeper knows a hell of a lot more about it than the infielder, who knows if it plays well, but he doesn't know *why*. If you use too much clay it gets too hard, and the holes that the spikes make are not repairable, and if you use a whole lot of sand so you don't get these holes, as I call 'em, or divots, then it's too mushy and the ball doesn't come up at all, skids and skips on 'em and goes under the glove. There's a happy medium and the smart groundskeeper knows how to reach it. Not all of them do. And some of the guys aren't able to get the real good soil to work with. I've had a lot of infielders come in from other clubs and take a sample of our infield dirt with 'em, to see if it can be matched in their home park. That's happened lots of times.

We use a mixture of four or five different bluegrasses. If you used just one strain a disease could wipe you out overnight. If you put in four or five, if one gets wiped out, you still have the others left. Another reason is to promote color. Some bluegrasses are greener than others, some more drug-tolerant than others, some heal quicker, some spread quicker. We're in a tough zone here in Baltimore, what they call a transition zone, too far north to be south and too far south to be north. It's a difficult place to grow either bluegrass or Bermuda or bent. We get terrible hot summers, which is terrible for bluegrass and great for Bermuda. We get cold springs and falls—I hear it's fifteen degrees wind chill tonight—and Bermuda would just brown out. So it's touchy. We get a lot of funguses we have to spray for continually, and environmentally you have to be very careful today what you spray, how you spray, what the runoff situation is. We have a lot of meetings to try to keep up.

There's seven or eight hours of baseball on a field every day. That's a hell of a lot, so you'd better develop some overseeding and top-dressing and that kind of thing. You get big bare spots and when it rains instead of playing on grass you're playing on mud, that's not too good. Then the sun comes out and it bakes like concrete. Where the outfielders stand they compress the spot, and we constantly seed it and top-dress it and keep that grade up. Otherwise, when it rains you've got a little puddle there.

It's a never-ending thing. It's not like a lawn. Look at a lawn in summertime. First it gets a little gray color, then blackish gray, then it starts turning brown. Well, everyone's lawn looks like that, so no one pays attention. Mother nature brings one nice big rain and the grass comes right back, and no one pays attention because that's the way it's supposed to be. But you let something that's as green as this field go to hell, the whole world notices.

This field will look the nicest in the middle of May. I'm not saying it goes downhill from there, but May is optimum in Maryland. A regular gardener would lose it in July and August. The first thing he'd do is—well, say it's dry this month, so he'd start watering the hell out of it, and the more he watered the more downhill it would go. That would leach out the fertilizers and everything else. Water *only* is not the answer whatsoever. The diseases and funguses would take over and he wouldn't know what to do about that.

We have crises constantly, but the average fan walking into the stadium don't know that. We get a lot of funguses you can't see from the stands. If you don't take care of them, they'll wipe you out. Pythium can wipe you out overnight. It's a spidery, saliva-type growth right at the crown of your grass, and it can be spread with the feet, so the ballplayers can walk it all over the ballpark, and it's just like a damn cancer. I'm just using that one fungus as an example. There's a million of 'em.

After years in the business you should know what conditions are likely to produce a pythium fungus—hot, humid, wet conditions. If you have little seedlings come up and you have a thunderstorm and tomorrow the sun comes out hotter than hell, you'd better do a maintenance spray for pythium, get it before it starts, knock the spores out before they take hold. The smart guy will do that. The guy that has a budget will do that, because it's extremely expensive to use a lot of chemicals. A case of just one chemical will cost four or five hundred dollars, and it won't last long.

We worry about the grass. We're very touchy about it. I don't like anyone to walk on it if they don't have a uniform. If you don't have a uniform stay the hell off the grass, and I enforce that. Reporters get on the grass a little bit around the batting cage, but that's it. I don't allow even our office people to cut across the outfield to the bullpen parties for season-ticket holders, sponsors. If everybody cut across the corner of grass, it'd be a cowpath in less than a week. That goes for police and everybody else. I don't tell them how to run their business and I don't want them telling me how to run mine—not as long as I'm as good as I think I am!

Maybe a lot of people think all we do is what they see us do after batting and fielding practice before the game. Zip, zip, the lines are done and we play ball. They don't know what was going on since early in the morning. Compare a ball field to a lawn or even some golf courses. It's *really* intensive care, and extremely expensive. There's no three acres in the country that costs what this costs. Especially after a rain when they do more damage playing than they would in three weeks of nice weather. When they go on the road we have to resod. We have a nursery in the back.

People say we're off for five months. But take last night for example, we worked eighteen hours. Normally we work fifteen, sixteen hours during the season. Nonstop. How do you like those apples?

Before the Colts football team left here three years ago, we took the whole field out every spring, the whole damn field, because pro football destroyed it. We still have about five football games here every fall, and we don't have to replace it all, but we have to replace some of it. The field looks like Iwo Jima. If there happened to be a football game in the rain, then you really are out of business. I prepare for a major uplifting in the spring, dig most of it up and start all over. We come in with graders and peel everything. We level everything with the transit, blue stakes and red stakes, just like a highway. Then all of February and part of March you're constantly between freezing and thawing, freezing and thawing. You've got to really, really hit it when you do get some decent weather in March, especially since we open as a southern field, of all things, in the first week of April. After we lay the sod we'll roll it lightly to make sure it has contact with the ground. A lot of time you'll have air under a piece of sod and hell, you know it's not going to grow with air under it, so you just firm it down.

George Toma in Kansas City is a hell of a grass man, and the fact that they gave him artificial turf to work with, I'd think he'd want to kill someone. I go way back to the Eastern League with George, when he was at Wilkes-Barre. His grass field in Kansas City *was* impeccable, just beautiful. In my estimation one of the worst things that ever happened to baseball is the artificial playing surface. It's *all* artificial: earned-run averages of the pitchers, batting averages, fielding averages are *absolutely* artificial.

The game itself is changed. Watch these players now: almost every batter after every pitch takes a walk out of the box. And our team is notorious for that. If you tried to walk away back in the early days, the umpire'd say, "Hey, sonny, we play ball *here*. Where're you going?" Not many people know this, but they wonder why we have three-, three-and-a-half-hour games.

The funniest statement I hear is the pitcher telling the manager, "I lost my concentration." I knew managers twenty, thirty years ago was likely to hit you standing on the mound if you said that. Can you explain to me how on the mididle of a baseball field in front of thousands of people and you're throwing a ball at a guy who's trying to drive it right down your throat you can lose your concentration? You can't. It's a copout. "I lost my concentration." What the *hell* are you talking about?

I've never had much money but I've learned how to do things that don't cost a lot of money. I'm a doer. Full of nervous energy. I even boxed for a long time, got knocked around. Was on the Navy boxing team, done pretty good there.

I do photography and color printing. I've learned how to dive—can't get enough of it. I could go down to the bottom and just lay there and stay there. No one to bother you. I'm a published chef. A lot of my recipes— French, Italian, anything—have been published. I've got a big garden at home, north of Baltimore. Earl Weaver and I had tomato contests every year. We planted them in the grounds-crew area. He had his tomato plants and I had mine. Hell, he never come close. He accused me of doing all kinds of funny things to his plants when they went on the road, urinating on the plants.

"Earl," I said, "I haven't touched your plants. I *watered* your plants exactly when I watered mine."

I didn't have to cheat to beat him! I pruned mine differently, fed them differently, cultivated them differently, things like that. I was close to my plants. I talk to them. I don't think they respond to a voice, but to music and sound, yes.

I'm an oenophile. Wine is one of the most important things in my life. I make all my own wines. We see the grapes on the vine in California before they're picked, then they're picked at the optimum time and flown here so we're making wine within hours. There's several of us who order the grapes from California. I really enjoy the wine-making, the gardening, the diving.

I'm a mycologist. Mushrooms. I've been pretty lucky, and damn careful. I'm this age and I've been eating them all my life.

J O E   M O O N E Y

It's a gorgeous day in the stands forty yards away, but he chooses to meet in a dingy storage room and seats himself across a formica table. A young kid comes in to ask how to work a paint gun. Mooney demonstrates with impatience, real or feigned. Other crew members enter and he answers all their questions in ten words or less. He is building and grounds superintendent at Fenway Park, and eyes me suspiciously.

It don't take an Einstein to put bolts into concrete and break out concrete with a jackhammer. That's the thing today: everybody wants to be an expert. They're all chiefs and nobody wants to be an Indian anymore. It's a way of life today. With the players it's the same way. The whole complex of living has changed.

I'm here for eighteen years; before that, ten years at RFK Stadium in Washington, D.C. The crew size here depends on weather and other things. Sometimes it's thirty, sometimes it's forty, sometimes it's twelve. That's the grounds crew, maintenance, painting, everything. The guy who works here the longest is on the mound, Jim McCarthy. Forty-something years. He does the mound and home plate, and the watering when the team's on the road. I don't know if it's his *specialty*. He does it.

During the game I do everything. I walk the stadium, check and see if the restrooms are all right, check for broken water pipes. This and that. Anything. The easy days are a lot more common than the hard days. The crew don't tell you about when they just come in and sit around all day doing nothing.

The field is Marion bluegrass, which is a good grass for this part of the country all the way down to southern Pennsylvania, Maryland; below that you might move into Bermuda. Various spots get worn and we re-sod during the year. Bluegrass goes dormant in the winter; it's often under snow, ice, whatever. You're in New England, remember.

The infield and baselines are a sandy soil mixed with Turface, which we cut in two or three times a year. Otherwise, just good topsoil everywhere. Anytime the team goes on the road we re-level the dirt part of infield, especially at the edge of the infield and outfield grass, otherwise they get a lip. We cut the grass every day. It's an inch in the infield. And the clay around the plate and on the mound has to be good. They have a lot of trouble in Florida because the clay's not good enough, unless it's shipped in. It has to be *clay*.

Ninety percent of your people think, "Oh gee, you're off all the time, the whole winter. You've got a hell of a job." They think we have like government jobs where we don't work half the time and they have to support us. They don't know all the big maintenance jobs are off-season, a lot of concrete work. Right now we're replacing seats. In mid-August we make a list and set priorities, and they know how much money they want spent and we go by that when we decide in September. Nine million things to do in an old ballpark.

Right now the engineers are looking at "plan three": new screen behind home plate, new press box, dining room, other stuff. Plus they're going around to evaluate and see how much to spend to keep up Fenway Park. Is it worth it? How long will the concrete and everything last? But it's not falling down! It's not even close to that. This park's always been well maintained. The Red Sox have always spent money to keep it up and keep it clean. You can find modern equipment in this ballpark you can't find in new ones. The offices have the first-class computers. But just like anything else—cars or bodies—you can only get so many years out of something.

There's not a groundskeeper on earth that won any games for anybody. The field actually has nothing to do with the ball game. You see the kids on the sandlots, the minor leagues, city-owned fields—the field is nothing. Nobody does nothing out there but the players themselves between the lines. They throw the ball, they catch the ball, they hit the ball. That's the secret of the game. I hear these experts say they done this and that, I haven't seen it done.

It's the same thing with guys you see bless themselves before they bat. The guy on the mound, he could be a Catholic, too. What the hell? What if they *both* bless themselves?

I don't even go near the players. Never did, never will. I know them very little. Most people in my position are hero-worshippers. Not me. They're no better than you, me, or anyone else. They put their pants on the same way. But does it happen? With twenty-six big-league clubs, I'll guarantee it with twenty-four of them. People go gaga over the players. I pitched batting practice for years in Minneapolis; Washington, too. People ask me who's the greatest player I've ever seen. How can you say who's the greatest? Well, you might say Mickey Mantle except for his leg, but he had that leg. I personally have never seen a better hitter than Ted Williams. Wade Boggs here today: he's a tremendous hitter, and he's worked at it.

I never get involved with the other departments. I got enough of my own business without minding other people's business. They're paying people to run other things. I think they're qualified. John McNamara does a hell of a job and proved it in '86 with the American League pennant. Now a few things go bad and he's a bum [and was fired shortly afterward]. That's how the public is, so why get all shook up about it?

What do I want to go into another ballpark for? I wouldn't go across the street to watch a game. They don't play the game like I like it played. Back in Scranton, Pennsylvania, we had a team that won seventy-two straight games. Red Sox used to own the Scranton franchise. I was an infielder, but my favorite sport was college football.

Boston? I couldn't tell you how many games they're out now, five or fifteen. I watched games for years in Minneapolis in '58, '59, but I don't watch anymore.

9
PICKING WINNERS

The night before we get together for breakfast in Chicago, the Montreal Expos' manager ordered an intentional walk for pinch-hitting Andre Dawson to load the bases and move the winning run to third.

"I wanted to get their pitcher, Rick Sutcliffe, who was hitting next, out of the game. I said in the dugout, 'It's penthouse or shithouse.' " The latter. Jerry Mumphrey, hitting for Sutcliffe, grounds a single up the middle. Just one more disappointment in a bad streak for the Canadian team.

I thought the team this year would be better than it was—*is.* I thought we had a chance to compete, but Tim Raines hasn't been healthy, our young pitchers have had problems. In '87, we lost Andre Dawson to free agency, Raines and Dennis Martinez out at the start of the season, and we had a patched up line-up. It looked bad but we couldn't convey that to the ball club. We had the attitude that if we could keep our head out of the water, we'd start getting guys back, and that's what happened. We won ninety-one games and were in the pennant race until the last week of the season, with a team that I thought, quite frankly, was going to be *way* below .500. After last year, I didn't want to believe that a lot of players had had career years. I knew Tim Wallach had had one, hitting .300 and driving in 123 runs when he'd averaged .265 and 80 RBIs before. Yeah, that's a career year. But we were the best two-out hitting team in the National League. We executed the best. We had a high percentage of getting runners in from third with less than two outs.

Same players this year! We're probably close to the *bottom* in those categories. You sort through. Where have we been remiss? Somewhere along the line we blew it.

We did get to within four and a half games of the Mets, and now we're sixteen or seventeen out, and that's in the course of five weeks, and not because the Mets were playing so great. They were playing about .500 ball. *That* is frustrating. You're losing and can't put your finger on it and can't do anything about it. We lost nine straight in August, starting with a double-header in New York and then out on the coast. The losses were 3–2, 2–1, 5–3. We were in almost every game. We weren't playing bad. We were just getting beat.

Getting beat is one thing, but beating ourselves is another one. The terrible game was just the other day, in New York. I've never seen anything like it. We had so many mental errors: a guy doubled off first base on a routine fly ball to right; a guy picked off second; a guy who hit a blooper down the right-field line stopped at first when he should have been standing on second base; a guy, the tying run, tried to steal third with two outs and a left-hand hitter at the plate; we threw to the wrong base.

One ball game! You can go half a season and not see this many mental mistakes. We made five of 'em. I take this personally. How can this happen after the way we've worked on this stuff? These were not bonehead baseball players doing these things, either—well, one of 'em is. I had promised myself earlier that we wouldn't have any more red-ass meetings, but after that game I had to change my mind. I had to have one more!

The only time I lose sleep is when I have something on my chest. In many meetings I've told the players, "This meeting isn't for you. It's for me. If I don't have it I'm going to lose another night's sleep."

I keep a pad and pencil beside my bed and I'll get up in the middle of the night and jot down notes for things I'll bring up in a meeting. You have to *prepare* for an effective clubhouse meeting. They can't be impromptu, where you're just ramblin' and screamin' and hollerin' out of control. You have to get some points over, bang, bang, bang. The approach to the hit-and-run, fear of failure, pitchers going for the perfect pitch every time. That's your objective. Never name names.

Most of your meetings are confidence builders. Most of the trouble you have on a ball club is that the players are trying too hard. The professional athlete is much more secure than the general public. They have to be, or they couldn't achieve this level. Sure the guys get doubtful at times—confidence comes and goes from week to week or month to month—but the inner *security* doesn't waver. The same applies to managers. I call a couple of pitchouts and two or three hit-and-runs and I get bad pitches and things don't come off. You get a little defensive for a while.

The manager is responsible for setting the tone, the winning attitude. That's your number-one job. The game itself is not life or death. The kids have to play loose, with a freedom of mind. Managing the game itself is the easiest thing in the world. That's *almost* mechanical.

Dealing with the pitchers is the key to managing on the field, but it's not difficult. I know pitching and I've got a pretty good idea when a pitcher's starting to lose his stuff. I show a lot of confidence in my catchers, too, because my managers showed it in me. But the catcher's not going to say, "He's throwing lousy." He'll say, "It's not moving quite as much as last inning." Or, "He's having trouble with the spin on his curve." I don't talk with the catcher in a place where the pitcher can hear. I don't tell the pitcher the catcher said he was through.

You always remember your screw-ups. John Dopson, the kid we got now, was just up from the minors, pitching his first ball game in Philadelphia, and he's ahead 2–0. He had just got them out very easy in the seventh inning and he's leading off the eighth for us. And instead of taking the seven good innings in his first start and getting him out of there, I let him hit and sent him back out and we ended up losing the ball game. That was 1985, my first year, and I've kicked myself in the ass for it ever since. I'll never forget it. It was dumb. I fell in love with the pitcher and I wanted him to get a shutout. Never fall in love with a pitcher.

I was going to get released by the Angels in 1970 when Bill Rigney, one of my former managers there, got the Minnesota job and called from the winter meetings to ask if I'd consider coaching for him. His last couple of years with the Angels he had told Jim Fregosi and me, "If you guys want to stay in the game, you can manage." I don't know why he felt that way, but he obviously saw we had an interest in the game beyond just drawing a paycheck. I was a catcher, and the catcher has got to think along with the managers anyway. Who's on deck? What bases are open? Will they pinch hit? Hit and run? You automatically do that. And my managers placed a lot of confidence in me.

I was thirty-one and planning on playing in Hawaii for at least another year, but I told Bill if he could get me $15,000, I'd coach for him. I'd been hurt for the past four or five years—broken fingers, hand looked like a pretzel. It really wasn't that tough a call. I was getting tired of coming back from injuries. I knew what I wanted to do and figured I might as well get into it rather than screwing around for another year or two.

I was the bullpen coach, then pitching coach, there for five years. Catching moves right into being a pitching coach. Catchers who become pitching coaches have a tendency to correct the delivery that they see. Sometimes, pitchers who become pitching coaches tend to mold everybody in their own image. That's not good.

The best thing that happened in Minnesota was I got fired. Otherwise, I would have stayed on as pitching coach. To tell you the truth, I was going in for a raise when I got fired. About two months earlier, Calvin Griffith had told me and Frank Quilici, who had taken over for Rigney, that if the club finished above fourth place, we had done a hell of a job. We finished a half game out of second, so Frank and I felt pretty good. I went in there to see Griffith and he started talking about an 0–2 pitch that somebody hit off [Bert] Blyleven in Chicago in April!

I said to myself, "Hey, he's going to fire me!" He never did give me a reason why. I must have done something.

Being fired forced me to go to the minor leagues in the California organization. Harry Dalton and his group had just come in with the Angels, and they offered me the job managing the A-ball team in Salinas, California.

At Salinas I just tried to be a fair manager, but not so that fairness could be mistaken for weakness. Give the guy the benefit of the doubt, but if he started to screw you, that was it. I've had guys, shortstops, who were afraid to go into left field out of fear of a collision. When the ball goes up, they'll run in place. That sounds silly but I've seen it. They think they're fooling somebody, and until you see it about three times, they are!

At the A-ball level, you're making decisions that change guys' lives. A manager down there can make and break some careers. We've got this thing a little ass backwards. You've got kids coming out of high school or college and we should have our *best* people at lower classifications, and not only to break them into a profession. You're playing a little bit of mom and dad, coach, a lot of roles at that level. Some players who should have made the major leagues never get out of A-ball because some manager scares the crap out of 'em right off the bat. They become defensive players, and it hurts 'em.

You get the homesick kid, the kid who just got a "Dear John" letter from his girlfriend, the wife who wants her husband to choose between her and baseball, the wife who thinks her husband is screwing around every place he goes, the wife whose husband *is* screwing around every place he goes.

I've had meetings with wives as well as ballplayers. The kid will come in and say, "My wife wants me to quit. Should I listen to her or do you think I have a chance to play?"

I've called in the wife and said, "It's very important for your marriage that your husband decides it's time to quit, and not you. It may be good now, but five years from now when he sees some of these guys in the major leagues, he's gonna say, 'Maybe I could have been there,' and he might blame you for making this move. Let your husband make the decision."

Most of this gets sorted out at the A-level. Amazing things happen. I got a call in Fresno, just before I went to the ballpark, from my pitcher Freddie Kuhaulua, and he says, "Skip, I can't pitch tonight."

"What's the matter?"

He goes through this long story that he just got a call from Hawaii. Last winter he and this other kid got into trouble and the kid got put in jail and the kid's mother was a mucky-muck with the voodoo and she put a curse on Freddie. Now he wouldn't move his arm. *Couldn't* move his arm.

So I called up my farm director.

"I need some help."

He had the attitude of "Yeah, I figured so. Big-leaguer managing in the minors needs help." See, some minor-league farm directors look at us former major-leaguers a little funny. Anyway, he and I called the woman in Hawaii and talked it out and she took the curse off and Freddie pitched that night.

If the money were the same, I'd rather manage in the minors. No doubt. It's more fun because you're *closer* down there. You're up at six eating breakfast in the coffee shop, standing alongside the bus at three in the morning peeing on the tire. In the majors you break off into little cliques; it's a different job.

Down there you have almost complete authority, and you have to be careful how you use it. For example, I've never said, "You'll never play in the major leagues." I've heard some managers do that, but I'm not that smart. I'd say, "In my opinion, I don't think you'll play in the major leagues."

When I told a guy we were releasing him, I considered that I was doing him a *favor:* "The bad news is that I don't think you can play in the majors. The good news is you've got the rest of your life to be a doctor, lawyer, mechanic, whatever you want to be. Don't waste any more time in this game."

Then the kid asks, "What'll I do now?"

"Well, what do you like to do?"

And we talk about his other interests, whether it's being an automobile mechanic or working with kids or whatever. And I might say, "If you believe Buck Rodgers and the California Angels organization is full of baloney, you can keep going and try to catch on with another club. I'm not going to say that would be right or wrong, but my suggestion is you go back to school."

From Salinas I went to San Francisco as the pitching coach and got fired. Then I managed in El Paso, then the following year to Milwaukee as the third-base coach. When George Bamberger had his heart attack in 1980, I took over the ball club until he came back. Then he retired that same year and I was named permanent manager.

Nineteen eighty-one was the strike season and the coaches and managers got reassigned and paid and the players didn't. Then in the players' negotiated agreement they got a $10,000 reward for going into the mini-Series. We made it, and that last out against Detroit to make it was the greatest highlight of my whole career. Anyway, the bonus wasn't paid to the coaches or the managers and I got into a difference of opinion with management over that. When 1982 came along, I wasn't in very good graces. The minute we dropped below .500 I was fired by Harry Dalton— barely fifty games into the season, and after you take the team to its first-ever playoff situation. In essence, I was gone before the season started. It was just a matter of *when*. We were in Seattle and about eight o'clock in the morning I got a phone call from the East Coast, where the firing had been announced, or rumored. They wanted to know whether this was true. I said, "Well, I'm not fired."

About nine-thirty Harry called me down and said he was going to make a change.

"Why?" Stupid question, but all managers ask it. Doesn't make any difference *why*.

When you're working with an organization and you're told that they don't think you're doing the job and they no longer want you, it's disappointing. Especially the first time. I wasn't shattered, but I was very down, even though I knew it was coming. The club was starting to come together after a string of injuries, and I thought I *might* get to where it would be difficult for them to fire me. But they got me first. I don't believe in crying in my beer. If you're going to be a manager, it's got to be on your own terms. You can't please everybody. You can't be a yo-yo manager. If what I bring to the situation isn't judged good enough, I'll get fired and take my wares someplace else. Everybody always asks the manager about the last game or tomorrow's game, but baseball is a business and a livelihood to a manager. I'm making pretty good money now but I know I'm subject to being fired, whether it's next year or three years from now. So you take the job and milk as much money out of it as you can and do the best you can. I enjoy it but I'm not going to cut my wrists if I leave.

And I did some things in Milwaukee that I don't do anymore in Montreal—handling players, mostly in matters that didn't pertain directly to the field. You can get paranoid about little things. You want everything to run like clockwork, but it's not going to happen. The fifteen minutes before the game you figure is *your* time, but there's five kids running around the clubhouse. On the bus after a tough loss and some nut starts playing his radio. I wasn't prepared for this stuff. As a first-year manager it bothered me more than it does now. There's some things anyone would like to do differently. Fortunately, I got a second chance. Now, I get these things settled *early*.

The players today are different in that the *situation* is different. When I started in the game—a few years back!—if we won we drew people, the club made money, we got a raise. If we lost we didn't draw people and the club didn't make money and we didn't get a raise. *Everything* was based on winning and losing. We didn't have statistical criteria set up ahead of time—top one-third, middle one-third, so on. It was win or lose, make money or don't make money, a $2,000 raise or a $5,000 *cut*.

Attitudes have changed, kept guys on the disabled list longer, kept guys from playing when they're "iffy." You ask a guy to hit–and–run, it's "Geez, I got to give myself up?" Some guys. This isn't across the board.

My clubhouse is a little different from most. I've got my coaches right out among the players, not isolated in a little room. My thinking is a player won't come around the corner to talk to the coach, but if the coach is sitting in the clubhouse, the player is more apt to come up to him with some problem or worry.

I like to talk to my players myself—one on one, in my office, before something festers into an all-out grudge between the player and me. I don't wait for them to come in. I've probably brought every player on my team into my office at least two or three times, whether it's a slump or he's not playing up to his potential or loafing, whatever. I'll say, "Looks like you're about to blow your top. Come on in and let's see what we can do about it." Always *before* a game. I never talk to a player *after* the game, in his heat of temper or my heat of temper.

One thing I pride myself on is I don't lie to my players. That's one reputation I have in the clubhouse. You may not like what Skip says, but he's not going to lie to you.

Sometimes a guy comes to me and wants to know why he's not playing more. That's the most common question. And if he's talking tough about it, I'll go right back in his face. "You really want to know why you're not playing more? Number one, you're not as good as the guy I've got out there. Number two, you're hitting .125 against left-handed pitchers. Number three, you're running the bases defensively, you're not getting a good jump in the field, and you're not really working on these things in practice, either. Now what else do you want to know?"

But if he comes in and says, "Skip, see anything I'm doing wrong? I just don't feel right." Then I'll say, "Okay, let's sit down and go back to the basics. The gun shows you're still throwing the ball 88 mph, so there's nothing wrong with your arm, but let's look at the film and maybe we can come up with something."

Billy Martin said you've got fifteen guys who like you because they're playing or pitching, five guys that don't like you because they're not playing at all, and five that haven't made up their mind. The secret of managing is keeping the first five away from the second five. There's some truth to that. You know the guys who don't like you and it's because they're not playing, unless you've lied to 'em or embarrassed them in front of the club. It's not that they don't *like* you, really. They're temporarily *mad* at you. Every manager will have players who are on edge with him. If not, you've got the wrong twenty-four guys.

You've got players who are never out—if they're caught stealing by ten feet, they'll always say they were safe—and these players you don't give the satisfaction of going out and making an ass of yourself arguing. Other players never argue unless they're right, and you back them up.

There's some good umpires and some bad ones and some that hold grudges. Those are the ones I don't like. Their attitude is almost cancerous to our game. They're the ones who think the game revolves around the umpire. Most of 'em are guys who couldn't make it as players and still want a portion of the spotlight. If they don't get it, they'll make it. You can't just sit back and take it all the time, from grudge calls, most of which will be balls and strikes. He'll look over into the dugout with a little smile and go, "Strike twoooo." Like that. You sometimes have a tough time not running out and grabbing him by the throat.

There's umpires whose strike zone changes the last three innings of the game; some in the last *inning*. They get the tight ass. There's umpires that can be intimidated. The biggest problem we have is umpires that are intimidated by the New York press—not the Mets, but the press, because those are the only papers in our league that name umpires, and the only time they do is when the Mets lose.

New York fans are toughest, too, no doubt. The whole Shea Stadium thing, the planes going over, the fans yelling and screaming—and there's just as many *un*knowledgeable fans in New York as anywhere else. I love to play the Mets because you have to enjoy the competition. No one in the division roots for the Mets. There's an arrogance, a standoffishness, that you have to have playing in New York because there's so many phonies around all the time, and it carries onto the field. They're a solid ball club. Like I've told *my* club, they win because they know how to play the game.

Baseball in Montreal is different. Some people like it and some don't. The one thing you have to remember as a baseball person in Montreal is that hockey is the number-one game. If you truly realize that, it's not bad playing in Canada. The ballplayers have mixed emotions. There's a tax problem up there. Some people feel there's a language problem, although I don't. I enjoy Montreal.

I think they have a higher degree of respect for authority in Canada than they do in the United States. You're the *manager*. But they still boo. But not like the minors. I was in Salinas with about three hundred people in the stands and I took the pitcher out and was walking back and this female voice yells out, "Rodgers, you're an asshole!"

I just stopped and looked up. The thing the fans can't stand is when you smile back. They're paralyzed.

HUGH ALEXANDER

Scout emeritus for the Chicago Cubs, he wears a huge gold ring honoring his fiftieth anniversary in the field. He travels 150,000 miles a year, all air, and at home in Florida he drives a "brand-new $36,000 custom gold-edition Cadillac."

He's a legend. Just ask him—or others in the game. And apparently he was that good a player, too, before the accident.

I'm recognized in baseball as being the number-one scout that ever scouted the game of baseball. I signed like sixty-three ballplayers that went to the big leagues, when I was an area scout for thirty-three years, signing free agents. For the last eighteen years I've been a big-league scout. I scout all the clubs, report on 650 ballplayers a year. You ask me about any ballplayer that played in the big leagues in the last two years and I'll tell you all about him, and I don't have to get my book.

You have to love it. You have to go home and have it out with your wife so she'll go along with your being a baseball scout, because there's been a lot of divorces in baseball. I've had six wives because I've never had one that really loved the game. They were always nagging me, "Hugh, why don't you get out of baseball? You're a hell of a salesman." All this stuff. I say there's no goddamn way I'm getting out of baseball and we're either going to get along or I'm going to tell you *adios*. The wife gets lonesome and goddamn you're *gone*. They can't travel around. They're a handicap. Every time my wife would say she wanted to go on a trip, I'd take her along and feel obligated to entertain her, so what I was doing was taking her to dinner instead of working baseball.

I signed in 1935 with the Cleveland Indians, and I played a year and a half in the minor leagues and then I went to the major leagues. I had just turned eighteen years old, and I'm not trying to brag but I put some numbers on the board that are out of this world. The first year I hit .348, hit 39 home runs, drove in 125—things like that. The next year I went to spring training with the Cleveland Indians in New Orleans and they sent me to Springfield, Ohio, and I played in 81 ball games and hit 31 home runs, hit .344 and drove in over 100 runs and went to the big leagues. It was almost unheard of in those days to go to the big leagues in a year and a half. Six or seven was more normal.

Then I went home to Oklahoma that fall and caught my sleeve between two big gears in the oil field and they pulled my hand down and crushed it off. I had just turned twenty years old. That was July 1937, and out of the kindness of the Cleveland Indians' heart—and it had to be, because there were only about twenty scouts in all of baseball back then—they gave me a job scouting. I'm sure they just felt sorry for me because of my being that kind of prospect and then losing my hand real quick. The general manager was a good friend of mine who had signed me as a player.

To show you how fate will play an important part in your life, I'm scouting for Cleveland at age twenty. The first player I signed was Allie Reynolds, the great pitcher. The second player was Dale Mitchell, who played left field for the Cleveland ball club for ten years. So I got off to a lucky start. My area was Oklahoma, Texas, Louisiana, Arkansas, Mississippi. Drove fifty, sixty thousand miles a year, scouting fourteen years for Cleveland. Then I went to the White Sox for four years, Brooklyn and Los Angeles for fifteen, the Phillies for sixteen, and this is my second year for the Cubs. My fifty-first year as a scout.

The game isn't as much fun today. There's too many changes. To the ballplayer today, it's all money. M-O-N-E-Y. But he plays just as hard and he's just as good an athlete, maybe better.

Scouts didn't make any money back when I started: $3,000. We were a little bit of a necessary evil, but I really worked at it. I think the hardest job in baseball is being a scout. It's hard work, driving up and down the damn highway sixty, seventy thousand miles in a seven-month period.

When I went to the Dodgers I became the supervisor of twenty-two states in the Midwest. I'd check out players, or if a scout was having trouble signing a player then they'd call me and I'd fly in and sign 'em. I knew the ins and outs of signing. Some of those ballplayers I helped on—I'm not taking credit for these players because other scouts signed 'em, I just helped —are Frank Howard, Steve Garvey, Billy Russell, Davey Lopes.

Frank Howard was a basketball player at Ohio State and we sent him to South Dakota and tried to sign him all summer. Must have had twenty or thirty meetings with Frank Howard. The next spring, Bert Wells and I was up in the room in Columbus, Ohio, and the phone rang at two o'clock in the morning. It was Frank Howard. He was all excited.

"Calm down," I said. "What's the matter?"

"I have to see you and Mr. Wells. I have to see you right now."

"Well, where are you?"

"In the lobby!"

He comes up the stairs and I say what's the matter, and he said he'd been talking on the phone for the last hour and twenty minutes to Paul Richards, the general manager of the Houston club.

"Richards said to me, 'Well, how much would it take to get you to sign with the Houston club?' I finally decided that if I put the money up so high, the Houston club would back off. So I said the lowest money I would possibly take would be $120,000, and Paul Richards said, 'I just signed you.' I said, 'What do you mean?' And Richards said, 'If you want $120,000, that's what you're going to get from the Houston ball club, so I just signed you.' "

Frank Howard told Richards no, he hadn't meant that. So then Richards said that Howard's word was no good. So now Frank Howard wanted to sign with us. Right then. He was really excited. You know, he's so big.

I said, "What kind of money are we talking about?"

He said, "If you guys right now will give me a $100,000 bonus and an additional $8,000, I'll sign right now. Right now."

He was twenty-one years old. That was an awful lot of money back then.

Bert Wells or I said, "Well, why the odd figure?"

He said he wanted $100,000 for himself and another $8,000 to make a down payment on a home for his mother and dad. So Bert and I went into the bathroom, and Bert said what do you think, and I said let's go out and give it to him. We were supposed to go only to $90,000, but Bert and I usually had the leeway of about $10,000, if we were talking about $50,000 or so, and what the hell's the difference between ninety and a hundred-eight, anyway? There's no difference. So we went out and said, "You got it."

Usually the problem is money. Ballplayer says he wants $90,000 and you're thinking in terms of $40,000, $50,000. You're a long way apart and you got to close that gap somewhere along the line. I never worked for a club that didn't have any money, or I couldn't have signed any players. It wouldn't have been any fun!

There's a lot of tricks in signing. One of them, if you're a good, conscientious scout, you'll be able to solve it, but if you're not, it'll go right by you and you'll lose the player. When you go in the house to do your preliminary work, you *must* find out who is going to have the final say in that family. About 75 percent of the time it's the mother, and you'd better figure it out. But I've been in the category a number of times when I thought the mother was going to be the deciding factor, and it turns out she wasn't. Could be the boy, could be the father. Sometimes you'd sit there and talk and talk and listen and the mother wouldn't say a word and I'd think well, she's not going to have any say in this, but the last day, that's when she came forward. This happened *fifty* times. You have to figure this out way in advance.

When a family was talking about a high-school boy going to college on me, I'd say, "Mr. Jones, Mrs. Jones, Jimmy. You're going to go to college, right?"

He'd say, "Yeah, I'm going to college unless I get X amount of dollars."

I'd say, "You know what's going to happen to you? The last three years you play in the big leagues are your most productive years, money-wise. You're at the top of your salary. Let's say you're a $500,000-a-year player, and you sign out of college after three years. You have lost three years in the big leagues and that's a million and a half dollars."

That's just a little ol' deal I used, but it's also about half truth.

The thing that used to scare me was when the boy told me he wanted to be an attorney, a doctor. I walked right away. You're inviting trouble. When he goes out and plays two or three years of baseball and doesn't do very good, he's going off to pursue that profession. They're having that problem with Bo Jackson, right? What does Bo want to do? Danny Ainge tried baseball, remember.

I've seen twenty scouts hanging around a house. What I used to do—and a lot of people thought I was wrong in doing this—I'd go in the house early and say to you, your mother, and your dad that you're a bona fide good prospect, and you're gonna have a lot of clubs in here after school's out, trying to sign you.

"Here's what I'm gonna do," I'd say, and it wasn't against the rules.

"I'm gonna keep out those clerks, those guys who are only going to muddy the water, who will come out here and spend four or five hours of your time and talk, talk, talk, and when all the talking's over offer five or six thousand. I'm going to start your money at *$40,000* bonus. Right now you've got that offer. It's my *first* offer, not my last. So when those scouts call you on the phone, you tell them real quick that you have an offer from the Los Angeles Dodgers for $40,000, and unless they want to go that high or higher you'd rather they didn't even come out to the house." Immediately I got it down to six or eight clubs. Then we'd fight like hell over the player.

The rule of thumb for scouting directors is to try to talk a scout out of a ballplayer. They'd question me and I'd say, "I can't cut him open to see what he's like inside, but if we don't go for this kid let's get out of the fucking business." My exact words. "We don't need to scout."

I'd feel that strongly about seven, eight, ten kids a year. I tried to keep away from the chance players, what I call nickel-and-dime players. Now those players are $10,000, $20,000 players, and they'll break you! You start signing them and the first thing you know there's twenty-five of 'em in the organization, and they'll play along four or five years. Maybe one out of that whole bunch, maybe two, will make it. That's not good enough odds. It really isn't.

When I found one with enough ability, I signed him. When I signed Dale Mitchell he could do two things. He could run like hell and he could hit with power. He couldn't throw a lick, and he wasn't a very good fielder, but I thought his speed and his bat would overcome that, plus the fact that he was a country boy and a gung-ho player, the kind of guy who gets his uniform dirty the first inning. That's the intangible you might not see in one game.

Most scouts in the winter would take an off-season job, be a substitute teacher, sell automobiles, carpenter's helper. But I never did. I got my four, five names of some real good college players and I'd invite them out to dinner. First thing you know I've got him signed for $1,000, $1,500. Then in spring the other scouts would come in and say, "You signed that Bryan kid!" and I'd say, "I damned sure did. While you guys were out working, I was working *baseball*."

College players didn't use to be emphasized as much, and for good reason. They didn't have real good coaching in those days; college baseball was a secondary sport. They only played about twenty games. It's not secondary now, when they play sixty, seventy, eighty games, then another fifty on one of those semi-pro teams in the summer. Before you're eligible for the draft at the end of your junior year you'll have played almost four hundred games as a college player, and you're ready to go play professional baseball. That did not use to happen.

When the spring opened up I saw my eight, ten, twelve top players religiously. If I still liked you I'd break you down and make sure you were the kind of ballplayer I thought you were. Then, long before you got out of school, I got to know all about you, all about your mother and your dad, your brothers, your sisters, the preacher, the principal, the coach. I knew everything there was about you by just going into town and asking questions. I'd tell people I was a scout and wanted to find out about you. I'd go to your girlfriend. When I was through I knew everything. The reason I tell you this story is I cut down on the mistakes. I didn't make a mistake on Mike Bryan. I did not.

Mistakes are made every day when they should not be. If I look at you and then get in a car to drive two hundred miles, I'm going to break you down right in my mind going at 70 mph: your arm, your speed, fielding, hitting, power—five things for a regular player. Break you down! If you have two or three minuses I'm going to walk away from you, and let somebody else make that mistake. But one thing that has changed in the last seven or eight years is that if the ballplayer can run and hit with power he can make the big leagues, even with a minus arm. Years ago he couldn't do it, when they stayed with the basic tools. Expansion has something to do with it, but more important, everybody is offense-conscious. The DH in the American League really moved in this direction.

The last real sleeper I found was down in East Texas. I had him hid out over there. This was 1967–68. The last week before the draft two scouts come up to me and said, "Hughy, we know about the kid you got hid over in East Texas."

"Oh, you do?"

"We sure do. Why don't you give us all the information because the old black coach over at Wiley told us about him?"

They were telling me this at the ballpark, so I'm telling myself that they'd heard *something,* but they can't pinpoint it, and they don't have many days to go. I say, "I don't have any player hid out over in East Texas."

Here comes that goddamn draft, I drafted that goddamn kid and he goes to the big leagues in about two and a half years! He turned out to be a bad kid.

Then there was Cecil Cooper. Only two scouts knew about Cecil Cooper. Did you know that? Red Murff and Dave Philley. Cooper went to a little bitty school outside of Beaumont, Texas. Just a few days before the draft I heard a rumor about a kid down in that country and I got on the phone and called about three or four coaches and finally one told me, "Yeah, that's Cecil Cooper." Well, by then he had one more game to play and I saw that game after driving all night from northwest Texas. Murff and Philley saw me drive up and said, "Where in the world did you come from?"

The Red Sox knew about Cooper. They had done their homework; all I had seen was five innings because the game was called on a ten-run rule. I could only put him down low and the Red Sox took him in the third, fourth round. At least I was there. If I had heard about him two weeks earlier, I would have done my homework.

About one out of ten players signed make it to the majors. The way I figure it out mathematically, and without a computer, the good scout has got to be right seven out of ten. I always was. The prospect who just goes to Double-A or Triple-A, hell, he's a liability, he's costing you money.

Scouting is not intuition and hunches. It's breaking the kid down. If he falters and gets released, the scouting director will tell the scout that signed him, "We're gonna release Mike Bryan." That bothers the scout. But then the director might say, "But it was a hell of a signing because Mike Bryan did everything you said he could do. What you couldn't do is cut him open and see what he was made of inside. That's where he failed. The game was too tough for him."

You're dealing with human beings. Always remember that. You're not dealing with animals you can train. By god, human beings have a mind, and they can get into drugs, or get girl crazy, or different things. And they'll fail. Or sometimes a kid will change. You walk away because you've heard some things and checked them out and they're true, and then he'll change.

Lots of fathers have asked me to go see their sons. "This boy really wants to play," he'll say, and I've gone to watch his boy play and then gone back to the father and said, "Your boy is a gung-ho player and he loves to play but he just does not have enough ability to play professional baseball. It's that simple."

I've had to tell a lot of fathers that, and it's hard to do, because the father loves the boy.

T I M   W I L K E N

He's one of the Florida scouts for the Toronto Blue Jays. I accompany him on an evening swing through the central part of the state, looking mainly at a third baseman in one game, a catcher in another. The third baseman is clearly bigger, stronger, faster, and better than anyone else on the field, even though he doesn't connect with a pitch. The catcher is new to the position but moves as if he had been born with the gear on; also hits a couple of long homers.

We're the black sheep of the industry, no doubt about it. We're the guys who come around and take the little kids away. We go to the University of Miami, a good college environment for baseball, and they're all prepped. An usher came up to me one day and said, "Who're you going to steal from us this year?"

It's not as though we're coming in and saying, "Forget your scholarship." It's not like you're not being compensated. In the pre-draft years a lot went on. Things got out of hand. But now everything we do is monitored by the commissioner's office. The player isn't signed until that office clears the standard contract. We can't alter it. We can't lie to the guy. He *has* to receive the money.

Within the organization people think we've got it made. Great life, lots of travel, glamorous. They think we don't do anything but "go to games." That's what [Reds' owner] Marge Schott says. The Reds may be all right for a while because her club was supplied with good players from the scouting system. Now the scouts are leaving. If the Reds don't replenish their supply, they'll slip. In the middle to late sixties, the Oakland A's had one of the best scouting staffs in the U.S. Charley Finley didn't care as much about his money, and they just rolled out some of the best players—Bando, Jackson, Fingers, Hunter, Odom—and guys who surfaced with other clubs, like Hendricks, Trillo, and a bunch of others. But somewhere in 1970 or '71 Finley started going to the bureau-type scouting, packing up his own scouts left and right, and the A's were okay as long as they had those other players in the big leagues, but as soon as they started retiring, Oakland really depleted because they had no minor-league depth.

My first day this year was January 14, and I'll be going at it every day, usually two games a day, up through the June draft. I send letters to high-school coaches requesting their schedules and rosters, and I enclose a self-addressed, stamped envelope. And I ask for suggestions on other players in the area worthy of mention. Sometimes they will mention somebody. If it's a sophomore or junior, that tells me they have a feel for that kind of player. If they mention a senior who's five-foot-four, 125 pounds, well . . .

You never know whether a coach is fronting for another school or bird-dogging for another organization. I know we don't give out money. It could happen, of course. I hope it doesn't happen. Pretty hard to do with the way word spreads; newspapers mention that scouts have come in.

I have about ninety-five days to see everybody. I do a lot of stuff right out of my head, and I have fairly decent recall. That's a prerequisite for a scout. This year I'll be doing some extra work in New England. We have a new man up there and he'll be scuffling and it won't be easy for him, and I'll try to help him out. If they have a rough spring, he'll have a harder time with rainouts. You might have to go on first impressions, practically. In Florida you'd think you'd have more opportunities, but now with the twenty-game season for the high schools, which is ridiculous, it's tough again.

Then come the signings of those players we get in the draft. After that come the summer assignments, whether it be amateur, minors, or majors as an advance scout. After that I try to hit as many junior colleges as I can in the fall, up to about the first week in November, then I go to Puerto Rico for fifteen to twenty days to cover the sixteen teams in that league, then I fly home for Thanksgiving and try to unwind for two weeks—as you can probably tell, I'm a litttle hyper. Then I can hit some baseball camps here and there in Florida in December, over the vacations, not really hard-type scouting, but, "Hey, this guy looks pretty good, maybe I'll catch him in the spring," or, "This guy definitely looks good, I'll definitely catch him later." Then from January first to the fifteenth I might get some time off. All in all there's six weeks when I can get some time off.

I'm single. Lately my free time has been going to all my friends' weddings. I wouldn't recommend scouting to anyone heavily into marriage and a structured nine-to-five-type thing. I drove forty-one thousand miles in Florida last year. I'm in hotels seventy-five to a hundred nights a year.

In 1979 I really wasn't doing anything with my degree in elementary education and child psychology—I guess I can deal with a lot of people I work with!—so I helped out around spring training at the Blue Jays' site in Dunedin, Florida. I had played amateur and pro ball in the area. Maybe they decided I had a pretty good insight into baseball and wanted to see if I could be a scout-type person. They sent me to California with Wayne Morgan, who's now the West Coast scouting director. I was out there with Wayne for three months. I had some knowledge because my father had been a part-time scout for the Pirates in the late sixties, early seventies, and had scouted for the Phillies before that, and he used to run some tryout camps, which used to be big before the draft. But to try to learn so much in just a few months just can't be done. A lot of things are instinctive.

But whatever the test was, I passed, and they decided to give me an area. Finally I went into both Carolinas, both Virginias, Tennessee, and about two years later, Georgia, Alabama, and the panhandle of Florida—quite a bit of area.

I moved to the Carolinas in '79 and that was quite a culture shock. I was twenty-four. Also, I had to find ballplayers. Billy Smith had had the area with the Houston Astros the year before and he was made director of our player-development system, so he gave me some names and we had some other names from guys who had run in and out before. I'd see those players, then others who might be interesting—high school, junior college, college. You talk to coaches, players. Newspapers, you read a little bit; if you read where a scout has been to see a player, well, there must be something there. But just because you read that a kid strikes out nineteen doesn't mean you're going to race off to see him. Your days are limited—from February through the draft in June—and I had a very large area and a car.

You try to correlate five, six, seven days in one area—up to ten days if it's a tough area to get to. Then back home to pay your bills, then get back on the road to another area. Sometimes I was a month on the road. You end up with a list of graded players. I write it all down on a sheet of paper, put down the kid's name and school and a little number next to it, 1 being the strongest, 5 the weakest—and that'll be my priority for seeing guys, looking for things like mental make-up which you might not have been able to pick up on a first look. I'd try to see a guy two to four times.

There's such a thing as a scouting rhythm and at first, in 1980, I couldn't find mine. I'd go see these guys and a lot of them didn't progress from the previous visit. Some players reach a plateau and that's it. But I couldn't recognize that. I was writing guys up too high. I was going into situations with too many assumptions. I struggled with schedules and I was homesick as hell in a yuppie, preppy area of penny loafers and Izods, which I had never seen in Florida. I was making a lot of phone calls home. They probably had thoughts about not rehiring me.

But somewhere right before that June '80 draft I started feeling more comfortable. I saw a guy named Butch Davis and I was certain I was right on him, and he did get to the big leagues with Kansas City. I was breaking them down better, thinking in terms of necessary but possible changes the player would have to make. I think the Blue Jays started detecting that. They gave me another chance and I went to Wichita that summer. It was a turning point for me.

Wichita is the summer version of a college world series. Over seventeen days I witnessed seventy-five to eighty games: sort of a mind-held-hostage tournament. Seventy-five to a hundred scouts were there. It really helped me to project on players. Kevin McReynolds, Joe Carter—tons of them were there that year. I might see a game at one, another at three, another at seven. I couldn't wait to get to the park early to watch batting practice, infield.

Next season I was seeing two players in West Virginia, in a town called Nitro just outside Charleston. I needed to get to a junior college tournament in Atlanta and see Herman Winningham, Mike Sharperson—whom we did draft—and Cal Daniels. The GM asked me if I could pump up to get back down there in my car. The clubs were bracing for the strike that year and were holding back on finances; any other year I could have flown. I left the West Virginia game at six P.M. and the first game in Atlanta was at nine the next morning. I drove as far as I could, got to Black Mountain, North Carolina, checked into the motel at twelve-thirty, got up at five-thirty, got to the game just in time for the first pitch. You find yourself starting to do things like that.

This is my tenth year of scouting. I now have three-quarters of Florida, the Bahamas, Puerto Rico in the winter, looking for trades and new players, and the Florida State League, looking for trades. I'm hooked. I'd like to be a scouting director or player-development director in the minor leagues, something like that. I managed part of one year in '82 in Bradenton, and I liked it, but there's something about scouting. There's a lot of independence to it. You can almost get to the point where you don't want to take instructions from the people in the front office. You have to step back and say, "Hey, wait a minute. I work for these people!"

The draft was created to level things out. Over 1,100 people were taken in 1987. A major-league club takes at least thirty draftees, and as many as seventy-five. You can keep drafting as long as you want to. Of course you won't sign all those guys. If a high-school draftee goes to a four-year school, we've lost him. But if he goes to a *junior* college—and more than likely we knew that's what they were thinking of doing—we have control of him until one week before the *next* draft. That's why teams draft so many players: if they go to junior college, then it's a hell of a position for us and the player.

The problem I have with colleges is the constant jacking-up of prices. If you can't compensate a guy for his education, you shouldn't even be there, but if you *can* give him at least that much, and maybe more, I think he should at least consider it. It's tough for a lot of kids to do two things at one time. I think their school suffers because of it. Do one thing at a time and do it well. I graduated at a later age and my grade-point average was a lot higher. I mention that a lot and it rings some bells with parents.

Last year I knew a little about a first baseman from St. Augustine. St. Augustine and Daytona Beach are not renowned for their high-school playing; they're getting better but it's kind of a dead area. But I saw this player who has aspirations of playing pro ball. He was also a very good student, with SATs like 1300, so he could go anywhere to college he wanted to.

Now, this guy had sent some information around to some of the better academic schools in the Southeast. No one really followed up because no one in baseball knew too much about St. Augustine. He was accepted to all of them, however. Meanwhile, I called his father in May and worked the boy out, and told the dad that his son really wasn't ready to go into minor-league ball right now because he really hadn't had enough baseball background, hadn't played enough. But maybe he would come on the next year and we could have the opportunity to sign him, if indeed he really wants to play pro ball. So an option for him was junior college. His father was worried about the academics, of course, but in the first two years you've got to get your basic requirements anyway, and St. Pete Junior College is like the third or fourth best junior college in the country, or so they say in their pamphlets.

We drafted him in the forty-eighth round, and then Auburn called, Georgia Tech called, someone else, saying, "We want to try to get him in here."

Where were they before?

He's now at St. Pete. I helped him get in there. So I get to watch him and he'll still have the opportunity to play, if he comes on. It's a showcase for the player.

That's why more clubs are drafting a guy who isn't ready but might develop. Go ahead and draft the guy and if he goes to junior college you have control rights—although they might change these rules. We took twelve to fifteen guys after that forty-eighth round who went to junior college. Now if just one of those guys pops, it's great for the Toronto Blue

Jays, and the others have gotten enough notoriety from being drafted that they may be set up pretty good, education-wise, with scholarships, whereas they might not have been if we hadn't drafted them.

Two years ago there were 144 players on the All-Star ballot; no pitchers. Of those players, 109 were either high school, junior college, or Latin. Thirty-five were college players, and only 18 were Division One college players. In the Mets versus Red Sox World Series in 1986, only two guys were college players: Spike Owen and Marty Barrett. However, the Twins are mostly college, or at least junior college. We're talking players only, not pitchers—they're a different breed.

A good scout, a very good scout, is only right 20 percent of the time on his main drafts. Ten percent is not bad. A scout can't feel too bad if the guy at least gets to Double-A. That's the biggest jump in baseball. After that, the ability *up here* takes over. The pitchers really pitch instead of just throw, hitters have to make adjustments or fail.

Some people will tell you it's a crap shoot, but I don't buy that. It's a science, but an instinct, too. There's a reason why some guys are more successful than others.

Take José Canseco. I wasn't involved with this, but he was one of two guys of some interest at a ball game. He was about six-foot-one, 160 pounds at the time. So was the other guy, Rolando Pino, who was drafted second or third round, while Canseco went in the fifteenth round. But Pino stayed about the same size and now Canseco's a behemoth. That might have been a case of performance versus projection. The higher pick would come out and show you everything you wanted to see, a very accomplished-looking player. Canseco was skinny and underdeveloped. But Camilo Pascual, the scout for Oakland, saw the potential.

Sometimes you don't know levels of competition. One 7-for-7 game can be awfully misleading when you don't have many at-bats. Plus you don't know who the scorekeeper is. If you have to rely on batting averages, you can be in trouble. Home runs? Well, you have to have a little strength to hit one in the smallest ballpark, so you might pay a little attention to that. Strikeouts, too, for a pitcher, if they're playing a good level of competition. If you're *not* striking out some guys, you wonder. Then again, the head of the aluminum bat is bigger, so that cuts down on strikeouts.

For an everyday player we're looking for agility, body control, hitting balance, a loose arm that might not be too good now but might improve with day-to-day throwing, running speed, bat speed, how he handles certain crucial pitches, adjustments he makes the second, third at-bats against a good pitcher. But maybe if he comes from a crude area he doesn't know any better, nobody's ever told him anything.

A lot of people say there's no competition in scouting. There *is* competition. That's what I like the most. When I first came back to Florida as a scout, I tried to figure out past drafts, clubs that have been dominant, what types of players they take, where they come from. Then I'd take this information into consideration when I looked at a kid. Is he a so-and-so-type player? How do I like him? Do we need to take him a round or so higher because some other team historically likes this kind of guy?

You're scouting other scouts!

I see scouts in other organizations feeling the pressure. There are guys who will run away from players simply so they won't be *wrong*. They won't be right, of course, but they won't be wrong. It's a no-decision.

Scouts can be just like players. They have their good days and their bad days. They can come in after long, tedious trips and not know what they're seeing. They're just at the game, that's all. I have been so wired out on diet cola when I finally got to a game in the Carolinas after a long trip they all looked good, or they all looked bad.

When I wasn't as familiar, I would low-profile it and I'd fit in the crowd because I was younger looking and I had my stopwatch here [he pats his pocket] and I rarely used the radar gun. If I wrote something down I just scribbled on this piece of paper in my back pocket. I didn't want to tip my hat to high-school players. I want to see them play without any inhibitions or anything. The stopwatch judges running speed, home to first. I use the radar gun at night when most of these parks have real poor light and everyone looks a lot quicker. That's where it helps me. In a day game I can generally guess every pitch within one mile an hour. When I look at pitchers I try to break down movement, location, feel for the mound, rotation on the breaking ball, and how they go at guys. Sometimes you can see makeup. You can see animation and emotion.

With aluminum bats, pitchers are more geared to throw away from batters. In pro ball it's just the opposite, throw *in* so they can't extend. If you try to throw in on the aluminum bat and get the ball just a little over the plate, the bat with its bigger sweet spot will drive that ball. The pitching game has to be completely reversed. And hitters look a lot better with aluminum. Maybe with wood the bat is broke, with aluminum the ball's driven for a double or triple. For high-school players, if we have a lot of interest and are wondering about his true pop with the bat, we'd arrange a workout session with a wood bat, two or three weeks before the draft.

There might be forty-five scouts stuck right behind the screen if a good pitcher's throwing; a collage of scouts. There's a lot of name-sharing among scouts. I still do some. Just of names, though, not of what you think. There's also a lot of decoying. Guys'll make up a guy's name if a certain scout has been yapping a lot to the college people, say. A guy might mention player Smith in East Egypt, and the Rona Barrett scout runs up to East Egypt and there's *nobody* there, much less Smith. That used to happen a lot.

In the ten years, I have personally signed maybe twenty-five, thirty players, and that includes a few we signed just to fill a roster somewhere. You don't tell people they're roster fillers—they have a chance to make it, after all.

A first-round draft generally dictates six figures. I've heard that some organizations allot about $300,000 for signing, so if they give $100,000 to your first choice, that leaves the other $200,000 to go around with the other twenty-five guys they hope to sign.

Some guys you take in the fifteenth round *might* get as much as a first-round player. We got a guy named Tom Quinlan, played at Myrtle Beach last year, eighteen years old, had a chance to go to the National Hockey League with the Minnesota North Stars. Our scout up there, Chris Bourjos, did his homework. Chris *knew* that Quinlan wanted to play baseball more than hockey, and he knew the other teams *didn't* know this, so we got him in the nineteenth round because those clubs stayed away. Quinlan got a pretty good bonus.

There's a lot of guys you'd love to have and you know you're right on 'em, but those are top-priority guys who have been evaluated by everyone. A hundred people have seen them. If they're picked in the first five rounds, you can accept losing any of them. But in rounds eight to twenty you feel like you've done your homework, you have a gut reaction—"Gosh, I want that guy, give him to me eighth, ninth, tenth"—but then you can't fit him in, or some other team trumps you and drafts him earlier, and he ends up in the big leagues. That's the one that eats you up, right there.

I truthfully believe that you have some kids who think about how they fit into an organization before they sign. Toronto has a reputation of signing Latin middle infielders. I've been in homes where the family knows who we have at every position at every level. They ask me whether their son can beat out so-and-so. This is *before* we've signed him. They've checked us out with *Baseball America* or whatever. Plus there's probably an agent giving them some kind of advice and giving them information. And I honestly say, "If you play to the ability I think you've got, you don't look at those other guys. Do what you got to do."

I have figured out before I go in where the starting point is. No one has ever told me, "We're embarrassed by your offer." Some people think we'll end up doubling our original offer, so if I start at five, they figure we'll end at ten. So they start at twenty! There are a lot of free-advice givers, too, and not just college coaches hoping the player won't sign. They'll say so-and-so was drafted by the Blue Jays and released. I've asked people where they got certain information about other players and they've said, "Well, somebody told me about it."

I like to have the kid himself in the early meeting to see his reactions. They're very tied up, usually. Sometimes the parents think the money's okay but the kid puts his foot down and wants more. I've never had an agent in the room, but I've been there when the phone rang and they'll say it's a newspaper guy but I suspect sometimes it's an agent. For the agent, most of it's long-term realization.

You've got to wonder why the player doesn't sign, especially if the money is good, but you're dealing with personalities here. Take Jimmy Key: a silent, confident person, runner-up Cy Young pitcher in 1986. Jimmy went in the third round out of Clemson, and I think that was a shock for him. There were two determinants why I think he didn't go higher: even though he knew how to pitch, he didn't put big numbers on the gun, and in a game against Wake Forest he jammed a guy and shattered his aluminum bat. A piece came out and I believe stuck in his shoe, and he had like eight stitches, and he was out for a period of time while the season was rolling along. The scouting directors and cross-checkers start their work in Florida and move north, and when they came through Carolina, Jimmy was out.

He told me he wanted to clear X amount of dollars after taxes. Well, he wasn't totally out of line, but it was a little high. And Jimmy just did not want to go to rookie ball; he thought he was definitely better than that. So I got to talking to him and said, "Jimmy, take this for example. Would you take somewhat less money to go straight to Double-A, rather than more and go in to rookie league?" He said yes, and it was a fairly significant amount of money. You see, he was one of the mission guys: I'm getting to the big leagues and prove to everyone I should have been a first-rounder.

Well, I talked to my bosses. It took about five days and there was a threat of losing him. Everyone was getting worn down and he could have gone back to school. He also wanted to hit—he was Atlantic Coast Conference DH of the year—and I said, "Well, I don't think we can do that, we're in the American League."

Finally we agreed that he'd take the higher figure and go to rookie ball, but if he threw good the first three or four times out of the chute, we'd move him. Sure enough, he did throw well, we moved him to A-ball later that summer and he threw good there. He spent the next year at Double-A and Triple-A, and the following year he was in the big leagues.

But the day we sign he doesn't come out of his bedroom! His dad calls him and he finally comes out with his head down and gives me the biggest dead-fish handshake. From a guy who's a hell of a competitor you wouldn't expect it. He signs the contract, turns around with his head down and goes back into his room. He was bummed out about going to Medicine Hat, out in Alberta.

The toughest thing for a family is when a guy comes in offering money for the boy to leave in ten days to go play baseball in, say, Medicine Hat, Alberta, Canada. It's a rookie league club, but the parents think it's a voodoo league. You say to a kid that he's going to be taken completely out of his environment, that's quite a shocker. He's being rushed into something he's not prepared for, regardless of the money. And in ten days the parents' *son* is going to be gone for two months until the end of August, in a lot of towns they've never heard of.

We've got a guy in Syracuse, Triple-A team, named Otis Green. The White Sox drafted him twice, and I found out he wasn't going to sign with them. After his signing period had ended, I called him the very next day. I said I had a pretty good idea what the White Sox had offered and I asked what it would take to sign him. He hemmed and hawed. I said we would like to make him the fifth pick in the secondary draft (we don't have that anymore), and he still wouldn't say anything. I went to his house and, same thing, he wouldn't say anything. I said, "Well, Otis, you're telling me you don't want to be our fifth pick."

He was one of two choices for us in that round and I told the staff I just didn't know his signability. Well, we took him, and I was authorized to fly him, his mother, and anyone else he wanted (his father is deceased) up to Toronto. I went to Miami and called him up and said, "I know it's short notice but do you want to go to Toronto? We have to go in the morning." He says okay. They're allowed forty-eight hours with a pro organization without losing their amateur status.

So I met him at the airport, took him to Toronto, worked him out, and he had a great workout. He must have mashed about twenty or twenty-five balls out of there. He put on a good show, and he looked all right fielding, too. Guys were yelling, "Give him what he wants! Give him what he wants!"

Bob Mattick and I took Otis and his mother out to eat at a real nice restaurant and started talking money with them. We said we just didn't know where to start. We came up with something, and Otis said no, he wanted more.

"How much more? We want to sign you, Otis. Don't be afraid to give us a number. It might be obtainable."

Well, he finally came up with a figure, and it wasn't so bad and we got it okayed. We went back the next day.

"Otis, we've got the money for you. Are you ready to sign?"

"Well, I don't know." And so on.

His mom stepped in and said, "Otis, you told the man what you wanted. Sign."

Boom! He took the pen and signed right there. A lot of times the mom is the main person.

HARRY DALTON

"I was all set to go to Columbia Journalism School when the Korean thing broke out. I enlisted in the Air Force and was stationed in Colorado Springs, and I went over and presented myself to the local club. I didn't want any salary. I just wanted to get some feeling for being in a baseball front office. Phil MacPhail, the general manager and Lee's brother, said, 'If you feel that way, come on.'

"Then it worked out that there was a job in Baltimore, as an assistant in the farm department. I had no scouting background at all."

He stayed with Baltimore for eighteen years, eventually becoming vice president for player development. He spent the next six years as executive vice president and general manager of the California Angels. He has had the same position with the Milwaukee Brewers since 1978. He watches the games from a bare-bones box above home plate, usually in the company of farm director Bruce Manno and other scouts.

"You have to push yourself to realize that there is another side to your life and that you have a family and you want to give them as much as you can, too. Baseball is a little bit of an addiction."

Most of the day is spent trying to do whatever it takes to make the team on the field today better tomorrow. Player evaluation, player acquisition, the farm system, which player is doing well, who should be moved up, who might be moved back or released. That's what we're working on. It's an inexact science. You're talking about human judgment trying to assess the future performance of human beings. It takes some imagination to do it. It takes some sense of baseball skill, some knowledge of people and the way they mature, and it takes some courage.

I'm not trying to overdramatize it, I'm just trying to say that I know that I can sit here and from my own mind derive a thought, put it into motion, make a trade or sign a player or do something, and it will actually lead to this club being more successful. I know that I might have missed something today that I could have done to make the team better three years from now. Maybe we won't get a guy signed because we didn't give him an extra $15,000 or $20,000, and four years from now it'll be a terrible mistake. I don't lose sleep over these things, but I don't treat this as a nine-to-five job where I'll worry about things tomorrow that I could be thinking about at six o'clock tonight. But to parallel the old saying, the general manager is never as smart as people might think he is when his club's winning, or as dumb as they think he is when it's losing.

Besides, I work with a staff of knowledgeable people, and picking them is what my main strength should be. *My* being able to see that this guy is a better player than that guy is not nearly as important as being able to pick my scouting staff and farm director and manager.

The greatest frustration is to see key players get seriously injured. We have this grandiose master plan and it's going to have our club set by year X. The scouting department starts looking at kids when they are fifteen and sixteen. We follow them for a couple of years and draft them and give them a bonus and send them to Bruce Manno's department to play for three or four or five years. We don't rush them and we finally get them here and then in the twentieth game of the season the guy breaks his leg or tears his rotator cuff and you don't have a replacement in kind because there's not that much extra talent in our league and there's not one thing you can do about it.

Paul Molitor lost an entire season and then forty games last year and then Robin Yount hurt his shoulder and eventually he had to end up in the outfield, away from shortstop. In 1982 we had traded for Don Sutton right before the August 31 deadline because I thought we had a good chance to win it, and we needed another pitcher. So we gave three kids for Sutton, which is the kind of trade you don't like to make unless you're pretty sure it's gonna buy you a pennant, or give you a good chance. We made the deal and the night that Sutton made his first pitching performance for us, Rollie Fingers went out with a bad arm, walked off the mound with a sore arm and that was it. I was sitting right here. It gives you an awful sinking feeling in your stomach. We went all the way through the seventh game of the World Series and lost. If Fingers could have helped us, we would have won. I'm convinced of that.

Pete Vukovitch won the 1982 Cy Young for us and then never really could pitch effectively again because he blew his arm out. It's just like crashes at Indianapolis. Every business has its hazards.

You can never get all your pieces together. You can *never* say, "We've got it," like General Motors. They work with the plans until they get the approvals and they've got quality controls stamped on the boards and here they go and it's all computer-operated and there are no glitches . . . and nobody picks up the paper the next day to see how many perfect cars were made.

I don't have a disciplined daily schedule but lots of mornings I'll be in here between six and six-thirty and study the box scores. Usually that's the first exercise of the day. I do a lot of reading early before the phones start: farm-system reports, daily game reports from the minor-league managers, their weekly pitching charts, statistics from the other minor leagues, our own professional scouting reports, and our own free-agent reports. If it's not important enough to remember you discard it, but some you remember. If you're looking to a possible move on the big-league club you're paying more attention to the reports out of Denver, our Triple-A team. Or if it's getting close to the draft you're trying to figure which free agents are most impressive, which you're likely to go after.

Right after eight o'clock here, I'll make calls to the East Coast when the switchboards open back there at nine, and get them out of the way: other general managers or scouts or whatever the matter might be on business, the player-relations committee, commissioner's office, league office, any of those. Then when nine o'clock gets here our switchboard is open, and the day doesn't always go as dictated, because things start happening. It's all really active and rapid but you may not make a decision in a hurry. You may contemplate something for a long time.

The real key is evaluating the performance of the team on the field on a *daily* basis. The nine innings themselves are the best part of the day. They've changed so little since I got into the business. Except for the designated hitter, and the mound has come down five inches, and they don't leave the gloves on the field anymore, it's almost exactly the same game as when I started thirty-five years ago, and that's enjoyable. I'm one of those people who, if I was outside baseball, would say, "Can you imagine working by going to a ball game every day of your life?"

I'm a fan *until* it comes to judgment time. Then I can't get emotional about the people playing. I traded Gorman Thomas for Rick Manning and Rick Waits in the middle of 1983, right after we had won the pennant in '82 and Gorman was a huge local hero. That trade really brought down a storm of protests. We knew that was going to be an unpopular deal, but I honestly felt that Gorman wasn't helping the club any longer, that he had started his downward path which wasn't going to reverse, and it was the time to move him and get rid of him and we did. I liked Gorman and he had helped our club, no question about that, and he was popular, but you just look at what you should do to help the ball club. It turned out Waits and Manning didn't do that much for us in the long haul. Gorman didn't do that much more, either, and then we finally brought him back after he got released in Seattle and he finished up the season with us, '86, I guess it was.

We might make thirty to forty player moves during a season. It depends on whether we're winning or losing, on injuries, and on how much help you think you have in the system. You might be going bad but you just don't think anybody in Triple-A is good enough to bring up, and you can't make a trade, so you don't have a lot of moves.

I don't think trading has the deviousness, the effort to be like horse trading, that perhaps it did twenty or thirty years ago. Some general managers we have a close relationship with, and we'll usually drop the fencing right at the start and be pretty open about who we might have available and who we might be after. At other times, with the fellows you haven't dealt with as much or you don't know as well, you are a little more guarded on what your real goal is. With twenty-six clubs and with the various contract restrictions on player movement, it's not as easy to trade as it used to be.

I'm also looking at individual performances on the basis of, "Are we *entertaining?*" You know, we're in the entertainment business. We have a pennant race every year and the professional part of us wants to win a pennant but the practical part of us wants to be an entertaining item that draws people who want to spend their money here. We can't guarantee a pennant every year, but you do want to be able to guarantee the entertainment. And if you have skilled athletes out there who play hard, you pretty well can. Then when you lose, people should still go out of here saying, "We had a good time tonight."

But if you consistently lose, it stinks. I could be stronger, but I won't. I don't care if all your friends are here and they say, "But it was a great game, don't feel bad." You *lost* and you don't go out there to lose. But there are nights when you know you've played a heck of a baseball game and that loss is a little easier to take than when you stink and are dull and boring. I know we haven't given the people their money's worth on nights like that.

After the ball game I go downstairs to the office, then I go to the clubhouse. Not every night. Some nights I'll go to the office, pick up the phone, call Treb [manager Tom Trebelhorn] and ask if there are any problems, if he needs to see me, discuss things that happened during the game that I don't know about that I should know about. Some nights I'll go downstairs anyway and just assess the mood of the players, maybe get a sixth sense, talk to Treb about a possible player move that I'm considering, a call I got that might open up a trade avenue, or a report from Denver on somebody we're looking at.

I stay close to the clubhouse and close to the players for two reasons. One, it helps break down their feeling that an uncontrollable source up there has total power to move their wife and kids three thousand miles *tomorrow* and they can't do anything about it. Two, it gives you a better chance to assess the players. You can see what they do on the field, but sometimes you can't assess mood and how they're reacting to winning or losing. If I'm down on their turf, they're comfortable and more inclined to say, "Can I talk to you?"

It doesn't happen a lot because the players take so many of their problems to their agents. I had a case a couple of years ago, when we were in the World Series. I got a call from an agent in California because one of our players had called him to say that his wife didn't have a parking space the night before. I thought it was kind of silly. But they may have some legitimate concern about the fact that they are not playing on a regular basis, or they've been struggling and when they struggle they always wonder about their security. It shows how important it is to get an encouraging word from somebody that they work for. It's in this organization from the owner on down.

With the four pennants and two World Series victories in Baltimore, I still honestly think 1982 with the Brewers was probably the most exciting year, and specifically that Sunday in Baltimore when Sutton beat the Orioles and we won the division, because we had gone in with a three-game lead over Boston, with four to play, and all we needed was one win. Friday night they slaughtered us in a doubleheader and Saturday they beat us again, and it looked like we were on the brink of a classic choke. But Sunday we came back and Robin Yount hit one out his first time up and Sutton took charge of the ball game and we won it. Then there was the playoff against California when Cecil Cooper got the base hit in the seventh inning and we beat them after losing the two games out there. That three-week period going down the line with Baltimore and then with the Angels and then with the Cardinals—one of the most exciting times in my baseball life. This whole city just responded. It was a wonderful feeling, being involved with something that made so many people so happy, so obviously happy. That's one of the wonderful things about this job and this business.

My biggest disappointment was not a single game or season as much as not coming closer than I did with the Angels for the six years that I was out there with Gene Autry. I really liked Gene. I wanted to win one for him but after six years there, this deal came up. But inside I think I had a bittersweet feeling, really, wishing that I had done a better job there. It turns out that a couple of years later the club was a pretty good club through a lot of the kids that we had signed, but I didn't stay there. I was already over here.

"KING"

"King" isn't his real name—or even his real handle. What he does is technically illegal—gambling on games. "But if it's so evil," he points out, "how come the tabloids run the lines every day?"

He apologizes for being late to our appointment, set up by a mutual friend, in the back room of a dark, almost empty restaurant on Manhattan's Upper East Side, and explains that he had to call in "half a dollar"—$50—on the Padres in their afternoon game againt the Mets. "Hope it pays for lunch," he says.

Seated with his back to the TV screen, he's upset when I don't immediately inform him of developments favorable to the visiting team.

If you've seen some of those Walter Matthau, Odd Couple–type movies, writers seem to spend most of their time figuring out what games to play that day. Too much time on their hands. I had just sold a script in 1982 and had some extra cash and knew guys who gambled and just thought it was a good time to plunge in. I felt ready. I was on a roll. Also, the previous fall, before I had a bookie, I took the Dodgers against the Yankees, got eight-to-five for the underdogs, and won $800. That convinced me I was a smart bettor. Through a friend, I was introduced over the phone to some guys who were running an organization and claimed they were the best. Someone recommends you to these people, and satisfies them that you're trustworthy. *They* are the ones who are taking the gamble at first, not you. They can't be sure you're going to pay.

There's a misconception that your local bookie is working out of a storefront somewhere, often mob-connected. Those guys exist, but there's another strata for the guys who want to gamble but don't want to deal with people who are, so to speak, crooked, who would prefer to deal with guys who treat it like a legitimate business. The guys I deal with came out of the financial world and know a good thing when they see it. Every once in a while you read about a gambling ring broken up, names confiscated, records showing a couple of million dollars in bets. You might pray they get raided if you owe a lot of money. And they worry about that, I'm sure. What's to prevent me from calling up the FBI? That's how most of those cases are broken: guys who owe money.

I was given a phone number and a code, "King," and my agent's code, say, "Muffin." My agent is the guy I would see any time money has to change hands. He knows my name. He inquires about my career: "Gee, you lost again, I assume you're selling a lot of stuff these days." Now I know his name. He doesn't care about that. I've been to his place to pay up. As best as I understand it, they have three or four guys answering the phones somewhere in mid-Manhattan. Every six months or so they change their phone number. I don't know if they've also moved offices. I envision a studio apartment with phones and a blackboard. I don't know their address and don't want to know. Their hours are six o'clock to eight o'clock every evening, and on weekends noon to two P.M. And for weekday games during the baseball season, also noon to two P.M.

I call and the guy says, "Hello," and I say, "King for Muffin." That identifies me and my agent.

"Okay, King, what would you like?"

"What are the baseball odds tonight?"

They read off the odds: "Met's seven-eight over Padres, Dodgers even-six over Phillies," and so on. This means that if you want the favorite, the Mets, you *lay* eight-to-five—put up eighty dollars to win fifty. If you want the Padres, you *get* seven-to-five—put up fifty to win seventy.

The vigorish is built in for the bookie, *if* he balances the bets on both sides. The worst he will do is break even, if the favorite wins, because he pays out fifty to the people who bet on the favorite, and he collects fifty from the people who bet on the underdog.

But if the underdog wins, he'll *make* money because he's collecting eighty from the people who bet on the favorite, but he's paying out only seventy on the Padres. That's why bookies like underdogs to win, usually.

Sometimes I'll call and they'll say, "Hold it, we're just getting the line." So it's coming from somewhere else. Maybe Vegas. I don't know. There may be a consortium of these offices, and as the betting action heats up, the odds may change. Let's say a hundred grand suddenly comes in on the Padres game this afternoon. That'll change the odds. They might drop to 6–7, trying to encourage bets on the Mets. They always want to balance the books. They want a line that looks attractive to both sides. But my bet stays at the odds I was quoted.

In extremely odd situations, baseball will have bets on runs scored, not odds. When the Baltimore losing streak got to fifteen or sixteen, the bookies were getting clobbered because people were betting against Baltimore until they finally won a game. So they finally posted "Baltimore plus two runs" against Detroit. Detroit won by a run. You could have won on Baltimore. But by and large, it's just too difficult to post runs for baseball. The averge winning margin is one or two runs, unlike basketball and football.

Every phone conversation is recorded. At the end of the week we total up, and let's say Muffin says, "Hey, you lost $625 this week," and I say, "No, I didn't. I only lost $525." They play back the tape recordings. I'm not allowed to bet more than a nickel—$500—on a game, I can't lose more than $2,000 for a week. (I'm at the low end of the scale.) Sunday is settlement day and if during the week I've gone over $1,000 I have to pay them something.

I can expect a phone call from my guy on Tuesday or Wednesday, saying I'm over my limit, what do I want to do. Meaning, when and where do I want to pay him. This becomes a negotiation. Some guys want total settlement every week. With my guys I might say, "I've got $600 on me right now, I can see you in an hour," and he understands that to mean, "I'd appreciate it if you would let me get by with just six hundred this week." That happens quite often, and it's one of the reasons they're good businessmen. So I pay him $600 and still owe $500. My job the next week is to keep it below $1,000, and hopefully get ahead. Anytime *he* owes *me,* he'll pay the full amount. I expect him to be like General Motors.

We meet on a street corner. Pick-up and delivery, they call it. The first time, he pulled up in a Porsche. I said, "Gee, I'm on the wrong side of this." His wife got the car in the divorce. Now he rides a scooter or walks up. One time I was to meet him right across from the Garden, on the northeast corner. I owed him $1,100. I look around and see him on the *southwest* corner, giving a guy an envelope.

I bet probably seven games a day, from $500 to $700 a day. Now why is that not so dangerous? I'll tell you why. I bet seven games for $100 each. If I go four and three, I'll make $100 or so. If I go three and four, I'll lose that much. It's real hard to go five and two, or two and five. You could *try* to lose five games and have a hard time. The most I've ever won was $600 on a basketball game. Took the Detroit Pistons on a whim, which is something I never do. Lost $800 on the Super Bowl one year, including $100 on the coin toss. For the Super Bowl they go crazy with bets, even open the office at half-time for second-half play.

I think baseball is the best game to bet because it's every day, for one thing. You can get a fix on teams. But there's *no* skill involved. Blind luck. These guys who advertise they can handicap games—if they could do that, why advertise to sell books or whatever? Just bet! I don't spend five minutes a day on it. Of course, I start calling the sports-scores number at eight o'clock. I probably spend several hundred dollars a year calling in.

But I do bet on pitchers. If Orel Hershiser's pitching on the road, I'll bet *against* him—even though I would have lost last night, because he beat Philadelphia. I like home underdogs because they're going to win some of those games and I might pick up an easy bet.

I do this to make money but I haven't made money. I've probably lost between ten and thirteen thousand. If you bet as many games as I do, over the long run, you can't win. The vigorish will clobber you. If I come out fifty-fifty, the vigorish takes away 5 percent of my money. I keep betting to try to get even. You've got to be optimistic. One year I came out ahead.

A friend used to have several bookies before he dropped about twelve thousand in a six-week period one summer a few years ago. He was hoping for a quick kill. Where else can you go, short of selling drugs, and make a phone call and the next day maybe have two or three thousand in your pocket? I can see the appeal, but I avoid those bets. Money *seeps* out of me. It doesn't gush out.

I don't root anymore. To be more exact, I root depending on my bet. Friends see me root against the Mets, they know I've got the Padres. I have a soft spot for some teams, but any adult who's a real team fan—what a jerk. Why would you have any loyalty to these guys? Twenty-five years ago —fewer teams, fewer trades, no free agency—maybe so. Plus you couldn't see all the other teams on cable. But today? The ballplayers are being paid.

They're trying to make as much as they can. Why not me? Sometimes I do bet *against* teams. Can't stand the Cardinals. Hate the Yankees, of course.

I love casino gambling but hate the slum by the sea—Atlantic City— and only get to Vegas on my way to or from the Coast. If I lived in L.A., I'd probably get to Vegas once a month.

Having time on your hands is what makes you gamble on games. When I'm very busy, I forget sometimes. That annoys me, of course, fig- uring those are the days I would have won. And I lay off at various times, sometimes for a month, if I go to L.A., say. And I have no trouble not playing when I'm under my limit for the week. Let's say I owe $900 on Saturday, and remember Sunday is pay-up day if I go over $1,000. I have no trouble not betting on Sunday. Or let's say I'm up $1,400 on Wednesday. I wouldn't bet the rest of the week because I don't want to blow the chance to collect. A lot of guys are much more compulsive than I am. I play fairly regularly, but I control it. Sometimes I make bets that in my heart and soul I know I'm going to lose, and I do lose. Then I say to myself, why didn't I change those bets. But it doesn't work out that way, for some strange reason.

I'm single. It's a hobby.

The Padres won the game. I paid for lunch anyway.

10

THE FOURTH
AND OTHER
ESTATES

For eight years he broadcast the San Francisco Giants games, and before that minor-league games and other sports. Then he joined Tommy Hutton on the radio play-by-play for the New York Yankees. After the '88 season he returned to the Giants.

We talk in the home-team dugout at Yankee Stadium. Players tromp past as they emerge from the clubhouse for batting practice. Dave Winfield shouts out to his teammates. Willie Randolph chats with young fans. Raphael Santana is quiet. They leave us alone.

I can say this because I've had eleven years of pro basketball, too: baseball is so hard to broadcast. It's hard because it is *not* an inherently exciting sport. It's a fascinating sport, a contemplative sport, but the moments of genuine excitement at a baseball game are few. People make the mistake of thinking basketball is difficult because it's fast, but that's the very thing that makes it easy. It's written out in front of you. You don't have gaps to fill. You don't have to be *entertaining*. In the course of broadcasting basketball, you're going to sound more exciting because you have to talk faster, you're in a confined space with a much higher noise level.

People talk about baseball as summertime and easy livin', but they're the same people who, because we're not yelling and screaming, say, "Gee, this guy sure is exciting with basketball, but I can't stand him with baseball. He's dull."

They just don't grasp what this is all about. It makes it tough sometimes. First and foremost I'm a fan of the game of *baseball*. The game will be played long after these guys are gone. Maybe there won't even be the Yankees in fifty years, but there will still be baseball. I'm a fan of the Yankees in that it's impossible to be around guys as much as we are and not want to see them succeed. It doesn't mean you've got to be a cheerleader in your broadcasts. At least that's my attitude. I once said to Bob Lurie, owner of the Giants and an extremely nice man, "You know, Bob, my job is not to make the Giants interesting. I have no control over whether they're interesting or not. *You're* job is to make the Giants interesting. My job is to make the *broadcast* interesting, because I do have some control over that."

I'm there to reflect excitement, not create it. I admire what Harry Caray can do in making every Cubs game sound like the seventh game of the World Series. He's marvelous and he's been in this game a lot longer than I have, but that's not my style. I can't work that way. My bosses here said to me, "We don't want a cheerleader. We don't want a 'homer.' You were hired because we like the way you do the ball games."

The listeners in San Francisco appreciated the fact that I was not a cheerleader, and a lot of people told me that New York would be the same way. But I confess to you that I have been somewhat shocked by the number of fans who have either commented in person when I was walking out of the ballpark, or sent letters saying, "How come you don't root for the Yankees? This is our ball club! You should be a fan like we are."

Maybe I'm making a little bit too much of this—maybe it's twenty-five letters—but the mere fact that people say that surprises me. Maybe the people who appreciate the fact that I'm not a cheerleader don't bother to comment. I've had a few such letters, but I'm a little surprised the other side has been more vocal. The Yankees themselves have never said anything to me about it. George Steinbrenner said, "Hey, if we screw up out there, say it. I say it. I don't want guys glossing over people's mistakes. I pay them a lot of money."

But if a guy makes a bad play, you don't need to bury him. If you can't get your point across without saying, "That's the worst play I've seen in thirty years of broadcasting," maybe you've got a problem.

The tide is moving toward boosterism. You're getting owners in the game of baseball who did not grow up with the game as part of the family business. Maybe they have less of an understanding of how the game is played, in the deeper sense, and are seeing it only from the merchandising standpoint, and the announcer therefore as an extension of that. Because we want to boost our product, we want a guy who says, "Hey, rah, rah! Hey, get out here! Hey, we gotta get 'em this inning, folks!"

Believe me, I have sympathy for the people in this business who are made to do that when it's not the way they want to do a ball game.

My interest in baseball began in Detroit, where I was born, and I got interested in broadcasting during World War II, when radio was *it*. I actually got started in baseball shortly after I got out of Syracuse University, which has been the breeding ground of a lot of guys in my business. The first job was with the Syracuse Chiefs, in the International League in the early sixties, including a few re-created games off the Western Union ticker—one of those exercises that left you with a tremendous feeling of confidence. If you can do that, you can do anything. After Syracuse I went on to San Francisco for a while, then Honolulu in the Pacific Coast League. That was an interesting experience and, again, there were more re-creates. Even though you were required to say at the beginning and the end that it was a re-created broadcast, a lot of people never knew, especially on the islands, where we dressed it up with crowd effects, sound effects. People would see me the next day and say, "Gee, I heard you last night. How'd you get back from Salt Lake City so fast?"

The trick is that key phrase in broadcasting: *word picture*. That's what you have to create. I used to do everything I could within the confines of the small booth in the studio to create an atmosphere which would enable me to bring a word picture to people, even though I was thousands of miles from the game. A simple thing: I'd get a photograph of a ballpark and hang it on the wall; once in a while I'd look up and see the flagpole in center field and I'd make reference to it.

In Syracuse, we got a record of the balls and strikes. In Honolulu, all we got was what the batter did, and we would make up the balls and strikes. The very first time I broadcast under that system I said, "Here's the first pitch, low and outside, ball one," blah, blah, blah, and the guy throws again, "called strike"—and now you're filling with some other stuff and all of a sudden you're about to have the guy throw the next pitch and you think, what's the count? There's nowhere to look. I started writing it down with a pencil. The next day I went out to a sporting-goods store and bought an umpire's indicator, and I kept the balls and strikes on that. Needless to say, we did not have a lot of three-two counts! The ball games did not run overly long. You could sort of tailor it to whatever activities you had planned the rest of the evening!

It was a test of your powers of concentration and what have you, but, yeah, it was a lot of fun. We had lined up someone in each city where the Hawaiian team was playing and have him call us from the ballpark periodically and just read off from his scorebook what happened. We'd record it over the phone and have it typed up: Jones grounds to shortstop, Smith flies to center, Brown singles to left, Green forces Smith at second, no runs, one hit, no errors, one left. They'd throw in a little pre-game stuff, including the weather.

By the time we went on the air, which was six o'clock in Honolulu, we'd have five or six innings piled up because it was nine or ten o'clock on the mainland, depending. By the time we were into two or three innings of *our* broadcast, we'd get the second call from the real game, and usually it would be over by then. Once in a while we'd have to sweat it out, waiting for that second call. So suddenly a brief shower passes by! That would be comparable to what we went through with Western Union when there might be a wire problem.

Talk about concentration. The thing I had to concentrate on was the sound of the ball hitting the bat. Here's the pitch and—pop! I had a musical wood block from an orchestra, and I'd knock it with a pencil. The problem was I'd make up in my mind, okay, he's going to hit the next pitch and I'm looking at my paper and saying, "Smith into the wind-up, the pitch"—and I'd swing and I'd *miss,* I'd miss the damn block! The rubber eraser hitting the table is *nothing.*

Throw it into reverse—"Oh, it's low and outside!"—and do it all over again. Concentration was important.

I worked in Hawaii twice, alone in '65 and then in '75 with a partner. From there I went to San Francisco. I'd done eleven years of pro basketball there, and had filled in occasionally doing baseball there on television, in 1972. One year I had cast everything aside on a whim and my wife and I left San Francisco and took a freighter and sailed to Australia where I had visited before and thought about living. That's how my years get broken up a little bit. Anyway, after the '75 season I came back to San Francisco, our station got the rights to the Giants games in '79, and because I had some baseball experience they included me as part of the two-man team, with Lindsey Nelson, who had come out from New York and the Mets. Lindsey and I worked together for three years, then he retired and I stayed on and did five more years, and I left, I quit, after the '86 season in which I guess could be described as a deteriorating relationship with the station I had been with for ten years.

Okay, that's enough, I said, it's a big world, let's find out what's out there. A month later I got wind of this job and went after it, sent tapes, all the things you do in this business. WABC was looking for an experienced guy at the major-league level, so that might have been one of the rare cases where experience was a plus. It was their first year with the rights to the game and it was a big thing for them. As they told me, "When it's the Yankees, you don't want tapes from Lincoln, Nebraska, or Grand Forks, North Dakota."

The Yankees' vast radio network goes into places where I lived, like Rochester, where I went to high school, and Syracuse, where I worked for several years. I've heard from people that I haven't seen in thirty years, people I went to high school and college with. There's kind of a thrill knowing those people are out there and feel a sense of pride in what you do.

My philosophy is, prepare every day for the worst game ever played. When I first came out to Honolulu in 1965 a sportswriter said to me, "The great thing about baseball is you come out here every night and see something you've never seen before." That's pretty darn close to the truth, but there are times when you have a feeling that some of the best jobs are in the dull games. Those are the games when you have to give the people a reason not to turn it off, because they don't know what the heck you might say next. They remember the great games because they were great games, not because of anything you said. Maybe you had the opportunity to call that home run in the bottom of the ninth that won it, but the call was the result of what the batter did. But in the 12–3 game, what you did to rescue that broadcast wasn't dependent on what went on out there, because the players weren't going to help you at all. You had to reach back into your bag of tricks and come up with some interesting anecdotes and stories. In a game like that every pitch isn't life and death, and you realize that. I had back-to-back years with the Giants when they lost ninety-six and one hundred games. You can't just say to yourself in June, "Oh, man, I gotta write off this season." The ball club may bring up new guys, but what are *you* gonna do? You're out there every day, sticking your head in that noose three hours a day, and you're still the only thing those listeners have. So I take the approach, forget the pennant race, look at each game as a separate entity, a contest to be won, and just view it as that.

Every day someone is listening to a baseball game for the first time, and I feel a responsibility to explain the game, throw in some background or history that 90 percent of the fans might know. Most of the game I'm going to appeal to that 90 percent, but I'm not going to forget that other 10 percent, or less, who may never have heard a broadcast. I may have some influence on their interest in baseball for the rest of their lives. *Mine* was influenced at age seven. I'm not talking about what number so-and-so wore, but refreshing people about who was where when Bobby Thompson hit his home run, or stuff that happened at Yankee Stadium with Ruth and Gehrig. I deal in the history of the game, because baseball has the richest history, and this ball club speaks for itself in that regard. As a kid I learned a lot listening to a guy who had played for the Detroit Tigers, a Hall of Famer, Harry Heilmann. I enjoy going into Fenway Park, or Tiger Stadium, which I remember as Briggs Stadium from when I was a kid. You just feel the history. It pumps you up. Even Cleveland. It's not the most exciting city in the world, and it's a dreary, old ballpark, but I grew up hearing about

Municipal Stadium, and I walk in and think, "Bob Feller stood on that mound. Kenny Keltner made two stops on DiMaggio that night in '41, threw him out on fantastic plays to help end that streak at fifty-six games." I get caught up in that stuff.

You have to convey a passion for the game. Make the fan feel about it the way you do, make him want to read more about something you talked about. Broadcasting is not teachable in a formal sense. There are principles to learn, certainly, but they can't teach you what you get out of going to a game as a young person, going to as many as you can get to before you're in the business, experiencing firsthand when something big happened, compiling experiences you'll be able to draw on years later. Nothing beats being there. *In your mind* it's a famous game. It doesn't have to be a World Series.

When I came over to the Yankees I had to bone up on the more recent history. I grew up in the East, so what had happened thirty, forty years ago I knew pretty well. The areas I was not as familiar with were things that might have happened ten years ago, when I was in the National League. Staying up on the National League was a full-time job. I'd look at American League scores, check an occasional box score, but I never read features on guys in the American League because I couldn't take the time, just as now I don't read about guys in the National League. I can't take the time from perusing last nght's American League games, in case there was an interesting play that happened that we might want to discuss.

Tommy Hutton and I were hired at the same time, and I knew him from the National League. He was a broadcaster at Montreal after he hung up his spikes in 1981. We had similar problems, learning the new league, new personnel, dealing with the designated hitter, which changes the game. This is an entirely different game than the National League. We had to stop certain aspects of our thinking about what managers might do when we'd realize, wait a minute, they don't have that decision to make. Sometimes you'd see the number-eight hitter in the line-up sacrificing, and you'd wonder why he's doing that with the pitcher up next and they don't look like they're going to pinch hit because there's no one throwing in the bullpen, and then you realize, wait a second, the pitcher doesn't hit anyway. Fortunately our minds were working faster than our mouths, so it didn't often come up, but it did come out in a simple thing like giving the line-ups, saying, "Batting eighth and playing shortstop, so-and-so, and hitting ninth and pit—uhh, hitting ninth and playing second base . . . " That *did* happen a couple of times.

I keep my notes on a sheet opposite the scoresheet. Some notes I've carried over. I might carry one around for two weeks. I keep files on every team, a general information file, oddball records, but I try not to deal in what I consider trivia. There's two different kinds of preparation I do. One, the day-to-day preparation of keeping up. The other is a labor of love: baseball research and history.

I'm an early riser, and my baseball day begins as soon as I get up. Unfortunately I can't get home delivery of all the papers I want—the *New York Times* is the only one that's delivered—so I go out to a newspaper store and buy three or four papers, including *USA Today,* for box scores I can't find in the local papers, and I start work. I have a little office upstairs with my books and files. I go over the box scores, clip out items of interest. If you find one or two items that might be worthy of interest, it's worth it. And, of course, *The Sporting News, Sports Illustrated,* and other periodicals. Three or four days before a new team comes into the stadium, I will clip the box scores of their games and look for little trends: batting streaks, relievers coming in three successive games. I read through all the PR notes put out by the other team, but the best work is what you do yourself. There's still a lot to learn if you put it in sequence. I try to do this in the morning because I'm totally useless after noon—which is tough when you play mostly night games.

Maybe in the afternoon I'll stretch out for an hour and pick up *Baseball Research Journal* or read a book about a certain team. This kind of rounds out your overall picture, and it's the part I enjoy most. Scanning box scores is informative and necessary, but it does set your eyeballs spinning after a while. When you sit down and read about the history of the game, that's really enjoyable.

The statistics books can be good and bad—bad if they're overused, like I hear from time to time, but excellent if you know what to take and what to use. The thing with statistics is that we have to humanize them. You can't just throw them out. I suppose you could say, "Ever wonder, folks, who won twenty games with the highest earned-run average?" and read off a list of ten names, but fans aren't going to remember once you get past the second name. So you say, "Well, you know, in 1938, Bobo Newsom with the St. Louis Browns, a team that no longer exists, now the Baltimore Orioles, Bobo won twenty games that year with an earned-run average of 5.08." There's a guy who won twenty of his team's 55 victories, and you tell a little something about the guy. Whatever you do, you can't just throw dry numbers at the fans, and that happens a lot. They'll say this guy hit such-and-such in late-inning pressure situations. Well, what the hell is a "late-inning pressure situation"? How much pressure was on the pitcher? Who was in the on-deck circle?

Part of baseball broadcasting is knowing when *not* to use the stuff you've prepared. A mistake a lot of people make is that because they have taken the time to look something up that morning at home, or have clipped this from the paper, by God, because they've put that time in, they're going to get every one of those things in on that broadcast. What you should feel is that it's nice to have that stuff, but that you don't have to look at it. You can build on what is taking place during the game itself, allow one thing that happens to trigger off something that you saw that's related from a game last year. You don't need to constantly refer to your notes. There will be a moment in that game or, if not, in the next game, where you can integrate that note into the action. But you can't take it out of context. It doesn't work that way.

Tommy Hutton and I live about a mile, mile and a half from each other over in Jersey, which makes it convenient. We drive to the ballpark and arrive by about four-fifteen, go in and talk to players if we have a question about something that happened in the game last night, or go over and see the other team. The ballplayer needs to feel comfortable enough with you so that he will answer whatever you need to know. That's about it. If I have a question about a play last night, or something about the pitcher who's going to work that night, than I can go to a guy and he can feel comfortable if he wants to go a little further, knowing that he can trust me. I need to be around so a guy doesn't say, "Let's see, have I seen this guy before?" But it's not necessary to run with them. I never have. If you walk in someplace and a guy's by himself, you'd walk over to him, and might sit down, but as far as making plans, no. That's not necessary, nor a good idea. There are enough other people—fellow media people, coaches. The players are entitled to go their way.

You can't spend every minute together as broadcast partners or broadcaster and players. On the road you spend a lot of time by yourself. Curt Gowdy once said, "It's a long season and a small booth."

To get a full picture of the booth you have to remember not just the baseball end of broadcasting, but the *broadcasting* end of it, the commercial part. You are just as preoccupied with getting in the commercial commitments, many of which run within an inning. The producer, who at the home games stands behind us, constantly reminds us to get in the ticket plugs, things like that. You're trained in the baseball end of it. The critic who writes about what you do doesn't care about what you know about broadcasting. He cares about what you know about baseball. You're concentrating on your knowledge of the game as it's played, the strategic and historical aspects, and suddenly that train of thought is broken, constantly, by what has become a necessary part of the broadcast, what we would call the extraneous material. Now even the scoreboard is sponsored. You used to just pick up the scores and read them, but now that's sold, too. Four times a night we have to specifically refer to the sponsor. So the atmosphere in the booth is a mixture of relaxation and confusion.

On the road, the producer is back in the studio and talking to you through your earplug. When you want to get in a certain story because it's just perfect for this moment, and suddenly there's this interruption, you've got to get this little commercial plug in, you might say to yourself, "Why do I do all this? Why do I prepare?"

I suppose the only way TV has changed radio broadcasting is when someone's watching TV and listening to you on the radio. Then, you'd better be right. You want to be right anyway. Television has also created an appreciation of what radio broadcasters do. Let's say you've got a couple of runners on base and a ball is hit up the alley and it's rolling. TV can't follow everything that happens, but you can. You can say, "Jones has scored, Smith's rounding second, Washington cuts it off in deep left center." Your eyes can move faster than the TV camera, or faster than the guy at home can assimilate what he sees, and you can actually give a better picture. If TV cut here and there it would be too disorienting.

The radio listener is totally dependent on you. The guy with the TV has some idea, but the guy at home has *you*. To the guy at home, I'm the Yankees, more so than Henderson, more so than Winfield. Unless I tell them what these guys are doing, they're not doing anything. The knowledge that this guy is totally dependent on what you're doing is why you do this work. I know when I'd sit there at night as a teenager, the lights off, I could picture through their descriptions the ballpark, so-and-so leading off first, the guy going into the stretch, looking over his shoulder. But I couldn't have done that if the broadcaster wasn't painting that word picture.

I did five years of radio and TV, going back and forth, and I enjoyed TV. You're supplemental on TV. You don't need to say, "Swing and a miss," but you do need to say, "Strike Two" because maybe the fan forgot the count. You don't tell the guy what he just saw. Try to tell him what he's likely to see next. For example, what are the consequences of the guy's being on first base in this situation. Is he likely to go? Watch the leg kick on this pitcher. Watch the manager in the dugout because there's a good chance that everytime he touches his nose he calls a pitchout. Try to stay a step ahead and lead the viewer. Many of these comments you would not make on radio, because the viewer can't watch the manager in the dugout.

The moment I remember the most was Willie McCovey's last at-bat in 1980 at Dodger Stadium. Fifty-six thousand turned out that Sunday before the All-Star game, and here was McCovey, whom I dearly loved, and the realization that after twenty-two seasons it came down to one last at-bat against the Dodgers, and here were 56,000 fans, 55,000 of whom were Dodger fans, on their feet applauding this guy who had represented the enemy to them on so many occasions, and yet in recognition of his great career coming to an end.

Goosebumps, absolutely, and also the knowledge that whatever it is you're saying at the moment might possibly be remembered, too. I almost resented that. I might have been more emotional otherwise. It was still a close ball game. Jack Clark was at third base, Rick Sutcliffe was pitching. They sent Willie up to pinch hit. He drove a long sacrifice fly to center field and Clark scored to put the Giants ahead, in a game the Giants won. It was RBI number 1,555 in McCovey's career.

I remember Joe Morgan, too, in the final game of the season in 1982 when he hit the home run against the Dodgers in San Francisco off Terry Forster, which in essence knocked them out of the race that year. There were fifty thousand on hand—the Giants had been in it until the day before—and here was Morgan, little Joe. You didn't realize it was going to be his last at-bat.

But the McCovey thing. Yeah. Yeah.

SHERM FELLER

Almost everyone in New England recognizes his gravelly voice. He hosts a Boston radio show of eclectic content, and eighty-one days or nights of the year he's the public-address announcer at Fenway Park, where his Yankee accent is unmistakable and his no-nonsense style a pleasant relief from the hyped-up performances in too many other towns. The man himself, however, is full of play.

It's not a big paying job. When I started I was taking a cab from the house to the ballpark for seven dollars each way. The first month I gave my sister the check—I'm a bachelor, I live with her—and she said, "You're only getting twelve dollars a day for the game. The cab is fourteen. You're losing two dollars a game." I said, "Yeah, but I see the games for nothing!"

I'd do it for nothing. I eat and drink thirty dollars' worth. The guys are great, the writers in one area of the park, the management people here, the scouts are over there, personal friends here and there, so it's a pleasure. I go to Winter Haven for spring training. To work? No. I just go to batting practice, then the pool, then a nap and a bath, then come out at night and meet the guys, and we drink. Then the wives come down and we behave.

They don't want me to be a star here, and I don't want to be. I just want to enjoy the game and inform the public. The baseball fan in Boston is much more discriminating than the fan anywhere else. The other team gets as much applause as the home team for a great play. However, this whole season [1987] has been very depressing. The team is good but we had an unfortunate start, contract troubles. The reason baseball is so big in Boston is that it's the only sport we knew in those days. Most of us weren't big enough for football and couldn't afford golf or tennis. But just one baseball and you had a game, or nearly.

They're very conservative here. No Chesterfield signs on the walls. No signs at all on the left-field wall. The old man [Tom Yawkey, the former owner] gave in to the other ads very reluctantly. Somebody talked him into it. He would have preferred all green walls, I'm sure. Still, Fenway's naked compared to most ballparks.

This year is my twenty-first. In the beginning I had nobody to copy, nobody to tell me what to do. In all my years in radio I made it a point never to listen to anybody else, so I wouldn't consciously or unconsciously try to copy anyone. I'm not interested, really. You can't change. It's like lying to your broad. A lot of guys put on a voice. It's a phony. Eventually it catches up. I don't have a television set. My sister doesn't watch it. If I decide to watch a road game I go to a bar.

The biggest challenge I got, really, is getting from the radio studio to the ballpark in time. I go one-way streets, anything. I had four cops after me one night, and finally they cornered me. Herb Score and the manager of the local Brooks Brothers store were riding with me. Score said, "They're going to shoot us." I said, "I'll stop, you get out." So Score got out and hurried off and the cop said, "Was that Herb Score?"

"Yeah."

"Son of a bitch, I could've got an autograph."

He didn't give a damn about my going down all the one-way streets and through the lights.

The first night a team's in town, I've got to get in maybe two minutes earlier to learn the names. The players get very upset if you don't pronounce their names right. How would you say D-E-V-O-N White? Well, I said *De*-von first. Then I found out. I have to pay close attention during the game. Say I know who *was* in the batter's circle so I presume he's going up to bat. I'm diverted for a moment, I announce his name. All of a sudden a new guy comes up out of the dugout and he takes Strike One before I realize the switch. The old guy and the new guy both get insulted. So now I have to say "Correction, please." I'm an idiot to everybody. The job's not like work, but I feel as badly when I make a mistake as though it were a job. I feel worse. But it's a human game. That's why the *E* is up on the board.

There are seven of us, sometimes more, in the booth, handling the computer board and the various scoreboards. That's why sometimes you see three different scores around the ballpark! I handle the balls and strikes and outs on the left-field board.

But I'm not too busy to enjoy the game. That's the whole thing. When we stay till one-thirty and we lose, that's a crime. The fans'll know I'm unhappy. The ballplayers know. They get mad at me when I say "Error!" too loud. "Don't you think they know I made an error?" Rick Burleson said that to me after I'd said, "Error, second baseman." He hated it. I don't blame him.

If I like the guy, I might make believe the mike doesn't work. I've got power up here, I suppose. With Yaz I never said his name, just "Number Eight." It didn't matter what I said anyway. They'd drown me out. Almost the same with Boggs. They drown me out. He likes it. He doesn't say anything to me but I know he likes it. I'm a show person and I know what they like.

When Reggie was here last week he took me to lunch. Did you hear about the tribute we paid to him? We played "Auld Lang Syne." He was really touched. Ted Williams and I are very close.

TOM MEE

He knew he'd never be a major-leaguer but he played minor-league ball anyway "because it was the best background you could have—or at least I thought it was. It got me every job I ever applied for."

With a radio and PR background, he was the first person hired by the Minnesota Twins when they moved to Minneapolis–St. Paul in 1960. He's now the director of media relations.

The media is vital. It can make or break you and you can't buy it. Way back when PR first started in sports, ownership was of the impression that you *could* buy it by taking the writers out to dinner, providing transportation. That might have been true at one time, but it's not anymore. We might do those things, but only to create a friendly atmosphere between us and them. My job isn't trying to get our name in the paper, like someone involved in corporate public relations, but trying to get what is in the paper about us to be favorable.

It's important that the guy in my position be on working and social terms with the people assigned to cover the Twins. It's not quite so important, maybe, for a general manager to be on those terms with them. Sometimes there's an adversarial relationship there. The GM has to be somewhat more difficult to approach than I am. I'm expected to be a buffer between him and them.

We're a service. We're not trying to sell anything. We make sure that anything a writer or broadcaster wants, we got it for 'em. But everyone looks at it from a different point of view. There's one PR guy who was a writer for a local paper before, and the writers who cover that team tell me that he's extremely difficult to approach. Maybe he feels that when he was a writer nobody had to do his work for him. I can understand how a guy who comes off the beat thinks, "I was my own man. I didn't go to the PR guy."

The job's easy in a winning season because everyone's happy. The players don't mind submitting to three or four interviews. In losing seasons the players get very testy. They don't want to sit down for one interview. I have to smooth things over. The player tends to look on me as one of *them* —the writers. Maybe a writer comes to me and says so-and-so won't talk to me. When I ask the player about it, he thinks of me not as his ally but as their ally. That's the problem media-relations guys have in baseball, and I suppose in all sports.

A lot of players are very wary of all media. You've got to understand that players have always been stars from the time they've been in high school. All the way up the line they've never read a negative word about themselves, until they get here. Now they're competing against the best in the world and there are days when they're not going to come off so well, and on those days the writers might say, "Player Smith dropped a line drive that opened the floodgates for a five-run fifth inning."

But player Smith wants you to write that the ball had a nasty spin or something. Don't confuse him with the facts! It's an ego thing. Their egos are easily fractured.

We haven't had a real problem on our club. Even Steve Carlton, when he came over, opened up to the media. We had a guy a few years ago I had to talk to: Roger Erickson. This was '77–78, when he won sixteen games as a rookie. About midway through the year he quit talking to the press. Started going into the training room, which is off-limits. I didn't know whether someone had written something, but I didn't remember anything. He was sort of the fair-haired boy. So I went into the training room one day and said, "You're having a good year and the club's having a good year and in your first year in the big leagues you can't start turning off the media. It'll come back and haunt you. Give them good positive answers and things will work out." He gave me some kind of answer, I guess, but I didn't make much headway. He still wouldn't talk. He's out of baseball now.

Sometimes writers can be tactless, too, when they approach a player. One thing today—and I think it's to the discredit of newspapers—is that they tend to assign the most inexperienced writers to the sports beat. Why, I don't know, but we see that in baseball. All the coverage guys today, with a couple of exceptions, are very young, not more than four or five years out of journalism school. And so many of these guys have been schooled in a Howard Cosell syndrome: they want to make a splash for themselves, create a controversy right off the bat. So they'll come into a camp and they will ask questions that are uninformed, either by accident or design. I think that's all right if the writer has been around long enough that the player respects him, but not with some young guy just on the beat. Players can get very upset. Managers can get very upset. And when you've having a bad season a kind of pall settles over the team. In baseball it's *every day,* and if you're losing practically *every day,* tempers run short.

Tom Kelly [the Twins' manager] still gets upset. He'll say, "Hey, that's a stupid question," and that upsets the writer because usually there are other writers around and this makes him look bad, but Kelly still pulls no punches. He feels if they're going to be covering this club they ought to know what's an intelligent question. This spring [1988] he thinks it's stupid to ask whether he thinks the Twins can repeat. Sure we think we can repeat. That's why we're here.

For the most part Tom doesn't alienate the press, especially the guys who cover the club. But he makes it clear to them and his players that his players come first. There are actually guys on Tommy Lasorda's team who resent him because they think he plays more to the media than to his players.

Kelly's players think, "He's for us. He's our man." He doesn't want anyone asking pointed questions about any of his players that would require him to make a critical comment. He won't do it. He values his players' attitude more than he values the media's attitude. In his role it should be that way.

In my role it's just the opposite, in a way. I've got to try to keep the media's attitude good. I'm a baseball purist. I like the game whether we win, lose, or draw. But the team and the media get down—although the media are the last people in the world who would ever admit to being fans. They get much more critical and negative when we lose. They claim this is objectivity. I claim they're really fans deep down inside, and it bothers them that their team loses. It's extremely tough to get the media to be kind to your athletes when they're losing.

I've gone to writers several times. One time, Pat Reusse, an excellent writer for the St. Paul paper, was in Milwaukee in May. This was years ago. The Bucks were in the NBA playoffs. The Twins got beat and there were only about seven thousand people at the game. Pat wrote something to the effect that those weren't seven thousand fans but seven thousand *idiots* who could have been watching the Bucks and the Lakers on TV; instead they came out to this miserable ball game. When the team came home I went to Pat and told him I would never, never criticize him for criticizing our team. That was his perogative. But, I added, while you certainly don't have to shill for our business, I think I do have a right to ask that you at least try not to *hurt* it. When you tell people to stay away, you're hurting our business. I just don't think you should go that far. He and I are good friends and I think he got my message.

Another part of my duty is running the press box for home games. I announce the scoring decisions and little bits of information that save the writers the trouble of looking them up. I've got to be objective. In fact, when we were in Detroit for the final game of the playoffs in 1987, I was busy keeping score and other records, and a friend came up to me after we won and said, "I gotta congratulate you." And I said, "Well, it's been a long time coming." And he said, "I don't mean that. I'll tell you something, when the last out was caught I looked at you and you had no reaction whatsoever. You showed me something."

I was too lost in my duties because I knew it was going to be hectic. I had to get downstairs to get Gary Gaetti, the hero of the game, to the interview room, and all the others. I was thinking of these things. Three innings before I had assumed we were going to win, with a comfortable lead. The thrill of winning was already past in my mind. I just didn't have time to get excited.

After the games the TV producers come to us for their interviews; the morning TV shows want their guys live and they need to know within minutes after a game who they're going to have the next day. That's probably the toughest job: getting the players to commit to things of that nature. If the interview is on the field and all you've got to do is go in the clubhouse and bring the player onto the field, no problem. But if you've got to get Gary Gaetti, say, to the ballpark by six-fifteen in the morning!

And Gaetti overslept.

JOE QUASARANO

After years of being in the broadcast truck himself, he's the executive producer for the California Angel television broadcasts in southern California. He hires and fires and oversees the whole operation.

"I didn't get into medical school, strolled into a TV station one day in Detroit, and they made me a booth announcer. Thirty-five bucks a day. Forget medical school.

"My first sport was hockey. I was a complete nonfan but it turns out to be one of the easiest games to do, as opposed to baseball. Any court game where the puck or ball is going back and forth is easier. If you've got a good camera crew you can fake it. If I had walked fresh into a baseball game, it would have been a whole different story."

With one exception, Yankee Stadium, where the control room is built into the stadium, you're in a mobile truck somewhere outside. At Anaheim Stadium it's out by the left-field bullpen. You arrive about two hours before the game and immediately go to the truck and make sure the set-up is proceeding okay. The first day in town, when you're on the road, you'll generally drive out six or seven hours before the game to make sure the truck is there. You just feel a little better knowing.

The technical director is in charge of the crew and he'll say, "Everything's fine" or, "We got a camera down," whatever. There's a crew of about fifteen people and they're all scurrying around. With a lot of the stadiums now, the cabling is left in place so it's a matter of plugging the cameras in, but sometimes you have to physically carry the cameras up to the positions, check them all out, check out all the microphone lines. Audio in baseball has gotten pretty fancy. In fact we're doing a lot of games in stereo now. There're a dozen microphones now, mikes down the left-field line, down the right-field line. It really adds to the ambiance, if you've got a stereo set.

If I know the truck and the crew are there and everything is going along fine, I'll call back to Los Angeles and say weather's good, weather's marginal—weather's bad, get some other programming ready. Then I get the PR person for the opposing ball club and get all the stat sheets so that the person doing the electronic graphics can enter in all the updated batting averages and what we call the hero stats: so-and-so is on an eight-game hitting streak.

At the network level there is a graphics producer, in addition to the operator. I think that's why the networks tend to have a ton of graphics. In fact, I think they get a little carried away with a lot of useless information. They may have ten pages for every ballplayer. I personally think that it is overkill.

The graphics operator is one position that often as not will be a woman. Not only do you have to know the sport, but you also have to be an excellent typist because you are putting in reams of data for two or three hours before the game and you've got to be able to get it back instantaneously.

They all use different systems, maybe tied in with the ballplayer's number. If your number is 12, say, they might log in your basic name and number under 120, your name, number and batting average under 121, name, number, and some sort of weird stat under 122. Whatever works.

Generally, the announcers are at the park about two hours before the game, too. We've had the same two announcers, Joe Torre and Bob Starr, for five years, so the three of us might talk on our ride out to the ballpark about whom we might interview in the pre-game show. Nobody turns down Joe Torre for an interview. He's not going to be a patsy, but he's not going to say to Billy Martin, "Hey, tell us about the last barroom fight." He's going to talk about baseball.

I have been lucky, announcer-wise, over the years. I started at KTLA with Don Drysdale, and nobody turns down Drysdale. Then I had Harmon Killebrew and he was a hero to everybody. Reggie Jackson didn't want to do a lot of TV in his early years with the Angels, but he wouldn't turn Harmon down. Billy Martin wouldn't turn Harmon down, either, whereas if I went to Martin, he'd probably say, "Nah, I don't want to do any TV."

When we've got the graphics going and we've figured out who will be the pre-game interview and what the announcers' remarks will be— normally pre-taped, so if somebody flubs, we can redo it—I'll sit down with five cameramen, audio man, two tape operators and the technical director, and basically explain—I hate to sound corny here—my philosophy of cutting the game. Those crews work for the local TV station or facility, and there are different teams and different directors rolling through every week. We might do things differently. For important games there's a lot of kidding, you know. They're talking about how their team is going to win. Some of these camerapeople and other technicians are fans. They love the game. They love to see the home team win but they're all pros, too. In the playoffs in Milwaukee in 1982, they were *really* fired up.

I also get a good amount of feedback from the crew about the local team, because these folks are there all the time. I'll ask about this new second baseman and I might just get some hints about the way he hits or the way he fields that may help me if I want to isolate on him. Maybe he always plays with his hat, his jock, maybe he's always wiggling. I may want to isolate on that if it's an otherwise dull game. Reggie Jackson used to squint and dance around and glare at the camera, that sort of thing.

It is not unusual for me to say in our pre-game meeting and occasionally during the game itself, "I want to hear more crowd sound." I don't want Joe and Bob to sound like they are in a vacuum. You get to a park and for whatever reason there are only eight thousand people there, it's a little tougher on the audio guy, but he can do it. And I don't think there is any deception here. But more than once over the years some fan has had a few too many beers and he's close to one of the mikes. You'll say to the audio person, "Try and find that mike and let's bring it down a little until this guy goes back to his seat." But basically the audio man is on his own.

For fifteen to twenty minutes we talk about camera assignments. Some of them are basic but it doesn't hurt to explain. The normal way baseball used to be shot, at least on the local level, was with four cameras: high home, high or low first base, depending on the ballpark and where you could put the camera, third base, and center field. Now most local outlets have gone to a fifth camera, which they either put at high third or at high first. That one often shags fly balls, as we put it. I'll say to the high third cameraman, "If there's nobody on base I want you to shag, follow the ball to the outfield."

I'll tell the center-field camera, "Your stock shot is over the pitcher's shoulder, but I'm going to isolate you, put you into the other tape machine, so when I leave you on the live broadcast, I still want you to follow the ball." This gives you another angle on the action.

Good baseball cameramen know the stock shots. A stock shot before the first pitch will get the batter as he comes to the plate. That's a waist-shot and you lay in the appropriate graphics, batting .298, that sort of thing. And generally you come back to that shot, especially if that at-bat goes on four or five pitches, cutting between close-ups of the pitcher and the batter. Another camera will do the close-ups of the pitcher.

The shot from center field generally is over the pitcher's shoulder, showing the batter and the umpire and the catcher, but if Joe Torre is talking about reading the catcher's signs, you might tell that cameraman to push in. The camera at what we call high first, up in the stands, is normally assigned to stay with the lead runner so that if someone is stealing a base or there's a squeeze bunt, he'll be with that runner so you can isolate into a tape machine. If you don't see it the first time, you can show it to the fans. And I might say, "Word of warning. This guy is going to steal every time he's on base, so be aware."

Cameramen have a little red light on their camera that tells them when they are on, and they also hear me saying, "Ready Camera Three." They know when they are free. They know when I'm not going to come to them right away because there's no baserunner on first, or whatever, and the real good ones will listen to the announcers and go find the shot for them. They have to know baseball.

Every once in a while you'll get a bad crew, but that doesn't happen much anymore. Without mentioning the city, I went into this park and found out that this crew had picked themselves based on seniority. These were guys who didn't want to do the local news that night and thought it would be neat to go out to the ballpark. And one cameraman in particular, at the high-first position, wasn't going to do anything unless you told him to. Rod Carew was on first base. I tell the tape operator, "You're iso-ed on the runner," and I tell this cameraman, "Give me a head-and-toe shot of Rod Carew."

So he does. We go back to the action, Carew steals and we go back to look at that replay. But this guy had kept the shot on first base. We see Carew run right out of frame. When things calmed down I said, "Why didn't you follow him?" He said, "You didn't tell me to." I knew that was going to be a long day.

At one time we cut in shots of the defense before the game—here's second, short, third—and one place I went into I gave the assignments rather quickly. We've got five cameras to find nine people and I said to Camera Three, "Get me a shot of the shortstop," and he asked me very seriously, "Which side of second base does he play?" Another long day.

We used to do a post-game show, where a third tape operator would build a reel of key plays. Again I don't need to mention the city, but the guy who built these highlights didn't understand baseball. Our color announcer, Ron Fairly, gets into the first highlight and the wrong play comes up. No big deal, so we come back to our audience and say we have a little problem there. Fairly describes another play and now the operator shows the *first* play, and I'm in the truck and I'm screaming at this tape guy. This was only my second year and it just looked terrible. After about five of these Ron says, "Well folks, it's obvious they're not going to show you what I'm talking about. Good night and we'll see you tomorrow."

We sign off. I called my boss to explain and he was so angry he hung up on me. Ron was so mad he kicked or threw a helmet and shattered it on the wall. He had saved it for me from Helmet Day to bring back to my nephew. Long flight home.

These are exceptions but they have happened. Occasionally there's some screaming in the truck. I tend not to scream unless things just get totally out of hand. Some of my counterparts are crazy from the first pitch on. I would go to a town and someone would say, "Jeez, so-and-so just left. Terrible three days. The guy just screams."

Right up until air time we're continually checking all facilities, making sure all the mikes work. One of the last and most important things I do is check my headset. I can talk to the five cameramen, the two slo-mo operators, the graphics operator, the audio man, and I can push a button and get either or both of my announcers. The headset also plugs into a telephone line to the station back here and a coordinator who puts in all the commercials.

Basically, during the game, you're trying to listen to the announcers and look at seven pictures: the live picture going out, the four other cameras that aren't on the line, and whatever the two slo-mo operators have for you. You trust them to find different angles on what you have just shown. Generally, Slo-mo A will be what the viewer just saw and, assuming we cut it properly, we can always go back to that at a much slower speed and show that the runner really was out at first. The second slo-mo operator is usually the better of the two. You give him some license. He has his own little switcher and can select any of the five cameras independent of what I'm doing. If there's a runner on base the operator knows who he's going isolate on. I don't even have to tell him that at all.

First batter comes up, we cut to a waist shot of him with a graphic, then cut to the center-field shot over the pitcher's shoulder for the first pitch, a called strike, cut back to the batter with a second graphic for him, then maybe a close-up of the pitcher, playing with the ball, kicking the dirt around, whatever, then back to the center-field shot. When the ball is hit to the outfield on the second pitch, not unheard of, we cut to the high home camera who starts to follow the ball, and then cut to the high third camera, the shag camera, who will have a close-up of the outfielder catching the ball. Now cut to a shot of the baserunner who realizes he is out and is trotting back to the dugout, then to a shot of the next batter with his graphic.

Ten seconds would be a long take during the game, maybe fifteen if a pitcher is real slow. Anything less than three or four seconds, except during a play, looks like a mistake.

Interspersed with this are shots of the crowd, which is where you get into personal philosophy. The game's exciting, you love to see people screaming, kids eating hot dogs, shots of a very pensive manager in a tight situation, that kind of thing, as long as you're not missing any action. You're very dependent on your crew to help find those things. You're thinking *variety*. There's a tendency for directors to get real cutesy when they're on the road and the game is dull, and find women in halter tops. The networks have what's called a T&A camera. One camera that does nothing but that, at least on the big games. I think it's overdone. I've never seen the research and I've got to believe the audience is a good deal male, but there's a lot of kids and there's a *lot* of shut-ins. I'm very, very sensitive to this. We don't want to offend anybody. I report to the station manager, who's a big sports fan and he's not adverse to calling me and saying: "You shoot too many women. Nothing wrong with it, but show us some kids, show us some old folks, show us a cross section, show us an enthused crowd."

There's very little chatter. The director gives the cues, the technical director actually pushes the buttons. Or you might just tell Camera Three, "If there's a pick-off at first, I'm coming to you," and then the technical director will push that button automatically. I don't hear much from the others unless there's a problem. "We lost Camera Three." Probably I hear most from the graphics operator, telling me that the graphic is good, no misspellings and it's the right one for this ballplayer. Then it's my option to put it in.

The announcers and I talk while we are in commercial. Bob or Joe might say, "Let's look at that last out. I think he was safe." During the broadcast I only hit the director-interrupt button when I want to alert them to something. At the very least I'm going to say, "Replay," just to get them to look down at the monitors because they tend to look at the field more than they do the monitors. If it's a home run, they know the replay is coming. I'll let the guy round the bases, let the crowd cheer, the tape's queued up and I hit the button and just say "Replay" or "Two replay," which means they're going to get it in slow motion and from another angle.

We are occasionally criticized that Torre explains the obvious. I don't agree because I think you have to cover the whole audience. There are a lot of astute fans, but there are people who don't know the subtleties of the game. We've also gotten criticized because Torre talks about spit balls or gouging the ball or throwing at batters. We'll get calls from fathers who are coaches of Little League teams saying, "This guy can't be throwing a spitter. It's not allowed."

Our stand is that Joe is both a former manager and a former catcher and if anybody knows, he knows. He can see it. He's *reporting*. I've rarely come down on him for that. We've had an on-going battle for Joe Torre's services. Everytime there is a manager's job open, he's generally approached. Prior to this season the Cubs were looking at him, and a few other teams. Now that he's got sixty games with us and thirty-five with a pay channel, the managing is looking less and less desirable to him. He's able to make a good living doing this, and it doesn't have the pressure that managing does, at least in his mind. We're willing to extend his contract for anything reasonable.

In addition to everything else going on in the truck, by the eighth or ninth inning you're also talking to somebody back here in L.A., and agreeing that if the game ends by 7:45, we'll get out and they'll run some sort of, I hate to use the word but that's what it is, fill program. They've got a variety of things to pick from here, maybe a *Happy Days* or *Laverne and Shirley*. On a Sunday it might be *The Three Stooges*. That's all laid out in advance, but if I cross, say, 7:47 or 7:48, they're going to want *me* to fill until the hour and start the movie clean at 8:00. So I may get into Joe Torre's ear in the middle of the ninth and tell him to be ready to do a post-game interview. He leaves Bob Starr and heads down to grab the player of the game. Say we've sent Joe down but now the game's been tied and goes into extra innings. We have to decide whether to start the movie late or dump the movie and get into an hour of extra innings. It would be really nice if there were a separate director and separate producer, like there is at the network level, but on the local level it tends to be the same person, for economics and other reasons.

It sounds corny to say, but the show is controlled chaos, and the producer-director is going to hear about it if it doesn't look right back home, no matter whether a cameraman screws up or an announcer makes a mistake. There's a certain amount of pressure there. *My* worst mistake was missing Rod Carew stealing home. I didn't even have it on replay. Right in the truck the phone rang. I knew who it was. The boss asked me if I was in the sauce, which is the last thing in the world I ever did prior to the game. Not even a beer, nothing.

I don't remember the details of the play but I guess there were runners on first and third and I was playing the odds, isolating on the runner at first. I should have known better. We weren't expecting it and by the time I cut to the play, Carew had already crossed the plate. We saw some dust.

WILLIAM WEISS

He works out of his house in San Mateo, California. Old pictures and files everywhere. Facts on the tip of his tongue: in 1949 there were fifty-nine minor leagues; today, seventeen. He's the statistician for the five minor leagues west of the Rockies.

I learned at a very young age that I was no athlete. If I wanted to have anything to do with baseball it certainly wouldn't be on the field. I was very much interested in baseball records and players' records—not just watching the game but the *statistics* of the game. Why does somebody want to be an actor? Statistics just seemed like a natural for me and it's what I decided I wanted to do in life.

One year I was trying to get the American League averages for a back year, and couldn't locate them. As you may know, the American League offices at that time were in Chicago, where I grew up. My father went up to the league office and asked if they had the averages I wanted. He got to talking to Dorothy Hummel, the American League secretary, and she said, "Why don't you have your son come down and see us?"

So I used to hang around the office on Saturday afternoons and go through the library of old record books and look up players' careers and that sort of thing. I was always more interested in minor-league players because you could find the backgrounds of the major-league players in *Who's Who in*

Baseball and *The Sporting News*. With the minor-league players you had to go back and pick them out year by year, going through the old baseball guides.

Then while I was in high school we had an amateur team and I was recruited by a friend who knew of my interest in record-keeping to keep the records, score the ball games, and prepare the averages.

After the war, when I was working in Chicago at a lot of odd jobs, the National Association, which ran the minor leagues and was located in Columbus, Ohio, sponsored a seminar for front-office personnel in the game, and hopefuls, because of the burgeoning number of minor leagues employing young men who had never had any contact with the business rules of baseball.

When you are job hunting you talk to anybody that looks promising. I struck up an acquaintance with another aspirant named Jim Burris, who later became president of the American Association, was general manager of the Denver ball club for many, many years, and is now in the real-estate business. Jimmy and I were standing on the street corner waiting for a bus, and a man not much older than ourselves—I would have been twenty-two by then—came along and asked, "Is this where you get the bus to go to 696 East Broad Street?" Well, that was the National Association address. We said yes and quickly introduced ourselves and this fellow turned out to be from Texas. His name was Howard Green and he was at that time president of the Class-D Longhorn League, which he had single-handedly organized the previous year. He was also half owner of the Abilene Blue Sox in the West Texas–New Mexico League. And so we got to talking and before I got off the bus I had a job.

He hired me to do the statistics for the Longhorn League and to work as his assistant with the Abilene Blue Sox, mainly running the box office out at the ballpark. This was my first job in baseball and I'll tell you it was a summer I'll never forget. Blue Sox Stadium is a great name but slightly grandiose for the facility, which had a big sign on the press box on the top of the roof that said DANGEROUS FOR OCCUPANCY BY MORE THAN SIX PERSONS. The offices of the Longhorn League and the Abilene Blue Sox were on the second floor of an old house near downtown Abilene, which was also where Howard and his wife lived. I had the spare bedroom, which also served as my office. It was *also* where they stored the surplus bats and tickets, and since there were twin beds in the room, I got to share the room with stray ballplayers that came and went, usually for their first night in town before they got situated.

I don't think I would trade that experience for anything. I got to see things both at the league level and at the club operation level. That Longhorn was quite a league. It had clubs in Ballinger, Del Rio, Big Springs, Midland, Odessa, Sweetwater, and Vernon, towns most people wouldn't even have heard of.

That was a great year, 1948, the year Bob Crues had sixty-nine home runs for Amarillo, which tied the then-existing record for the most homers by a player in a single season. He should have had seventy and the seventieth would have been in the Abilene ballpark, but you know how bad lights were back then, and the outfield lights in particular. The Abilene ballpark had a scoreboard above the center-field fence. If a ball hit the scoreboard it was a home run, even if it came back on the field. We had a center fielder, a young man from Sacramento named Gus Stathos who had the nickname of Grandstand Gus, the Galloping Greek. Crues hit a ball out to center field and from the stands you couldn't pinpoint exactly where it hit. The umpire said it hit the fence and was in play and Crues only got a double. After the game Stathos said the ball had hit the bottom part of the scoreboard. It should have been a home run.

And we had probably the two most one-sided consecutive games in baseball history between Midland and Del Rio. Del Rio was in last place from the day the season opened. Midland defeated Del Rio 31–0 and 40–4, and they had won 29–10, I believe, the day before the 31–0 game. In that 40–4 ball game, one pitcher went the whole game for Del Rio. Only 29 of the runs were earned. I didn't see it but I've got the scoresheet.

I don't really care for hot weather. We didn't have air conditioning in Abilene, and I think I spent the summer there, at least two and half months, without ever taking the bedspread off at night. I just flopped down on the bed as is. I started writing letters.

At that time, the statistics for the baseball leagues operating on the West Coast—the Pacific Coast League, California League, Sunset League, Far West League, and Western International League—were being kept by the Howe News Bureau in Chicago, an outfit that is now in Boston. I thought that I could sell those leagues on the idea that it would be more advantageous for them to have somebody locally situated. I came out to California to talk to the presidents. The Longhorn League season ended in Albuquerque and I got a ride west with Lynn Stone, our third baseman who lived in Long Beach and became the president and general manager of Churchill Downs race track, a far cry from playing third base with the Abilene

Blue Sox. He and his wife and their infant baby and all their household possessions and all my Longhorn League records were piled into an old Plymouth and we drove nonstop from Albuquerque to Los Angeles. I got off downtown. And to sum it up without taking all evening, by the next winter, the winter of 1948–49, I was hired by the California League and the Far West League to do their statistics and also to work in the office in San Francisco.

Then the next year I got the big plum, which was the Pacific Coast League. Again, the good fortune of just being in the right place at the right time. When I had first passed through Los Angeles I had gone up to the Pacific Coast League offices and become acquainted with the public-relations director. The following winter I was coming out to San Francisco from Chicago but there was a bad series of snowstorms and the trains were re-routed by way of Los Angeles. So I stopped over and went to see my friend and while I was sitting there Clarence Rowland, the league president, walked in. He said, "Do you think you'd be able to do the Pacific Coast League records, too?"

The Pacific Coast League is right next to the major leagues and when I was able to get my breath back I said yes. I also picked up the old Sunset League, so I left the job as an assistant to the president of the California and Far West leagues and my folks came out here from Chicago—I wasn't married at the time—and we bought this house in San Mateo and settled in. That was 1950, and I've been here ever since.

We have done different leagues over the years, but right now, and for some time, it's been the same ones: Pioneer, Northwest, California, Pacific Coast, and this year we've added the new league they are starting in Arizona, a short-season league at the rookie level for the signees out of high school and Latin America who are not quite ready for the Pioneer or the Northwest.

The Howe bureau in Boston does the statistics for all the minor leagues east of the Rockies, and Elias does the major leagues. The Elias bureau is the premiere sports statistician, period.

I can't say that I've ever been that fascinated in the type of thing that Bill James is so well known for, a greatly expanded idea of what statistics are and what they mean. I don't think you can do much in the way of *predicting* from statistics. Statistics tell you what has happened, period. It's a tool. A friend of mine once worked for the Oakland A's and likes to tell the story about Charley Finley and the late Ray Swallow, his farm director. This would be probably around 1969, 1970. Ray would come into Finley's office and give him all these statistics about a particular player they were thinking about bringing up and Finley would sit there and listen and fidget and then say in this stentorian voice of his, "Cut the crap. Can he play or can't he?"

I think James is all wet regarding minor-league players, saying on the basis of what they did in the minors what they should have done had they gotten to the major leagues. No way. Fresco Thompson was the farm director for the Los Angeles Dodgers for many years and he summed it up very well, I think, in referring to players who seemed to do exceptionally well in Triple-A, say, and never cut it in the majors. Thompson's phrase was, "He has reached the level of his competence."

However, some of the things that they do with baseball statistics are certainly of interest and of value in evaluating a particular player, like why one .280 hitter is a lot more valuable than another .280 hitter. One of the most fascinating statistics of that type is what Pat Tabler with Kansas City does with bases loaded. It's amazing. He has a batting average of over .500. One of the really weird statistics of present-day baseball is that man's ability to get base hits with the bases loaded.

The fascination with this whole thing is watching the players day by day, week by week, month by month, year by year, how they progress or fail, how well they do in certain circumstances, the streaks, the spurts, the slumps, all facets of the game, players' career records as well as the day-by-day happenings.

The basics of the job are still the same: batting records, pitching records, fielding records. There has been an expansion in the number of columns, partly because of rule changes such as the game-winning RBI and saves, which became a part of the official rules in 1969, but the biggest change is in the transmission of information rather than in the information itself. Everything used to come by mail, so they couldn't be real up-to-date.

The official scoresheet is filled out by the official scorer at each ballpark. Depending on whether you have a 1–0 or a 14–12 game, it takes anywhere from twenty minutes to an hour for him to put that all down on paper. Then he sends it in here on the FAX machine. This is kind of an odd operation because it's in my home. We have the FAX machine up front because all that stuff comes in at night and we're usually up in the front part of the home at night and it's easy to hear the beeper. I like to see the reports as they come in to make sure that the transmission was okay, and that, at first glance, they didn't leave out the fielding records and that sort of thing. It's a standard form. The major leagues use a similar form. The column headings are the same and in the same order throughout baseball.

Then sometime between midnight and two A.M. I sit down and go over each report to see that it proves out, to see that there isn't some mistake. You add the columns to see if the addition is correct, check the one team's offensive statistics against the other team's pitching and defensive statistics. They have to equal out. Putouts have to equal three times the number of innings pitched, and so on. You go horizontally and make sure that each position in the batting order has a proper number of plate appearances. Sometimes the scorer will just put a figure on a wrong line and you'll wind up with a batter in the number-three position having four plate appearances and the batter in the number-four position having *five* appearances, which can't be right. If there's a problem I just type out a note and send it out on the FAX machine the next morning to the ball club office for the scorer to give me the correction.

We'll have probably five games in the Coast League, five from the California League, four in the Northwest, four in the Pioneer, and two in the new Arizona State League. Steve Puccinelli works for me, and the Northwest League and the Arizona State League are his exclusively. I just hand Steve the scoresheets in the morning.

After we get the scoresheets checked, the information is entered onto the individual player's record. I hope we will have computers in place a year from now, but at the present time we are still doing it manually. This has been a labor-intensive occupation, but not a very costly product to produce. Calculater, typewriter, duplicater, and FAX machine are all you need. The rest of it is your time and elbow grease.

Each player has his own sheet with the same column headings as the official report. That information is posted each day. My wife does that, then she gives me the sheets and I sit down and bang out the calculations, the percentages, the ERAs. Once a week all of this is tallied and we prepare and send out the weekly statistics.

Of course, you always get phone calls during the day from people wanting some specific information. For instance, at the beginning of a home stand the home team needs some statistics on the visiting team that they can't get from the club itself. Well, it takes me about fifteen minutes to do that and send it to them on the FAX machine. And there's always the call asking for something specific about a given ballplayer or a team for some reporter who's preparing something for radio or television or for a newspaper story.

For the California League I've been writing a weekly newsletter, and that's a lot of fun. It goes to media, major-league organizations, the national publications, *The Sporting News, Baseball America,* the ball clubs, of course. I'm always on the lookout for fodder for the newsletter. I subscribe to a lot of newspapers that I go through at night picking out things that I need for future reference.

I get to see some California League games from time to time down in San Jose, but I miss being closer to the field. For about twenty-five years here I was president of the Peninsula Winter League, which was started by some of the major-league clubs for some of the amateur players there were interested in, and some kids from the farm system that weren't going to one of the other winter leagues. But they kind of lost interest and it just passed out of existence a few years ago because we couldn't get enough teams to make it go. But that was fascinating because I got to see so many players who became major-league stars before they ever signed a professional contract—Keith Hernandez, and, going back to the first days of the league, Jim Fregosi, Tommy Harper, Willie Stargell, Joe Morgan, Larry Bowa, Bud Harrelson. All these players were in our winter league right here in San Mateo county before they ever became household names.

Winter is more of the same except you don't have game reports coming in every day. It takes a couple of months to get the final official averages ready and bring the record books up to date, and before you know it it's time for another season. It's a little less hectic and you don't put in as many hours during the day and there's more freedom. If you want to shut up shop for a day or two and go somewhere you can. Can't do that during the season. I enjoy historical research and last winter I was doing something on the old California League, going back to the nineteenth century. For example, in 1892 the San Jose ball club played a 177-game season, and except for three or four games, *two* pitchers pitched the entire season. One pitcher pitched over 800 innings. That's a career for most pitchers nowadays. I don't know what their arms were made of. One of the two actually got to the majors. His name was George Harper. The one who pitched the 800-plus innings, J. D. Lookabaugh, kind of disappeared a couple of years down the road. Probably threw his arm out.

B U S   S A I D T

A baseball writer whose first love is baseball broadcasting.

No one really knows how I got the nickname. My father and I were both Harold, and the "Bus" isn't short for Buster or anything.

I was born and raised in Trenton, New Jersey. My friends called me "Mr. Baseball." I played the game at the American Legion ranks, obviously was not good enough to play the game professionally, but I was determined to do something in the baseball structure, someway, somehow. I went to work as an accountant for the city of Trenton, at the same time stringing for the *Trenton Times* newspapers, covering all sports, including the professional club in Trenton at that time, in the Interstate League. This is before World War II.

In the service I was a cryptographer in Algiers for a little more than three years. We had the good fortune to have a commanding officer who felt that baseball was very, very crucial to the morale of the troops. Playing in the North African GI League we had a pretty good ball club, which included the MPs, the pill rollers [medics], and us. We were called the Lids —the "lid" was the keying device for Morse code. The commissioner was a great old ballplayer named Zeke Bonura. Ray Shore, a minor-league pitcher and now a Phillies scout, was on our team—the Bob Feller of North Africa.

We won the league, and since we were a radio outfit we set up a radio network. By this time I wasn't playing so I broadcast the game riding around in a jeep from first to third base, and back behind home plate. And lo and behold, inasmuch as most of the fellows weren't used to hearing baseball broadcasts, they enjoyed the broadcasts and I said to myself, "I can do it." I had always been a student of baseball broadcasters, techniques, and styles— Mel Allen, Red Barber, Ernie Harwell, the giants of the business.

After the service I had in the back of my mind, "I can broadcast baseball." Of course as a kid I had invented my own baseball game, sitting up in the attic, and I called my own games. *Before* the war, by the way, games weren't broadcast nearly as broadly as people imagine. For example, there were no broadcasts in Philadelphia until 1936, nor in New York till '39. The three New York teams had a working agreement among themselves not to broadcast baseball. There was a deep bias against broadcasting in some elements, particularly in the Northeast, under the assumption it would cut down attendance. In 1939 Larry MacPhail told the others he was going to break loose and he brought Red Barber in. Then they all had to go that way. Lo and behold, they found that it *increased* attendance.

After the war, WBUD went on the air in the Trenton area and I applied for the job as sports director. They called me over there one day late in 1946 and the guy said, "Read me something out of the *Philadelphia Inquirer* sports section."

So I read him something.

He said, "Fine, you'll hear from me later."

A month went by and I called up and asked how I made out in the audition. Guy said he had one more person to hear. At four o'clock one day he called and said, "You know we're on the air today and you're the sports director. You have a fifteen-minute show at six P.M."

I was in that job for twenty-two years, until 1969. We did the Trenton Giants, owned by the New York Giants, and it was an excellent team, turning out Robin Roberts, Curt Simmons, George Kell. By today's standards it would be a Double-A team, at least, and it was a B-team then, a designation based on the population of the city. No one had heard radio broadcasts in the area, so it was virgin territory, and the public's reception was fantastic. I was everything, play-by-play and engineer. I put the equipment in the back of the car, went on the air all by myself. I never made more than $10 a game, and if I was out of town they deducted what I would have been paid for my regular sports show, which I couldn't do. It never occurred to me to be upset by this because broadcasting baseball was such a pleasure. I was *learning* the game. I went to Florida for the first time in the spring of 1950, where the Giants' minor-league teams trained in Sanford. I was doing interviews every day and I was in *heaven*.

I was privileged to dine with Mel Ott, Carl Hubbell, Leo Durocher. When we were on the road we'd go up to the manager's room after the game—hot summer nights—and drink a beer, talk baseball, talk game situations, hit-and-run, why they did this, why they did that. Nothing more charming in the world than talking with a veteran manager like Tommy Heath or Frank Genovese, Willie Mays's first manager.

I was the first broadcaster to put a microphone in Mays's face. Willie Mays joined the Trenton baseball club in May of 1950. I went to the railroad station with Bill McKechnie, Jr., who was the GM of the club, to pick up *Junior* Mays, nineteen years old, just in from Birmingham, Alabama. We drove him to Hagerstown, Maryland, which was the farthest outpost in the Interstate League—below the Mason-Dixon Line. Mays was the first black player in the Interstate League, and the reaction was . . . mixed. I did the first broadcasting of Mays in his first year in organized baseball.

I have auditioned for many, many broadcasting jobs in the major leagues. I never learned how to get over the final barrier. I knew people in high places, in advertising agencies. Mel Allen worked very, very hard for me, trying to get me into a major-league spot, because he had heard me and was impressed by my enthusiasm. I auditioned for the Yankees in 1951, when Curt Gowdy left Mel Allen to go to Boston. Also in that audition— just to show how baseball broadcasting was going in those days—was Bill Frawley, from *I Love Lucy,* and Bud Palmer, the former Princeton basketball star who also played for the Knicks. He was a greeter for the city of New York and had never broadcast a baseball game in his life.

They selected a guy named Art Gleason, who had been an old buddy of Casey Stengel's in California.

Then the jock suddenly started to appear in the broadcast booth. I had never dreamed I would have to fight ex-ballplayers. Phil Rizzuto came in, and then other players. And the minor leagues began to distintegrate as TV began to emerge. Sadly, sadly. By 1953 there was no Interstate League. The Trenton club died after the '59 season because they couldn't get a lease.

After the New York audition, Mel Allen told me to hang tough because something would come along. My audition material, taken right off the air, was accepted by many people: "Hey, you're our guy!" But all of those offers seemed to be lateral moves.

Then I had some really heartbreaking experiences.

I was hired by Binghamton, New York, in the Eastern League in about 1953, which in those days was a major step to New York, and I was about to go to spring training with them, when suddenly the guy lost his broadcast rights. Then I was hired to broadcast the St. Paul Saints, the Triple-A ball club for the Dodgers, and the GM called me up and said a one-time Dodger pitcher named Rex Barney, who had pitched a no-hitter in the big leagues, had decided he wanted to be an announcer, and they were going to use him.

Probably the greatest disappointment was about 1960. The Phillies fired Gene Kelly. This looked like the real opportunity. I was well known in Philadelphia by this time. All the strategies were in motion. My father was the media-relations director for the American Legion for the state of New Jersey, and in that capacity he worked with John Farrell, the president of Ballantine Beer in Newark. They were a major sponsor of the Phillies. My father came home one day that winter and said, "You got the Phillies job. Farrell just told me at lunch. He didn't know you were my son."

Nobody told *me,* though. Within the next seventy-two hours I had calls from Philadelphia sports editors saying, "Hear you got that job."

It never happened. Went to a broadcaster named Frank Sims, with no explanation. Not that they owed me one. Nobody with the Phillies had ever told me I had the job. But how did the rest of the world think I was going to be the broadcaster?

So then it began drifting away. I blame myself as much as anybody. I didn't make myself a nuisance enough to get someone to say, "Ah, go ahead." In 1964 I had the opportunity to move into the newspaper business as a daily sports columnist for the *Trentonian,* the morning tabloid—my first full-time job outside accounting. I was still doing the radio talk show. I did the column for two and a half years.

In '67 I went with the *Trenton Times* newspapers, and I've been there ever since. I'm a combined columnist and writer. I cover a baseball game every day of the season, either Philadelphia or New York: the Phillies when they're home; when they're on the road I go straight to New York—the Yankees usually, because the Mets are usually gone when Philadelphia is. I'm always on the road: the Yankees are 150 miles away; Philadelphia about 76 miles round trip. Shea Stadium out the Brooklyn-Queens Expressway? There's no such thing as an easy way to get there.

I get to the stadium in Philadelphia for a seven-thirty game about five o'clock. At Yankee Stadium I'm there about three o'clock, because of the traffic conditions on the George Washington Bridge. Pretty much the same at Shea, because of the hazards getting there. Fill the time talking to other writers, ballplayers.

If one of the teams is in contention by the third week in August, we switch our attention and I travel on the road with the team that has a chance to win the pennant. I've covered every World Series since 1946, plus play-offs, winter meetings.

I see 180 baseball games a year, and every time I write about it, I want it to be special. I do very little play-by-play, very little description in my columns. Pick up the *Trenton Times* any day after a Phillies game the night before, and if my column works, the angle will be interesting to you. The score will be there, the key plays, but the rest is column. Right there, finding the angle, is what separates the men from the boys, whether you're a good columnist or just a columnist working at a job. Something *always* happens. It's always there. You just have to call on your vast reservoir of experience. I'm proud to say this: the late Dick Young, the epitome of the hard-nosed, hard-working, down-in-the-trenches sportswriter, had no facility for turning phrases, but he rarely if ever wrote a column that wasn't interesting. I'm not the dinosaur he was, but I hope that everything I write is challenging to the reader, informative, but with a light sense of humor. I'm a tough critic of myself, and I want to be regarded as one of the best.

To paraphrase Will Rogers: "I've never seen a ball game I didn't like, but I'll make an exception in this case"? I don't feel that way. There's never been a *day* in the years I've been doing this that I haven't looked forward to going to the ballpark. It's still so much fun. In winter meetings, we sit around and make up trades ourselves, follow the rumors. Baseball probably only needs three weeks of spring training, but I'm happy it's longer. Renewing friendships with scouts, managers, the whole social aspect of baseball is terrific. My wife comes down every spring. Pre-season *football?* It's like watching paint peel.

The tradition in baseball. It has its phonies and jerks, but the game withstands all the donkeys, in a lot of cases, who administer and run it—the frauds and carpetbaggers. I'm not a Peter Ueberroth fan. I'm scared to death what he might do before he moves on. He might champion inter-league play. I don't like it. I'm an unabashed baseball purist.

I have a reputation for being very caustic about Steinbrenner, whom I only refer to as "Steinbrenner the Owner," never anything else. I think George kind of likes me, but our problems go back to when he introduced the by-invitation-only press conference for major announcements. It began with the firing of Dick Howser in 1979. The press conference was held at Tavern on the Green in Central Park. Lo and behold, Steinbrenner the Owner invites *thirteen* people. All the suburban newspapers that cover the Yankees, including me, are excluded. Now, I've been driving over there for almost twenty-five years. What kind of statement is he making to my newspaper and its readers, the Yankee fans of central New Jersey, when he absolutely bars my participation in a major announcement?

I was very, very upset and knocked off a three-page, single-spaced letter to him. And a column, of course. He responds to me with a very kind letter, saying that I was absolutely right, that he had something in mind that didn't work out, and that all he can say is that he'll certainly try to see that it never happens again. Well, this letter got into the hands of an editor at the

New York Post, and "Page Six" one day ran a thing that said, "Veteran New Jersey scribe bests Steinbrenner," or something like that—"earns apology" —which is big news I guess.

This "private"press conference business has happened *again* and *again* and *again*. I have a drawerful of letters, always apologizing. So what do I make of this?

The more the team wins, the better the whole atmosphere, the easier the job. More people are reading the stuff. And we're all egotists in one way or the other.

Baseball writing today is much better because the writers approach the game better. Read pre–World War II baseball writing. Those writers wouldn't be caught dead in the clubhouse. They wrote from their own expertise and frequently it didn't make any difference because they didn't know why the manager did a certain thing. Ballplayers will tell you today, "You saw it, go ahead and write it." In those days, they did. Pull out their typewriters, get the Western Union man over, and twenty minutes after the game they were having a martini.

The *clubhouse* writing began late in the forties as television began to have an impact. Writers, led by Dick Young and some of the famous New York by-liners, understood that they had to get something else, a different angle.

Most of the writers today have a better education. Without disparaging the old-time writers, most of them got their jobs as office boys. Branch Rickey once said there wasn't a baseball writer in the world he couldn't buy for a steak. Well, that's bull. But there is a buddy system in journalism today. The guys make a conference call every week and exchange information: so and so has a bad heel, so-and-so got locked up for being drunk. Then you can see the same column in different form in Boston and Dallas.

But the truth is that among young fellows, younger writers, the job of baseball writer is not a great job anymore. Newspapers have a lot of trouble getting guys to cover major-league baseball because it's not conducive to a happy marriage. I'm divorced and re-married, and baseball had something to do with it.

Too many young guys have the feeling that baseball was invented as a vehicle for their writing talent. And in my opinion there are far too many quotes in baseball writing. Way out of line. But that's peer pressure. If you don't get quotes, your editor or somebody is going to say, "Hey, aren't players talking?" But you *know* what the guy's gonna say out of the cliché catalogue: "Well, I just wanted to stay within my limitations and give it my best shot while just looking to put the ball in play." Every fourth day the player says exactly the same thing. Frequently I don't even go down to the clubhouse, often because of the deadlines.

My late friend Moe Berg, a major-league catcher from about 1924 to 1940, primarily with the White Sox and Red Sox, was probably the first Ivy League graduate to play in the major leagues. He was also a graduate of the Sorbonne and spoke eight languages. A PBS documentary is being made of his life. He died in 1972. He was a lawyer, licensed to practice before the Supreme Court, but baseball was the overwhelming passion of his life. We used to talk about the subject of quotes. He ridiculed them.

The players could also be a factor why young baseball writers leave the job. A lot of time you feel as though you're walking up hat in hand: "Please, Mr. Gibson, would you kindly help me . . . "

"Nah! Not today! Get out of here!"

There is too much of that stuff. The player who knows how to handle this is the happier player with a better shot at everything. Definitely. Baseball is filled with very sharp young guys. That's a pleasure.

In many cases it's a very uncomfortable atmosphere in clubhouses. *Adversarial* is the right word. My own credo is that when I approach a baseball player and he acts in any way as if I'm bothering him, I just say "Thank you" and walk away. I don't grumble, like a lot of my colleagues, about what a jerk he is. I'll find somebody else.

Jerry Grote probably had the worst reputation. I remember going in there after a guy pitched a one-hitter against the Phillies, and I went over to Grote, who caught the game, and said casually, "I guess you'd like to have the one pitch back. What happened on that? How were you pitching to that guy?"

He says, "What the . . . No matter what I say you, you wouldn't write it right anyway."

I say, "You ever read anything I wrote?" The ballplayers have no idea who wrote what story, nor do the readers.

"No, but you're all the same."

There's a lot of misunderstanding about all this. Major-league teams are having clinics with their players. This is excellent. And baseball players are very insecure for good reason. I remind my readers that the ballplayers' peak earning period is very short, and it hinges on every pitch. That accounts for a lot of strange behavior. Plus the Latins feel uncomfortable because of the language difficulty.

But there's still too much of the Willie Hernandez business—throwing water on the writer. That's subhuman behavior. Now you read that Jim Campbell, the president of the Tigers, when asked about it said, "Well, I didn't see it." Bill Lajoie, the personnel director, says it was a fun thing. And where's Ueberroth? When boors do something like that they must be punished.

I'd only change this job for baseball broadcasting. I daydream: Bill Giles, the owner and president of the Phillies, says, "Oh, we've got a little problem here. Harry Kalas, our number-one man, has to do a Notre Dame basketball game, and our other man, Andy Musser, is doing something else. We don't have anybody to broadcast the game." I say, "Hey, tomorrow? I'll do the game, don't worry about it." He giggles and that's it, but I've always maintained if anyone put me behind the mike at a major-league baseball game I could stay there as long as there was baseball.

But there are only a couple of hundred writers in the baseball fraternity. Feature writers are not members. I value the card. I'm proud and privileged to carry this card, the same as a licensed engineer or M.D. or CPA. As I said, I wanted to be close to this game, and when I got my first Baseball Writers' Card I wrote a column saying just this: I'm not a lawyer or CPA, but I'm a baseball writer, and I've got the card to prove it.

11
PLAY
AT THE
PLATE

Like a lot of catchers today, he doesn't look like one, and he bristles at the persistence of the old image. Medium height, medium weight, medium talent —he's your basic ballplayer on a rollercoaster in Atlanta. The Braves set the record for consecutive victories to start a season (thirteen in 1982, tied by Milwaukee in '87) and the National League record for losses at the start (ten in 1988). He was on the All-Star Team in 1983 and was unceremoniously benched in '84. He has a wisecrack for every situation, and a sharp insight to go along with it.

In 1976 I was playing what you would call semi-pro ball in Eureka, California. We played whoever we could get a game with. It's way up north where you find yeties and Big Foot and things like that roaming the mountains. A guy named Lou Bonomi, notorious in that league, had found me just through word of mouth from some people that had played with me the previous summer in Virginia. Lou was a great guy. I worked in his little neighborhood grocery store as the meat-cooler guy during the day and then played ball at night.

This was the summer after my third year at the University of Nebraska at Omaha. I wanted to play baseball but you don't know anything about pro ball or who drafts you or what. My dad called me up at Lou's grocery store and said, "You got drafted."

"What round?"

"Fifth round."

"Who?"

"The Braves."

"The Braves? Never heard of them."

I had talked to the Mets—the guy came to my house, checked my eyes and everything—but they ended up drafting a catcher from Missouri instead of me. And my dad was sort of a bird dog for the Cardinals. The Braves kind of took me by surprise.

The Braves bring all their draftees in for a couple of days and work them out, so my dad and I flew down to Atlanta and I walked into the clubhouse and put on a uniform. I caught eighteen innings that day. I was a little tired at the end but you had so much excitement because everybody was watching you, and after the second day of the workout Bill Lucas, who was general manager of the Braves and is deceased now, met me and my dad up in his office.

He said, "This is what I've got for you," and the total package came to about $25,000. He talked to us and then said, "I'll leave you alone for a few minutes," and he walked out.

My dad looked at me and said, "Well, you want to play or you don't. Sign it or not."

I said, "We came to play," so we called him back in and I proceeded to misspell my name on the contract. That's how excited I was. The thing about that is, as I'm sure you are well aware, you've got a little bit of bargaining power when you are a junior because you can threaten to go back to school for your senior year. But I wanted to play.

I had started out as a center fielder, actually, but when you are little you play them all, and our catcher didn't show up one day for practice so I said, well, I'll put the stuff on, and I've had it on ever since. I kind of liked that ball beating at me; and my dad, who was a pitcher in the minor leagues for ten years in the Yankee and Cardinal organizations, told me if you want a chance to get a college scholarship, catching or pitching is the way to do it. That's what they still say.

A couple of times, when I was getting hit by the ball just about every other pitch and guys were stealing and running all over hell, I thought maybe I'd like to be in the outfield stepping on bees, you know, but then I'd say no, not really, I wanna be hit by the ball, I wanna be taggin' guys out at home, 'cause you get your picture in the paper and it goes all over the country!

I was just average size for a catcher, and I think I'm just average size now. That stigma or that label that you have to be some big bruiser, or the fat, stubby, muddy guy, or the guy who got the short straw in order to catch, those have all sort of gone by the wayside. It's a little bit more of a glamor position than it used to be.

I went to Kingsport, Tennessee, in the rookie league and we played at Kingsport High School. You're playing on a high-school field again and your training room is the science classroom and you don't have a locker. We had two-a-day practices and then we played that night. Stayed at a place called Sheila's Townhouse Motel. What a spot! All it was was a room and on the side of the wall was a toilet and outside was a Coke machine and a phone booth for almost daily calls to Mom and Dad. I lived with the short-stop on our team, Jim Wessinger—great guy, he got to the big leagues for a cup of coffee and that was it. We had no refrigerator or anything. We kept a big ice chest filled with meat, cheese, milk, juice, stuff like that. We didn't really have a car and walked everywhere and, God, we were really rich. We cleared about $176 dollars every two weeks. The motel was $100 a month.

Welcome to pro ball.

I'm telling you, that's where a lot of people are weeded out because they have gone to these fabulous baseball institutions in college and the next thing you know they are sitting on a bus for ten or fourteen hours every three or four days and that's a shock, and you're handing them seven or eight dollars a day to eat on, and they're on their own for lodging and that country-club thing is gone. But it didn't make any difference to me. I was a pro ballplayer and no matter what it was, it was great.

I threw out the first twelve or thirteen guys that tried to steal, something like that, and I ended up throwing out nineteen of twenty-five, so I got moved up. I was only there three weeks. No, about four weeks.

So I left Sheila's Townhouse Motel and I was going to Greenwood, South Carolina. One of the club people—can't remember his name now—picked me up at the airport and we went back to his place and I stayed with him in a trailer about the size of a . . . it wasn't very big. He said, "Here, you sleep in this room," and there was a mattress sitting on some cement blocks. That was it. He was a smoker and you could have taken an empty cigarette package and thrown it in the drawer, shut the drawer, and I'm sure the mice would have had it shredded by morning. That's where I stayed.

Welcome to A-ball.

We rode around in an old school bus called the Blue Bird, which was legendary because it had been around for 250 years and it had no air conditioning and the seats were straight upright. The only time you got some sleep it was beer-induced.

In Lynchburg, the Mets had these guys about eight feet tall throwing about 200 miles an hour, it just seemed like. Boom, boom. They were all trying to beat Seaver and they kicked the hell out of us. One night, we played in the mud and put our shin guards and all of our stuff on top of the luggage rack and the ride took so long that everything dried out. So dried-out that sand and dirt started falling down on top of our manager Gene Hassell's head, and he thought that we were throwing mud at him. We get home about two-thirty in the morning and here are the wives out there waiting to take their husbands home and Hassell's mad because he thinks someone's been throwing dirt balls at him, so he kept us in the clubhouse for about an hour trying to get someone to admit to doing it. Finally a pitcher named Lamar Jones said, "All right, Skip, I did it. Let us go."

Our man Gene. He was great. Tiny little man with a big voice, real loud and boisterous, demonstrative-type person. We called him the little general. Early Times man. And this is weird. He had played with my father, and his first wife—he was now on his second marriage—took my mother to the hospital when I was born! How about that story? Now I'm playing for the guy! Every time I'd come around third he'd go, "Your daddy would be proud of you, boy. I'll tell your daddy you're doing a good job."

I don't think I hit that good there, only about .230 or .240, one homer, a couple of doubles, seven or eight RBIs, but I was catching real good, so after about three weeks I went to Savannah, Georgia, Double-A. I went to three classifications in one year: Rookie, A and Double-A. That was fast. They just wanted to see what I could do at other levels.

It was August in Savannah and Grayson Stadium was just a sand pit. I thought that the mosquito and the gnat were co-captain state birds of Georgia. Oh God! There was only one thing that could get them away from you, and that was called Skin-So-Soft. The Avon lady used to come to the ballpark and sell us this stuff. It had this horrible odor to it and it was just like putting Raid on. I mean, everybody was just taking a bath in it and I'm not so sure the Skin-So-Soft people enjoyed that, but it worked like a charm, I'm telling you, it really did.

The manager was Tommy Aaron, Hank's brother who died of leukemeia. He was a helluva guy. I played the rest of the season there and hit about .280, .288, and played pretty good.

I got invited to the major-league camp in the spring, very exciting stuff. I was nervous and I didn't know anybody or anything about the big leagues. I was just happy to be there. We had a utility infielder by the name of Craig Robinson. We were hittin' one day and I picked up his bat and started swinging with it. He looked at me and he said, "Rookie, don't ever pick up my bat again unless I tell you it's all right."

Boy, that scared the shit out of me. I remember it like it happened yesterday. I thought, Jesus, this guy's a little testy or something, but really he was just doggin' me. I didn't know. I didn't know what the attitude was and I was seeing guys I had watched on TV and I'm in camp with them, you know.

Dale Murphy, who was catching then, was ahead of me. They were trying to get him ready to go to the big leagues but he really faltered in that spring training. He screwed it all up. He played so bad they had to send him back to Triple-A, so that's why I went to Double-A in 1977, in Savannah. I spent the whole year there and got Double-A player of the country, catcher of the country, and Topps Bubble Gum Double-A player of the year. I was starting to get the feeling that I was good enough to play; I could make it, maybe.

We were in the playoffs and Hank Aaron came and watched our game and I went 4 for 4. *The Sporting News* ran a big article on me and Hank said I was ready to play in the big leagues. I was getting a reputation as a line-drive hitter and a great defensive ballplayer—well, not great, but a really solid defensive catcher. We played 142 games back then and I caught 125 of them. I was pooped at the end.

I had spring training with the big team again in 1978, and I thought that I would play the whole year in Triple-A in Richmond because I needed the experience. Murphy was still the phenom catcher but he was having trouble throwing the ball. He had this mental block about throwing to second base—wild, you know, one hop into center field—and he tore his knee so they eventually had to get him out of there. And then Biff Pocoroba got a bad arm.

So on August 16 we were playing Tidewater and we just got our brains beat in and Tommy Aaron called everybody in and told us to sit down. We thought we were going to get yelled at. But he said, "I want everybody to congratulate Bruce Benedict because he's going to the major leagues." You know, even when I talk about it now I get kind of misty. When you're in the minor leagues you're so close to these people you play with because you don't have much money. You depend on each other for rides and meals and stuff like that. I can remember that after a ball game in Double-A in Knoxville, say, we'd go to the concession stand and buy up all the popcorn and all the hot dogs and all the beer and put it in sacks and share it with everybody on the bus. Those are the things that you remember right there. In the minors, the *only* thing you have to offer each other is your friendship. You were growing together, learning together. You did have more fun.

Up here, everybody gets in their big car and drives to their big house and stays in it, and they have families. You have some friendships, but nothing like in the minors. Lifelong friendships are developed in the minor leagues. Rick Mahler and I have been buddies since 1976, best of buddies. We played together almost every year. Glenn Hubbard, with the Oakland A's now, I did play with him *every* year that I was in pro ball, from 1976 up till this year.

So anyway, everybody congratulated me and it was the longest ride back to Richmond that I had ever taken in my life. I just wanted to get packed and go, you know. I put on my three-piece denim and flew to St. Louis. Top of the world. I called my dad and I got a telegram from my high school girlfriend saying, "We made it." We weren't together at the time, but she sent me that telegram. I got to St. Louis on the seventeenth of August and didn't play that day. I remember just walking in and sitting down and not knowing anybody, being afraid and insecure. Guys came up and said, "How're you doing?" You know. They try to make you feel comfortable but you're scared to death, you're absolutely scared to death. You're so intimidated that you just start all over. You've left those warm confines of your minor league team, your buddies, too, and you kind of feel like a lost child for a while.

The next day I was sittin' in the bullpen and we were losing 5–2, 7–2, something like that, it was in the ninth inning and Bobby Cox calls down: "Send Benedict up here. He's the fourth hitter."

Two quick outs, then Darrell Chaney, with two strikes, got a base hit to right field.

Clear as a bell in my mind: standing in the on-deck circle, walking to home plate for the first time, walking up there, Ted Simmons the catcher for the Cardinals, guy by the name of Tom Bruno pitching, big right-hander. I step in the box, give Teddy this kind of sheepish look, you know, I'm scared to death and say, "How ya doin'?" I was standing on virgin territory and swung at the first pitch, a fast ball, and lined a base hit to left field—the first pitch I saw in the major leagues.

On my twenty-third birthday I got the hit that you work your whole life for. Once I got that hit, it didn't make any difference anymore. Nothing mattered anymore. I said to myself, I don't know how long I'm gonna play or how well I'm gonna play, but I've fulfilled a dream of sorts and do what you want to with it, now.

That girl who sent me the telegram that said, "We made it" is now my wife. Her name is Kathleen and we have three kids.

In 1979, I spent the whole year in the major leagues, though I didn't play regularly. We had Joe Nolan, Pocoroba, and myself. I was the third catcher and I don't remember how many times I batted, but I hit .225. I was happy because I was still learning at another level. Poco's arm wasn't right and Joe Nolan was not an everyday player and I thought if I hang on here, I'll get my chances.

So I got married at the end of that season and had a great spring in '80. On March 28, my son Christopher was born, about one week before we left spring training. I went to Bobby Cox who was managing and said, "Bobby, do you mind if I drive my wife to Atlanta? She's just had a baby and I don't want to leave them."

He said, "You're asking the wrong manager. You need to be asking the Triple-A manager."

"Why?"

" 'Cause we don't have room for you. We think Pocoroba's back from his arm operation and we're gonnna give him a chance to play every day. Joe Nolan's gonna be our back-up catcher. We want you to play every day because you didn't get to play that much last year and we don't want you to go backwards. You're an everyday player.

"If something happens to Pocoroba, I guarantee you'll be called back up and play every day."

And so down to Richmond I go. I was disappointed, which you should be, and unhappy, but not mad. The thorn in my side was that my wife and I had had the *foresight* to come to Atlanta before spring training and get an apartment. We had the baby's room all set up. So we had to take a trailer and go back to Atlanta and pack up some stuff. We kept the apartment, though.

A week after we got to Richmond and to the minute when we got everything set up in an apartment, to the *minute,* I'm out there telling the grounds-crew guy after the ball game on a Saturday afternoon about how to fill up these deep holes in the batters' box and the general manager comes out and says Atlanta just called and Pocoroba's got a bad arm.

"They want you in Atlanta tomorrow night."

So I put my wife and *two-week-old baby* in the car with the trailer and we go to Atlanta and arrive at four in the morning. I knock on Gene Garver's door—we were buddies—and we stayed with him.

I was really starting to believe in baseball and the organization. I had heard that promises weren't kept all the time. Bobby Cox kept his and I went out and played every day. I hit .250 or .260 and it was the start of a real good three- or four-year period. In 1981, the strike year, I made the All-Star team and then in '82 we won the division championship under Joe Torre. That year I hit a grand slam off Fernando Valenzuela in Atlanta, and I'm telling you ten times a week people *still* come up to me and say, "I was at that game. I saw it."

We had gotten this guy named Matt Sinatro—another catcher, who's now playing a little bit for Oakland—and they gave him the job for, like, six weeks and said, "The job is yours. See if you can keep it." Well, he couldn't, so they came back to me, and in the third or fourth game I was starting, the Dodgers walked Glenn Hubbard to load the bases to get to me. First pitch a curve ball in the dirt. Next pitch a grand slam off the fat

Mexican. Dusty Baker's playing left. He watches it go over the fence. I got it on tape. I cry every time I see it. Darrell Chaney, the best man at my wedding, was announcing for the Braves, he and Ernie Johnson. I hear them, and the crowd's so loud. It helped us go on and win the pennant on the last day, but we lost to the Cardinals in the playoffs. I hit .390 over the last month and a half of the season. I remember standing in the clubhouse in San Diego listening to the Dodgers game. Bill Russell grounds to third base and I hear Vin Scully say " . . . and the season is over for the Los Angeles Dodgers." That means we win. It was just a euphoric feeling. Then in '83 I made the All-Star team again.

Those were four good, real good years. I was walking on the mayor's lawn right there. It was as good as it gets.

Then after the 1983 season I got separated from my wife and we got divorced. The next season was hell for me. We traded for a guy named Alex Trevino, who's playing with the Astros now, and he hit like .450 the first month. They couldn't get the guy out and I lost the job. I thought I was gonna kill myself drinking that summer. Here's my wife living in a nice house, dating a guy, raising my two kids and I'm struggling with baseball and living by myself. I was unhappy not being married to my wife and not being a father to my kids. Rock bottom. Great copy.

Guys knew that I was having a tough time but didn't say anything to me. I mean, what were they going to say? We fired Torre and Eddie Haas came in.

I didn't play much in '85. They had decided they weren't happy with Alex Trevino and traded him but they got Rick Cerone from the Yankees for Brian Fisher and he played most of '85. I didn't care for that at all because I was still reeling from being a good player and, having a little bit of an off-year, not really being given any time to recover.

Just lost your job.

Boom, you're out.

If you haven't had the constant, constant pressure of having to beat somebody, or the fear of being beaten, there's no way that you can under-stand what an athlete goes through. It's in the papers, it's on TV, you either do well or you don't, you beat or you get beaten. People who don't play sports don't understand that.

"They're playing the game for the money, that's why they are doing it." I hear that so much and it might be the number-one thing that makes me mad about fans. If I sign a hundred autographs and can't sign the 101st, the guy says, "The money you're makin', you ought to be ashamed of yourself." You know, stuff like that. And you know who's created that? The media created that monster, by putting the salaries in the paper every-day. It bugs players to hear that money thing all the time. I make $665,000 this year and Paul Assenmacher, say he's making $80,000 or $90,000. I guarantee you he's gonna try as hard as I am, or I'm going to try as hard as he is. What's money got to do with it?!

Go in and look at Bruce Sutter, look at his shoulder. He got $48 million, or whatever, from the Braves to pitch and his arm is shot, nerve-dead in the shoulder. He has an operation and with $48 million bucks in the bank he works for two years, eight hours a day to come back in this league. You're an athlete! You're a competitor! If I'm playing tonight, which I think I am, am I going out there to face Nolan Ryan thinking about my bank account? No. I'm thinking about hitting a line drive over his head. Money has *nothing* to do with it.

I went to the organization. "Come on, I played pretty good here three, four years and you just gave my job away. I've seen more devotion to a guy you *didn't* like."

But they wanted more power, more power, they said. They constantly had this need for more power in the organization. They were going to find somebody to hit for some power, twenty to twenty-five homers. I've got seventeen *career* homers, so that leaves me out.

I spent that season trying to get back together with my wife. One day over the winter I was staying at my place and there was a knock on my door and it was her, Kathleen, and she said, "I've been giving it some thought. Why don't we try to put this thing back together? Why don't we try to live together this winter and see if we can work out our problems?"

We went to spring training together and got married on March 22, 1986, a little wedding down there with Dale Murphy as my best man. We spent the weekend at a real nice hotel on the ocean. Chuck Tanner was our new manager. On Thursday I went in—my first spring training with the guy!—and explained that I had been married at one time, divorced, and we wanted to remarry and we wanted to do it this weekend. Can I have a day or so to get the arrangements together?

He looked at me and said that is one of the greatest things I've ever heard. You've got two children and you're gonna remarry. If I see you before Monday I'm fining you a thousand dollars. So that story has a happy ending. Now we have another child, the third.

We had traded for yet another catcher, Ozzie Virgil, and Chuck Tanner didn't play me, either. Period. I didn't talk to him about it because I didn't want to go in there and say, "We're not doing very well and our other catcher's not doing very well, how come I'm not playing?" Maybe I didn't want to know the answer. Maybe I didn't want him to tell me he thought I was horseshit and the only reason I was there was because I was making a lot of money and it was guaranteed. I had just signed a three-year contract. They couldn't afford to really let me go but they didn't want me to play every day. It was kind of a catch-22. Maybe I didn't want to hear that.

I still shake my head and wonder why, after 1984, they didn't say, "Why don't we go back to this guy?" I still don't understand, but there comes a certain point where you have to stop thinking about that, you have to let it go and move on. You have to quit complaining and bitching about it. I accepted in my mind that I was going to be the back-up catcher. They wanted somebody with power. But I always leave the door open, thinking if I play hard and play well enough I might get my chance back. You hope but you don't dwell on it. I can still play for two, three, four, five years.

Bobby Skinner, an assistant coach under Tanner, told me about a back-up catcher they used to have with Pittsburgh. "He could have still been with us but he always wanted to run his mouth." So I thought that was Bobby's way of telling me that if I wanted to stay with this club, stay quiet, stay out of the papers. I did, but I was going to do that anyway because I want to see our organization win, I want to see our city do well, and I didn't want to go to another city. Why do I want to spend the summer in Seattle or Cleveland or Detroit? Nothing against them but I'd rather stay at home and hope that I get my chances to play.

Boom! Russ Nixon is the manager now [June 1988] and I'm getting a chance to play, so maybe it worked out. I played the first games after he got here and I've played about every other day since that point.

I've had seven managers in the majors. I'm one of three guys with the Braves today that have been on the club that set the National League record for consecutive wins *and* consecutive losses at the start of the season. We are a roller-coaster bunch, there's no doubt about that. Changing managers, changing catchers, gee, you know, *constantly*. Sure, players talk about what's been going on. When we were hitting in the cage underneath the stadium one of our hitting coaches was reading a magazine and the other was asleep by his locker. Yeah, this is noted. We only had one coach to throw batting practice. *I* threw batting practice to my own team—unheard of. I think we're on the right road now. I think now the Braves have finally made some sound baseball moves in hiring Russ Nixon.

When you don't play for long periods of time it's frustrating and you kind of lose your sense of teamsmanship. The more I play, the better I do, there is no doubt about that. I'm not an "impact player" where I have great strength or great speed. My contributions are measured over long periods of time. I handle pitchers well. I'm a line-drive hitter. I don't strike out much. I hit and run. I throw pretty good. I just want to be remembered as the guy who came to the ballpark and played hard every time. That's the kind of player I am. You can't say, "Boy, that son-of-a-bitch could hit some homers!"

It gets to be a job sometimes, but I always love hearing my name in the starting line-up. In Atlanta the PA announcer says "Bruuuuuuce Benedict," and when I go into a restaurant people say "Bruuuuuuuce Benedict." I like that and I've got my speech all ready for when I'm done playing. They're gonna say, "What do you have to say, Bruce?" and I'm gonna say I'm grateful for three things. I'm grateful for Ted Turner and the Atlanta organization for giving me the opportunity to play. I'm thankful for the fans in Atlanta who have really been great to me, even when things weren't going good. And I'm thankful I got to watch Dale Murphy play. Those are the three things, and they are not stock answers, either.

I've been thinking about retirement a little bit. I think I could do some announcing. A guy offered me a job in his insurance company. I do *not* want to go to the low minor leagues and manage. I don't want to be away from my family for long periods of time riding a bus for $10,000 bucks. I'm not getting down on the people that do it, they really love the game and they are working their way up, but I don't want to. I would coach in the major leagues if somebody offered me the chance, preferably in Atlanta.

This is my free agent year. I bet I stay. I bet I'm here. But when it *is* over, I hope that I can say, "It's over, I had a good ride, an up-and-down ride but a good ride. See ya!"

He had 236 ABs in 1988, a .242 average, no homers. After the season he signed a one-year contract with the Braves.

M A N N Y   M O T A

He holds the major league record for total pinch hits with 150, and compiled a .297 batting average pinch hitting with the Pirates and the Dodgers. His lifetime average is .304. He's now the batting instructor and first-base coach for the Dodgers. He enunciates his words carefully and emphatically, with an honesty that invites respect.

On some occasions I might swing the bat hard and miss the ball *on purpose*, just to get loose. A lot of times, or most of the time, I used to get behind in the count, like one strike, two strikes, and that helped me to be a better hitter. I knew I had to bear down and make good contact. If I'm gonna strike out, I'm gonna strike out swinging. The worse thing that can happen to a pinch hitter is to get called out on strikes. When they put you in there they want you to swing the bat.

When Walter Alston told me I was going to be the pinch hitter for the Dodgers, I prepared myself mentally and physically to approach the game from a different angle: running more, taking a lot of extra hitting to keep my timing sharp, learning every pitcher in the league. I tried to have a book in my mind about every starter and reliever, about the guy who I was supposed to face in the late part of the game. I knew I had to discipline myself because I was only to hit once. I had to be ready. After the fifth inning I started getting myself loose, going into the tunnel do some running, or into the batting cage to take a few swings. I never let the manager surprise me. I believe if you are a baseball player you belong to the field. I never went inside and watched TV because I didn't think that would help me. I'd rather be at the bench watching every move they make, watching the catcher, watching the infielder, watching the outfielder, watching how they pitch a different guy, maybe the same type of hitter as myself, to have an *idea* what to look for when I go to the plate.

I loved to hit in a clutch situation because I learned how to control myself and not put on any kind of pressure. I loved to hit with men on base. Just try to relax, don't let anybody bother me and just concentrate on the guy on the mound and let him release the white ball. You check to see how they play you. You have to know the situation. In some situations you go for the fly ball, in others you go for the ground ball, or you go for the base hit. Walter Alston used me in situations where he really needed a base hit. In a wide open game, he tried to use somebody else. He knew I could not provide him with a long ball but he could depend on me to try to bring the guy in from scoring position, second and third base.

You cannot make mistakes. You gotta be aggressive but by the same token you gotta be selective. You gotta put everything into that one at-bat. Total concentration and positive thinking.

The fans play a big part when you pinch hit, the way they receive you when you're announced by the PA system. That gives you motivation to do well—don't let those people down! When you see so many people behind you they give you inspiration. That was Dodger Stadium.

I have some big pinch hits and I also have some other ones which I don't want to talk about. One time in '77 or '78 I had a pinch hit double against Philadelphia during the playoff and we came from behind and won that game. Eventually we went to the World Series. That was one of the biggest. Also, when I tied Smokey Burgess with 144, and then when I broke the record with 145. The double, I think it was kind of a breaking ball. I don't know if it was a split finger or slider change-up, something like that. I think Gene Garver was the pitcher. Number 144 was a fastball against Joe Sambito; 145 was a breaking ball off Lynn McGlothen. I can see it in my mind. Those are the three biggest pinch hits for me, I'd say.

One time in 1977 we played an exhibition game against the New York Mets in my home town in the Dominican Republic. I pinch hit with the bases loaded and I hit a grand slam off Tom Seaver. That game was televised back to L.A. That was one of the greatest feelings I ever had as a pinch hitter because it happened in front of my home people. The fans went wild and I was so happy, so pleased to come through in front of the fans from Los Angeles and from all Latin America and the Dominican Republic. The pinch hit record doesn't belong to me, it belongs to all of them and all of the people who are rooting for me and all of the people who made it possible.

I don't miss pinch hitting because I enjoy coaching and being the hitting instructor. As the hitting instructor, the main thing is to tell the guy to make good contact, even the power hitter. Don't overswing. Go with the pitch and try to hit it hard. If you make good contact you got a chance. What they do at batting practice, they've got to take into the game to apply. They've got to have concentration, desire, and they have to discipline themselves as a hitter. They have to learn the strike zone. A lot of hitters think about hitting every pitch to one side of the field, but you can use *both* sides. A lot of power hitters realize they don't have to pull everything to hit it out of the park because they are capable of hitting the ball out at every angle. Pedro Guerrero, Mike Marshall, they use the whole field.

I'm behind the cage during batting practice. If I see them trying to lift the ball, if they try to overcut, I just remind them. I even call from the first-base coaching box if I see them do anything wrong, like pulling down or coming up, or pulling away. Usually I leave them alone and let them concentrate on the game, but if I see anything I think can help at that moment, I will do it. Sometimes the skip wants me to stay with the team at the bench and let somebody else coach first base, so I can communicate with the hitters before they go to the plate and after they come back.

I'm here to build confidence and not destroy confidence, so there's no reason for me to get mad. If you fail seven out of ten times you are still a good hitter. You've got to make him believe. You've got to know the best time to approach a hitter. By the same token you have to let him know that slumps are part of the game. I don't remember one player in this game who never went through a slump, I don't care how good a player was.

I got out of a slump without thinking of being in it. I just tried to make good contact and use the whole field. I suggest to the guy in a slump that he try to hit the ball the other way. Doing that, you wait longer and while you wait longer you see the ball better. Sometimes you bunt. There's a lot of ways to get out of a slump. The worst thing to do is just try to overdo it, try too hard, try to get four hits in one at-bat. You gotta go little by little, and you cannot run before you can walk.

As the first-base coach, I have to know the situation, tell the runner about the pitcher's move to first, about how the outfield is playing, and how well the outfielders throw. I have to memorize all the signs and be sure that the runner *got* the sign. If I have any doubts, somehow I communicate with the runner. Still, an awful lot of times we miss them with the kids, and sometimes even with guys who've played in the major leagues for a long time. I don't think established major-league baseball players should miss a sign.

This is my life, this is my bread and butter, this is my family support. I enjoy every minute and every second. I give everything I have to the organization which I work for and I'm very fortunate to be part of the organization. Also I have the opportunity to communicate with our coaches, other coaches, and the manager, and we have a different view and philosophy of the game. You put it together and then you might learn something.

I live in Santo Domingo, where I manage a ball club in the winter league. I love managing. Not everybody thinks the same way, not everyone has the same kind of temperament when you manage. You have to know them to know how to treat them but you gotta treat everybody with respect.

BRUCE FROEMMING

Irascible on the field, he's left alone by the players, for the most part. That's the way he likes it, the way he thinks it should be. Besides, things are calmer than in the old days: "The players now have these two- and three-year contracts. They're not as competitive as they used to be. They don't fight the umpires as hard as they did when I came into the league. No question about it. It is much easier to umpire with the athlete of today."

In my rookie year I had a tough situation in Houston. I was working with Al Barlick, John Kibler, and Paul Pryor. Bases loaded, Deron Johnson for Philadelphia hit a shot and the second baseman flipped it to Roger Metzger for one out, and Tim McCarver, who was running from first to second, hit Metzger with a football block, way out of the base line. The ball ended up in center field, the guys on second and third scored, and Philly is up 5–3 or whatever. I called interference, double-play, the runs came off the board. I knew I had the play 100 percent right, but the Phillies went absolutely berserk. Remember, it was my *rookie* year. They came not just from the dugout. They came from the bullpen. I've got twenty-five guys at second base screaming at me. At one point I had the argument under control. I got to Frank Lucchesi, the first one out, and said, "I can't talk to twenty-five guys, Frank. Let me explain what happened."

"All right," Frank said, and held his arms up. "Let him talk! Let him talk!"

As I started to explain what happened, his coach, George Myatt, said, "He's a damn liar." I threw Myatt out and then forget everything else, the place went nuts. We had a really, really, rough argument. Fifteen minutes. I had to throw four guys out. We always call the league president after an ejection. On a normal ejection over the weekend you don't call till Monday, but Barlick said this was not normal. I called Chub Feeney, who was at a party, and he chewed me out for calling him over the weekend and said, "Give me to Barlick." Then Barlick got on and explained what happened and Chub calmed down and called me the next day and said he was sorry he had jumped on me.

One of the really wrong theories about officiating is that a good official is one you never notice. The umpire who made that statement was probably a real poor official who tried to get his paycheck and hide behind his partners and stay out of trouble all his life. *Control* of the ball game is the difference between umpires that shows up for the players and managers. Some umpires might have slightly better judgment than others, but you're not going to get to the big leagues with *bad* judgment.

The Augie Donatellis, Al Barlicks, Shag Crawfords—those guy were *involved.* They called the balks, the obstructions, the interferences. They threw the guy out on occasion. They were high-profile. *And* they were the guys put into the big games.

In my third year in the league we were in the pennant race. I'm working second base in Pittsburgh with Ed Vargo at the plate. Dave Giusti's the pitcher, Manny Sanguillen's catching. It's a passed ball and Lou Brock's trying to score and he was going to be a dead duck but he kicked the ball out of Guisti's glove when he slid. Sanguillen's trying to put the ball back in Giusti's glove. There was dust everywhere. Vargo, an excellent umpire, called him out. I'm at second base. Vargo's argument. I don't have to see anything. But I saw the ball on the ground.

The Cardinals erupted from the dugout because they had seen the ball, too, and Ed had all he could handle. You're gonna have arguments with two or three guys, but when an entire dugout erupts, something might be wrong. And Vargo, being an excellent umpire, picked up on that. Then when I closed in from second base Eddie picked up on this and says, "Bruce, you got something?" and I say, "Eddie, I got the ball on the ground. The guy's safe."

That good umpire being the guy who is never noticed? He'd have walked out to center field and turned his back on the play.

Bob Prince, the Pirates announcer, just murdered me. Not about whether the call was right or wrong, but where the call came from. How can the second-base umpire overrule? The next year Bob Prince and I went at it real hot and heavy in the lobby of the Shamrock Hilton in Houston. He gave me a "Hey, how ya doin'?" and I said, "I know what you did to me last year. Don't give me ——" and *again* his argument was that it wasn't that I had the play wrong, but how can you call that play from there?

Taking charge. That's what umpiring is about. That's what I try to tell the young guys working with me now. The other day Gary Darling fined a guy for throwing his bat and helmet—you fine him, not throw him out for that—then the guy got sassy and cussed Darling and Darling threw him out. I was at second base and my heart just started pounding because you don't see that much in young umpires. You see them try to tiptoe around those situations. I was really fired up about it. You can teach that, but to get anybody to *do* it is another thing.

The easiest thing to do is throw a ballplayer out. The hardest thing is to keep him in the game, but if somebody *wants* trouble, *handle* it. Speaking for myself, the argument ends when it gets personal. The guy gets into personalities, he's out of the game.

Billy Martin thinks it's cute to kick dirt and throw dirt, and then the league president comes down with a *three-game* sentence on it. It's incredible. That's not what the game's about. That's not what managing's about. That's not what umpiring's about. I respect the players and the managers and I expect the same thing. If I don't get it, I'm gonna get rid of 'em. Consequently, there's not many guys that talk to me that much. Probably that's the reason I don't chase a lot of guys during the year. I have arguments like everybody else, but we're gonna do it right or we're not gonna do it at all.

Right is "Hey, I think you missed the play. How come he's safe? How come he's out?"

But, "Listen you sonofa——" That's the wrong way, and he's gone. And there's no *warning*. That's it. He's done. And everyone knows that. They know who's got the short fuse, which would be a person like myself, a Tata, a Pulli, a Runge, a Wendelstedt. A newer fellow maybe will be easier because, hey, you gotta feel your way. It's not something you pick up right away. But like I told Darling, "If a guy cusses you, you get him right now. No *warning*."

You've got guys you'll tolerate a lot longer than other guys. Example: Pete Rose vs. Tim Foley. I choose Tim Foley because he's no longer in the league. With Foley, he just had to open his mouth and he had a problem, and probably would get thrown out. Pete Rose'll get a longer argument. Steve Garvey. Willie Stargell. Billy Virdon. John McNamara. Don Zimmer. You respect them because they have respect for you. I'd say 97 percent of the players are really decent guys. Most of the problems you have are with the same couple of guys on every team. When there's trouble, you can look at them to be at the head of the class, comin' at you. And we know who they are. I won't list them, obviously.

If I didn't give my boss, Bart Giamatti, the respect he wants, he'd get rid of me. If you don't get respect from your kids, you're gonna discipline 'em. People *beg* for discipline. Run a guy over and he doesn't do anything, you lose respect for him. Guy runs into you and you say, "Hey, back up or you're gone," the guy's not gonna run over you next time. That's my theory.

I never make a call and then think about it. Just like when I had the Ike Pappas near-perfect game in 1972. They wanted me to call Strike Three on the twenty-seventh hitter. He walked. Lou Boudreau and the writers came up to me and said I wasn't a fan. They said, "Gee, you could have become famous as the twelfth umpire in history to have a perfect game." I asked Lou who the *eleventh* guy was, he said he didn't know. I said that's how damn famous I would have been. What seemed important yesterday is not important tomorrow. Think about that sometime.

Was the pitch close? They're all close but I don't call pitches "Close!" It's either a ball or a strike.

In the 1977 playoffs, I had the controversy with the Davey Lopes play. He hit a ball to Mike Schmidt who threw to first on a very close play. If he's out, the game's over and the Phillies lead the Series. He was safe and the Dodgers went on to win the game, then the Series.

The next night I had the plate. There were death threats. They had to take my wife out of the stands. Fred Fleig came to the dressing room and said he had looked at the replay *fourteen* times, stop-action slides, and said he still couldn't tell if he was safe or out and I said, "Fred, I had one look at it and I called him safe and I guess I must have been right."

If *you* think you're wrong, you're going to get an argument because they'll think so, too. Everybody's got an ego and I think umpires really got big egos because you're commanding the game. You want people to see you because you want to be promoted. You have to think that you're a really good umpire and better than just about everybody else. But we want to better ourselves, just like the players do, so I'll wait a couple of innings and I'll go to my partner at the base next to me and I'll say, "Whatdya think of that play at first base?" and he might say, "I thought the guy had it." Which means that maybe I missed it. But *at the time* you think you're right. If you're out there guessing, you're going to have a lot of problems. The players pick up on that. You're a salesman.

I went to umpiring school in 1958, the winter after I graduated from high school. As a freshman I had been cut from the varsity baseball team at Custer High School in Milwaukee. It was a shot in the dark to go out for second base as a freshman anyway. I was overmatched because of my size and being so young. There was an ad in the paper for umpires. Four games a day, $3.50 per game, four days a week. Nice money for a freshman and I liked it right away. I was part of the game. I had hollered and griped a lot as a player because I was supercompetitive, and I still am today. I don't play cards just to pass time. If we play cards I wanna beat you. The same with bowling, golf. I wanna beat you. That carried over into my arguments with officials. I was known as a hot dog. Umpiring, I was now seeing the game from a different perspective. But I made the high-school team my sophomore year, so that ended my umpiring career then.

When I graduated I really didn't know what I was going to do. I came from a poor family. My dream was to go to teacher's college and become a teacher-coach for the rest of my life, but it wasn't gonna happen. I was an average student at best. I took a ball to school and I took a ball home. I was all sports. To take books home at the end of the day was the extracurricular activity.

There was an ad in *The Sporting News* about a couple of umpiring schools. One was the Al Somers school in Florida. Harry Wendelstedt bought that school out years later. In January I went down there to Daytona Beach, which was also the winter camp for the Cleveland Indians. We spent a week or ten days learning the rules, taking tests on stuff you never even heard of until you went into umpiring: interference, batting out of order. Then we were on the field for four weeks, where you're graded on your field work, your bases work, your plate work—all with a two-man system, because that's how you start in the lower minor leagues. You don't get three umpires until Double-A ball. And they don't even teach four-man because it's going to be a long time before you even *think* about the major leagues.

The average age in that class was twenty-eight to thirty. All backgrounds. Now you have a younger group trying to get into umpiring because it has made such great progress, through our association. The job at the big-league level is very attractive financially now, but when you're in school, then or now, you don't even think of that. It's just the excitement of being involved with the profession. You want to be an *umpire*. Today, there are almost three hundred students in the two schools. Twenty-two will get jobs. Durwood Merrill, an umpire in the American League, was a high-school principal in Hooks, Texas. Why would you leave the security of being a principal and take the long shot of being a major-league umpire? A love for the game. Paul Runge's a very successful real estate agent in San Diego. One partner I had during the school was a former pilot with Eastern Airlines and he had a lot of money and he wanted to get into umpiring. He had an airplane and we used to go from Daytona Beach to Miami once or twice a week to go to the dog track or have dinner. To me, coming from as poor a family as I did, this was another planet.

We played games daily in the school—when you weren't umpiring, you were playing, in order to create playing situations. Augie Donatelli, a guest instructor that year, told some of the Cleveland guys who were around that they should get this guy—me—to *play* ball. Forget umpiring. I was probably at the peak of my own game at that time. When the school was over the Indians did invite me to spring training. They didn't mention money or anything. But at the end of school I was offered an umpiring contract with the Nebraska State League, a Rookie League. I couldn't believe it. There were seventy-five students for twenty-eight jobs. I was the youngest chosen. I passed up the chance to go to spring training and took the umpiring job, and wound up with that fellow with the airplane in the Midwest League for six weeks before I started in the Nebraska State League in June 1958, where I was the umpiring chief. They thought I was going to be a guy with experience. I was eighteen and looked like fifteen.

A guy in those years could go eight or nine years before he got to the major leagues. Dutch Rennert went seventeen years in the minor leagues. Jimmy Odom, who went to the American League, spent nineteen years in the minor leagues, which is an absolute lifetime. I was in the Nebraska State, Midwest, Northern, Northwest, and Texas leagues, then five years in the Pacific Coast League. Thirteen years in the minors, with the *top* pay being $3,200 per season, when I was umpire-in-chief in the Pacific Coast in 1969 and 1970. An umpire in Triple-A today makes less than *$5,000,* maybe another $8,000 expense money. An umpire starts in the major leagues at $42,000, with an $8,000 bonus his first five years. You can see why a guy would want to get up here. There's survival here, and there's not in the minors. Baseball loses a lot of good umpires because a guy can't hang in there. He's got a family. He's got kids. There's a lot of sacrifice, and probably more on the woman's side. I'm *doing* something I enjoy. She's at home with the kids, the problems. There's strains in those minor-league years. The boy's sick and you can't get home because you don't have the money. On and on and on. No different from any other life except that *you're gone.* People say, "Geez, look at that, what a life," but behind all that there's stuff that you don't bring out.

Fortunately I got good jobs in the winter, with a trucking company or whatever, in order to *get through* the summer.

You have a lot of pitfalls and tragic things that happen in the minor leagues—plays or arguments where a club or a league will want to release you, and if you're released, you're *done*.

In 1964 a development program for umpires came into being—a system where they monitor you much better than it was done before, although the supervisors are not all qualified, and I say that with no reservations whatsoever. There's not *one* supervising umpire in the development program today who ever got to the major leagues.

The program is good for umpires *now*, but it hurt me because Ed Doherty and then Barney Deary, when he took over, were going to weed out the *old* thoughts, the old guys—and that included me, even though I was young—and were going to train umpires to be the way they wanted them to be.

The attitude when I started was to go out on the field and battle 'em. They gave you the basics of this in umpiring school, but they cannot teach you what live action can. The real action is in the league where guys are fightin' for their jobs and to win the game, where nothing is make-believe. They fight you harder at the grass roots than they fight you in the big leagues. Some weeks every night was like the Fourth of July. There were fireworks all over the field. You were learning just like the players were.

I had my own ways. I didn't take any abuse. I was *too hot* for the development program people. They were looking for the type of umpire who stood out there and took a lot of abuse, to be more tolerant than what a Bruce Froemming was at that time. I clashed with their machinery. They tried unsuccessfully two or three times to have me released.

I had had a play in Tulsa in 1965 in the Texas League playoffs. Tulsa, the home team, had the tying run on second base. Bobby Pfeil was the runner. I still remember it like it was yesterday. A ball was hit down the left-field line and the third-base umpire went down the line to cover it. I had the plate so I went out to pick up the runner coming around third to see if he tagged the bag. He missed it by two or three feet. I called the guy out on appeal. That turned the playoff around and Tulsa lost it. We got run out of town. Don Denkinger and I, my partner that night along with two other umpires, had to have police protection till we got on Highway 66.

Chief Bender, who is still a scout with the Reds, Bob Howsam, Vern Rapp—they were all standing at the chicken wire where we were dressing, *climbing* the chicken wire, saying I was a no-good so-and-so and, "We'll get your job." They went to the World Series that year up in Minnesota, and they went to Ed Doherty and said, "Hey, get rid of this guy." That's how it started. And then some people didn't have the balls to do what was right. That's saying it like it is.

The Cardinals and Bob Howsam went after my throat with the league president at that time, Hugh Finnerty. This story is known by all my peers from the time, Dutch Rennert, Paul Runge, Hugh Finnerty, who still lives in Tulsa, John Ferguson, the writer for the Tulsa *World*. In the Tulsa paper the next day Ferguson quoted some retired major-league umpire, as saying, "Those are plays you should never see."

Now you tell me how to respect that. I'm there to do an honest job. I've never turned my back on anything I've seen on the field.

I saw Ed Doherty three years later at Phoenix, the first time I had been able to talk to him privately, and I asked him if I was being held back because of the controversy, and he said, "There are certain things you don't see and hear, Bruce, if you wanna move up in this game."

I took that to mean that he wanted me to cheat, or to not hear guys cussin' me. I said, "When a guy calls me such-and-such a name, I'm not supposed to hear it?"

He said, "That's baseball talk."

So I lost all respect for him.

I can't say that if I hadn't seen that play and instead had ruled the guy safe, I would have made the major leagues earlier. I do know I would have lost all respect for myself that night. I do know they tried to grind me in the ground because I called that play.

In 1965, Jocko Conlan was given a job, after he retired, as supervisor in the National League, and he came out to the Texas League to look at my partner and me—to look at my partner, and he *tripped* over me, because I was with my partner. This was the summer before that playoff game. He later showed me a letter that he sent to Warren Giles saying that he considered me a diamond in the rough. That story is also in the last chapter of his book. So my fortunes changed from being a guy recommended to take *right now* to a guy who didn't get here until '71, six years later.

I was in the Pacific Coast League in '66, '67, and '68, and when the major leagues expanded in '69, the wheels were turning. "Who are they gonna take?" And you saw some guys going, you know, who you didn't think were better than you, or whatever. You wondered when you would get your break. Then the National League signed a couple of guys from a low classification, which we questioned.

That's when Al Barlick came in. The National League gave me ten spring-training games in 1970 to pacify some people, and Barlick worked one of them with me in Vero Beach, with the Senators under Ted Williams playing the Dodgers under Walt Alston. Barlick was supposed to have the plate but he switched with me because I wanted Al to see me work. After the game he said, "What the hell is wrong? Why haven't you had a chance to go to the major leagues?"

I told him about the development program. He went to bat for me with Fred Fleig, the supervisor of the National League umpires. Barlick's credibility was just incredible, and Fleig, who had heard nothing but bad about me from the development people said, "Gee, Al, we don't have very good reports on him."

Barlick said, "Fuck the reports. Let's give him a shot. Let's bring him to spring training and see what he can do." It was Al's persistence that paid off and I give him almost all the credit, going to bat for a guy he didn't know.

At spring training in 1971 there were two job openings and I was one of seven people trying for them. One guy, Jerry Dale, was going to get a job. Four of the guys in the group were already on option. If it was a horse race I'd have been an eighty-to-one shot. And I knew I was eatin' those guys up in spring training. If it was just umpiring, I knew I had a chance. If it was politics involved, I didn't think I had a chance. I was working mostly games in the St. Petersburg area, where the Mets were, and the New York press was very favorable, wondering where the hell I came from.

Fred Fleig called me to the Holiday Inn in St. Petersburg about the twenty-fifth of March. Al Barlick had already told me they were gonna give me the job. Just to show you how the wheels turn and how a guy really knows what he is in life, when Mr. Fleig sat down he said, "Bruce, I know you're a very bitter person. I know your feelings about the development program and what has happened." He said that he was sorry he listened to certain people, but then he said, "Now you're here. One thing I want to do with you is for you to put aside all your feelings about what has happened in the past and I want you to look forward from here."

I said, "I respect what you just said, Mr. Fleig, but as long as I live I will never forget these people because they hurt my family. They didn't just hurt me. They hurt my chance to make a better living for my family, only based on personalities, likes and dislikes, nothing to do with my ability."

He said, "Well, we'll go from here, you and I will. Welcome to the National League."

As I sit here with you today I can exactly remember the booth where we sat and him telling me to forget this, and the bitterness and the *hurt* just came right out of me. Those people were creeps. To this day I have no respect for Barney Deary and the program because of what they did to me and other umpires like me. I don't have to tell you what my ratings are, but I know I'm in the upper third of the class. And here's people who were saying they didn't think I was a prospect.

So finally getting the job was an anticlimax. I was wore out. I really was. When they run over you with a steamroller and you got scars, it's for somebody else to say, "You made it. Forget it." But when I left Mr. Fleig and went back to the bar at the Holiday Inn and all the boys were there to congratulate me—because everyone knew what was going on—I turned the bad water off, to a certain extent. It'll always drip but I said, "I'm going forward."

If I had to start over, I wouldn't do everything the same, but I'd go into the profession. How many people in life can say they're at the top of the job where they wanted to be when they started as an eighteen-year-old kid? If I umpire ten more years I'll have over forty years in the game, more than two-thirds of my life, and I'm very happy. I can even say this—though people might say, "Geez, you've got to be half-crazy to say that"—I really enjoyed those thirteen years in the minors. The people! Life is people and it's what you make of it. If you want to hang your head and mope—and the easiest thing for me to do was feel sorry for myself—okay. But I said bullshit, I'm gonna make it.

We've got a great relationship on this crew right now. We talk baseball all the time. "Did you see that?" "Can you believe they brought that guy in?" We do some managing out there. We're into the game. We don't go to the newspapers and I wouldn't say anything to a player 'cause it'll get back: "Hey, Froemming's out there managing."

If you're sensitive, you wouldn't wanna be working with us. The needle is out. Everyone's fair game, including me, and I'm the crew chief. The guys know I like to play the game that way. I like to tease and I don't mind being teased, and I think it gives the crew a good attitude. You've got to be in that dressing room for an hour, an hour and a half, and you can't just sit there and get dressed and stare at the wall. If you do, I don't think you'll do a good job on the field. For the most part, umpires have fun-type personalities.

The pride in umpiring has really come forward in the last couple of years. I couldn't say enough about Bart Giamatti, and not because he's a friend, not because we signed a good deal. That has nothing to do with it. The guy has *time* for us. We've got a working relationship we've never had before. I've got an interview with him on my desk now. He's talking about complaints he hears about the umpires. "Hey," he says, "I *love* the umpires."

▬▬▬▬▬▬▬▬▬▬▬▬▬▬▬▬▬▬▬▬▬▬▬▬▬▬▬▬▬▬▬▬▬▬▬▬▬
R E X   B A R N E Y
▬▬▬▬▬▬▬▬▬▬▬▬▬▬▬▬▬▬▬▬▬▬▬▬▬▬▬▬▬▬▬▬▬▬▬▬▬

He's one of those big, gnarled-looking guys who turns out to be a "very sentimental Irish person." As the public-address announcer at Memorial Stadium in Baltimore, he can have a hard time getting through some of the introductions at old-timers' games. He's an old-timer himself, the starting pitcher for the Dodgers in Jackie Robinson's National League debut.

"I never did really live up to expectations. It spoiled me all my life. I pitched one no-hit, no-run game against the Giants and I pitched four one-hitters. Career record is fifty-seven wins, twenty-something losses. I really don't know, but it should have been two hundred wins. I broke my leg severely sliding into second base at the end of the 1950 season. I never got back into the same motion. I pitched in '51, then just a little bit in '52, then that was it." He was twenty-seven.

In April of 1943 I was eighteen years old and pitching in high school, and I went to Durham, North Carolina, after being signed by the Dodgers. I'd made a deal with the draft board so they'd let me finish one season of professional baseball. I played in Durham just one month before they sent me to Montreal, the equivalent of Triple-A, for a month. Next thing I know I'm in Brooklyn. It was the first time I'd been in a major-league city, really.

Mr. Rickey—anybody who ever played for him will call him "Mr. Rickey"—owned the ball club and he called me in the office one morning and he said, "Son, we know you're going to be drafted as soon as the season's over. You might get in an inning or two if we're ahead 15–1, or behind. We want you to get acclimated to the major leagues." That was ten o'clock in the morning and we're playing at one-thirty. I go to the ballpark.

Leo Durocher says, "Kid, when'd you pitch last?"

"Five days ago."

"All right, you start today's game."

Boy, I'd have been happy to go back to Omaha, I was so scared of all these major-league guys—Dixie Walker, Billy Herman, Paul Waner. But I pitched and left with a 2–2 tie in the seventh inning.

The third game was really the highlight of my career. Eighteen years old, keep in mind, and we're playing the *hated* New York Giants—but I didn't know they were hated then. I probably hadn't been east of St. Louis in my life. I pitched thirteen innings, left in a 1–1 tie, and we won in the seventeenth.

Several years ago there was a story about that game and several young guys brought the clipping to me and said, "This can't be true, pitching thirteen innings when you were eighteen."

I said, "Are you crazy? In those days, if you felt good, you kept going." Hell, one day a few years later I won a doubleheader. I pitched seven innings and we were ahead and we won that game, and in the second game Durocher came to me and said, "Kid"—he didn't know my real name for about five years—"Kid, could you pitch an inning or two in the second game?" Well, I did and I won that one, too.

Anyway, I was in the army on October 3, 1943, and served overseas for two years in a tank outfit. When I signed with the Dodgers, Mr. Rickey had given me $5,000, which is the most he gave anyone, I think. My parents thought he was crazy. "They're going to *pay* him to play baseball?" And I remember saying the same thing: "You're going to *pay* me to play baseball?" Honest, I was so naïve.

But the bonus was going to be paid one half before I went into the service, the other half if I came back in one piece. After I came back I had to work out for a couple of weeks to prove that I could still throw hard.

That's what I was, a hard thrower. Very wild. A couple of sayings from the New York papers: "If the plate were high and outside, Rex Barney would be in the Hall of Fame." Dick Young started that. Then someone wrote, "Rex Barney could throw a ball through a brick wall if he could hit the brick wall."

In *USA Today* I was voted one of the twenty-one all-time hardest throwers. In all modesty I was voted *one* of those twenty-one, but they listed us in alphabetical order! People thought I was *the* hardest thrower. But I would trade it all to have had great control. Mr. Rickey took me out at eight o'clock one morning during spring training, put a patch over one eye, a patch over the other, thinking maybe I was jerking my head.

The thing I'll think about all my life—the frustrating thing—is what that lack of control cost me. Bullshit on that throwing hard. True, you can make a lot of mistakes and get away with it throwing hard, but control, that's what Koufax and Newcombe and Gibson had *as well*. Sure, it felt great to hear the crowd "oooh" when I'd strike out the side. One of my great thrills was in 1947, when I was like the eleventh man on a ten-man pitching staff in the World Series, but I got to start a game—unheard of. I walked the first three hitters I faced and thought, "Well, you always wanted to be in a World Series, but that's it." But they left me in and I struck out DiMaggio, Henrich, and Keller. When I walked off that mound I was twenty feet tall. I know that.

That year I also pitched the first major-league game Jackie Robinson ever played in. I had gone to a Jesuit high school, Creighton Prep, and then Creighton University, and we played with and against blacks and thought nothing about it. In 1946 there were rumors that Jackie was going to join the club. He was in Montreal at the time. We had several rednecks on our club who swore they'd never play with a black player. Lo and behold, the day before Opening Day in 1947, Jackie joined our club as a first baseman. Utter chaos. Terrible. He was a super human being, had to be, and of course Mr. Rickey knew this. He had researched the whole thing and Jackie was the guy they chose. A lot of guys could never have survived.

I started that first game against the Boston Braves, in Brooklyn, and the reaction wasn't too bad. He was a Dodger, after all. But on the road things were a little different. They called him every possible thing they could. Asinine things. He used to tell us not to worry about it. "I'll handle it," he said.

I'm not going to mention the name but we had one player who wrote Mr. Rickey a letter saying he did not want to play with a black man and preferred to be traded. About halfway through the season that player wanted that letter back. It dawned on him that with Jackie we had a chance to win it all; we'd come close for several years. But Mr. Rickey said, "No, young man, when the season's over you will get your wish. I will trade you to a last-place club. But you'll be on this club the rest of the year." And he *was* traded after the World Series.

The guy who did the most for Jackie Robinson was Pee Wee Reese, who was from Louisville, Kentucky. At first Reese's theory was, "With this guy, we'll win," but they became very close friends.

I knew the ax was coming in Vero Beach, but you never *believe* it. You think you're going to wake up the next day and it'll all fall into place. I saw guys older than me still playing. Ralph Branca, who was my age and roommate for six or seven years, pitched four or five years after I was done.

They want to send you to A-ball or something, and your pride is hurt. The toughest part of the game for me, even now, is going into a clubhouse knowing that a player is going to be sent down. No matter how young or how old the guy is, it tears you up. They all think they're the best out there. I don't care how old they are. They never think their career is over. Never.

I had had a tough war—shot in the back, in the leg—and I thought the transition would be tough. It was—call it battle fatigue or whatever— but I got out of it and thought I would never experience anything like that again. Then all of a sudden nobody wants you, you can't throw hard any- more, everything hurts. You're out. There's no sentiment in this game. None. It's not what you did for me yesterday or will do tomorrow. It's *today*.

All those people who said, "Come see me when you're through"? They're out to lunch or having a meeting. I sat in many a hotel room many a night trying to figure things out, how I would make ends meet. That's the sad part of the game that these guys today may never experience, because they make so much money. If they have any kind of agent or any kind of brain they'll end up all right. The transition won't be as hard for these guys. But in my day there were a few suicides; a few ended up on skid row, men who just couldn't get it together. It's sad. It hurts me. I had enough gump- tion, I guess, to pull myself up. I worked very hard. I went to a speech teacher when I got to the Triple-A level to get my voice better. I'm an original member of the baseball pension plan. I draw a pension and I'm very thankful for it. I don't have to have it, but so many people I know would have such a tough time without it.

In 1952 they offered me jobs coaching, managing, but that part of the work never got to me. But I can remember Red Barber, the great announcer that he was, doing interviews with me saying, "You know, when you're out of baseball you ought to think about going into radio."

Well, I went to Vero Beach and worked at a little radio station down there, and I did some play-by-play at Daytona, then I moved up to Charles- ton for a couple of years.

Mutual Broadcasting had a game-of-the-day back then, and I got that job for three years. That was the greatest schooling, because I might do a Cubs-Pittsburgh game today and a Detroit-Yankee game tomorrow. You did this seven days a week. We lived on airplanes. Then the Giants and Dodgers went west in '57 and I joined WOR-TV broadcasting National League games in New York. Then I went back to Charleston, and I came to Baltimore in 1964, doing sports shows and a little TV. Then in 1967 I did my first public address job. The regular guy was sick and they took me out of the stands.

I did some radio and TV—I was the guy in the bullpen—and I did the

PA when I could. I took over full time in '69. In 1983 I did radio all year, when the Orioles won it all, and now I do cable games, mostly on the road, and I do the public address work at home, and I do my radio shows.

People think mine is a great job, and it is, but you'd better watch what's going on. I've had times when other guys have taken my place doing the PA but they do one game and then come to me—this is after *begging* to do it—and say, "Don't ask me to do that again!" It's more demanding than you think. You've got to watch the field every second to spot changes. It's all very technical.

You develop techniques. About ten, twelve years ago we had our annual pre-season meeting and we were talking about how to get the fans more involved, and I mentioned something I had seen in the minor leagues when a fan caught a ball on the fly. The announcer said, "Give that fan a contract!" and the usher would bring him a mock contract. Everyone else in the meeting said, "That's corny as hell," and I said, "Yeah, it is, but it's something to try." I think that was 1979. So we tried it, and I thought I would specify man or woman or boy or girl in my announcement. Well, on the very first night I see the ball come down and a lady catch the ball.

"Give that *lady* a contract!"

The toughest-looking, ugliest guy with hair down to *here* turns around. I thought I wouldn't get out of the park alive. From that moment on it was, "Give that *fan* a contract." And it caught on. I had a couple of ushers upstairs to give me signals on balls I couldn't see. The next year we decided to cut it out. The phone calls and mail were unbelievable! We brought it back.

One night we were doing a game here and I said, "Will the owner of an automobile with New York license plates, number . . ." Well, the reaction from the fans! You know, the fans here, like in most parks around the country, hate New York. So sometimes in order to liven up a game I'll just make up a New York license plate.

Years ago I said, for some reason I don't remember, "*Thank* yooouuu" after an announcement, and now when I walk down the street people will say, "*Thank* yooouuu." I *have* to do it in the stadium. We all get our own identification remarks.

On June 23, 1983, I had a severe stroke, brain seizure, cardiac arrest. I was in a coma for five days, thought I was dead a couple of times, came out of it and my right side was paralyzed, but with a lot of hard work and a lot of prayers I have absolutely no sign of anything. They said I wouldn't work for a year or eighteen months, or ever, but I was back in six months. I knew I could do it! I'm a better person for it. I'm more considerate than I was. Everyone has a lot of problems you don't know about. Some are more severe than my own. But I'm very proud of what I did. I just got hardheaded about it. I love my game and my job. You're not going to put me in a wheelchair.

I hear writers, broadcasters, players complain what a tough job they have. That's bullshit. It's not a job. You know why? Every player in baseball from the time he was four years old lusted to be a major-league ballplayer. Eight million kids a day are on a playground in a city, and they all think they're going to be a big-league ballplayer. *One* of them might make it.

I never complain. I don't care how hot or cold it gets. I love the game very, very much. It's new every day. It's so captivating. Otherwise, how could a man like Mr. Rickey, a great man, stay in it all his life and love it? Willie Stargell—what a great guy—has a couple of quotes I'll never forget. "I know one thing about baseball," Willie said. "The umpire says 'Play ball!' I've never heard 'Work ball!' yet."

The other one was, "No one made me play this game. I asked to play it."

That's my theory. I would like to see some of the guys drafted into the army for a year or two, or go into a factory or a coal mine for a year. What do you think they'd say then? Yes, it's a difficult game, but I can't call it or any job related to the game real *work*. How many jobs are there where you can come and go as you want? Sure there's pressure to produce, but I think there's more pressure on the guy or gal driving the school bus with fifty kids screaming in the back, or a guy or gal flying an airplane. Baseball beats working! It beats carrying that lunch bucket! It beats driving that school bus. It beats flying that airplane. It beats a lot of stuff because you're still playing a game.

The *everydayness* of baseball. I've seen millions and millions of games and I'm not saying every one is new, but the next game I see may be the best game I've ever seen. I saw the last game of the 1983 playoffs when Tito Landrum hit the home run for the Orioles to beat the White Sox in Comiskey Park. But what impressed me more was Britt Burns pitching ten innings and shutting the door on the Orioles. One of the most magnificent games I'd ever seen in my life. I was doing the television. I looked down when he finally gave up the home run and the Oriole players, almost all of them, got up on the top step of the dugout and applauded him. Bitter foes. Bitter enemies. Trying to get into the World Series. But they knew he should never have lost that game. Home run. Tenth inning. Whew! Things like that just tear me apart.

People ask me what was the greatest catch I've seen. Well, I don't think I *have* seen it, even though I saw the catch Al Gionfriddo made off DiMaggio in the World Series. I was in the bullpen that day. I saw Larry Harlow make a catch—I swear to God, I've never seen anything like it—he was like on a teeter-totter, half on the fence, half off, and he caught the damn ball. I saw Paul Blair knock the gate open with his body and catch the ball out of the ball park. Those were two nondescript season games. Every day in some ballpark in this great country somebody is making the greatest catch someone else ever saw.

The big difference with *players* today—and I truly mean this—is that we really did have more fun. There's no question about it. You know, I go to a lot of old-timers' games around the country, and a lot of them won't ever go to a ball game, because they think there's a lot of jerks playing the game now. I find some bitter people. The highlight of their lives was on the field, and they may never adjust.

Another thing that's turned it around is all the money and the long-term contracts. I would like to say that if I got a five-year contract for five million I would bust my fanny to do good every year, but I'm not so sure. Statistics show that there are more guys on the disabled list on the first year of their long-term contract than in the following ones. Each year it goes down. On the other hand, there are a lot of players with long-term contracts that give their all. I'm totally engrossed by people like Dave Winfield, Cal Ripken, Jr., Eddie Murray, Boggs, Mattingly, Bell. Reggie: He may not have been a popular guy but I'm going to tell you something, he gave you everything he had at all times. But there's a lot of guys who don't. I can see it in the clubhouse, on the field, off the field. I can see complacency.

Viewers ask me about animosity in the clubhouse, and I have an answer for that. You show me a club that does not have some animosity, and I'm going to show you a loser. I saw the Oakland A's have fights in the clubhouse. I've seen problems in *this* clubhouse through the years, guys pushing each other. I see that happen. Stop to think. A married couple, together all the time, day and night, you can't tell me they don't have arguments. I'm not saying fisticuffs, but arguments, and they might push each other once in a while. How are you going to get twenty-five guys living together to be lovebirds all the time? It doesn't happen! I never worry about arguments.

Earl Weaver was a great manager but a cantankerous man. I've seen

some things with him, players pushing him around, him yelling and screaming. It's a highly emotional game. It is. They're still a bunch of little boys
playing a little boy's game. Campanella said it: "What does it take to be a
major-league player? You've got to be a real man, but you've got to have a
lot of little boy in you."

Think about it. They all have unbelievable egos. You've got to be
selfish.

12
THEY
ALSO
SERVE

She's known, especially in the Seattle Mariners organization, as the lady who took Mindy, the white Maltese, to spring training. "I guess she became a legend, so when a ballplayer saw me in the office in Seattle he'd look around and ask, 'Where's that dog? Don't you bring her to work here?' No, I didn't."

Before the 1988 season she gave notice to the Mariners. "I wanted to be in D.C., where I grew up, and there's no team there, so I was prepared to go to work for politicians and things like that. I knew that would be tough, but I was prepared. I could still go to baseball games, and read *Baseball America*, *The Sporting News*, and *USA Today*, and get all the gossip."

Then came a call from Dan O'Brien in Cleveland, who had been her boss in Texas and, for a while, in Seattle. She changed her mind about retiring. Now she's the Indians' administrative assistant for baseball administration.

I guess I'm the keeper of the information, any information the president or general manager of the ball club needs. It has sort of become a legal secretary position, except it's baseball law, and baseball law's not like any other. There are three sets of baseball rules: major-league rules, professional-baseball rules, and National Association [minor league] rules, and they all intermingle. And then there's the basic agreement [the union contract]. I don't know who started all of this. I'm still not comfortable with all the rules, because they change, and now you can't change any rules without the players' association approval.

I also do all the regular secretarial duties, answering letters, answering phones. One of my main responsibilities now is all the major-league contracts, for the forty-man roster plus the manager, coaches, trainer. I have been known to do the minor-league contracts, too.

Off-season is our hectic time of year, starting September 1, when you can recall your option players and expand your active roster. There's a lot of paperwork. Every time a player moves you have computer work and paperwork. Every time a player goes on the disabled list you have paperwork. At the end of the season you compute all of the performance bonuses. You've got to make sure that those are calculated correctly. The computer will often just light up and tell you if you've made an error, and you get phone calls from the league office or the player relations committee and you think, "Now what did I do wrong?" Usually it's just minute things like crossing the *t*.

In December we have to tender the contracts, and after that all the negotiations start, and players with three years' service are eligible for arbitration. It's hot and heavy in January and February for my bosses, who are on the phone all the time. And spring training's coming.

I have to keep track of length of service and options, although the new computer system almost does that now. Once in a while *we* catch errors. You have to be aware of when a player has, say, two years and seventy-five days going into a season, because he'll become a three-year man during the season and you can't outright him without waivers. If you do outright him and he doesn't want to accept the assignment he becomes a free agent then or at the end of the season. So that's an important date. Then when he becomes a *five*-year man you can't move him without his permission, other than to another major-league club. You have to be aware of when a player becomes a *six*-year man, too, because then he's going to become a free-agent at the end of the year.

I need to keep track of the salaries of other players. That used to be hush-hush within your organization, but now it's all pretty much public—printed all the time, if not confirmed. But within the clubs, we are given that information by the player relations committee and the league office. We have an electronic mail program that all the clubs input information into, and each day we receive updated information.

When I'm typing a player's contract, I usually get some notes with the basic salary information: the player is going to make such-and-such for each year of the contract, however long that might be; performance incentives; awards incentives, All-Star team, Cy Young. Some contracts are just two little numbers, one on the front, the minor-league rate, and one on the back, the major-league rate, but some of them are twenty pages long. Guarantee clauses usually take three or four pages. Usually that's all just written out on a yellow sheet of paper and I sit there with five or six other documents and work them together on the word processor and pound it out. A lot of the recommended language has been done for us by the player relations committee, and that's on file.

I rough it out and they—Dan O'Brien, my boss, and Hank Peters, our president—go over it, and then I do it again. It could take a couple of hours, or days. Then you have to "promulgate" the contract. You have to be sure the right people have copies. You have to "tender" the contracts by December 20, certified with the post office, unless the player is in the middle of a multiyear contract. When a player isn't signed and you don't tender him by December 20, he becomes a free agent. It's just one of the rules. If that happened, I probably wouldn't be the one blamed publicly, but I certainly would feel responsible.

I have to keep track of waivers, and that system has just changed the past few years, so it's a little harder for me now. Throw out the old garbage, bring in the new! The language is legal language, and it's not always clear. Mistakes are made all the time. In order to outright a player of certain service to the minors, you have to get waivers from the other teams. Then there's a time of year, from July 31 to September 1, when you have to have major-league waivers before you can *trade* a player to another major-league team. We made a deal in Seattle once, with Boston. We were getting Ray Quinones, Mike Trujillo, and Mike Brown for Spike Owen and Dave Henderson. But Boston didn't have waivers on Mike Brown and Mike Trujillo. Those two were at the minor-league level, but Boston still had to have waivers. So we didn't get those two players for one week because of the technicality. With a lot of talking and thinking and discussing with the league office, we found a solution. Stephanie Vardavas thought of it, even though it wasn't her job at the time.

Waivers are kept very confidential because most of the time a player wouldn't understand. I think he'd think the club didn't want him. You can request waivers on Monday through Friday before two o'clock Eastern time. You do this through the computer, and every day on the computer, by about four o'clock, there's a list of players on which waivers are sought. I run this off and circulate it. If you want to claim someone, you enter on the computer that Cleveland wishes to claim so-and-so from Seattle, say. You are awarded players on a waiver claim by the standings in reverse order, so if you're in the basement and claim a player along with the Yankees, who might be in first place, your club is going to get the player. At the end of the period after waivers are asked, the club is told whether a player has been claimed, and by whom. We don't know who claims players on other clubs. We only know who claims ours. Then the club has forty-eight hours in which to decide whether they want to *withdraw* the waiver request. Most of them are withdrawn.

There are twenty-four players on each of the twenty-six clubs' active roster, and the average player will have waivers requested at least twice every year, just in case you need the waivers for a trade opportunity, or a move to the minors. You want to be ready in case of the blockbuster deal where somebody wants to trade his whole club for Don Mattingly. I would say that a majority of clubs, when a new waiver period starts, ask them on *all* the players, just to be ready. But you can only request waivers on seven players a day, so it takes four days to get them all for your whole team. On those first days of a waiver period, I don't take time off.

I'm an organized person, and all this is a challenge to me. And I like the game. My dad was visiting clubhouseman for the old Washington Senators. He was a bat boy in 1924 and '25 when they won the World Series. I grew up hearing about Walter Johnson, Sam Rice, Goose Goslin, Joe Judge. My brother-in-law was drafted by the Chicago Cubs, and my grandfathers and my nephew have played baseball. I'm a third- or fourth-generation Washingtonian, depending on which side of the family, and I have to tell you this: my mother's grandfather, William Andrew, was the engineer who put the top on the Washington Monument.

I'm a fan but I don't go to all the games. Part of my excuse in Cleveland is I've been getting settled. If I go to the game I'll sit up in the box with my boss, or downstairs with friends. I'd hate to see them build a dome here. The Kingdome in Seattle is just a big cement mushroom. Maybe they're waiting here to see how the retractable dome in Toronto does. There's nothing like sitting out on a Sunday afternoon when the weather's about seventy-five or eighty and watching a baseball game and eating a hotdog and having a beer, too. But I hear that it's always twenty degrees colder inside the stadium here—which is fine if it's ninety outside. I don't know why everyone talks so demeaningly about Cleveland. "The mistake by the lake"—I don't see that.

I got into baseball in 1962. I worked for a federal union and I was driving to work one day with this lady I worked with and she mentioned that a friend of hers working for the Senators said they were looking for a secretary. My aunt worked for the attorney for the Senators and I got the job. It wasn't very interesting at first, just typing the same letter over and over again. But then I eventually moved over to promotions and advertising, and did that for six or seven years. Joe Burke was general manager at that time, and he asked me if I'd like to come down there. "Down there" was the other end of the hall where the baseball department was. So I moved to the baseball end of it, in October 1969. I've been doing major-league work ever since.

In 1970 or so, David Eisenhower came to work for us—a summer job, really—helping Hal Keller with the draft and doing a lot of statistical work for us. He *loves* baseball. He played those board games and I just read in *USA Today* that he still does. Every baseball fan wants to work in a front office. They come in all the time. Not just David Eisenhowers, but the average Joes, and they don't care what they make. They just want to work in baseball.

We didn't have much room so David and I shared an office. We became baseball buddies, chatting when there wasn't much to do. I wasn't married at the time, and was sharing an apartment with Joan Flanagan, one of the girls I worked with. One night, Joan wasn't home and I was in the bathtub and the phone rang. I came running out with a towel around me and there I was standing in the kitchen with just a towel and this voice says, "One moment please, the White House is calling." There I was in my birthday suit and the White House was calling. I looked down and thought how glad I was they don't have televised telephones. David had left his wallet at the office and asked whether it would be safe, with a couple of hundred dollars in it. I said we'd had a lot of break-ins at the stadium. So he said, "Would you mind meeting me there so I could get my wallet?" This was about ten o'clock at night. I called a friend and had him meet me and we went over and David and Julie pulled up in a White House limousine with the Secret Service. We went upstairs and I forgot all about the alarm system. I opened the door and the alarm went off and all I could see was getting off the elevator with the Secret Service waiting down there with guns drawn. But they never heard the alarm.

About seven of us from the front office moved with the Senators to Texas after the 1971 season. Dan O'Brien came in at the end of the '73 season. I did the same work for him, then he left in 1979 to go to Seattle to become the president, and I went with him. Then he was fired in 1983 and Hal Keller was promoted into his job. Then Hal was either fired or quit in 1985, and I stayed on when Dick Balderson came out from Kansas City to take the job.

I enjoyed very much doing the minor-league work, too—did it two years in Seattle and *loved* it. It's sort of a little family off the overall family, and you are the contact for all the managers and coaches and trainers and scouts. You have game reports coming in every day and you can see what the young players are doing. It's fun to see the development of the kids you sign, eighteen years old, or seventeen. Jimmy Presley was seventeen when they signed him in Seattle, and his parents had to sign his contract. I didn't know that and I sent the contract in and the National Association sent it back and said his mother had to sign it. Sometimes you learn by your mistakes.

I don't know the players here in Cleveland very well yet, because I just started, but in Seattle, especially with the ones we signed, I almost felt like they were my sons. I go to spring training every year, and I'm usually the one typing the contract, and if the boss isn't there I'm the one who goes over it with them and explains it and gets them to sign it. I help them with their insurance. They're all so young and just starting out in the world and they don't understand hospitalization and workman's comp. Minor-league players are covered by Prudential Insurance, and major-league players are under their own benefit plan. There are rules as to which one you're on. It confuses me sometimes, so I can imagine what it does to a twenty-two-year-old. Then they get married and of course start having children, and we have to make sure they have the proper insurance.

If they had a question they called Ethel. I'm sort of their baseball mother. I don't have any children. I'm divorced. I guess I've sort of adopted them. I check the standings, read the stories, look at the box scores to see how my babies are doing. There's a lot of them still in Seattle, but also Darnell Coles in Pittsburgh, Phil Bradley with Philadelphia, Spike Owen with Boston, Dave Henderson with Oakland, Matt Young with Oakland. Gosh, there's a lot of 'em out there. I can look at most teams and there's somebody there.

Baseball—sports—are a little chauvinistic, and you either accept that or you don't. Some people have a hard time with it, and they've left. I don't, most of the time, maybe because I'm older, or maybe because I grew up in the business. But you just make yourself miserable by fighting it. I have no desire to have a job where I would have to go in the clubhouse, because that's the players' domain, but a lot of business gets conducted there, and I have to send a runner down or ask my boss or our traveling secretary to get something signed or acknowledged. In some ways it would be easier if I could go, but it's not necessary.

I know the mechanics of the game off the field, but I'm not an expert of the game on the field. I'm not qualified to evaluate talent. I couldn't be a general manager, but there is a place for women in baseball. There are a couple of men in this position; Lee Pelekoudas, who used to be the traveling secretary, replaced me in Seattle.

Most of the women in baseball are doing the secretarial jobs. I don't mind being called a secretary, but I know my job's more than that. I know I have some expertise. I also know that out there in the real world there's not much call for it. There's only twenty-six of these jobs.

Maeve Burkeridge, who worked for Hank Peters for twelve years with the Orioles, and works for Roland Hemond now, is doing the same thing I'm doing, and I had been talking with her on the phone since I worked for the Senators, but we had never met. I love to talk to Maeve, because she is from Ireland and I'm part Irish, and she has this wonderful Irish brogue. I could listen to her forever. I had been talking to Stephanie Vardavas in the league office, now with the commissioner's office, for I can't remember how many years, seven or eight, but I'd never seen her, either. We were just friends on the phone. Two years ago last Christmas the three of us made a date to meet at lunch at the harbor in Baltimore. I drove over and they were late, and I'm going back and forth, back and forth, and I had no idea what these people looked like. We finally met and sat down and had lunch and it was wonderful. They weren't like I pictured them at all, and I'm sure I wasn't, either. Now the people from the various organizations meet at the computer seminars: Arlene with the Cubs, Lesley with the Angels, Rhoda with the Padres, Sandy with the Brewers. It's fun to sit down and talk about the problems, and how they're handled.

I've met so many wonderful people, a lot of famous people, in all walks of life: Ted Williams, Joe DiMaggio, Charley Pride. He's a big fan of the Rangers.

The greatest highlight was my first Opening Day in D.C., when John Kennedy threw out the first ball. On Opening Day in 1971 I was in my office, running around, and there in my office, little ol' me, was Hubert Humphrey and Rogers Morton—majority leader or whip at the time—and the secretary of agriculture, I can't remember his name. Joe Cronin was standing there. J. Edgar Hoover. They were there for a luncheon. I don't think I'd have had the chance to meet all these people and make such wonderful friends if I worked for IBM or General Motors.

AL FORESTER

He was in the florist business (five greenhouses and two shops) with his four brothers in Boston, but he had played ball semi-pro and also in the Navy, and he wanted to get back into the game. Shortly after he applied for a job on the grounds crew at Fenway Park, his predecessor had a heart attack. That was 1957.

During the games I'm stationed down at what we call "canvas alley." That's where our crew stays. It's a box seat, first row, you know. We're down there for two things: in case something happens on the field, and for the fifth-inning drag. Other than that, anytime it rains we all run out and get down the canvas. If you put it on a couple of times, it gets heavier and heavier because the canvas picks up the dirt as we're dragging it. It makes it that much heavier so you need twenty-five, thirty guys. I might be one of the senior members but we're all grounds crew. We're all equal. We all have to push that tarp out.

I have the seat right beside the ball boy. Some of the kids don't have any interest in watching what's going on, but I watch every inning. I can call a base hit anytime. Little bloopers, whatever. When the ball leaves the bat, I know.

The infield is the main thing. That's where the bounces are. You don't get many bad bounces off of grass. The dirt is maybe two feet in some places, three in others. What happens sometimes is we just add onto it, and then I take the Rototiller when the team is away and Rototill it all just like you Rototill your garden. Just mix it up: take the top and put it on the bottom. The bottom comes up to the top. So in other words, it's just like a man plowing your garden. I do that maybe twice a year. Then we just rake it and level it off a little and roll it and rake it again and roll it until it gets right back where you want it.

If I see a bad hop during the game, I blame it on the infielder. I don't know if you've ever heard of Marty Marion. He used to play shortstop for the St. Louis Cardinals. That man always walked around between pitches and base hits, always moving his feet around. If there was a little divot out there he would just scratch it up and level it off with his shoe. People can't see how many holes there are out there, divots from spikes. When a ball-player goes in for a ground ball and takes the shot and cuts to the left, cuts to the right, what's he doing? He's digging up a little bit of a divot with his shoe. So, I mean, if he doesn't go back and just fill it up again, well that's his own problem. Just go out and scratch it up with your shoe. You've got a spike on there, so level it off and now you won't get that bad hop.

Bad hops don't come from pebbles. That's all *dirt* out there, screened dirt with a mixture of loam, sand, and clay. After the game is over, we have two fellas go out with this aluminum drag. It fills in all the divots. The following morning when I come into work I put some water on to wet the infield and all the dirt along first and third. After it's wet I take an infield pull machine, like a sand-trap machine they use at golf courses. I bring out what we call a nail drag—it's got three hundred nails on it—and attach it to the back end and just drag that thing, make like a figure eight, up and back, working my way from first to third. Then I'll go the long way, back and forth, till I got it all scratched up. And now we've got a little cushion out there. Joe [Mooney, the superintendent] comes along with his rake and gives it a level job. After that the kid comes along and puts a cocoa mat on it, which is just like a rug mat you see in front of a home. It's made out of rope. And he'll take that and smooth it all out, and then another kid will come along with a roll, a light roll, and roll it, put the water on it, and we're all set to go.

The mound dirt is altogether different. That's all red clay from New Jersey. Red clay, from about the position of the pitcher when he starts out, about two feet in back of the rubber, down to about nine feet down in front. He wants something *solid* for his follow-through. Eventually he'll make a hole there but it's not going to be a big hole. But if you put in the same dirt as you have on the infield, no way. You wouldn't last four innings in a ball game.

If you have a lefty pitcher for our team and a righty for their team, it may end up that every time the opposing pitcher gets out there, he'll scratch our Red Sox pitcher's hole, so naturally it's going to get a little bigger and bigger and eventually they may say to get out there, the hole is too big for the Red Sox pitcher. You go out there with a rake and a pounder and scratch it up, fill it back in and just pound it down and that's it.

After the game you take a broom out there and sweep out the holes in front of the rubber where they follow through, put a little water on them with a watering can—clay gets sticky when it gets wet—and then you come in with your new clay, which is in a bucket, and pound it down. Just like making bread dough. You got to pound it down and fill that hole back up, then scratch around and fill it all up and that's it.

The same thing with home plate. Where the two batters' spots are, left and right, plus the catcher's spot, plus the umpire's spot—all red clay. If it was dirt the ball would never get in play. The hitter wants it hard. He's always scratching because he wants a little bit of a hole there so when he puts his right shoe, if he's a righty, in there, he's got a spot where he can really let go. His whole motion is forward and his back foot will never give because he's got a little bit of a hole there, just like putting your foot up against the wall to brace yourself and then you take off. They all have their own spots, but, generally, they all go into the first hole unless they want to move up in the batter's box.

I'm here at six-thirty in the morning and I may leave an hour after the game. Right now the only time we have a day off is on weekends when the team is away. Some of the younger fellas stay on weekends just to water. I think the most I've ever worked is somewhere in the vicinity of 102 hours in a week—if we have six night games and then a Sunday game. Overtime pay, sure. During the off-season we just work forty hours and that's it, unless something comes up. Somebody needs a ride to the airport, I can just drive them, or pick them up. Ballplayers get hurt, sometimes I have to go to the airport to pick them up, like the time Bill Lee got in that fight in New York with the Yankees. I had to pick him up and take him to the hospital out in Worcester to be checked out.

Sometimes I even go up the wall in left and get those balls up there in the net. You just can't let anybody go up there. You only have so much time to get up there and get down before the ballplayers come out to play the game. If a kids goes up there and he's frightened, now it's going to take maybe half an hour to get him down. So, I mean, different jobs come up at different times. If I had a job in a machine shop and had to watch some tool go around a thousand times, I would have quit a long time ago.

It's really a great experience to be in a ballpark and meet the people. You're talking about fans, you're talking about ballplayers, you're talking about—I've been out there at a festival we had, the mayor's field day. Bob Hope was the umpire. I had the opportunity to put his chest protector on him. And then he kind of hugged me a little bit, just a little joke. We used to bring the little podium for Arthur Fiedler to stand on. We had opening day for the Harvard band. Ted Williams, a fantastic man. He used to have this fellow pitch during batting practice, and he had the ground crew shag the balls. We used to go out and do it on our lunch hour, instead of eating a sandwich. One day I was out there playing right field when he hit the ball over my head, you know, and I caught it before it went into the grandstands. He kind of blasted me because he wanted to see if it would go out. But other than that he's just been great. I went down to Cooperstown with him when they inducted him. The fellas in the clubhouse, Mr. Yawkey, Ted Williams, we all went down in the same bus.

In 1987 the Red Sox gave the three DiMaggio's a tree and I was out there, just holding up the tree while they had their picture taken. Joe, Vince, and Dom. I've been out there with Yaz on his three thousandth hit, four hundredth home run, whatever. And even when he retired I was out there, driving this Suburban, towing a boat that the Red Sox gave him. I've seen a lot of them come and go.

The Red Sox took me and my daughter to California for the playoffs in 1986. And then when we came back I went to the World Series at Shea Stadium. I was there throughout the Series, so I saw them all. What can you do? Things happen. There is nothing you can do about it. The ball is going to bounce somewhere and it just bounced that way. We just lost it, that's it. No way of bringing it back.

P E T E   C E R A

A little round man, he celebrated his fiftieth anniversary in the game in 1987. We talk above the roar of the washer and dryer in the Philly clubhouse.

Never had to work in a factory. Baseball's all I did all my life. It gets in your blood. Been with the big club for fifteen years now as assistant equipment manager. I'm seventy years old right now and I've been single all along. Still lookin'!

I work from February 5 through October 15. In the off-season I live in Hazelton, Pennsylvania, up near the Poconos, a resort place. During the season I live right near the stadium in a private home, Italian people like I am, walking distance just right around the corner. I was supposed to be there a couple of days and this is my fifteenth year! Some friend of mine was looking for a room for me in 1974, they got to like me and I stayed. I eat there a lot.

We split the road trips and I go with the equipment on the plane. Five thousand pounds is our maximum, and only once have we had a problem. I make sure everything is on, then make sure everything gets off and onto the truck. Then we go to the hotel with the personal bags. Some of the guys then go with the truck to the stadium to unload, but I don't. I don't have to. They have the people to do the work. Then I'm just "around" until we load up again at the end of the series.

In Philadelphia my main duty is the laundry. We have two washers and two dryers run by computer cards. In the minors sometimes I had a wringer washer and no dryer—I hung the stuff outside. Every player's uniform gets washed every day, just about. I'll use fifty pounds of soap in a couple of weeks. After we're done with the uniforms we give them to our minor leagues and they use them. The big difference between the minors and the big leagues is that everyone up here has at least two sets of uniforms for home and road each. In the minors, if I had thirty uniforms I started suiting the guys from the smallest up. They weren't tailor-made.

The uniforms are better now. Them days they were wool, now they're double knits. Conditions are better. Players get their shoes free. Minor leagues, they have to pay, or get hand-me-downs from the big clubs. They're only too glad to get a pair. We send them used baseballs, too.

I go to the stadium at ten o'clock and leave about midnight, at least. I'm not working all that time but I'm here, you know. I usually watch the games on TV, or maybe go over to the visiting clubhouse and see old friends. I should have kept a diary myself, I could have wrote a book. The biggest thrill was after the World Series going down Broad Street, and another was shaking hands with Connie Mack. I still correspond with some players from thirty, forty years ago. I've got all the rosters and keep up with who's out of baseball, who's died. There's such a big turnover, there must have been a thousand players at least. My favorites have been Richie Allen, Greg Luzinski, Pete Rose—Mike Schmidt, of course. He's the only one left from when I was a trainer in the minor leagues—Double-A at Eugene, Oregon.

I started in baseball in 1938 as the trainer at Hazelton, Pennsylvania, which was Class-A baseball. Then I went to Wilmington, North Carolina, where we played inside a race track, and then to South Carolina before I went into the army for three years with the engineers. We built the monument for Ernie Pyle on Okinawa. Maybe you've read about him: wrote about GI Joe; killed by a sniper on his last day.

I come out of the service and went to Scranton, Pennsylvania, in the Eastern League and we won the pennant by eighteen games. In 1953, I worked for the Washington Senators, the last year they had a pro team in Scranton. I've been with the Phillies since 1954, in Terre Haute, Indiana, in the Carolina league. Then at Williamsburg, Pennsylvania; Little Rock, Arkansas; Macon, Georgia; Reading, Pennsylvania; and Eugene, Oregon. I was in Little Rock when Richie Allen was the first black player to play there. Fans weren't that bad, not as bad as everyone thought it would be. In the South the black players would have to stay with a funeral director or a schoolteacher or something like that; they didn't even allow them in hotels.

I guess I would have liked to stay a trainer in the big leagues, but I don't have the degree. They say it's because of malpractice suits. But every team has a doctor right there. It's just a new rule they got.

I could retire and get Social Security plus a pension, which ain't as good as the ballplayers', but it's good. I've got a lifetime pass here now, but I haven't used it yet. I've got two World Series shares and I'm hoping to get another one. Winners share in our last World Series was $85,000, just $65,000 to the losers. It's a big difference. It keeps going higher and higher. Shares are usually voted to trainers, equipment men, and coaches. Coaches aren't allowed in the meeting when the players vote, but they automatically get them. When Pete Rose was here he gave the coaches a new jeep as a gift for doing extra work with him. Then he won $23,000 a few years ago when he had that streak of hitting, and he split that nine ways, he gave each one of us $2,500. The whole $23,000 he gave away! All he wanted was our Social Security number, you know. Why should he pay the tax on that? That's the biggest tip I ever got. The second biggest tip was twenty $100 bills from Richie Allen. Some of the players are more friendly than others, but they're all okay as far as working with, you know. Some of 'em don't tip at all.

J A C K   M U L L A N Y

He's a fixture at Shea Stadium in New York, one of the ushers assigned to the choice section behind home plate, where the players' families and assorted VIPs sit. Besieged with requests for autographs, introductions, *seats*, he betrays no reaction whatsoever when approached by the hopeful fan or gatecrasher. He's a stout Irishman who has seen it all and has a multipurpose, monosyllabic answer to most requests.

I have my eyes all over the place. These are prime seats. If we get somebody who's not supposed to be here, we can be fired, *on the spot*. It has happened. Or you could get a week's suspension, two weeks' suspension, *month's* suspension. I missed the '73 playoffs because of a little incident, but I'd rather not talk about it. I don't really watch the games. Many a night I'll go home and put the replay on and watch it. My wife will say, "Didn't you see enough baseball today?" No! You don't really see the game, certainly not how the pitcher's pitching to the guy, stuff like that.

I started at Ebbets Field forty years ago, before the Dodgers moved west, and my brother was there previous to that. That's how you get started. Somebody in the family, somebody you know. It's the Licensed Ushers and Ticket Takers Union. We have all of the major sporting houses in the city. We used to have all the fight houses, but today they're all closed down. We have the Garden. At Yankee Stadium we have the ticket takers. We don't have the ushers. That's about the only house we don't have. Different union. Con Ed [Consolidated Edison, the power company for New York City] had an offshoot union and those guys moonlighted up there and formed a union.

Each house has its own seniority list. You shape and shape and shape and, hopefully, ten years from now, you get work. Here at Shea we have maybe 400 men on the list, and there will be a call for 150 men. The head usher and assistant head usher make up the worksheet the night before. They're part of management. It's hard to move up. When I started with the

Mets I was number forty-four. Twenty-seven years later I'm fifteen, and I've only moved up in the last five years. The guys above me, sixty-five, seventy years old, they're dyin', you know. My own brother just passed away this past April. He'd been with the Mets also these twenty-seven years. He was number eight on the list.

The seniority only puts you to work. There's no guarantee *where*. Through the years and all you get into spots like this behind home plate. But say the boss didn't know I was comin', he may put somebody else here and if at the last minute I come in, he could be nasty and say, "Hey, I didn't know you were comin', so you work upstairs." I haven't worked the upper deck since Shea Stadium was built. I had to go up there *one* day, to deliver a message.

We're paid per game, and almost double for doubleheaders. Used to be we got an extra dollar for the second game, but now that the union has progressed over the year, it's not bad. There's also a bonus system, you get so many days' pay if you work so many games. If you work sixty-five, I think it is, you get like ten games' extra pay, which isn't bad. Christmas present. If the games goes after midnight, and some have of course, they give you "supper money," with which in New York you could maybe buy a good *breakfast*.

We're here two and half hours before the game. You make sure people are in the right seats, watch for guys poppin' off, smokin' pot, stuff like that. If I can't handle it, I get a special cop. It's not really a *job* job. It's more of a fun job. Sometimes you get a little trouble. Just yesterday, there were eight people, four seated on one side here, four on the other. They all wanted to sit together. Kept bothering me about sitting together. I told the guy *three* times, "You know, I got a boss upstairs and if he looks down and sees me move you, he thinks I'm *doing something*, know what I mean?" The fourth time I finally said, "Now strictly between you and me, I'm really getting teed off. Sit in your seats and that's it."

You get all kinds, all sizes and shapes, the good and the bad. One day it was raining like heck here and the drains weren't working right, so water was pouring like a waterfall out of the mezzanine into the loge right above us. I hear all this yelling and screaming and people lookin' up, so I go down to the front to look up and there's this guy *completely naked*, taking a shower.

A lot of times the players' families—wives and kids—only come out in the seventh, eighth inning. They have a room for them, also. Mothers and fathers usually let me know who they are. We had a ballplayer here one time whose parents got divorced, and his wife's parents too. Then all four got remarried. So it took awhile to figure who's who and what's what. One day the wife's mother came in, and the wife started to introduce me and I said, "Sure, she's in California, in real estate." They were amazed. I'm very good at faces. I can place faces. Names—don't ask me.

One day Dani Folquet—she was on *PM Magazine* on TV—came in and introduced herself. We got to talking and finally she said, "You know why I'm really here?"

"No," I said.

"I want to meet Lee Mazzilli." She knew this was the players' family section, and she knew I knew them all.

"Well, he's out in center field," I said, and I laughed. But then I said, "But I'll do the next best thing. His brother Freddie's here, I'll introduce you to him and he can take over."

Now she and Lee are married.

Some of the guys are really, really friendly, and some'll walk right past you. You say hello and it's as if they don't even see you. Gary Carter, one of the nicest guys on the club. Always stops and talks. Roger McDowell. Mazzilli. Buddy Harrelson, I've known him from Day One.

For the playoffs and the Series you get more of the celebrities, people who aren't, really, baseball fans. All your Hollywood types, Billy Joel, Christie Brinkley, people like that. Only time I ever see them! At the World Series. So I wouldn't really call them baseball fans. Richard Nixon comes more often.

And when they're cold, they're *cold* . . . you know, tipwise. Generally the big people just say thank you. Most don't really tip. The average working guy takes care of you better. If I *averaged* fifty cents a seat for all my seats I'd be very happy, but I don't do that.

13

PEANUTS!
POPCORN!
SEASON TICKETS!

He's what they call a gamer: shows up every day, plays hurt, can't get him out of the line-up, not afraid to get his uniform dirty. Once worked eight straight years at Comiskey Park without missing a game. The Iron Man of the vending business.

You don't have to think much, but still there's a lot of theory about how you vend. If you're stupid you're not going to make as much as a smart vendor who knows where the sales are: who's ready to drink. If you go up the same aisle somebody else has just been up, that's stupid. You gotta watch for the other vendors.

I never really expected that I would be doing this for almost twenty-five years. I wanted to be a writer, a lawyer, I was going to college at the time and I thought I might go into advertising and I was worried about going into the army, too. The lottery saved me. That was probably the single most exciting day of my life, to see that my lottery number was like number 211 or something.

My uncle had a stand at Sox park and was a vendor a long time ago, in the fifties. He got my brother a permit card with Local 236, Service Employees Union of the AFL-CIO. My brother wasn't a baseball fan much but I went with him to some games just to watch. I always loved baseball. I'm a crazy White Sox fan. I always wanted to play in the major leagues. My brother wasn't athletically inclined, and vending is a very physical job, so I don't think he liked it very much, and, anyway, I applied to be a vendor myself in 1965, when I graduated from high school. Vending wouldn't be as good as being *on* a baseball team, but at least I could come to the ballpark every day, see the game, and then make money, too.

There was a big waiting list to get into the union. Meanwhile, my brother was away at school and he said why don't you use my card and go in my place. So in July 1965, I went down and I vended under the name *Ronald* Rutzky.

I worked under my brother's name in '65 and I made about $10 a day selling pop, which wasn't too bad if you're seventeen years old and you're working two and a half hours and you're at the baseball game. I only worked Sox park 'cause those were the years when the Cubs were real terrible.

In 1966 I went to apply to get the job and they looked up my brother's record—which was really *my* record—and they said, "Well, your brother worked a lot of times last year, maybe you'll work as many times as he did. We'll give you a card." I had a real big debate with myself whether I should join the union. If you didn't join the union you paid fifty cents a day to work. It cost $50 to join and you had to pay $5 a month for the dues. I was eighteen years old and it sounded like a lot of money to put out for nothing. I joined because I figured I could get better items to sell, with more seniority.

I went to Columbia College in Chicago and started working a lot of games selling pop. I started making a little more money—$20 a day, maybe; $30 a day, sometimes—good money in 1967. In 1965 Leo Durocher took over the Cubs and he finished eighth and he said, if you recall, "This isn't an eighth-place team." In '66 he was proved right. They were a *tenth*-place team. What they've drawn this year so far [June] they probably drew for the *whole year* then. You still could probably make money, although at the time I really didn't know that much about vending. You'd think that only if they draw a lot of people will you make money, but you can still make money if there are small crowds. It depends on how many vendors come. So I started working both parks.

I liked vending even though I was a very small kid, only about five-foot-two and I was very thin. I didn't have that much physical strength, so after I sold a load of pop I would have to sit down. I couldn't walk for three weeks. Normal people don't climb up and down stairs for three hours. I guess I was growing, so my muscles weren't really that well developed. For the first five or six years, in March I would start climbing up and down stairs a little bit, so I would be more ready when the season started. I felt like it was spring training myself. Nowadays, I've done it so long, my legs muscles are developed to such a degree that I could work four hours. I might get hungry or something but basically my legs just don't get tired. If there is a sale at the end of the day I'm ready to run for it. I have vended as much as eleven straight hours and I never stopped once. Eleven hours walking up and down, all at Comiskey park, a twi-night doubleheader and they had a three-hour rain delay and each game was like three hours and something.

I'm sort of famous. I don't have more seniority than *any* vendor, but almost more than anybody that is still working. I've been in the union twenty-two years. There's other guys that have been around longer but they haven't worked as many games. This isn't supposed to be your whole job but this has been for me for the past fifteen years. I've been able to get unemployment compensation in the wintertime, except for one year.

When I started I was making a dollar a load selling pop. I was seventeen and I could live on $20 a week. I didn't need any money because my parents took care of me. Now I make $10 a load on beer, but of course that's twenty-five years later—inflation. And I'm older and I've got to make more money anyway. Up to two years ago I didn't have that many cares. Then I got married. My wife's a season-ticket holder at Sox park. My brother met her in Jamaica and introduced her to me at the ball game on Memorial Day, three years ago. And now I'm a parent myself, too, so . . .

I'm in a streak of thirty-four straight days without a day off, and that includes thirty-seven games in those thirty-four days. I try to work 162 ball games—eighty-one at each park. At this point there is no other vendor who has worked every single game at both parks selling beer. There's another vendor who worked every game but one day he sold pop at Sox park. My daughter was born last year and I missed two games for that, and I missed two games here because I got in a little trouble. I was accused of selling beer to a minor and they said they had it on tape. Those things happen. It's almost impossible not to sell beer to a minor, especially if you're an aggressive vendor and you're trying to sell as many as you can. Sometimes you get carried away. But I wasn't sure. They said they had the evidence. If they could prove it they could suspend me for thirty games. So they said why don't you just take two days off and we'll just forget it. I didn't like it, you know. It hurt me real bad and I was real sorry that I screwed up. I lost a couple of good days. It was a real streak. I was making almost $200 dollars a game. You never know how much you're going to make and it turned out the first day I missed it was real cold so I was happy, I was relieved. The year before I missed no games. There was a streak at Sox park I worked eight-straight years without missing a game. I only missed a game to go to my high school reunion. That's how I stopped my streak. It was kinda like I *wanted* to stop my streak.

I still watch the games. Those guys who have beer stands underneath make a lot more money than I do, but to me that's like having a real job. They may tell people, "I work at the ballpark and I go to every game," but they're *down there!* That's no good. My favorite player of all time was Richie Allen. I was a Richie Allen fan before he came to the White Sox. When he came to the White Sox it was like the greatest thing that ever happened. The first year he came he was MVP. There was never a player I had seen who could excite the people so. He hit so many home runs at home, and the balls he hit were like off the scoreboard, or off the upper deck roof. I wouldn't go get another case if he was coming up. I would stop completely for that; when he would come up. I would also make sure I never went up into the upper grandstand, because up there you couldn't see the ball if it went over the roof. It was such a thrill. I guess that's why people love baseball. If you think about why all these people are just sitting around and get so happy when somebody hits a ball out of the park, it's hard to believe.

A vendor's dream is to be the only vendor and have every sale. My theory of vending, my strategy, is to come every day no matter how bad it is. I've driven in horrible rainstorms and it's cold out and everyone thinks I'm insane when I tell them I'm going to the ballpark. They think nobody's going to be there, you're not going to make a dime. The reason I go in horrible weather, no matter what, is because I want vendors to know that I'm going to come, that they *can't* think that they are going to be the only vendor, 'cause I'll be there. One time there was two games and I went from the Cubs to the Sox and there was a phenomenal rainstorm between games and there was no way on earth they were going to play. It was absurd. The Sox had like three thousand people but we only had four guys on the third-base side—no, we actually had twelve guys but a bunch of the vendors were playing cards. I sold over twenty cases, which is pretty good. Nowadays if we do twelve or thirteen that's real good.

One day I did fifty-one loads. It was a doubleheader, but not that long, and I cut myself and I didn't even have the best beer and I was in the upper deck in left field. We had bottles at the time; with bottles you could really open them and pour them. People were really thirsty. The first hour I sold twelve cases—one every five minutes. At the time I was getting $5 a load so I made $255. I since have surpassed that as my best day in money terms, but I've never sold more than fifty-one cases. Other guys have.

My body is well suited to it. I love being outdoors. I had another job three years ago in a video store. It was pretty good money. I'm a real big movie fan. My favorite movie is *The Godfather*. I've seen it over twenty-five times. I know most of the dialogue. And my second favorite is *Part II*. My third favorite is *The Graduate*. I was interviewed by Gene Siskel and I auditioned at ABC to be a movie critic, and then Channel 5. I've been on WGN radio talking about movies several times. I don't get paid but once every two months I get called up. What I really want to be is a movie critic. Well, actually I want to be a movie *star*. I was in *The Untouchables*. I was in the scene—there was like two hundred of us—when Robert DeNiro punched his attorney. I jumped over seats and I was yelling at him. You could see me pretty good. I worked for three days and I made $200 doing that.

It's really dangerous right around home plate. Those foul balls come over your head and you really gotta watch it. I've been hit a couple of times. If I hadn't been watching a lot of times I could have gotten seriously hurt, or at least my beers knocked over which is a catastrophe in itself. You have to have the right temperament for vending. You have to get through the crowd and you have to watch it so you don't knock people down or hurt 'em, or they're gonna come after you. People are gonna shove you, too, and some people try to cheat you. I'm hustling as much as I can. There isn't anyone who hustles more than me. It's hard to believe that I can pour two beers faster than they can open their wallet. They say "Two!" and I pop the cans open and start pouring and then I got the beer and their wallet is still not even open. That irritates you really bad because, you know, another vendor is going to take that sale on the next aisle. I want to finish this sale and serve these people and I want them to have the beer but I also want to get out of there and get rid of them and get to the next sale. Volume, volume, volume.

There used to be a lot of regular customers at White Sox Park. Every day on every load I knew that I could sell at least half my load to my regular customers—guaranteed sales. But they don't have the season-ticket holders they used to have at Sox park. I think that baseball's such big business and the sets are so expensive now that the season tickets are more the corporations, and they just give them away to their customers or families or whatever. They used to drink a lot harder, too. Whole bars would come, and that was the best. They used to call Sox park the biggest tavern in town. Friday night there would be a hundred bars and they'd all come down on buses and drink out of their minds. More families come to games now, and the Sox aren't drawing all too good. Eight, ten thousand people. I've been averaging $90 at Sox park. Here at Wrigley I'm averaging about $130 a game.

You'd be surprised how honest the fans are. They will give me the money back if I give them too much, and I'll give them the money, too. At one time if people had given me more money I might have kept it, but many years ago I just became more—I don't know, something in me wanted to be more honest with people and I would give them the money back. Like last week somebody gave me two twenties stuck together. I easily could have kept it, but I just gave it to him right there.

There are fans who have tried to rip me off. They say they gave me a twenty and it was only a five. Just last week somebody did that. Then he says, "Hey, didn't I give you a big tip?" I said, "No, what do you mean? Yesterday I gave a guy back twenty dollars." I don't put the money into my other bills until I walk away. I learned that the hard way.

You don't want any trouble. There's two words that are so valuable:

"I'm sorry," or "Excuse me." If I bump somebody I go out of my way to ask if they're okay, make sure they're not going to make out a complaint or something. If you get bumped I think it's a natural instinct—hey, you want revenge or something—but if I instantly say, "Excuse me," it's incredible what power those words have to make people relax or forgive you. *If you say it nicely.* There's guys who walk through yelling, "Excuse me! Excuse me!" Those "Excuse me's" aren't the same. I know vendors who have been fired for smashing someone in the head. You've got to watch it if you want to keep this job. You don't want to miss any games, or any innings, or any outs.

I try to make vending more like a game. Like, I keep lists of how all the vendors do in the upper deck, which is where I work if it's open. [He shows me the list.] This is the left-field side, this is the right-field side. I did sixteen cases, tied this guy for high. I'm usually second or third. But for the year I'm number one, because these guys don't come every day. A lot of these guys have other jobs. This one works in insurance, this one at the post office, this guy's a social worker, this guy's a musician, a guitarist, yesterday he played at a wedding. He used to wear a badge until they made him take it off. He would tell everyone, "I'm the sheriff. Buy from me." People would wait for him. Some of the guys will sort of beg people. "You want a beer? You ready for a beer?" Some guys will start pouring a beer before you've even said you want one. I won't push it like that.

I like seeing the beer, pouring the beer. It's a soothing effect. I like people drinking it. I would like to have a drink of it sometimes, it looks so good. I like beer.

PAT GALLAGHER

An irreverent kind of guy, of whom there aren't that many in the front offices of the baseball world. The senior vice president for business operations for the San Francisco Giants, he learned the hard way about the baseball business when he hired the Great Wallenda to perform on the high wire between games of a doubleheader against the Mets in 1977. The fee was $6,000. The umpires established a special ground rule in case a ball should hit the wire strung across the field, 150 feet up.

"Wallenda was seventy-four and could barely walk off the airplane, and the wind came up at Candlestick and it started to rain. I said to him, 'Hey, I'll make up an excuse. You don't have to do it.' But he said the show must go on and all that. He got up there and walked across. In the middle he stood on

his head. You could have heard a pin drop; nobody left their seat. He took a baseball out of his pocket and threw it as the first pitch of the second game. I had the traditional shaker of martinis for him when he got to the other side. He toasted the crowd and everybody cheered and we were on the front page of every newspaper the next day. Plus we had sold eighteen thousand tickets, probably twice what we would have otherwise.

"I was just beaming when I went down to talk to Spec Richardson, our general manager. He reamed me up one side and down the other! Wallenda was *too* good. Too interesting. Nobody had gone to the concession stands! Spec said we probably *lost* $25,000."

Postscript: Despite the problem at the concession stands, Wallenda was hired to return to Candlestick the following year. He signed and dated his contract on March 19. On March 20, in Puerto Rico, a high wind blew him off his wire. The following day, Gallagher received the contract in the mail.

I got into baseball pretty much by accident. I played as a kid, but in Southern California I started surfing and doing the other things you would do there. I was not a red-hot baseball fan.

I was an art student in college, and it took me four years of college just to realize that commercial art was not what I was cut out to do. At the same time I was working at Sea World in San Diego in a variety of capacities— sweeping up cigarette butts, training animals—and so when I got out of school, I just went back to work there. It was one of those companies where you got a chance to grow real quickly. They moved me around the country. I returned to California in 1974 with a company called Marine World/Africa USA.

In 1976 the Giants came within a couple of hours of moving to Toronto and Bob Lurie stepped in and bought the team. After about six months of operating it, he decided he needed a marketing guy. The Giants had never had a marketing guy; there were only one or two guys in the game who had a "marketing" title. Bob decided he wanted somebody who had experience in the entertainment business who did *not* live and die with the team's win-loss record. My charge in coming here really was to start from ground zero in developing reasons for people to come out to the game. It was one of those deals where all of a sudden you say, "Now what do I do?"

You have to have a sense of humor because, on the one hand, we're trying to develop all these things, like the Great Walinda, and, on the other hand, the players and management and the media are talking about what a lousy place Candlestick Park is. I kiddingly say we're going to have a Rolex watch day, everybody gets a new Rolex President watch, and people say,

"Yeah, but I've got a watch, what do I need a watch for, it's a long drive"! I've never had another baseball job, but it just doesn't seem like the people in the other cities have as tough a time as we do. Maybe they do.

We're a tenant. The city is our landlord. The way they operate Candlestick Park and the way it's maintained is really a disgrace. The ability to control the whole experience is a pretty powerful thing, and we don't have that control here. In order to get something to eat or drink you actually have to walk *outside* the stadium. You walk into the restrooms and the urinals are overflowing. The escalators that bring people to the upper deck break down.

If my theme-park background has taught me anything it's to try to inject into baseball some of the feeling and some of the philosophy of people like Disney. I'm not talking about just the glitter and entertainment, I'm talking about how we service the people who come in and make it a better, a *predictable* experience.

The Dodgers are sort of like the McDonald's of baseball. Every time you go there you have a pretty good idea of what the experience is going to be like. When you drive into Dodger Stadium there's a smiling person there to direct you. When you walk up to the gate there's a ticket taker there who smiles and tells you where you are supposed to go. When you want to get something to eat it's easy and convenient. When you walk out you're not worried about whether your windshield is broken or whether some jerks are going to charge you to get back in your car.

I don't care whether we get a new stadium. If we can't achieve a predictably good experience of going to a game, it's not going to be better. The ballplayers complain about playing out there, but to tell you the truth I have more sympathy for the fans. All that money sort of eases the pain a little bit for the players.

The situation does sort of beat on me after a while. When there's things that you don't have control over, you start not only expecting the other people's excuses, you start making excuses of your own, and I have to admit I think we do that here sometimes.

I thought this job would be a neat thing to do for a while and I've been here twelve years. I had no idea it was going to last this long. My title now is senior vice president but I'm really a salesman. If the team does well that just gives me an opportunity to sell more and do a better job. I don't mean that in a callous way. It would be nice to have a World Series ring, but the last thing Bob Lurie needs is a marketing guy like that, who lives and dies with the team. If things are going great everybody is celebrating. If everything is going bad, we've got twenty-four guys on the field hanging their heads. You don't need everyone else to do that.

Unfortunately, the teams during those first years were pretty awful. We incrementally increased the attendance but never really in my mind made the kind of impact that we should have. In '82 we did come very close—finished a couple of games out behind the Dodgers—but in '83 we just decided to take a different tack, and rather than try to convince people that this was a wonderful place, we thought we would *challenge* them to show up. We said to Bob Lurie, "Look, people are saying a lot of these things about Candlestick anyway. We don't have enough money to make this place any warmer. Why don't we just try to make people feel better about being here by recognizing them in some way?"

With the help of some advertising people we came up with this little button, the Croix de Candlestick, like the famous award for bravery and courage. We would give it to people for what we would consider the ultimate act of courage, being a Giants fan and staying until the end of an extra-inning night game at Candlestick Park—a badge of courage separating the front-running fans (admittedly we have a lot of them here) versus the hard-core fan. The purple heart of being a Giants fan. We did a series of commercials that were exaggerated to a point where they were set in what looked like Valley Forge, guys sloggin' through the snow.

Our theme that year was "Giants Hang in There" and all that really promised was that we were going to show up and play and it also promised that you had to have a sort of a special kind of guts and determination to be a Giants fan. Frank Robinson was our manager at the time. We asked him what kind of a team he had and the only thing he could really say about them was it's one of those kind of teams that hangs in there and just doesn't give up and we thought that was pretty neat and so decided to take that and embellish it.

It all seemed to work together. The Giants "hanging in there" and the Croix de Candlestick became sort of the rage that year. We did have a few extra-inning night games and we gave away the button. Attendence that year was up, about a million-two. The radio spots won a Cleo, which is like the Oscar of advertising, which we were all real proud of. I mean, it's not like winning the World Series, but it was one of those things where you get recognized. But from then on people expected us to do something sort of offbeat. Just by working in San Francisco people think you are weird and baseball people think what we are doing is kind of weird. I guess a lot of the guys around the league are sort of rooting for us, privately. None of them have owners that would let them do the stuff that we get to do. I can't imagine George Steinbrenner letting somebody from the Yankees talk about how lousy Yankee Stadium is and daring people to show up. If there's anyplace where they *ought* to dare people to show up, it's a stadium in the Bronx.

In '84 we took the idea of the team mascot. One of the things about baseball is that when somebody tries something new and is successful, other people follow. It's like the cows standing around the lake: one goes down and drinks the water and if he doesn't fall over dead, all the rest come down and drink. The San Diego Chicken is the premier mascot, and the Philadelphia Phillies came up with the Phillie Phanatic, which was pretty good, but then there was just a rash of awful, fuzzy mascots. We did this survey in town and loaded the question. "If the Giants had a mascot, would you boo it?" Sixty-eight percent said yes, they'd boo it. That's all we needed. John Crawford, one of the guys who develops our advertising, came up with the idea of Crazy Crab. This guy in a crab costume was sort of the Rodney Dangerfield of mascots. It started out as a TV commercial: the crab's agent had gotten him this new gig as the Giants' mascot, and when he came out on the field and did his little act to this dumb music, the fans, because they are so sophisticated in San Francisco, wouldn't put up with anything as dumb as a mascot and booed him off the field.

At that point we had not planned to put him on the field. The whole point was to demonstrate that Giants fans were different. About two weeks into the campaign we decided to see what the reaction would really be, so we trotted him out in the fifth inning—big crowd—and damn! Just as we had conditioned people, they booed him off the field, so that became the shtick. Every game he'd come out and dance and people would boo him— give them a chance to get up and clear their lungs—and he'd give the high sign and walk off the field. The only bad part about 1984 was we lost ninety-six ball games. Frank got fired and the whole thing was pretty sad. Toward the end of the season people were sort of taking out their anger on the mascot. They started throwing bottles and everything else on the field. The guy inside the crab costume said, "You don't think anybody out there has a gun, do you?" And I said, "Oh, Jesus, I think maybe it's time to close this act." We put Crazy Crab on ice after that.

We decided to take *another* different tack. If night games are so bad out here, how would people feel if it was day games out here? We'd had writers who for years would say, "Why don't you play more day games?" and we said okay, let's do it. We became the Chicago Cubs of the West. We scheduled about 75 percent of our games as day games in 1985. Our theme was, "Real grass, real sunshine, real baseball," and our television commercials portrayed this place like Honolulu. You know, we had Samoan beer vendors with grass skirts, girls in bikinis, guys with surfboards, a Beach Boys style of music. It was kind of a fun deal. We put the grounds crew in Hawaiian shirts.

But it was just another awful year. Real grass, real sunshine, real baseball: by the middle of the season one of the writers said, "Well, two out of three isn't bad." You have to admit it was kind of a character builder. We brought back Crazy Crab for a weekend series to try and change our luck and we got swept, so we permanently retired him. Sometime in there we had a kite day. We figured with all this wind . . . but damn it, that day we had no wind. What can you do? We lost a hundred ball games. I wish I could remember who came up with the best description of a losing baseball season that I've ever heard: "A Broadway show that ought to close but can't."

Now we're thinking, "Okay, we've sold cold baseball, we've sold hot baseball, the only thing we haven't had to sell is *competitive* baseball."

At the end of the season, 1985, Al Rosen and Roger Craig showed up on the scene. I think that at the time everybody said great, any kind of a change is gonna be better than what we've got here, but nobody was really all that enthusiastic.

Al Rosen: great player in his day, had been with the Yankees, been with the Astros, was he a retread?

Roger Craig: one of the famous pitchers on the Mets staff, lost twenty games, played on some championship teams, but not noted as a really successful pitcher through his career.

All of a sudden something magical happened. Rather than keeping some bum around because he had a big salary, Al just dumped him—"Hey, we can finish in last place without these guys." He brought a lot of kids up and there was an effect on the rest of the organization. You could feel it. Hey, wait a minute, something's going on here. He brought Mays and McCovey back into the organization. And in our first meeting he told me that he had done some research on me and the stuff that I had done here and all he wanted to do was let me do my job and hoped he could learn something. I walked out of there about ten feet off the ground. I said here's a businessman who understands what's going on. And when we presented ideas to him after that, he could be a demanding guy, but he understood what we were trying to do and if anything he encouraged us to do things with *more* flair. It was like a dream come true. Don't do anything disrespectful, or anything that would be taken in the wrong way by the fans, but have some fun.

So we're sitting here and trying to figure out how to sell this thing. Listening to Al and Roger, their enthusiasm was pretty contagious, but I'd sort of been through that before. It's easy for them to say whatever they want, but as a sales guy, as a marketing guy, I don't want to come up with some sort of dumb slogan campaign that we are saddled with as we're sliding into the second division.

In looking at what we had, we'd always come up with a column of strengths and weaknesses. The only thing we could figure to say about the team this year was that they were young, so the theme became, "You gotta like these kids!" The rationale was that maybe people would stay off their backs while they're learning how to play. I mean, "You gotta like these kids" doesn't really promise that much, but it became a positive.

This was 1986, and all of a sudden these underdog rookies, the Mike Aldrettis and Robbie Thompsons and Will Clarks and some of the pitching guys who had been struggling—Mike Krukow and people like that—all of a sudden things were happening. Roger Craig told them to have fun and play and they all respected him. He was a prophet. Everything he said came to pass. I don't know what it is, but it's like he manages *everybody* in the organization, me included.

So 1986 just breezed by and it was a wonderful year. Before the '87 season we sat down with Roger and just let him talk. This term "humm baby" kept coming up. He called everything "humm baby"—pretty girl, bottle of wine, great play. I was sort of afraid that it was something that you could really drive into the ground. Humm baby. Humm baby. Jesus. We agonized over it but finally decided hey, here's something that's so real and so good it's too good to pass up.

I asked Roger, "How do you spell 'Hum baby'?"

"I don't know."

"Is it 'Hum baby'?"

"No, it's 'Humm baby.' "

The slogan became, "Humm baby, it's gonna be fun."

The season started and, I don't know, it was just one of those things that captured people's imagination. They were saying it all over town, all over the country. And we don't take any credit. All we take credit for is maybe listening to Roger. After we put it out there the fans grabbed it away from us and took it for themselves—one of those things you always hope for.

In '87 you had, on one side, people talking about how bad things are and how lousy the stadium is and how we gotta move, and, on the other side, we're setting attendance records. As the marketing guy for something that people are always saying is lousy, all of a sudden to have it be good and have people want it, was the greatest thing that could ever happen. I mean, it's like the guys who tried to sell Extra-Strength Tylenol after the ladies got poisoned. That's how we had felt about it sometimes—trying to sell something that couldn't be sold. All of a sudden it was just a miracle.

It didn't take a genius to figure out that "Humm baby, it's gonna be fun" ought to be "Humm baby, let's do it again" for 1988.

Our advance sales for the season went from 450,000 to 1,200,000. Incredible. We look at each other and laugh. Last year in September when we were going for the playoffs, all of a sudden people realized they didn't have any way to get tickets for the playoffs, so we came up with this thing where we allowed them to plunk down a $120 deposit on 1988 season tickets in order to qualify to get post-season tickets. I called it our amnesty program: people saying, "Okay, I admit that I'm a front-runner, but please let me in."

We said, "Fine, we'll let you in, it will cost you $120." We had 15,000 people plunk down the bucks. It was incredible. I don't know if it had been tried elsewhere. It was certainly the first time we did it. Some people said, "You're extorting the money out of us," and we said, "Yeah, you're right, we are, but do you want to come to the playoffs or not?"

The players are sort of our shills to sell all these different promotional things that we have. They really get a kick out of it because it's pure Hollywood. We've got the big 35mm cameras and we build a set. I've never had a player come and say, "Hey, I want to get paid for doing this," because they are all afraid we *won't* ask them. Jeffrey Leonard gave us a problem one year and I said, "Okay, I'll just use the one that we did of you last year," and I laughed at him. What am I going to do, slash my wrists because he doesn't want to do one of these commercials? Go push around some clubhouse guy. I don't care enough for you to push me around. Let the writers and the broadcasters and all these guys take it seriously. We're not going to take it seriously in these terms of how people look at it because this is the *entertainment* business.

I think a lot of people are intimidated by baseball players. Heck, I know I am in certain cases. You think, geez, here's a guy, his life is twenty-five times more exciting than my life. Well, it really isn't that way, and once you realize that you get to be on more even terms with them. We've got PR people in our office who are making one one-hundredth of what the players make and who work about five times as many hours *plus* take shit from the players in the process, and to hear some of these players complain about an extra-inning night game followed by a day game is comical. You have to have a sense of humor about it.

I don't begrudge the players for anything they get. They are the entertainers. Nobody pays to watch me do my job. What may bother some people is the difference in the *scrutiny* given the dollars. It seems like such a big deal on this side to give somebody a $1,000 raise, while a guy who just hit .220 making $400,000 gets a raise the next year to $700,000. That sort of gets to people. They comment on it.

For many years the way front-office folks were treated was, "Hey, there's a ton of people out there who want to do those jobs," and if somebody complained loud enough, just pick the next guy in line and put him in that position. I think that's starting to change because owners are starting to realize that it is a business and you've got to get good people rather than a washed-up sportswriter. But in some cities there still are guys who sort of get the short end, and they allow themselves to get that because they want to be involved with the game.

Something else that's really unfair in baseball is this tampering rule. I could understand it if a front-office guy is under contract, but in order to hire somebody from another organization, you've got to get permission of that ownership. There have been many instances where a guy might have had a chance to move, either in a lateral move or upward, and has been prevented from doing so because the owner won't give someone else permission to talk to him. A lot of times the person doesn't find out about it. I think that is absolutely criminal. In a way it was that same kind of mentality that got the players to react to management in the way they did. Somebody in a front office will challenge this rule somewhere along the line. It's not right and it's probably illegal.

ARTHUR D'ANGELO

Surveying the ballpark across the street, he calls himself the mayor of Fenway. He's not boasting, but speaking with pride.

He explains the sadness around the eyes: Henry, his beloved brother and

business partner in Twins Enterprises, has recently died. In fact, Arthur plans on taking a brief vacation because he's depressed. But his love for baseball and selling baseball soon takes over the conversation.

We came to this country from Italy in 1939 and we started selling newspapers in front of the ballpark. We lived in walking distance, five miles. We were twelve or thirteen. The only thing we could say in English was "two cents." Newspapers were two cents in those days. If they asked us questions —what street was it?—we would just point this way or that way. We didn't know what we were talking about, but we did know the value of money.

Boston College used to play football games here and we used to sell flowers. In those days fans at college games wore yellow mums. And as we got older we started selling ice cream in front of here. Then in 1944 we were drafted and spent a couple of years in the service. We got out in March 1946, with limited education. We really had no training, no jobs. So we started selling pennants. You'd never seen pennants at *baseball* games prior to 1946; only at football games. This was around May, when the Red Sox had a fifteen-game winning streak, so we felt maybe we could sell some. Basically, believe it or not, we are the originators of selling pennants at baseball games.

In 1946 the Red Sox won the pennant, and we'd done well. After the baseball season was over, we had nothing to do and the government of the United States sent a train throughout the United States showing copies of the Constitution, the Bill of Rights, the signing of the Japan surrender. So we thought, well, why not make a buck? We made copies of the Bill of Rights, the Constitution, and the train itself, on a pennant, and we sold them to the people who were going to see the train. We had some big crowds. We traveled throughout the United States, every city over ten thousand people from October through April, and then the following winter, too. I can still name you every state capital, the biggest cities, the rivers, you name it.

We also made pennants for Dewey in the 1948 presidential election. Dewey was the favorite, he was going to sweep the country with votes and win it. We couldn't sell the pennants! I wouldn't be surprised if we have some around somewhere. Truman was selling much better. We backed the wrong guy and took a bath. We haven't done that since. Sports is our bag and we enjoy it and that's that.

Until 1967, they didn't buy much here. Only when Ted Williams was here. We used to sell a lot of Ted Williams goods. We made T-shirts of Ted Williams, we made pennants of Ted Williams. People didn't even recognize the Red Sox team; they recognized Ted Williams. And that kept us alive. But after he retired, from about 1961 to 1967, they had very little attendance. We almost got out of the business of selling. We used to come here and gross $12, $15.

Fans will only buy when the team is winning. It makes a lot of difference. The percentage of business is 40 percent less per game; when the team loses. Fortunately in 1967 the Red Sox got revived. They won the pennant and we started selling more merchandise. We ended up buying a building and opening up the store. That was 1968, I believe. And, naturally, from pennants and novelties we went to sweat shirts, T-shirts, jackets, and so forth. After a team wins the pennant, you've got a couple of good years because they sell a lot of tickets. Then they start falling apart again and it goes bad two years and then if the team rebuilds you start to do well again. So we also had some lean years before the Red Sox won again in 1975. We are fortunate that the Red Sox win it about every ten or twelve years. There are some teams that haven't won it for many, many more years.

Right now, this is positively the largest store in the United States as far as baseball or sports. Wrigley—there's a fairly decent one there. We sell to them. And there is one in Detroit. Otherwise, there is no one who sells all the different style hats of every major-league team including baseball, basketball, football. We probably carry two hundred different types of logos. If the workers aren't sports-minded, we don't want them working for us. Live baseball, eat baseball, sleep baseball. We want them involved with it. A person comes here, it's not just selling the merchandise. If they want to ask questions, give them the answers. Everybody asks, "What's happened this year to the Sox?" So you have to tell them stories, that's all.

Inside the ballparks, prior to these years, they used to sell little bats and caps, nothing else. When the Red Sox saw what we were doing on the outside, they went into the business. Rightfully so. What the hell, everybody wants to make a buck. And then every concession in the United States started selling those souvenirs. In turn, we got stopped and we went to legal battles with the Licensing Corporation of America, the clubs' licensing company. But they were pretty good about the whole thing. They gave us a piece of the pie, really, they gave us the okay to sell, paying a percentage. And from then on we started wholesaling, too, because we felt we knew the business as well as anybody, if not better. We had the experience. We started selling in small quantities to other ballparks throughout the United States.

Take baseball caps. In 1967, '68, like I said, we had a few dollars, and I started going overseas myself because the caps made in the United States were getting too expensive. So I went to Korea, Taiwan, mainland China, made some connections there and I started bringing in three or four thousand dozen a year. More than that. The first year was about ten thousand dozen —of different teams, not just the Red Sox. One thing led to another. Now we are selling probably 500,000 dozen a year. We are shipping some goods now to Italy, to England, to the Netherlands. There are other wholesalers now. I think we're one of the biggest, comparing ourselves with Rawlings and MacGregor.

When we sell a new item we have tried it out for a year or two. If we think it's right, then we pump it into them. When I say "pump it," well, we feel we are the experts in this business. In baseball people used to buy novelties—little bats, little gadgets, key chains. No longer. Right now the things that are good are wearable goods. It has all changed in the past seven or eight years. Mothers and fathers, grandmothers and grandfathers, they will buy for their children, not only because it's a souvenir, but they can go to school in it. Back in '46, there were 2 percent women going to ball games. Today, you probably see 40 percent. I would say 25 percent of the fans will buy *something* during the season.

This ballpark is extremely hard for a concession, even though they probably do the best job of anybody. They cannot put big displays inside the ballpark. The ballpark is too small. If you go to Anaheim Stadium, it's like they built it for concessions. You go to Metropolitan Stadium in Minnesota, it's built for concessions. I've been to every ballpark in the country. I've seen ball games in practically every state of the union. The poorest concessions, believe it or not, are the *inside* stadiums. Seattle is very poor. I personally don't think that closed-in stadiums are good. I don't call them stadiums. I call them arenas. It's not baseball. People recognize that on Saturday and Sunday they want to go to an outside game. They want to see the skies during the day.

New York is a more rowdy crowd than most cities in the United States. I guess Boston has more finesse, what I call a subway fan. Most of the other ballparks—with the exception of St. Louis, right in the heart of the city, and now Minnesota—are nearly all out of town. You have to drive to get there. Here you can get smashed, you don't have to drive home. You can take a streetcar. What happens in most stadiums today, there are buses of people coming from seventy-five, eighty miles away—the surrounding states. These guys or women, they do a little drinking on the buses and by the time they get to the ballpark, they get a little wired. I'm not saying the majority, but this happens throughout the United States. Go to the ballpark

in Minnesota or Kansas, there are people going to the game from the Da-
kotas. And by the time they're there, they're really smashed. But they do a
good controlling job at Fenway Park. In the Middle West they do a lot more
drinking. There are a lot of beer drinkers.

I haven't missed a game at Fenway since 1946 with one exception, in
1960, when we went to the Olympics in Rome. We sold baseball pennants,
but they said, ROME 1960 OLYMPICS. They'd never sold pennants before in
Italy. We doubled our money.

I go to every game from the second inning on. I go in after the crowds
go in and I come out in the eighth inning because the crowds come out. I've
had the same season tickets, the same seats, for many, many years. Box
thirty-eight, first row, between first and home. I think I could be a scout
and be as good as anybody else. And believe it or not, I've never played
baseball. I never had the opportunity to play. We played soccer in Europe,
but when I came to this country, it was just work, work, work. Nothing
else.

I'm here from seven in the morning. I see if everybody is in and so
forth, check out the store, see if it is well stocked. If it's not, go to the people
who do the stocking—now that I've reached an age of no return. My brother
and I used to do all the stocking. I stay till when the ball game ends, till
midnight, or sometimes till one or two o'clock in the morning. It's a long
day. I enjoy every bit of it.

Like I said, my brother and I were inseparable. We held our meetings
during the ball games, because we were never bothered by anybody else,
and every half inning we'd discuss what we were going to do the next day.
Baseball is a very, very leisurely sport. Football is spontaneous, you're in
action every minute. In baseball, you have three or four minutes every half
inning to relax your mind and think about other things instead of sports. It
gets exciting, the home run, you know, but it only lasts a few seconds and
then your mind relaxes. The sixth game of the World Series in 1975 was the
most exciting time—the home run by Fisk. I'm very friendly with Fisk and
it was one of the most exciting games. But there's been so many! You know,
you're losing 3–2 and all of a sudden somebody hits a single . . .

Naturally we do much, much better when they are winning, but it's
not just the money itself. Besides, believe it or not, in the World Series, in
the playoffs, they're not the true fans. The true fans don't get the tickets. It's
people that know somebody and somebody who knows somebody who has
the tickets. Some of these people will never see a ball game again. They do

buy souvenirs but they're not our regular customers. You see a lot of people with neckties, suits, which that's not a baseball fan.

I'm the mayor of this area. I feel that I am. Maybe I'm not voted, but I do feel it inside. We're part of Fenway, just like a building. All the ballplayers come to our place when they're rookies. They all want their own posters made and their name up in lights, or whatever you call it. Once they become stars, they're out of the picture. Naturally my number-one man was Ted Williams. He was just super. Jimmy Piersall—see, I keep going back because I'm that old. Lately, Yastrzemski, Rice, Boggs, they're all very, very nice. They're all friendly. I don't go over to the clubhouse. I could go. The owner—we have a very, very good relationship. I can go whenever.

You know, a lot of mornings I just sit here and look at the ballpark and reminisce. Just look at it. There's no ballpark like it. You can sit in any seat and see a ball game. It's just super. I'm not going to live forever but as long as I live I want to see this. And even my kids are so mentally involved with Fenway Park. They're baseball nuts. Oh, maybe I created them, or in turn they accepted my way of life. It's the Red Sox. We feel we're family.

I used to see Mr. Yawkey go upstairs into that door right across the street, in the early mornings. He came in May when the weather used to warm up. If the team did well he stayed until the end of the season. If the team did poorly he used to leave around the end of August. But Mr. Yawkey was always very good to us.

JIM MURPHY

The florid-faced, red-haired Irishman is the proprietor of Murphy's Bleachers, directly across the street from the real bleachers at Wrigley Field. He wears shorts and sneakers and drinks a Bud Light as the crowd begins to fill up his beer garden prior to the one-twenty game against the Reds. Hamburgers sizzle on the open grill. The El roars past every few minutes. Inside, the young women behind the elaborate old wooden bar wear Cubs pinstripes. The television shows Cubs highlights. Rock songs alternate with patriotic Cubs cheers.

This was the first drive-up hot dog stand in Chicago. Ernie Peretti built the bar here back in 1940. One guy used to park his car, tip a couple of bucks to a cop, go into the Bleachers, put his bets down with the local bookies that were hanging out, go to the ball game, sit in the bleachers, drive back to

Lincoln Avenue. Nobody knew who he was until he finally got killed. He was John Dillinger.

I started renovating these properties across the street from the park in about 1972. I built the first roof deck—real elaborate, with Astroturf, barbecue, bathrooms, shower. I lived in the building. The idea was to watch the game with a refrigerator full of beer. I was a policeman, a detective, gang-crime unit. You're only good at that for about ten years, then they burn you out pretty heavily. I retired in 1980 and bought the saloon. I could see the place could be profitable. It was called Ray's Bleachers then. The tavern was from the brick wall forward. We added on the upstairs, the beer garden. You used to need a shotgun to take your garbage out. A lot of the places were what we would refer to in police terms as a bucket of blood, most of 'em, with a fight every day, walk in the door to someone giving you a crack in the side of the head with a ball bat. You'd get a killing a night up here. About 1976 there was a dramatic change. I was the first guy in here renovating property. Then things got a little yuppie and everybody started following suit, building roof decks. Now the Cook County treasurer lives in one of the apartments. Another guy, he's a salesman out of Boston, keeps an apartment here and a house in Boston. We've got a dentist on the first floor. I live here.

Totally different crowd now. Upgraded situation. Drinking all across the country has changed. I can remember when people would be urinating at the bar in here. Now, there's next to no rowdiness. You're looking at a new generation of fans. We've got families, kids, people in their sixties and seventies. It crosses all age barriers. It's America. There are a lot more girls coming out to watch baseball, and that's helpful. It has a quieting effect on the male population. And food's important, too. You can't just have a drink in the hot sun. We do 50 percent food. You can't be solely in the liquor business, but we sell an awful lot of Budweiser. We're rated as one of their best accounts.

Most of the games are one-twenty. The fans start coming in between eleven and twelve o'clock. By one o'clock you won't be able to move. Not many local people during the week because obviously some of us have to work. There'll be a couple of dozen people left during the game, and then it'll be wall-to-wall again after the game. I've never taken a head count but it's hundreds, *several* hundreds. We take out all the bar stools after the game, all the furniture goes. Then we have something called the holy hour, which they have in England and Ireland—my overseas relatives, shall we say. When we feel everyone's had enough to drink—hour and a half, two hours after the game—we simply close the place for an hour, send everyone home. We call it the Murphy Shuffle. We mop the floors, clean the whole place, then let people back in—and check everybody out very closely. We allow people back in who can handle it, usually neighborhood people. The others are on the way home. We close at two in the morning. I'm 100 percent "hands on." I sleep here, I live right above the place. You can't get any more hands-on. It's necessary if you're going to show a profit.

Baseball is 100 percent of our business. It's eat, sleep, and talk baseball. But *we're* not selling baseball. It sells itself. All these people in here grew up with the game. It carries right through your life. I don't think I'd ever leave. There's too much excitement. All that we do is have a lot of fun along the way. We're kind of an offshoot to baseball: get a great sandwich, have an ice-cold beer, have some fun, go to the ballpark and watch nine innings of great excitement and hopefully watch the Cubs win.

We took a position on the lights that we don't want the Cubs to leave Wrigley Field, for obvious reasons, and if the lights is the issue, then we should concede some lights. I don't think eighteen games is any big deal. If anyone thinks a major-league team won't leave Chicago, watch the Sox. They're going. I'm positive. I'd be very surprised if they don't [they didn't], and that should be a lesson we should learn. Or how about the Dodgers? "Oh, they'll never leave *New York*." Boy, did they pack their bags, huh? How about the Baltimore Colts moving to Indianapolis? A major-league team leaving the East Coast in the middle of the night! The Cubs have fans all over the country. They could move this team anywhere and be an instant draw. If we're sure that lights will keep 'em, fine, we want to keep 'em. We'll do less business for night games than we do during the day.

What happened here was a lot of these people who were involved had political ambitions and were trying to use this as a stepping stone. That's a bunch of bullshit is what it is. Most of these people involved in the no-lights issue are transients. The attorney for the no-lights group moved to Kenilworth. The president sold her home for $250,000 and moved to the western suburbs. They ended up all moving out, even before the issue was resolved.

Where else can you go to work and have so much fun with a lot of people every day? I've done it the other way as a detective, where you've got to play *Starsky and Hutch* or whatever that TV show is, and I'd much rather come to work and have a good time and a couple of beers. I'm sure I could sit down and write a book about it. Every day is another chapter. We used to have Bill Veeck in here every day; he could tell stories for hours and hours. When the players come over you're privy to a lot of the things going on, and when you get to know them as well as we do, when someone gets traded you lose a good friend.

Players come in almost every day. No problem with the crowds. We've got a little roof deck so they can get away, wait for the traffic to die down and maybe have a cold brew and a sandwich. Keith Moreland used to come over all the time and sign autographs and replenish his vital fluids. We usually have a day when the ballplayers come over and guest bar-tend and we donate all the money we take in to charity.

The playoffs [in 1984] were unbelievable. Never in my life did I imagine it could have been like that. There were seven, eight thousand people in the streets, hanging off the lampposts. I had the governor in one room, Channels 2, 5, 7, 9, 11—I had 'em all here. As one sports reporter said, "I'd give $100 to anyone who didn't start his interviews at Murphy's Bleachers." We had a thousand people standing outside the fence, waiting to get in.

But I knew the Cubs were going to lose. I could smell it. I predicted in the second inning of the last game that these guys weren't gonna make it. Sutcliffe was pitching at the time. I could just see that he was a little off and everybody else was a little off. They weren't jelling the way they should. A little intuition, I guess. People thought I was crazy; I said, "Uh, uh." If they didn't put enough runs in front of 'em right away, I knew they weren't gonna make it.

JIM TOOMEY

He's a jack-of-all-trades in the St. Louis Cardinals front office, now semi-retired.

"Opening Day this year [1988] will be my sixth World Series ring. I'm wearing the one from 1982 now. All full-time employees receive the ring. Everybody makes a contribution—what the hell."

About twenty years ago a fellow who wound up being a pretty good friend of mine came to me and said he needed a job. He was working for the same big electronics company he's still with, but not in as big a role. He's a district manager with a big slice of the United States for his area. But he was making a lot of money then, too.

"I need a job in baseball," he says to me. "I've got to be in baseball. I can't stand *not* to be in baseball. I don't care what the job is. I'll do anything you want to have done and I don't care what the money is."

"You don't really mean that."

"What do you mean I don't mean it?"

"A lot of people *say* this, but I'm afraid your interest, as you describe it, would last until the first payday."

"Oh no, no."

"Well, I'm going to do you a favor."

"What's that?"

"I'm not going to give you a job, and I'm saving your ass so you can do what you're doing now and what you probably do very well."

Even those of us who work in baseball day by day can't really grasp how deeply a lot of people get involved, how deeply they want to be a part of it.

Another time, many years ago when we were still at old Busch Stadium, the telephone operator calls me and says, "There's a man out here and I don't know who the hell should talk to him. Maybe you should come out."

I ask what he wanted. She says, "Come out and see, will you?"

So I go out and I see this guy and he introduces himself to me and he's an undertaker.

"What can we do for you?"

"Well, I have here in this box"—and he shows me the box—"the ashes of a man named"—I don't remember—"and one of his last requests was that he be cremated and his ashes buried in right field where Enos Slaughter played. He was a great admirer of Slaughter."

Well, now, we didn't own the stadium. We were a tenant. I wonder what the hell to do with *this* one. I go to our owner, Fred Saigh, and ask him.

He says, "I don't know."

I say, "If I keep quiet about it there wouldn't be any harm in letting him do it."

He says, "I guess you're right. Let him do it—what the hell."

So I call up the groundskeeper and say, "Bill, get a shovel and meet me out in right field."

We interred this guy's ashes out where Enos Slaughter played in Sportsman's Park. When we left that park, Busch donated it to a Boy's Club and they built another baseball diamond and a gymnasium there, and God knows if those ashes have been disturbed.

I've never watched a game as a *fan*. I sit and watch the games and never say anything and I never yell or shout. I just sit there and watch it. During the '82 World Series, Bob Wirz, the PR director with the commissioner's office, sat next to me for all seven games and I never did anything—never shouted, never screamed, never said anything. In the seventh game, I think in the seventh inning, we were behind and Keith Hernandez hit a line drive to right-center field. A hit would tie the score and that ball was hanging up there a little bit. It looked like the outfielder had a chance and I said, "Get down, you son-of-a-bitch." Wirz looked at me funny and said, "I thought you were going to go through the entire World Series without ever saying anything."

I said, "Well, I think in the seventh inning of the seventh game you're entitled!"

Post-season play is a rock crusher, anyway. I went to the general managers' meeting this year and I was sitting there at a table with Andy MacPhail of the Minnesota Twins. I said, "MacPhail's gotta be chairman of the group." I pointed out that he had won the World Series. "You *remember* that, don't you, Andy?!"

The truth is, *I* really don't remember the World Series. I don't know what happened. You go through the Series and people start talking to you about things that happen and you have no sense of them having happened at all. You don't know what the hell they're talking about because you're so immersed in the damn thing, you got so many people talking to you, asking you questions, distracting you, so many things on your mind, so many things to do, you never get the fun out of actually watching the games. Even when you win you don't have any sense of having any fun because you don't remember what happened.

I was an usher in the World Series in 1934. The Cardinals had not drawn any people all year long to speak of—340,000, with 35,000 of those on the last day when the Cardinals clinched the pennant. So they were looking for ushers and I got a job because I wanted to see the games and didn't have enough money to buy a ticket. This was the Depression. Maybe 10 percent of the people in my section around home plate were movie people in from California. From St. Louis west there was no major-league team.

Fifteen years later, in 1949, I was a sportswriter on the *Star-Times* in

St. Louis, a newspaper no longer in existence. The guy covering the Cardinals on a daily basis for the *Post Dispatch* was named Bob Broeg, who may know more baseball history than any man alive. Fred Saigh, the owner, knew Broeg well and offered him the public-relations job. Broeg said he didn't want the job, and he put in a good word for me.

I did that job until about 1967 and then I became assistant to the general manager and did that for ten years, and then I was asked to go back and do public relations again, and I did that through 1986. Now I'm a consultant or something like that. My main function this year is to give [General Manager] Dal Maxvill help wherever he needs it. I don't anticipate being on the scene much.

When I started I was a one-man department, then I hired another guy to help me. We didn't do all the things they do now—extensive promoting and marketing. At first, we didn't even have a mailing list. Early in the season, we passed out little postcards and let people write their name and address on them and we built a mailing list of the people who were interested in baseball, and then we started sending out a little newspaper. We built a list of about forty to fifty thousand people over a period of about a month.

Among the early things we did were team nights and giving away orchids. Giving away an orchid was something better than it is now; they were a symbol of something at that time. Back then, the fans came to the stadium *to see a ball game,* to see Dizzy Dean pitch, to see Stan Musial, Red Shoendienst, Enos Slaughter, Harry (The Hat) Walker. Who else did we have? Oh, I don't know, but we had a good team. In 1949, my first year, they drew more people than they ever drew in history in a ballpark that effectively seated fewer than 30,000 people. We drew 1,430,000 people.

Nobody in St. Louis had a television set, or very few. People listened to the games on the radio. The broadcasts were done by almost anybody who wanted to show up with a wire hung around him. We had about three stations broadcasting the games. In 1949 the Cardinals sold the rights. Harry Caray and Gabby Street were the broadcast team, and we had a network of 110, 120 stations. We went to Tulsa, Wichita, Memphis, Little Rock.

Caray was an exciting announcer, a controversial man—still is, you know—and he was in his prime then. Harry was giving his opinions, Gabby was telling stories. We got all this interest in the Cardinals because of this radio network. But the thing that's really responsible for the growth of this game more than anything else is television.

Anheuser-Busch bought the ball club in 1953 and they put the power of their public-relations people behind it and applied some of their advertising concepts. We did well but not as well as we should have done because we didn't have a winning team and basically this business is winning.

The thing has really taken off since Whitey [Herzog, the manager] came into the picture. Whitey had a couple of concepts about the kind of team he wanted. The ballpark is too big to find a couple of guys to keep knocking the ball out of it, so he assembled a bunch of guys who could run and slap the ball around. And keeping the ball in play makes for exciting baseball. He not only got guys with talent who could do what he wanted to do on the field, he also got together a bunch of guys who were compatible and who would not be stirring up problems all the time. He has about five rules. They're not hard rules: show up on time, run out the ball, stay in shape. That's about the extent he asks of a guy.

Another reason you've got bigger crowds is you've done things to accommodate bigger crowds. You've got bigger stadiums. We have better facilities for people: the seats are wider, the aisles are wider, the space between the rows is bigger. It's more comfortable. I don't miss the old parks. One of the guys that likes things like that is Bob Costas, whom I knew from when he wasn't known. He came to St. Louis as a little skinny kid and was going to do basketball on KMOX. He's one of those guys who talks about the nostalgia and beauty and charm of the old stadiums, and to an extent that's true, but the old stadiums also have narrow seats and bad sight lines and some seats behind posts. And as I told Costas, "The reason you like the old stadiums is because when you sit in the press box you never have to stand in line to go to the john or get a hot dog." Fenway Park is a beautiful old park, but most of the seats are pointed out at the fences. Underneath the stands at Fenway, the concourse is often slick. And it slopes like *this*. You have to walk very gingerly when you walk under the stands at Fenway! That's true of most of the old ballparks, even the old one in St. Louis.

Now, Busch Stadium is perhaps architecturally the best stadium in the big leagues because it's got some *design* to it. It's got the arches. It was designed by one of the great architects, whose name I might remember . . . Edward Durell Stone. He carried out the arches from the arch on the riverfront. He gave it some style—more than the Atlanta stadium, for example, which was built at the same time, more than Candlestick Park, which was built earlier, more than Dodger Stadium, which has no design at all but is really pasted up against a hillside. Dodger Stadium, don't get me wrong, is a fine stadium except for one thing: their fans can't see a ball game sitting down. Everytime a pitch is made or a ball is hit, everybody stands up. Did you ever notice that? I don't want to sit in the box seats at Dodger Stadium because every play everybody stands up and I don't want to stand up.

There are a lot of ballplayers whom I consider very good friends—as nice guys as you would want to meet—but you really can't, in any job in baseball, let yourself go overboard in your admiration of them. You gotta stand back from it. If you start falling in love with the people that are out there performing, you're not going to do your job right. You're not going to be able to make the right kind of judgments. You talk to a guy on a club about one of his players, about making a deal, and the guy's got a very, very excessive value on this player's services. He's simply mixed up his personal feelings for the guy with the ability on the field. You can't get that close to it.

On the other hand, though you're not going to cut your throat over it, you know it's more fun when you win. The best thing about baseball is that there's a game every day. I often wonder how the people in football put up with having to be morose over a big loss for seven days before they have another shot at somebody. I remember a season that I thought probably could have been the worst ever. We were at the All-Star break and we were below or just barely at .500, going nowhere, and it continued on that way. Then we went out to the West Coast in August. We've got the Dodgers beat in a game that might have helped us turn it around a little, then we get a bad hop and I'm cursing and moaning about it. Vin Scully comes in the press box and I said something to him to indicate I was pissed off and he said, "Well that's the way the ball bounces," and I said, "That's an easy damn thing for you to say. You sit here and win all the time." I got very upset with him.

Anyway, we left L.A. and went to Houston after that series, and I get a phone call on Monday and it's from Bing Devine, the general manager, and he's just been fired. It looks like it's gonna be as bad a season as you can get. And I'm a son of a gun if we didn't turn it around and start playing well, for one reason or another.

The St. Louis radio station had the Dodgers–Phillies game on when a fellow from the National League office called me up about some business. I said, "Just a minute. I want to see what's happening in the ball game."

"What ball game are you talking about?"

"The Dodgers–Phillies game."

"Why is that being broadcast in St. Louis?"

"There's interest in it."

"What do you mean? The Phillies are seven games out in front!"

"Well," I said, "I'm going to tell you something that I haven't told anybody else but we're going to win this damn thing!"

And he laughed at me.

With two weeks left we were still six and a half games back. But everybody, the whole team, knew somehow it was going to happen, that it was impossible but it was going to happen. It got to the point where you could see the momentum rolling and you knew it was going to keep going. Gene Mauch started getting too smart, the way he managed the Phillies, and they collapsed and by God we wound up winning the thing.

That was 1964. My *first* pennant! It was a long time in coming—fifteen years. There were sixteen teams then, so you ought to win once in that time spread. It was frustrating because we had a lot of times that we finished second and that doesn't make you very happy at all. We played the Yankees in the Series that year and beat them in seven games. You want to be there at the end because if there's any reward in this business, that's mainly it.

14
YOUTH

World's youngest general manager—looks even younger than his twenty-three years—and tied with numerous others for most enthusiastic. I meet him in Orlando, Florida.

I grew up in Washington, D.C., and went to Lake Forest College in Chicago, and during my summers at Lake Forest I interned for the Twins in Minneapolis. Last year [1987], after I graduated from college in May, I spent the whole summer in Washington, just kind of goofing off, basically, playing tennis every day. I thought I'd begin looking for a job in Washington on September 1. I was going to try to get on Bush's advance team. You know, fly around the country two weeks ahead of him and coordinate everything. Then on August 3 or 4, the Twins called me and said they wanted me to become the post-season coordinator. Dave Moore, who's the Twins' vice president of operations, was assigned to have the post-season stuff but he couldn't do it all, so he said we're gonna have to hire someone to do it.

"Can you be here Tuesday morning for a meeting with the American League representatives?"

"Yeah, what the heck?" and I hopped on a plane. I felt that I was very well prepared for the job and I knew they had the confidence in me. I had to handle all the logistical arrangements for the ALCS [American League Championship Series] and the World Series—you know, put on the whole event, coordinate all the transportation, all the hotels, all the catering, all the construction outside the stadium, I mean everything. It was a million-dollar project in six weeks. It was unbelievable, but a lot of fun. You had to learn on the spot and I took a crash course in a lot of things and just before Christmas they asked me if I would come down here to the Double-A club in Orlando in the Southern League and be the general manager. I guess they were pleased with my performance. The former GM here, Bob Willis, had been here for twenty-five years, a very loyal employee of the club, but his health was failing him. He was sixty-three. It was time for a switch.

My grandfather used to own 47 percent of the Twins. Then he sold out four years ago, five years ago, whatever. It's one of those things, you know, where I thought about, after college, going into banking, insurance, some of that professional stuff. But it would always be in the back of my mind, "Why didn't I try it?" Baseball. It turned out I loved it, you know. I absolutely adored it. And whether or not I'm in this game for the next fifty years is another story, but at least I'm making a go of it now.

I'd seen one minor-league game, in Pittsfield, Massachusetts, when I came down here January 8. I've been down here for about seven weeks now. I didn't know anyone here, I'd never been here. I didn't have a secretary. There wasn't a typewriter which actually worked. I had to go out and charge on my Visa. We didn't have any legal pads.

So far it's been sort of a honeymoon. I go to a lot of receptions and so forth, and that's all well and good, but now's coming the hard part. Now I've really got to start thinking, "Christ, how am I going to put people in the park this year?" Now the pressure is kinda beginning to settle on me a little bit. I mean, this is really an undertaking for me, a much bigger one than I expected. To be honest with you, I don't know a lot of stuff yet. Someday soon somebody will say, "Jamie, you know we gotta do this." So then I research it a little bit and learn about it and do it the next day, you know. I'll learn some things, definitely. This year I'm gonna have to keep a diary because I'm sure it's gonna be a lot of fun.

I walked into meetings in the beginning and said my name is Jamie Lowe, and they said, "Well, where's your boss?" or "Who the hell are you?"

"General manager of the Orlando Twins."

"How old are you?"

"Twenty-three."

They start laughing. Then they ask, "How can we help you this year?"

My age was really on my mind—and everyone else's—but now I think people kind of get a kick out of it. I just think you have to come with a lot of confidence at a younger age—not cockiness, but you have to be pretty self-assured. People have the perception that if you're younger you don't have any experience, but although I'm young I do have four good summers of baseball experience under my belt. I think people find it kind of refreshing, from what I understand, seeing some young kid come in and try and talk them into something.

I officially represent the club in all the municipal organization meetings down here in Orlando. Now we're negotiating with the city for a new lease. Right now we're divided up—our minor-league complex in Melbourne and our big-league complex up here. That doesn't make any sense 'cause you're shuffling guys back and forth. We'd like to develop some land or whatever for our own financial benefit here in Orlando. Ft. Myers is offering us a lot of land, plus a whole facility. If we position ourselves correctly and we sell ourselves correctly, it'll be a new era, a whole new beginning. If you have one complex you create kind of a big-league atmosphere and the younger guys think, "Hey, big-league camp!" and they learn. We'd like four or five fields and we'd like to double our grandstand capacity by about 5,000 chair-back seats. It holds 2,400 now. The rest, a little over 3,300, is bleachers. This whole weekend I've been preparing briefs; our first session is tomorrow morning with the mayor.

We'll have the mayor out here to throw out the first pitch. Invite the right people, put up some bunting. I'm gonna try to line up some fireworks if I can find a sponsor.

Selling is what it is. It's promoting. You've got to sell yourself, you've got to sell the product. You've got to educate the community. We have to co-promote a lot of events. Our attendance last year was the lowest in the Southern League by a very, very large amount. Season attendance in Memphis is a quarter million and we were at 70,000 last year, for seventy games. So we have a long way to go, you know, but the city of Orlando poses so much opportunity.

We never really had an advertising budget so I just created one. I had to put together where I wanted to spend the dollars and how much it was gonna cost and set a goal. This year our goal is 100,000 people. This community has a million people. It's growing by 7 percent annually. One hundred people a day move to Orlando. You have all those kinds of numbers, and they are staggering figures, but we can only draw 70,000 off of that? You gotta be kidding me! I mean if almost defies logic.

A giveaway costs about $4,000 bucks per night. The greatest thing we have done right now is we're giving away a car each month through a Ford dealership. It'll be the Fan-of-the-Month drawing and that person gets to use a new Mustang for a month. Actually, you have a lot of Florida gaming laws, so lotteries have to be open to everyone. We can't make it so that you have to buy an Orlando Twins ticket in order to become eligible. But you do have to show up at the stadium, so for another four bucks you might as well get in. Our goal is to fill each date with a promotional night, group night, or some kind of special event. Every night.

During spring training we expect 85,000 people to come here to witness our fourteen spring-training games. People will begin lining up here at eight, nine o'clock in the morning, waiting in line to buy tickets to come see the Twins play. So that means they'll be standing around here for a couple of hours bored stiff. One thing we are going to do this year, which we haven't done in the past, is open an *Orlando* Twins ticket booth and sell advance tickets. If I only sell a hundred tickets doing this, it's a hundred more than I would have sold otherwise.

You have to have that kind of mentality, I think. I'm in the frame of mind where I'll try anything once. If it doesn't succeed, hey, at least I tried so I have that peace of mind. And one of the beauties of this position is that there's only one way to go right now, and that's upward.

In 1981, we won the Southern League and we won it with Gaetti, Viola, Bush. You have to tell people that Orlando is a great proving ground for major-league talent in the sense that *ten* Minnesota Twins from last year's world championship team played in Orlando—that's in addition to Tom Kelly, who managed the '81 championship team here, and Rick Renick, our third-base coach, who played here in '65. So it's great caliber baseball and we offer a very wholesome, fun, exciting entertainment product at extremely affordable prices: front row for four bucks! You can't go to the movies for that kind of money. Weather is considered a problem. I understand it rains every day at four o'clock. People look outside, they're coming home from work—"Well, I guess it's rained out tonight." But at four-thirty it's perfect outside, but they've already made other arrangements.

It's a small staff and that's one thing which we will increase in the coming months. The budget is roughly half a million dollars. On Tuesday we have a retired couple coming in and they'll head up our novelty operation for spring training. Especially with the World Champions, we'll have three novelty booths open. We've lined up five or six people to sell novelty items during the games in the booths and two more in the stands to walk around and hawk some souvenirs. We have a PA announcer. I just hired the cleaning company to clean up the stadium after the games and after practices. Before it's really never been very consistent; we've had some people, charitable groups, come in and so we donate them some money, but they don't do the most professional job, understandably.

Many minor-league teams are very, very profitable. Minor-league baseball in general, I think, is a very profitable business. If you've noticed the selling prices for minor league franchises over the past couple of years, the numbers have just soared. Franchises are becoming more and more valuable because people are realizing that baseball is a beautiful game which appeals to everyone and is such an affordable game, at this level.

It's very beneficial for me to be owner-operated by the Twins because, having worked up there, I know everyone. I'm tying in to some of their promotional nights. They have a glove day, Wheaties will have a glove day for us, for a thousand people. I can get beach towels at *their* prices, because of their volume and sell them to a sponsor down here, you see.

Obviously I'm not a scout. I'm not an evaluator of talent, and I don't profess to be. On some clubs, some GMs have that responsibility, do some more of that baseball stuff. But at this point I'm not even gonna try. I mean, obviously you try and learn as much as you can. It's just a matter of watching. But one thing, I think you handle the players somewhat personally. If they are having problems or they are discouraged or they're down or they're doing well, whatever, I think you try and develop somewhat of a relationship along those lines. More like a guidance person, you know.

In the beginning I'll travel just so I can familiarize myself with the Southern League and various people and various parks, just because I want to learn as much as I can about everyone and about the people and about how the league operates and about how minor-league baseball operates in other cities. The Southern League is Birmingham, Charlotte, Chattanooga, Columbus, Greenville, Huntsville, Jacksonville, Knoxville, Memphis, and, of course, Orlando. Bus rides absolutely everywhere. I just figured out that we are going to travel twelve thousand miles this year.

I was making out our hotel rooms the other day—that's one of my responsibilities. Say we have to go to Columbus, that's four hundred miles away. Now in order to save costs we can't leave here right after the game 'cause that means we'll get to Columbus at, say, four A.M., which means I'll have to pay for an extra room that night—or morning. So we'll have the guys hang out here till one o'clock, so we'll arrive at Columbus at six A.M., so I don't have to pay for the extra room. That's brutal and tough on the players but it's one of those things, just the way it is in the minor leagues.

The average player's salary is about $1,500 per month and you get paid for the months you play. You're not paid year-round, which means during the winter you've got to go find another job. These guys aren't making any money! So we're staying at some Sheratons, we might stay in a Hyatt in Greenville, which is one way of taking care of them, anyway.

Dave Moore and I worked very closely in putting the whole post-season thing together in Minneapolis last year.

It was a massive job for two reasons: we had no idea how to do it and no idea how much it would cost. You're given a manual by the commissioner's office, and you try and follow the manual, obviously, but each club's gonna do it variably. I'd call up the Mets and say what was your budget. I'd call up Anaheim, Kansas City, whomever. But the size of each city is so different, and the cost of living in cities like New York and Boston is so much more.

At the *end* of the World Series we put together the budget.

First we had to build auxiliary press boxes in the stadium. We had to have banners. We had to paint logos on the field—a lot of inside-the-park operational stuff. Security is unbelievable. You've got to arrange for all the media booths, all the media seating, where each member of the media is going to sit, assign phones. I had nightmares, I swear to God, about phones. To a member of the media, the phone is probably the most important thing. If he has thirty inches of space for his typewriter or his computer and a phone, he's set. Providing them that with thirty inches of space was no problem. Providing them with the phone began to be a problem. The networks' phone needs are actually tremendous. You start overloading. So I'd have nightmares every night about the phones—phones not working, the phone company not keeping up, all the lines would go dead. That would be the end of me!

Unlike the Super Bowl, where there's lots of civic things going on outside, with the Series everything goes on *inside* the stadium. We thought we needed to incorporate the town, set up festivities as much as possible. We had not been in the playoffs or the Series since 1965. What can you do? So you work with the Chamber of Commerce, you work with the state tourism board. I co-chaired a Twins post-season committee trying to generate all this enthusiasm.

We started this planning, but there was no guarantee we'd be in the playoffs! We had to secure nine hundred hotel rooms. We'd say, "Well, we'd like to block one hundred rooms here."

They'd say, "Money up front."

"We can't do that, but if we're in it, first of all you'll make a lot of money, but if we don't make it, you've only committed a hundred rooms."

Some of them would say they blocked the rooms and then a week before the ALCS started, they've taken the hundred rooms from underneath you and they didn't tell you! The Holiday Inn took away a hundred rooms without telling us because they didn't think we'd make it. So now you're a hundred hotel rooms short.

Dave Moore and I were in a glass-enclosed booth for all the games, and I carried around a little beeper in case the commissioner had questions. The first day the commissioner arrives, Northwest Airlines loses his luggage! Each morning we'd have a meeting with him and he'd critique and evaluate the previous night's performance, so you're on the firing line. He'd say, "Why was there a beach ball in the left-field stands last night?"

What are you gonna say?

Another example. Each night you would have a pre-game and a post-game party. The pre-game party would be for all the VIPs, owners, people like that. Post-game would be for everyone—members of the media, friends of the ball club. You're given a lump sum by major-league baseball for the parties. I can assure you it covered maybe the gala party *alone*. The rest was on us, so the Twins really incurred a lot of expenses. Every party was at the same location downtown—logistically, you just had to do it that way. So one night the director of security at the Strutwear building, where we're holding these parties, goes up and asks the commissioner to sign his homer hanky. All right, that's fine. The next morning at nine A.M. Ueberroth asks, "What kind of security force do you have? The director of security comes up and asks me last night to sign his homer hanky!"

Now I have to go back to this guy in the afternoon and patch things up and say, "Well, please, let's not do that in the future." And he says the commissioner's bodyguard gave him permission.

The next day the commissioner brings it up a second time and I'm looking at the commissioner's bodyguard, knowing full well that he gave the man permission. While we're getting chewed out, he's not saying a word.

So you have little things like this going on. The whole thing was awesome. I studied political science but I guarantee you don't take a course in this stuff. One thing I learned is to write everything down. Keep great lists. Think ahead. The first time you're gonna make a couple of mistakes. I did then and I will now, but you just have to realize that you're young, you're gonna make mistakes, you have to keep going.

The Orlando Twins drew only 70,000, but in seven fewer dates than the previous year. The team was 66–75. "It was the best year of my life," Lowe reports. He'll be back for '89.

SHARON PANNOZZO

Don't ask her a question if you're not prepared for a blunt answer. She's a straight-talking PR person, assistant director for media relations with the Chicago Cubs, a title that doesn't begin to describe her duties.

I go on about a third of the road trips. I'm the only woman in baseball who travels at all. There was another one, but they took her off the road and fired her. She expected to be treated like one of the guys. She has filed a discrimination suit now.

The first time anybody sees me get on the bus, like a new player, I see *the look*. "What the hell's she doing on the bus?" With the wives, it's curiosity. What is she doing on the bus? Who is she? Once it's explained, it doesn't bother them. On the team charters, I'm the only woman besides the two stewardesses and they always come up to me and ask me what I'm doing on the plane.

When Don Zimmer was first here he kicked me off the team bus. I took taxis everywhere, which actually is more convenient because you could go when you want. Ball club had to pay for it. For about a year I did the cab routine. I did get to take the charter bus from the airplane, and then he loosened up a little bit and let me get on the bus to the hotel from the game. I sort of grew on him. Now he offers to carry my computer for me!

I went into the clubhouse *once,* on the road in New York. I'd been with the Cubs about two years and I had to go in and get an interview—at the time we did our own audio hotline kind of thing. It was the first time I had to do this. I figured, all right, I'll go. So I knocked on the door, walked in, and I just stood there—and they're all standing around in towels with no clothes on, in their underwear. I felt the redness, the heat on my face. I knew I was blushing badly. I turned around and this one particular ballplayer looked back at me and he started blushing and—you've heard of Yosh Kawano, our infamous clubhouseman. He sees me standing there and he rushes over and turns me around and says, "What are you doing here?"

"I have to do this. I have to get this."

"Well, who do you want to talk to?"

"I have to talk to Keith Moreland."

"Stand outside."

So I stood in the runway right outside the clubhouse in New York and next thing you know I got Keith Moreland standing there dripping wet wearing a towel. I stuck the microphone in his face, asked the question, and walked away, and said I'll never go in there again. I don't have any reason to. There's enough other people running around. If I need someone I'll call them on the phone.

You still find women very apprehensive about going into the clubhouse. We have four women writers out here on occasion and they all come to you and ask how do you want me to handle this. They don't want to cause any trouble down there. They just want to do their job. They're embarrassed just as much as the guys are embarrassed by having them down there. We've got a couple who after a while got used to it and the players got used to them. They just go in the clubhouse and don't feel apprehensive.

We just had a new sportswriter, a woman from UPI, start recently. She wanted to know what she should wear. She was worried about all these things, but they are things you have to be worried about. You don't want to look too conspicuous. There's things you have to take into consideration being female down there, as opposed to being one of the guys. You'll never be one of the guys. You'll always stand out.

I found I've had the best results by maintaining a low profile, letting people get used to you, not being pushy, not being perceived as a bimbo. We've had female interns around here that come dressed in fishnet pantyhose and what not—a big joke. You have to try to be professional. I don't date any of the ballplayers and never would. I've always said I would never be the subject of clubhouse chatter.

We have our own computer system that produces intelligence reports, like clutch hitting and one-on-one statistics—how Andre Dawson has batted against Nolan Ryan over the past five years. It's a system that I've taken three years to put together, with the help of a computer person. I told them what we wanted and baby-sat the system through its growth. And I'm the only one who knows how to do it. I never knew much about computers but I'm an expert now. This system is close to state-of-the-art. Different managers and different general managers have different views on statistical systems. Davey Johnson's really into it. Jim Frey liked it. Gene Michael was a fanatic for it. A lot of the older baseball guys don't use it as much, but they're beginning to realize there's some history to it, and it can make a difference. That's what I spend a lot of my time doing, because it involves putting in the information, producing these reports which the masses don't see. They're considered *intelligence* reports. For instance, the other day Nolan Ryan was pitching, and when Don Zimmer was doing his line-ups he noticed in the big books I prepare that Jody Davis only has one hit off Nolan Ryan in twenty at-bats in his career. So Jody Davis didn't start that game. Berryhill did.

I also help take care of media requests for interviews, media requests for tickets, and just picking up the phone. Every position in our department is a troubleshooter. Whoever happens to pick up the phone and there's a problem somewhere, he takes care of it, basically. Calls from the public get to us, too. If someone wants to know what uniform number Hack Wilson wore in 1923, we get the call and try to find the answer. If someone wants statistical information, we take care of that. If the operators don't know where to send a phone call, we get it. If you actually sat and wrote down everything you did in the course of a day, it would be a very long list. And the next day the list would look entirely different. We could be twenty games out and it's not going to affect the mood in our office. We're gonna still do the same things and take care of everybody. Granted, it affects the on-field personnel, so it affects your dealings with them. Let's put it this way: when you're going on a road trip, you just pray that you win on getaway day, because you don't want to get on a bus or a plane with all these people who aren't in a good mood.

On the average day we have about fifty people in the press box, a good twenty-five radio people, and then the TV crews which you don't even see because they generally don't come to the press box. They pick up their passes, roam around the ballpark, go down to the photo bays. We handle all their credential requests, parking requests.

Until I got into public relations I always thought that sportswriters do a lot of work. I never realized that we were doing their work for them. They have the best job in America! You hand them the game notes. You've seen them: you could do everything off the game notes. Granted, they do a few interviews here and there, and some of them are very good journalists and some work extremely hard, but there's a lot of them that can slide by with the information we provide them. I never realized you have to give them lunch and snacks during the game. I never realized they got all these free tickets. We have at our disposal eighty tickets, forty of which are freebies, forty of which they can buy. We sort of have unwritten rules about who gets comps. If you are here thirty or forty games a year and you want free tickets, fine. If you're somebody who just shows up out of nowhere, then you can buy your tickets with twenty-four hours notice. I'd tell Harry Caray the same thing if Harry walked in. I would. Then he'd get on the air and he'd rip me!

On the road, one person does what five people do at a home game, but scaled down. From about eight o'clock in the morning until you leave your room, somebody's calling you for something, somebody needs tickets, wants an interview—the phone never stops ringing, especially if you're doing real well. You have to leave your room to get away from it.

Then you get to the ballpark, and you're on the field beforehand setting up interviews, running around, and Harry Caray shows up ten minutes before the game and says, "I need two tickets for my limo driver."

"All right, what's his name?"

"I don't know. Just put them under 'Limo driver.' "

"Okay, Harry."

During the game you have these forms that go to the computer system and have to be filled out. You also do the scorebook, the day-by-day books, *all* the game notes (whereas at home someone does page one, someone else page two, someone else page three). After the game you finish updating the books and this and that, you stay with the writers to make sure they don't need anything, and you're out of there about an hour and half after the game's over. Then you get up in the morning at eight o'clock and try to do the whole thing over again.

We have the largest promotional caravan in baseball. We do these hot stove luncheons and dinners in the winter—five guys on a bus, three buses in three different directions, four stops, come back three days later. One bus hits the local Illinois area, Joliet, Gary, places that are an hour, two hours from here. Then we send one bus through Illinois to downstate Iowa—no one wants to go on this trip. That's a long haul, four hours between stops. The buses get back late on Tuesday night and then on Wednesday we have a big media thing here, all the players are here, we invite all the Chicago media, 150 people, and we have a big cocktail party over in the stadium club to wind the whole thing up.

I get stuck organizing the thing every year. No one ever wants to go on this trip. Whichever players will go, go. They don't really like doing it —well, it's not that they don't like doing it, but most of them don't live in the Chicago area, and no one wants to fly in for three or four days in the middle of January, so you sort of get on the phone and beg them. They are paid very well for their time. But the thing is, a lot of the guys who have gone on one will call and ask to go again, because they had a good time. It's getting them to go the first time.

You ought to see the buses we travel on. We have a guy in Wisconsin, Dick Hammann, who's a big Cubs fan who donates these executive buses, and actually drives one of them himself. These buses have stereos, microwaves, showers, couches, tables, video games, VCRs. I mean, these things are incredible. We stock the bus with food and booze. It's like a party for three days.

When we get on the bus to go to Iowa, it's like this is no man's land. These people wait for us to show up. They want to finally meet people they've heard about. It's funny. They'll start calling me about the caravan probably in July. Which day are you coming? I'll get calls in July about which day we're coming in *January*. It's a big deal. We get police escorts when the bus hits the town. The mayor gives everybody a key to the city. People ask *me* for autographs. That just goes to show you. They really can't wait till we get there.

An average turnout at one of the functions is like 700 to 800 people.

After the '84 season it was phenomenal. The turnouts averaged 1,000. We've had up to 1,500—that was like half the town!

It's set up as fund-raising for a local civic group. We go to them and say we'll pay all the expenses, you organize it at your end and find us a place to have the dinner and all this, and you guys can charge $5 or $10 a ticket and have the money for a local baseball group.

Part of the concept of the caravan is also to have this press conference, before dinner or autographs or anything. All the local press can do one-on-one interviews with Andre Dawson or Rick Sutcliffe or whomever, and they wouldn't often get the opportunity to do that in the off-season, whereas someone from the *Chicago Tribune* will call me and ask for Rick's home phone number. It's a good way for these people who work for little dailies in Davenport, Iowa, to feel like they get treated like the guy from the *Chicago Tribune,* even though they don't do it as often.

And for the average fan in one of those places, it's like the ultimate fantasy. The ballplayers sign autographs, answer questions.

On the bus I had last year were Shawon Dunston, Les Lancaster, Jim Frey, and Dewayne Staats, one of our announcers along to act as emcee, the bus driver, and me. The PR person takes care of everything. You're the tour guide, make sure the bus goes, you give the ticket-sales spiel, everything else.

Between the publicity and possible ticket sales, they're worth it. Those people come up to Chicago with big groups in big buses. The goodwill alone is just phenomenal. People write letters to thank you for coming. They understand that you went all this way just to see them, and they appreciate that.

In 1981 I was a sports-management major at the University of Massachusetts, and part of the curriculum was you had to do an internship. I worked for the Red Sox for six or seven months, from January to July. It was a lot of gofer work, but they gave me the opportunity to work with the media guide, and I met a lot of people, sportswriters, et cetera. I realized that basically that's what I wanted to do. I could have been a lawyer or a doctor or something like that, but I decided I wanted to do something that was fun. I don't consider myself a real fan, but I find it interesting, I find the statistical aspect of it interesting.

However, jobs don't come very easily, so I decided I'd go back to school and get a masters in business administration because the degree I had was worth nothing, basically, you know. When Dallas Green took over the

Cubs, there was a Black Monday, all these people were fired and the PR department was cleaned out and reorganized. A friend knew I was sort of looking for a job in this area and she called me and said all these people were fired. The PR director at the time was Bob Ibach, so I called him up and talked to him and he said "Well, I need to hire somebody by Friday." This was on a Tuesday.

"I'll be there Friday," I said.

I called an airline and it was $1,000 at that time for a spur-of-the-moment trip. So I drove all night, got here at nine o'clock in the morning, got lost all over the city—never been here before in my life, surprised I found the ballpark. Spent the whole day here, talking to Bob, to Ned Colletti, the assistant at the time. They couldn't believe I drove all night. I'm falling asleep. They took me to lunch. *They* got lost. They wanted to see if I could write a press release. The whole ordeal took all day.

At five o'clock I said I was leaving. I told Bob Ibach I'd driven all that way and now I was driving all the way home unless they wanted to hire me. I could start on Monday. I gave him a number to call me at on Saturday morning. He called and said the job's yours. I showed up on Monday, went back home the following week to pack my bags, and came out for good. That was 1982. That was extremely fortunate. Opportunities don't happen like that all the time.

I have other options, job offers from PR firms, but I've just never taken them. I enjoy what I do. But after working thirty days straight and you're tired, you wonder what you're doing here. You sit there and commiserate in the press box. "What the hell?" When other people are out on Memorial Day weekend having barbecues and you're at the ballpark, you sort of resent that people have off Saturdays and Sundays and holiday weekends.

Nineteen eighty-four was a magical year, even though you worked every day and put in all kinds of hours, and the media kept on growing every day as we kept winning. It was fun to win—the best time I've ever had here. Maybe I'm just hoping for that to happen again. Ned and I always joke that we'll quit the year after we get our World Series rings. I could be here until I die waiting for a World Series ring. The playoffs were disappointing for a short time but then you realize what a great year it was. We sort of rode on the coattails of that for a long time. We still are, as far as attention and fans go. Everybody always talks about '84. Until there's something else to talk about, everybody always will talk about '84.

You know, the thing is, with the hours you work in professional sports, you'll never be compensated for what you do. I'll never forget when Terry Barthelmas, who at the time was vice president of stadium operations, told me that there was a glamour factor figured in the salary. I'm waiting. I haven't seen this glamour factor yet! To me it's always been a job. I'm not a big baseball fan. I've seen at least 1,500 baseball games. When you have to work at something, when it's something you have to do every day, it loses it's uniqueness, it's not fun anymore. I'm a season-ticket holder over at the Bears, nice seats on the thirty-yard line. I enjoy going to football games. I like auto racing, all these things, but now all of a sudden I don't like baseball anymore. Maybe because now the game is a job; sometimes too much knowledge takes the fun away. If you know all these statistics, it takes the fun away. It's not *just* baseball anymore.

I've decided I have to make an effort to try to like baseball again. I know the PR people at the Brewers real well, they're always bugging me, "Why don't you come up to County Stadium?" So I'm going up for the weekend, gonna have some beer and sit in the bleachers. Maybe I'll like baseball again. Gotta try something.

Pannozzo reported she had a great time in Milwaukee—"crashed a few parties"—and came home rejuvenated.

BILLY FAGAN

He's one of the game's budding entrepreneurs, a quick-witted, sharp-tongued burr-headed kid from Florida who claims to know the worth of every baseball card ever issued—and who are you and I to differ?

Mike Scott? His rookie? That card right there is worth five dollars. Not worth much because people don't want him. One of the first cards, a tobacco card from the 1800s sometime, is a *$20,000* card. Honus Wagner. There was only a couple made. Wish I had that one.

I'm twelve. I've been collecting about two, three years. My brother bought me some and I found out what they were worth, at least five cents apiece, and some are worth more than $40 or $50, and you get at least fifteen cards in a pack. My whole collection is about 10,000, worth a couple thousand dollars. Most of the kids I know collect. The average size collection is 2,000. I'll end up with over 25,000, I'm sure, because I'm going to keep collecting the rest of my life. Then I'll give them to my children when I grow up, so they can collect.

I try to put them in sets, or teams, and put them in little plastic bags once I got the sets, so they don't get ruined, so they'll still be worth a lot.

Different sets have different numbers of cards. Now there are Topps, Donrus, Fleer, Score—that's a new set this year. They make about 20,000 of each guy.

I got an unsealed set of '87 Donrus, but a sealed set is worth more because they're untouched. But they're not as much fun because you can't ever see them unless you open it up. But if you collect them out of packs you can see every card, you know. I got that set for my birthday and it's worth $50, and it will be worth a whole bunch soon because it's going up and has Mark McGwire's rookie in it.

You can order factory sets or collect them out of packs—get them at Pik Kwick, Circle K, any kind of store like that. I do both. Topps comes with bubble gum, Donrus with a puzzle, Fleer with a sticker, Score with a little trivia card.

Prices go up, or they drop if the player starts to slack off and do bad. It's both how he does and how many people want him. Some sorry guy, he's just worth twenty cents.

All rookies are worth twenty cents to start out. Now Darryl Strawberry's rookie is about $15, $20.

A Mickey Mantle '52 is worth more than $4,000. Some people pay that. I'd like a Wade Boggs rookie. I like him and I want his rookie card, worth about $25, $30.

Gary Carter's rookie—1975 Topps—is worth $48. Keith Hernandez's rookie is $26.

I got a McGwire, autographed, worth about $50, $60.

Don Mattingly, '85 Topps? Nine dollars. But his Donrus is worth $16.

Keith Hernandez '82? Twenty-five cents. Common card.

My favorite players are Mark McGwire, Kirby Puckett, Eric Davis, Barry Larkin, Tony Gwynn. Those are mainly my favorite players because they're good players. Tony Gwynn's cards aren't worth much—except his rookie—but they should be because he batted .370. I think cards are priced by if they're black or white. Gwynn batted .370, Wade Boggs is under him, but Boggs is worth more. Blacks are never worth as much even if they do better than the others. I think it's that way. But old Henry Aaron's and Willie Mays's are valuable.

I've got over fifty autographs I get at spring training games. When I go I don't like to watch those games. I just like to get autographs. I only watch on TV and see on the cards what they bat. I know a lot about each guy. I've got Mark McGwire's and Pete Rose's autographs at card shows. If you get a Pete Rose on a ball, or any other superstar, don't get any other autographs or they hurt the value. I paid nine dollars for that Pete Rose, it's worth $100. Superstars are worth a lot if you get their autographs.

Or it might be worth only one or two dollars—Buddy Bell, say. There's not a market for him, really, but when they retire the autograph's worth a lot because they're major-leaguers and they're famous.

I play center field. I'm an excellent fielder but I can't hit good at all. I can hit better now than I could in my first year. I want to pitch, but I'm not very good. The umpires make a lot of bad calls. Out-at-bases is fair, but the strikes and balls are pitiful. Some are pretty good, but some stink really bad.